America Firsthand

SIXTH EDITION

Volume One
Readings from Settlement to Reconstruction

Robert D. Marcus
*Late of the State University
of New York College at Brockport*

David Burner
State University of New York at Stony Brook

Anthony Marcus
University of Melbourne

BEDFORD/ST. MARTIN'S
Boston ♦ New York

FOR BEDFORD/ST. MARTIN'S

Publisher for History: Patricia A. Rossi
Director of Development for History: Jane Knetzger
Developmental Editor: Sarah Barrash Wilson
Production Editor: Arthur Johnson
Production Supervisor: Jennifer Wetzel
Marketing Manager: Jenna Bookin Barry
Editorial Assistant: Rachel L. Safer
Production Assistant: Tina Lai
Copyeditor: Mary Lou Wilshaw-Watts
Cover Design: Donna Lee Dennison
Cover Art: "Train traveling on suspension bridge," 1859. © Hulton-Deutsch
   Collection/CORBIS.
Composition: Pine Tree Composition, Inc.
Printing and Binding: R.R. Donnelley & Sons Company

President: Joan E. Feinberg
Editorial Director: Denise B. Wydra
Director of Marketing: Karen Melton
Director of Editing, Design, and Production: Marcia Cohen
Managing Editor: Elizabeth M. Schaaf

Library of Congress Control Number: 2003101706

For information, write: Bedford/St. Martin's, 75 Arlington Street, Boston, MA 02116
(617-399-4000)

ISBN: 0–312–40361–5

Acknowledgments

Bracketed numbers indicate selection numbers.

[2] "The Conquest of New Spain" from Bernal Díaz del Castillo, *The Conquest of New Spain*, translated with an Introduction by J. M. Cohen. Penguin Classics, 1963. Copyright © 1963 by J. M. Cohen, 1963. Reprinted by permission of Penguin Books, Ltd.

[3] "Announcing the Discovery" from Stephen Greenblatt, ed., *New World Encounters*, University of California Press. Copyright © 1993 The Regents of the University of California. Reprinted by permission.

[5] "Testimony of Pueblo Indians" from Charles Wilson Hackett, *Revolt of the Pueblo Indians of New Mexico and Otermín's Attempted Reconquest, 1680–1682.* Copyright © 1942 by Charles Wilson Hackett. Reprinted by permission of the University of New Mexico Press.

[12] "A Man of the American Enlightenment" from Frank Luther Mott and Chester E. Jorgenson, eds., *Benjamin Franklin: Representative Selections.* American Book Company (1936).

This book is dedicated to Robert Marcus, who died in October 2000; he was one of the two creators and coeditors of America Firsthand. *At the time of Bob's death, his doctoral sponsor Robert Wiebe—soon to pass away himself—eulogized that Bob had "a first-rate mind, was ingenious, versatile, and brimming over with fresh ideas." We remember Bob as an original thinker, a thoughtful scholar, and a true friend.*

Preface

This sixth edition of *America Firsthand* continues to pursue the goal of previous editions: to give center stage to ordinary Americans who speak directly of their own lives. As much as possible, individuals speak in their own words and in selections long enough to be memorable, personal, and immediate. The accounts of indentured servants, Southern aristocrats, runaway slaves, Western explorers, civil rights activists, immigrants, and many others expose students to a wide range of American life and human experience.

In addition, this revision retains two features unique to *America Firsthand*, the Points of View selections and the visual portfolios. The part-opening Points of View sections pair counterpoint readings on a specific event or topic, exposing different viewpoints and offering opportunities for analysis. For instance, students encounter both British and colonial accounts of the Boston Massacre, as well as the contrasting testimony of an independent craftsman and a manufacturer on industrialism in the late nineteenth century. Critical-thinking questions help students sift through the evidence, make connections, and analyze the readings in relation to each other. The four visual portfolios in each volume provide students with the opportunity to extend historical analysis from text to images. Focusing on a theme such as "Slavery and Freedom" or "The Western Landscape," each portfolio is accompanied by a short introduction, a brief narrative describing the images, and questions to help students make comparisons and draw inferences from the visual depictions.

The team of authors for this new edition was changed by the untimely death of Robert Marcus in October of 2000. Robert Marcus and his longtime collaborator David Burner brought the series into the world and developed it over five editions. Marcus was a scholar and educator whose lifelong commitment was, as he wrote in the preface to the fifth edition, to "include people from many groups whose experience has been, until recently, largely lost in mainstream history." In attempting to uphold this commitment to inclusiveness and pedagogical excellence, Robert Marcus's son Anthony Marcus joins David Burner in producing this sixth edition. Presently a lecturer in cultural anthropology, he has taught college students for over ten years and has published on race and ethnicity in Latin America and the United States. Anthony collaborated with his father once before on the two-volume documentary history of U.S. trials and court proceedings, *On Trial.*

This edition of *America Firsthand* features an entirely new final part in the second volume. With five new readings and a visual portfolio about September 11 and its aftermath, this section reflects the passing of post–World War II America and the arrival of a new set of challenges and historical problems in the post–cold war era. The opening Points of View selections offer the views of an Arab American woman who argues in favor of racial profiling at airports alongside those of an African American man who insists that racial profiling is an injustice. Part Seven also includes selections on undocumented Mexican immigrants, the Rodney King beating and riots, Matthew Shepard's death, and September 11.

The new Points of View readings at the end of the second volume join two new Points of View sections in the first volume. These include Bartolomé de Las Casas and Bernal Díaz del Castillo's conflicting views on European contact with natives of the Americas as well as views of the Mexican-American War from opposite sides of the battlefield. Like those Points of View pairings that were retained from the previous edition, these new selections present differing perspectives and offer opportunities for critical thinking.

This edition also includes three new visual portfolios, each connected to a number of the preceding selections and carefully annotated with background information and questions that link the images presented with the readings. The first volume incorporates a new visual essay on colonial architecture, and the second volume includes new portfolios on advertising in the 1920s and on September 11.

Throughout, we have retained readings that users wanted to continue teaching and dropped less successful ones. New selections in the first volume include a description of the Revolutionary War and its aftermath by an African American loyalist soldier; dispatches from an officer in New Mexico during the Mexican-American War; a presentation of everyday life on a nineteenth-century Connecticut whaling vessel in the southern Indian Ocean; the remarkable tale of Henry "Box" Brown, a slave who mailed himself to freedom; an account of a sixteen-year-old who helped John Brown free slaves in Kansas; and the correspondence of a black Civil War journalist who experienced the fall of Richmond in 1865. Fresh selections in the second volume include Jane Addams on industrialism and the Pullman Strike; Kate Richards O'Hare's statements in her own defense during a World War I sedition trial; the comments of a journalist at *The Nation* about the Scopes trial; remembrances by a member of the Puerto Rican radical group the Young Lords; and a memoir of being held hostage in the American embassy in Tehran in 1980.

As in previous editions, carefully written headnotes before the selections prepare students for each reading and help place personalities in their times and places. Questions immediately following the headnotes enable students and instructors to give attention to specific passages and issues that can provide points for discussion as well as material for testing or essays. Glosses within the accounts identify unfamiliar names or terms.

America Firsthand, Sixth Edition, presents the American experience through the perspectives of diverse people who have in common a vivid record of the world they inhabited and of the events they experienced. We hope that the readings will serve as fertile ground in which students can begin to root their own interest in history and deepen their understanding of the times in which they live.

ACKNOWLEDGMENTS

We would like to thank all the instructors who graciously provided helpful comments for improving *America Firsthand*: Jamie Bronstein, New Mexico State University; Elizabeth Clement, University of Utah; Benton Gates, Indiana University–Purdue University, Fort Wayne; James W. Hilty, Temple University; D. Carol Hunter, Earlham College; Anne Keary, University of Utah; Cynthia A. Kierner, University of North Carolina–Charlotte; Molly Ladd-Taylor, York University, Toronto; Jennifer A. Lee, University of Florida; Kathy S. Mason, Southwest Missouri State University; David McCreery, Georgia State University; Beth Ruffin McIntyre, Southwest Missouri State University; Kelly A. Minor, University of Florida; David W. Moore, Loyola University, New Orleans; Penne Restad, University of Texas, Austin; Rebecca S. Shoemaker, Indiana State University; Julie L. Smith, University of North Carolina–Pembroke; Cherry L. Spruill, Indiana University–Purdue University, Indianapolis; and David Stowe, Michigan State University.

We also wish to extend great thanks to Jo Sanson, whose assistance enabled us to produce the best sixth edition possible. Cary Wintz and Timothy More also provided valuable research to the project. The many people associated with Bedford/St. Martin's who worked on the sixth edition need to be acknowledged as well: Joan Feinberg, Denise Wydra, Patricia Rossi, Jane Knetzger, Sarah Barrash Wilson, Rachel Safer, Amy Langlais, Elizabeth Schaaf, Arthur Johnson, and Donna Dennison.

Contents

PART FOUR

Defining America: The Expanding Nation   **145**

PART FIVE

An Age of Reform: Rearranging Social Patterns   **197**

Points of View: Nat Turner's Rebellion (1831)

PART SIX

Civil War and Reconstruction: The Price of War   263

PART ONE

Indians and Europeans

New World Encounters

The contact between two worlds, a "new" one and an "old" one, permanently changed the way people on both sides of the Atlantic Ocean lived and thought about themselves. For Europeans who had spent centuries in the impoverished western margins of the Old World, Christopher Columbus's "discovery" of the New World afforded fresh opportunities to amass unimaginable fortunes in precious metals, exotic spices, and new intoxicants. (Christopher Columbus's letter to the Spanish monarchs he sailed for allows modern readers to better understand how he viewed the new land and its peoples.) More importantly, the emerging European nations of the North Atlantic would eventually reconfigure the entire world, shifting its center away from the great civilizations in the East and building global empires from the land, labor, and high crop yields of the New World. This age of discovery, exploration, and conquest would touch off a scientific and commercial revolution, making Western Europe the cosmopolitan center of the world by attracting new ideas, new technologies, and new forms of wealth and redistributing them across the world.

For the native peoples of what would come to be called the Americas, "discovery" was a catastrophe. European settlers, soldiers, and missionaries, along with Africans, introduced new plants, animals, and technologies that disrupted and radically reoriented life in the New World. Within fifty years of contact, Old World pathogens like smallpox had killed some thirty million natives of the New World, taking advantage of their lack of immunity and the brutal disruptions of European conquest.

The Dominican friar Bartolomé de Las Casas's report of the Spanish conquest of the West Indies — islands named by explorers who wrongly believed they had found a Western passage to Asia — captures the horrors of that first colonial encounter between Europeans and American Indians. This pattern of brutality, violence, and subjugation of indigenous peoples would be repeated many times over the following five centuries. Yet, as the Spanish soldier Bernal Díaz del

Castillo shows in his tale of the conquest of Mexico by Hernán Cortés, the campaign was not merely one of violence and slavery but also of politics and persuasion. For centuries following Columbus's voyage, various Indian nations played independent and sometimes powerful roles in the diplomacy of the Western Hemisphere. Their adaptations and cultural exchanges with one another and with European settlers continued, even while many tribes maintained distinct political and cultural identities into the present. The visual portfolio "New World Contact" (page 43) illustrates the way that Europeans viewed Native Americans and suggests some of the early transformations of the New World and its people.

The Pueblo Indians' accounts of their revolt of 1680 illustrate the Spanish empire's uneasy mix of Indian and European religions and interests. Captain John Smith's description of Virginia's Indians also shows cultural differences between Europeans and natives. And Father Paul Le Jeune, representing the French empire in the New World, suggests how little understanding existed even between friendly whites and receptive Native Americans.

Indians throughout the colonial era and well into the nineteenth century provoked fear and mystery. Stories about what happened when whites were captured by Indians, beginning perhaps with John Smith's account of his supposed rescue by Pocahontas, remained popular for more than two centuries, making captivity narratives among the first best sellers produced in this country. Mary Jemison's account of her captivity among the Seneca illustrates how Anglo-Americans domesticated their anxieties about Indians and wrapped them in an aura of romance.

POINTS OF VIEW
Contact and Conquest (1502–1521)

1

Destruction of the Indies
Bartolomé de Las Casas

Bartolomé de Las Casas (1474–1566), a Spanish colonist and later a Dominican friar, saw Christopher Columbus in 1493 when the explorer passed through Seville on his return to Spain after discovering the Americas the previous year. Las Casas's father and two uncles sailed that year on Columbus's second voyage. As news spread throughout Europe about what was believed to be a western route to the East Indies, rumors of an

Francis Augustus MacNutt, *Bartholomew de Las Casas: His Life, His Apostolate, and His Writings* (New York: G. P. Putnam's Sons, 1909), pp. 314–21.

abundance of gold, spices, and other valuables attracted adventurers and others in search of fortune. The Spanish built small colonies on the island of Hispaniola (now the Dominican Republic and Haiti). In 1502, Las Casas himself traveled to the New World to serve as an officer of the king. In exchange for his services, he was given an encomienda, an estate that included native people to labor for him. Several years later, he was moved by a sermon given by a Dominican priest denouncing the treatment of the Indians by the Spanish. Las Casas returned his serfs to the governor and probably was the first priest ordained in the New World.

Las Casas spent the rest of his long life attempting to protect the Native Americans against the massacres, tortures, slavery, and forced labor imposed on them by their Spanish conquerors. In 1515, Las Casas returned to Spain and pleaded before King Ferdinand for more humane treatment of the native people. His passionate defense of the indigenous Americans influenced Pope Paul III to declare the natives of America rational beings with souls. Las Casas traveled throughout Spain's new colonies and in the 1840s became bishop of Chiapas (now southern Mexico).

His powerful writings created the image of Spanish conquest often called the "Black Legend," a vision of destruction and cruelty until that time unparalleled. Most modern scholars accept the accuracy of Las Casas's shocking portraits of devastation, many of which he personally witnessed, such as the violent and bloody conquest of Cuba. Today, however, many view these horrors not as the outcome of some peculiar Spanish cruelty but as characteristic of the bloody "Columbian encounter" between Europeans and other cultures in the age of exploration and conquest. Las Casas wrote the following treatise in Seville in 1552.

BEFORE YOU READ

1. Do you think Las Casas's view of the Native Americans was accurate?
2. Do you judge his criticism of the Spanish empire to have been fair and accurate?
3. Throughout his life Las Casas remained fiercely loyal to both the Spanish monarch and the Catholic Church. Can you reconcile these feelings with his condemnation of the Spanish empire's actions in the New World?

SHORT REPORT OF THE DESTRUCTION OF THE WEST INDIES

The Indies were discovered in the year fourteen hundred and ninety-two. The year following, Spanish Christians went to inhabit them, so that it is since forty-nine years that numbers of Spaniards have gone there: and the first land, that they invaded to inhabit, was the large and most delightful Isle of Hispaniola [present-day Dominican Republic and Haiti], which has a circumference of six hundred leagues.

2. There are numberless other islands, and very large ones, all around on every side, that were all—and we have seen it—as inhabited and full of their native Indian peoples as any country in the world.

3. Of the continent, the nearest part of which is more than two hundred and fifty leagues distant from this Island, more than ten thousand leagues of maritime coast have been discovered, and more is discovered every day; all that

has been discovered up to the year forty-nine is full of people, like a hive of bees, so that it seems as though God had placed all, or the greater part of the entire human race in these countries.

4. God has created all these numberless people to be quite the simplest, without malice or duplicity, most obedient, most faithful to their natural Lords, and to the Christians, whom they serve; the most humble, most patient, most peaceful, and calm, without strife nor tumults; not wrangling, nor querulous, as free from uproar, hate and desire of revenge, as any in the world.

5. They are likewise the most delicate people, weak and of feeble constitution, and less than any other can they bear fatigue, and they very easily die of whatsoever infirmity; so much so, that not even the sons of our Princes and of nobles, brought up in royal and gentle life, are more delicate than they; although there are among them such as are of the peasant class. They are also a very poor people, who of worldly goods possess little, nor wish to possess: and they are therefore neither proud, nor ambitious, nor avaricious.

6. Their food is so poor, that it would seem that of the Holy Fathers in the desert was not scantier nor less pleasing. Their way of dressing is usually to go naked, covering the private parts; and at most they cover themselves with a cotton cover, which would be about equal to one and a half or two ells square of cloth. Their beds are of matting, and they mostly sleep in certain things like hanging nets, called in the language of Hispaniola *hamacas.*

7. They are likewise of a clean, unspoiled, and vivacious intellect, very capable, and receptive to every good doctrine; most prompt to accept our Holy Catholic Faith, to be endowed with virtuous customs; and they have as little difficulty with such things as any people created by God in the world.

8. Once they have begun to learn of matters pertaining to faith, they are so importunate to know them, and in frequenting the sacraments and divine service of the Church, that to tell the truth, the clergy have need to be endowed of God with the gift of pre-eminent patience to bear with them: and finally, I have heard many lay Spaniards frequently say many years ago, (unable to deny the goodness of those they saw) certainly these people were the most blessed of the earth, had they only knowledge of God.

9. Among these gentle sheep, gifted by their Maker with the above qualities, the Spaniards entered as soon as they knew them, like wolves, tigers, and lions which had been starving for many days, and since forty years they have done nothing else; nor do they otherwise at the present day, than outrage, slay, afflict, torment, and destroy them with strange and new, and divers kinds of cruelty, never before seen, nor heard of, nor read of, of which some few will be told below: to such extremes has this gone that, whereas there were more than three million souls, whom we saw in Hispaniola, there are to-day, not two hundred of the native population left.

10. The island of Cuba is almost as long as the distance from Valladolid[1] to Rome; it is now almost entirely deserted. The islands of San Juan [Puerto Rico], and Jamaica, very large and happy and pleasing islands, are both desolate. The

---

1. **Valladolid:** a city in northwestern Spain.

Lucaya Isles lie near Hispaniola and Cuba to the north and number more than sixty, including those that are called the Giants, and other large and small Islands; the poorest of these, which is more fertile, and pleasing than the King's garden in Seville, is the healthiest country in the world, and contained more than five hundred thousand souls, but to-day there remains not even a single creature. All were killed in transporting them, to Hispaniola, because it was seen that the native population there was disappearing.

11. A ship went three years later to look for the people that had been left after the gathering in, because a good Christian was moved by compassion to convert and win those that were found to Christ; only eleven persons, whom I saw, were found.

12. More than thirty other islands, about the Isle of San Juan, are destroyed and depopulated, for the same reason. All these islands cover more than two thousand leagues of land, entirely depopulated and deserted.

13. We are assured that our Spaniards, with their cruelty and execrable works, have depopulated and made desolate the great continent, and that more than ten Kingdoms, larger than all Spain, counting Aragon[2] and Portugal, and twice as much territory as from Seville to Jerusalem (which is more than two thousand leagues), although formerly full of people, are now deserted.

14. We give as a real and true reckoning, that in the said forty years, more than twelve million persons, men, and women, and children, have perished unjustly and through tyranny, by the infernal deeds and tyranny of the Christians; and I truly believe, nor think I am deceived, that it is more than fifteen.

15. Two ordinary and principal methods have the self-styled Christians, who have gone there, employed in extirpating these miserable nations and removing them from the face of the earth. The one, by unjust, cruel and tyrannous wars. The other, by slaying all those, who might aspire to, or sigh for, or think of liberty, or to escape from the torments that they suffer, such as all the native Lords, and adult men; for generally, they leave none alive in the wars, except the young men and the women, whom they oppress with the hardest, most horrible, and roughest servitude, to which either man or beast, can ever be put. To these two ways of infernal tyranny, all the many and divers other ways, which are numberless, of exterminating these people, are reduced, resolved, or sub-ordered according to kind.

16. The reason why the Christians have killed and destroyed such infinite numbers of souls, is solely because they have made gold their ultimate aim, seeking to load themselves with riches in the shortest time and to mount by high steps, disproportioned to their condition: namely by their insatiable avarice and ambition, the greatest, that could be on the earth. These lands, being so happy and so rich, and the people so humble, so patient, and so easily subjugated, they have had no more respect, nor consideration nor have they taken more account of them (I speak with truth of what I have seen during all the aforementioned time) than, — I will not say of animals, for would to God they had considered and treated them as animals, — but as even less than the dung in the streets.

---

2. **Aragon:** an ancient kingdom in what is now northeastern Spain.

17. In this way have they cared for their lives—and for their souls: and therefore, all the millions above mentioned have died without faith, and without sacraments. And it is a publicly known truth, admitted, and confessed by all, even by the tyrants and homicides themselves, that the Indians throughout the Indies never did any harm to the Christians: they even esteemed them as coming from heaven, until they and their neighbours had suffered the same many evils, thefts, deaths, violence and visitations at their hands.

OF HISPANIOLA

In the island of Hispaniola—which was the first, as we have said, to be invaded by the Christians—the immense massacres and destruction of these people began. It was the first to be destroyed and made into a desert. The Christians began by taking the women and children, to use and to abuse them, and to eat of the substance of their toil and labour, instead of contenting themselves with what the Indians gave them spontaneously, according to the means of each. Such stores are always small; because they keep no more than they ordinarily need, which they acquire with little labour; but what is enough for three households, of ten persons each, for a month, a Christian eats and destroys in one day. From their using force, violence and other kinds of vexations, the Indians began to perceive that these men could not have come from heaven.

2. Some hid their provisions, others, their wives and children: others fled to the mountains to escape from people of such harsh and terrible intercourse. The Christians gave them blows in the face, beatings and cudgellings, even laying hands on the lords of the land. They reached such recklessness and effrontery, that a Christian captain violated the lawful wife of the chief king and lord of all the island.

3. After this deed, the Indians consulted to devise means of driving the Christians from their country. They took up their weapons, which are poor enough and little fitted for attack, being of little force and not even good for defence. For this reason, all their wars are little more than games with sticks, such as children play in our countries.

4. The Christians, with their horses and swords and lances, began to slaughter and practise strange cruelty among them. They penetrated into the country and spared neither children nor the aged, nor pregnant women, nor those in child labour, all of whom they ran through the body and lacerated, as though they were assaulting so many lambs herded in their sheepfold.

5. They made bets as to who would slit a man in two, or cut off his head at one blow: or they opened up his bowels. They tore the babes from their mothers' breast by the feet, and dashed their heads against the rocks. Others they seized by the shoulders and threw into the rivers, laughing and joking, and when they fell into the water they exclaimed: "boil body of so and so!" They spitted the bodies of other babes, together with their mothers and all who were before them, on their swords.

6. They made a gallows just high enough for the feet to nearly touch the ground, and by thirteens, in honour and reverence of our Redeemer and the

twelve Apostles, they put wood underneath and, with fire, they burned the Indians alive.

7. They wrapped the bodies of others entirely in dry straw, binding them in it and setting fire to it; and so they burned them. They cut off the hands of all they wished to take alive, made them carry them fastened on to them, and said: "Go and carry letters": that is; take the news to those who have fled to the mountains.

8. They generally killed the lords and nobles in the following way. They made wooden gridirons of stakes, bound them upon them, and made a slow fire beneath: thus the victims gave up the spirit by degrees, emitting cries of despair in their torture.

9. I once saw that they had four or five of the chief lords stretched on the gridirons to burn them, and I think also there were two or three pairs of gridirons, where they were burning others; and because they cried aloud and annoyed the captain or prevented him sleeping, he commanded that they should strangle them: the officer who was burning them was worse than a hangman and did not wish to suffocate them, but with his own hands he gagged them, so that they should not make themselves heard, and he stirred up the fire, until they roasted slowly, according to his pleasure. I know his name, and knew also his relations in Seville. I saw all the above things and numberless others.

10. And because all the people who could flee, hid among the mountains and climbed the crags to escape from men so deprived of humanity, so wicked, such wild beasts, exterminators and capital enemies of all the human race, the Spaniards taught and trained the fiercest boar-hounds to tear an Indian to pieces as soon as they saw him, so that they more willingly attacked and ate one, than if he had been a boar. These hounds made great havoc and slaughter.

11. And because sometimes, though rarely, the Indians killed a few Christians for just cause, they made a law among themselves, that for one Christian whom the Indians killed, the Christians should kill a hundred Indians.

2

The Conquest of New Spain

Bernal Díaz del Castillo

The discovery of the Americas by Columbus in 1492 set off a speculative frenzy in Spain and Portugal. Merchants, nobles, and military men rushed to equip ships and send soldiers in search of the gold, slaves, and spices promised by this vast new economy. Everybody expected that there were incalculable riches in these new lands, but nobody

Bernal Díaz del Castillo, *The Conquest of New Spain*, trans. J. M. Cohen (Middlesex, Eng.: Penguin Books, 1987 [1568]), pp. 107–113, 183, 216, 234–235.

*was sure what they were or where they would be found. Twenty-five years after Colum-
bus's discovery, the big payoff still remained elusive. The Spanish colonies in the New
World were little more than a few Caribbean islands with sparse populations of settlers,
African slaves, and Taino natives, who with increasing frequency died of disease contracted from their captors soon after being enslaved. All this changed with the conquest
of New Spain (present-day Mexico and Guatemala), which brought Europeans into
their first face-to-face contact with the major civilizations of the New World and
demonstrated to both sides something of what they could expect from the other.*

*Hernán Cortés, who led the conquest of New Spain, was not unlike many of the
adventurers and businessmen who crossed the Atlantic in the first century after Columbus. In 1503, at the age of eighteen, Cortés traveled to Santo Domingo, the capital of
Hispaniola, on a convoy of merchant ships. Using his training as a lawyer and his family connections, he became the colony notary and received a* repartimiento *(a form of
colonial slaveholding). In 1511, he left Santo Domingo and helped Diego Valásquez
conquer Cuba, becoming clerk of the royal treasury, mayor of Havana, and a wealthy
owner of land, Indians, and cattle. In 1517 and 1518, two expeditions to the Yucatán
brought back rumors of gold and a great inland empire. Valásquez asked Cortés to command an exploratory expedition to the mainland. From the outset Cortés was clearly
imagining far more than scientific exploration: he mortgaged everything he owned to
help equip a fleet of 11 ships, 16 horses, and 508 soldiers.*

*When Cortés's army—of which twenty-one-year-old Spaniard Bernal Díaz del
Castillo (c. 1498–c.1584) was a part—arrived on the mainland, he found an Aztec
empire in deep crisis. Rapid expansion from the center of power at Tenochtitlán (present-
day Mexico City), the world's largest city at the time, had stretched the empire's rigid
political structure and low technological development nearly to the breaking point. Unable to fully integrate the vast agricultural hinterlands into the empire, the Aztecs had
resorted to increasingly brutal ritualized terror, human sacrifice, and militarization to
keep control.*

*With the help of Malinche, an ambitious native woman who became Cortés's lover,
advisor, and interpreter, Cortés and his men swept through town after town, defeating
local armies, abolishing human sacrifice and tax collection, and carrying out mass con-
versions to Christianity. By the time the Spanish finally arrived in Tenochtitlán,
Cortés and his mistress were feared and admired as mythical liberators. The conquest
required two more years of political maneuvering and bloody battles, culminating in the
siege of the island city of Tenochtitlán in 1521 by Cortés's army, his forces bolstered by
as many as two hundred thousand members of indigenous groups disaffected by Aztec
rule.*

*After serving in Cortés's army, Bernal Díaz later became the governor of Santiago
de los Caballeros in Guatemala. He wrote* The True History of the Conquest of
New Spain *in 1568, at the age of seventy, in response to wildly exaggerated histories
written by Cortés's personal secretary and others who had not been part of the conquest
and who accepted Cortés's claims of godlike dominion over the Indians. The shifting political alliances, friendships, betrayals, negotiations, and battles in the conquest of New
Spain that Diáz describes represent a pattern that would be repeated by colonists many
times during the first three centuries of European settlement in North America.*

BEFORE YOU READ

1. How important was military might, as opposed to political negotiation and alliance, in the conquest of New Spain?

2. Why do you think Bernal Díaz was determined to refute accounts that depicted Cortés as godlike in the eyes of the natives? What problems might exist in Díaz's account?

3. Was Cortés a liberator or an oppressor of the natives?

THE STAY AT CEMPOALA[1]

We slept at the village where these twelve Indians had prepared quarters for us, and after getting good information about the road we must take to the town on the hill, we sent word to the *Caciques*[2] of Cempoala, very early in the morning, that we were coming to their town and hoped they would be pleased. We sent six of the Indians to carry this message, and kept the other six as guides. Cortes also ordered the guns, muskets, and crossbows to be kept ready for use, and scouts to be sent ahead. The horsemen and all the rest of us kept on the alert, and thus we advanced to within three miles of town. When we came to this point twenty Indian dignitaries came out to welcome us in the name of the *Cacique*, and brought us some cakes of their very finely scented rose-petals. These they presented to Cortes and the horsemen with every sign of friendliness, saying that their lord was awaiting us at our lodgings, since he was too fat and heavy to come out and receive us. Cortes thanked them, and we continued our march; and as we came among the houses we saw how large a town it was, larger than any we had yet seen, and were full of admiration. It was so green with vegetation that it looked like a garden; and its streets were so full of men and women who had come out to see us that we gave thanks to God for the discovery of such a country.

Our mounted scouts had come to a great square with courtyards where they had prepared our lodgings, which appeared to have been lime-coated and burnished during the last few days. The Indians are so skilful at these arts that one of the horsemen took the shining whiteness for silver, and came galloping back to tell Cortes that our quarters had silver walls. Doña Marina[3] and Aguilar[4] said that it must be plaster, and we laughed at his excitement. Indeed we reminded him ever afterwards that anything white looked to him like silver. But enough of this. When we came to the buildings, this fat *Cacique* came out to receive us in the courtyard. He was so fat that I must call him the fat *Cacique*. He made a deep

---

1. **Cempoala:** in the modern Mexican state of Veracruz; now an important archaeological site of Totonac culture, one of the many ethnicities dominated by the Aztecs at the time of conquest.

2. *Cacique:* a village chief or political leader.

3. **Doña Marina:** also known as Malinche; Cortés's native lover, translator, and trusted military advisor.

4. **Aguilar:** Jerónimo de Aguilar, a Spaniard who had been shipwrecked off the coast of New Spain several years before Cortés arrived. Taken as a slave by the natives, he learned their customs and languages and later assisted Cortés after being liberated.

bow to Cortes and perfumed him as is their custom, and Cortes embraced him. After leading us into our fine, large quarters, which held us all, they gave us food and brought us some baskets of plums, which were very plentiful at that season, also some of their maize-cakes. As we were hungry, and had not seen so much food for a long time, we called the town Villa Viciosa.[5] Others named it Seville.

Cortes gave orders that none of the soldiers should leave the square or annoy the inhabitants; and when the fat *Cacique* learnt that we had finished eating, he sent to tell Cortes that he wished to pay him a visit. He came with a great number of Indian dignitaries, all wearing large gold lip-rings and rich cloaks. Cortes also left his quarters to receive him, and greeted him with a great show of affection and flattery. Then the fat *Cacique* ordered a present to be brought of golden jewellery and cloth; and although it was a small and of no great value, he said to Cortes: "*Lope luzio lope luzio!* Please accept this; if I had more I would give it to you." I have already explained that in the Tononac language *lope luzio* means lord of great lords.

Cortes replied through our interpreters that he would repay this gift in services, and that if the *Cacique* would tell him what he wanted it should be done for him, since we were vassals of the Emperor Charles,[6] a very great prince who ruled over many kingdoms and countries and had sent us to redress grievances, to punish evildoers, and to command that human sacrifices should cease. And he explained many things concerning our holy religion. On hearing all this, the fat *Cacique* heaved a deep sigh and broke into bitter complaints against the great Montezuma[7] and his governors, saying that the [Aztec][8] prince had recently brought him to subjection, had taken away all his golden jewellery, and so grievously oppressed him and his people that they could do nothing except obey him, since he was lord over many cities and countries, and ruler over countless vassals and armies of warriors. . . .

. . . [T]hey told us that every year many of their sons and daughters were demanded of them for sacrifices, and others for service in the houses and plantations of their conquerors. And they made other complaints; so many that I no longer remember them. They said that if their wives and daughters were handsome, Montezuma's tax-gatherers took them away and raped them, and that they did this in all the thirty villages in which the Totonac language was spoken.

With the help of our interpreters Cortes gave them such comfort as he could. He promised to help in any way that was possible, and to prevent these thefts and crimes, since it was for this purpose that our lord the Emperor had sent us to these parts. He told them to stop being anxious, and to see what we would do. His speech seemed to give them some consolation. But their hearts were not relieved, for they were too much afraid of the [Aztecs].

---

5. **Villa Viciosa:** city of abundance.
6. **Emperor Charles:** Charles V, king of Spain.
7. **Montezuma:** ruler of the Aztec empire.
8. **Aztec:** originally translated as "Mexican," "Aztec" is used here to denote the inhabitants of Mexico City and their closest allies, a militaristic society that dominated many of the peoples who lived in what is now Mexico.

While these conversations were going on five Indians came in great haste from the town to tell the *Caciques* who were talking to Cortes that five of Montezuma's [Aztec] tax-gathers had just arrived. The *Caciques* turned pale at the news. Trembling with fear, they left Cortes and went off to receive the [Aztecs]. Very quickly they decorated a room with flowers, cooked them some food, and made them quantities of chocolate, which is the best of their drinks.

When the five [Aztecs] entered the town, they came to the square where the *Caciques'* houses and our quarters were, and passed us by with cocksure pride, speaking not a word to Cortes or anyone else they saw. They wore richly embroidered cloaks and loincloths—for they wore loincloths at that time— and shining hair that was gathered up and seemed tied to their heads. Each one was smelling the roses he carried, and each had a crooked staff in his hand. Their Indian servants carried flywhisks, and they were accompanied by the *Caciques* of the other Totonac towns, who did not leave them until they had shown them to their lodgings and given them a meal.

As soon as they had dined, the tax-gatherers sent for the fat *Cacique* and the other chiefs and scolded them for having entertained us in their villages, since now they would have to meet and deal with us, which would not please their lord Montezuma. For without his permission and instructions they should neither have received us nor given us golden jewels. They continued to reproach the fat *Cacique* and his nobles for their actions, and ordered them to provide twenty Indians, male and female, as a peace-offering to their gods for the wrong that had been done.

At this point Cortes asked our interpreters why the arrival of these Indians had so agitated the *Caciques*, and who they were; and Doña Marina, who understood perfectly, explained what was happening. As soon as Cortes understood what the *Caciques* were saying, he reminded them that, as he had already explained, our lord the King had sent him to chastise evildoers and prevent sacrifices and robbery. He ordered them therefore to arrest the tax-gatherers for having made such a demand, and to hold them prisoners until their lord Montezuma was informed of the reason: namely that they had come to rob the Totonacs, to enslave their wives and children, and to do other violence.

When the *Caciques* heard this they were appalled at his daring. To order them to manhandle Montezuma's messengers! They were far too frightened. They dared not do it. But Cortes insisted that they must arrest them at once; and they obeyed him. They secured them with long poles and collars, as is their custom, so that they could not escape, and they beat one of them who refused to be bound. Furthermore, Cortes ordered all the *Caciques* to cease paying tribute and obedience to Montezuma, and to proclaim their refusal in all the towns of their friends and allies, also to announce that if tax-gatherers came to any other towns he must be informed, and would send for them. So the news spread throughout the province. For the fat *Cacique* immediately sent messengers to proclaim it, and the chiefs who had accompanied the tax-gatherers scattered immediately after the arrest, each to his own town, to convey the order and give an account of what had happened.

The act they had witnessed was so astonishing and of such importance to them that they said no human beings dared to do such a thing, and it must be the work of *Teules*. Therefore from that moment they called us *Teules*, which means gods or demons. . . .

After these events the *Caciques* of this village and of Cempoala, and all the Totonac dignitaries who had assembled, asked Cortes what was to be done, for all the forces of Mexico[9] and of the great Montezuma would descend upon them, and they could not possibly escape death and destruction.

Cortes replied with a most cheerful smile that he and his brothers who were with him would defend them and kill anyone who tried to harm them; and the *Caciques* and their villagers one and all promised to stand by us, to obey any order we might give them, and to join their forces with ours against Montezuma and all his allies. Then in the presence of Diego de Godoy the Notary they took the oath of obedience to His Majesty, and sent messengers to all the other towns in the province to relate what had happened. As they now paid no more tribute and the tax-gatherers had disappeared, they could not contain their delight at having thrown off the tyranny of the [Aztecs]. . . .

. . . [I]n this town of Tlascala we found wooden cages made of lattice-work in which men and women were imprisoned and fed until they were fat enough to be sacrificed and eaten. We broke open and destroyed these prisons, and set free the Indians who were in them. But the poor creatures did not dare to run away. However, they kept close to us and so escaped with their lives. From now on, whenever we entered a town our captain's first order was to break down the cages and release prisoners, for these prison cages existed throughout the country. When Cortes saw such great cruelty he showed the *Caciques* of Tlascala how indignant he was and scolded them so furiously that they promised not to kill and eat any more Indians in that way. But I wondered what use all these promises were, for as soon as we turned our heads they would resume their old cruelties.

When our Captain remembered that we had been resting in Tlascala for seventeen days, and after all we had heard about Montezuma's great wealth and flourishing city, we decided to consult all our captains and soldiers whom he felt to be willing to go forward; and it was decided that we should set out without delay. But a good deal of criticism of this decision was expressed in the camp. Some soldiers said that it was very rash to start attacking this strong city when our numbers were so small, and harped on Montezuma's very great strength. But our Captain replied that we had no alternative. We had so constantly asserted and proclaimed that we were going to see Montezuma that any other course was useless. . . .

. . . [W]e left Iztapalapa with a large escort of these great *Caciques*, and followed the causeway, which is eight yards wide and goes so straight to the city of Mexico that I do not think it curves at all. Wide though it was, it was so crowded with people that there was hardly room for them all. Some were going to [the city of] Mexico and others coming away, besides those who had come

9. **Mexico:** the Aztec empire.

out to see us, and we could hardly get through the crowds that were there. For the towers and the *cues*[10] were full, and they came in canoes from all parts of the lake. No wonder, since they had never seen horses or men like us before!

With such wonderful sights to gaze on we did not know what to say, or if this was real that we saw before our eyes. On the land side there were great cities, and on the lake many more. The lake was crowded with canoes. At intervals along the causeway there were many bridges, and before us was the great city of Mexico. As for us, we were scarcely four hundred strong, and we well remembered the words and warnings of the people of Huexotzinco and Tlascala and Tlamanalco, and the many other warnings we had received to beware of entering the city of Mexico, since they would kill us as soon as they had us inside. Let the interested reader consider whether there is not much to ponder in this narrative of mine. What men in all the world have shown such daring? But let us go on.

We marched along our causeway to a point where another small causeway branches off to another city called Coyoacan, and there, beside some towerlike buildings, which were their shrines, we were met by many more *Caciques* and dignitaries in very rich cloaks. The different chieftains wore different brilliant liveries, and the causeways were full of them. Montezuma had sent these great *Caciques* in advance to receive us, and as soon as they came before Cortes they told him in their language that we were welcome, and as a sign of peace they touched the ground with their hands and kissed it. . . .

When we arrived near the great temple and before we had climbed a single step, the great Montezuma sent six *papas*[11] and two chieftains down from the top, where he was making his sacrifices, to escort our Captain; and as he climbed the steps, of which there were one hundred and fourteen, they tried to take him by the arms to help him up in the same way as they helped Montezuma, thinking he might be tired, but he would not let them near him.

The top of the *cue* formed an open square on which stood something like a platform, and it was here that the great stones stood on which they placed the poor Indians for sacrifice. Here also was a massive image like a dragon, and other hideous figures, and a great deal of blood that had been spilled that day. Emerging in the company of two *papas* from the shrine which houses his accursed images, Montezuma made a deep bow to us all and said: "My lord Malinche,[12] you must be tired after climbing this great *cue* of ours." And Cortes replied that none of us was ever exhausted by anything. Then Montezuma took him by the hand, and told him to look at his great city and all the other cities standing in the water, and the many others on the land around the lake; and he said that if Cortes had not had a good view of the great market-place he could see it better from where he now was. So we stood there looking, because that huge accursed *cue* stood so high that it dominated everything. We saw the three causeways that led into Mexico. . . .

---

10. ***cues:*** temples or pyramids. The Temple of the Sun, just outside of Mexico City, is by volume the largest pyramid in the world.

11. ***papas:*** priests known for their widespread human sacrifice and cannibalism.

We saw the fresh water which came from Chapultepec to supply the city, and the bridges that were constructed at intervals on the causeways so that the water could flow in and out from one part of the lake to another. We saw a great number of canoes, some coming with provisions and other returning with cargo and merchandise. . . . We saw *cues* and shrines in these cities that looked like gleaming white towers and castles: a marvellous sight. All the houses had flat roofs, and on the causeways were other small towers and shrines built like fortresses.

Having examined and considered all that we had seen, we turned back to the great market and the swarm of people buying and selling. The mere murmur of their voices talking was loud enough to be heard more than three miles away. Some of our soldiers who had been in many parts of the world, in Constantinople, in Rome, and all over Italy, said that they had never seen a market so well laid out, so large, so orderly, and so full of people.

FOR CRITICAL THINKING

1. Díaz presents the native population of New Spain as political agents whereas Las Casas tends to depict the population of the West Indies as relatively passive victims of conquest. How much do you think these two portrayals derive from the different realities of conquest in the regions, and how much are they products of the distinct world views of their authors?

2. Las Casas based his argument that the lives and property of the native peoples of the New World should be protected on the assertion that they were rational beings with souls. Do you think Díaz would have agreed with Las Casas's view of the natives?

3. How do these two descriptions of encounters between Europeans and natives compare with the now-popular views of encounters between Native Americans and European Americans in the United States?

---

12. Many Aztecs referred to Cortés by the name of his lover and translator, Malinche (Doña Marina).

3

Announcing the Discovery
Christopher Columbus

When Christopher Columbus sighted land on October 12, 1492, he was convinced he had achieved his goal of reaching Asia—a belief he clung to even after three more voyages in 1493, 1498, and 1502. By what one scholar has described as "a giant geological trick [played] upon the admiral before historical time began," the Caribbean islands he discovered were positioned much like the islands off the coast of Asia that appeared on the medieval maps he had long studied. These maps, based on both the Bible and reports by such European travelers to Asia as Marco Polo, led him to identify Cuba first with Cipangu (Japan) and then with Cathay (China). Similarly, he erroneously identified Hispaniola and Jamaica with the islands in the China Sea. Some of the landscapes and climates Columbus encountered conformed as well to the geography of Asia firmly fixed in his mind. And many religious prophecies confirmed his various interpretations of his whereabouts. For instance, in a later voyage he believed that part of the coast of South America was the portal to the terrestrial paradise assumed in medieval theology and geography. He would go to his grave in 1505 without ever having been aware that he had reached a New World not described in any of the geographies or drawn on any of his maps. Columbus's descriptions of the New World, as in his "Letter to the Sovereigns" in 1493, were heavily colored by the expectations of Asia that had propelled his journey.

Columbus (1451–1506) seems the most representative of Renaissance men with his scientific interests in navigation and cosmology, fascination with ancient texts, urge for power and domination, and truly overwhelming lust for gold, honors, and fame. Yet he was even more complex than that—a medieval man, as well, and an intensely religious mystic. He emphasized with special symbols in his writings that his first name, Christopher, meant "Christ-bearer." Although he never took vows, he would sometimes dress in the severe robes and rope belt of a Franciscan monk. He led his various crews through innumerable religious observances and struggled constantly to justify his behavior toward the Indians in Christian terms. He wrote extensively about the location of the earthly paradise, argued in a letter of 1498 that the earth was not round but pear-shaped, and wrote of the earthly paradise "which no one can enter except by God's leave . . . [lying] at the summit of what I have described as the stalk of a pear."

Margarita Zamora, "Christopher Columbus's 'Letter to the Sovereigns': Announcing the Discovery," in Stephen Greenblatt, ed., *New World Encounters* (Berkeley: University of California Press, 1993), pp. 3–8.

Columbus's first letter to Ferdinand and Isabella was written when Columbus feared that his ship was going down in a storm. Sealed in a barrel and tossed into the sea, it was never found. The "Letter to the Sovereigns," excerpted here, arrived at its destination by more normal means but then was apparently suppressed by the royal court and lay lost in Spanish archives for almost five centuries. A revision of this letter, doubtlessly the work of court officials, circulated in two similar versions all over Europe, providing educated readers their first glimpse of the new discoveries. In the original letter, wholly removed from the announcement to the world that defined the historic voyage for half a millennium, was the goal Columbus never abandoned: financing a crusade to reconquer Jerusalem from the Arabs, "for which purpose," Columbus reminds his sovereigns, "this enterprise was undertaken."

BEFORE YOU READ

1. How accurate is Columbus's account of the lands he discovered? What do you find convincing and what doubtful?

2. What does this letter indicate about Columbus's motives for his journey? Do you find any contradictions among his motives?

3. The royal court, in publishing a revised version of Columbus's letter, suppressed his discussion of using the riches of the world he had discovered to finance the reconquest of Jerusalem from the Muslims. Why do you think the court omitted this part of the letter?

LETTER TO THE SOVEREIGNS OF 4 MARCH 1493 ANNOUNCING THE DISCOVERY

Most Christian and lofty and powerful sovereigns:

That eternal God who has given Your Highnesses so many victories now gave you the greatest one that to this day He has ever given any prince. I come from the Indies with the armada Your Highnesses gave me, to which [place] I traveled in thirty-three days after departing from your kingdoms; after fourteen of the thirty-three there were light winds in which I covered very little ground. I found innumerable people and very many islands, of which I took possession in Your Highnesses' name, by royal crier and with Your Highnesses' royal banner unfurled, and it was not contradicted. To the first [island] I gave the name of San Salvador, in memory of His Supreme Majesty [Jesus Christ], to the second Santa María de la Concepción, to the third Fernandina, to the fourth Isabela, [and] to the fifth Juana. . . . After I arrived at Juana I followed its coast to the west and found it to be so large that I thought it was probably not an island, but rather a mainland, and most likely the province of Cathay; but I could not verify this because everywhere I arrived the people fled and I could not speak with them. And because I was unable to find a notable settlement, I thought that by hugging the coast I could not fail to find some town or great city, such as those who have gone to that province overland tell it. And after following this land for a long while, I found that I was veering away from the west and it was leading me to the north . . . , and so I turned back. In the meantime I already understood something of the speech and signs of certain Indians I had taken on the island of San Salvador, and I understood [from them] that this was still an island. And thus I came to a very good harbor, from which I sent two men inland, three days' journey, with one of the Indians I brought, who had become friendly with me, so that they could see and determine if there were any cities or large settlements, and which land it was, and what there was in it. They found many settlements and innumerable people, but no government of any importance. And so they returned, and I departed and took certain Indians at the said harbor so that I could also hear or learn from them about said lands. And thus I followed the sea coast of this island toward the east one hundred and seven leagues to where it ended. And before leaving it, I saw another island to the east, eighteen leagues out from this one, which I later named Española. And then I went to it and followed its coast on the north side, just as in the case of Juana, due east for one hundred and eighty-eight very long leagues. And I continued to enter very many harbors, in each of which I placed a very large cross in the most appropriate spot, as I had done in all the other [harbors] of the other islands, and in many places I found promontories sufficient [for this purpose]. So I went on in this fashion until the sixteenth of January, when I determined to return to Your Highnesses, as much because I had already found most of what I sought as because I had only one caravel left. . . .

Besides the above-mentioned islands, I have found many others in the Indies, of which I have not been able to tell in this letter. They, like these others, are so extremely fertile, that even if I were able to express it, it would not be a marvel were it to be disbelieved. The breezes [are] most temperate, the trees and fruits and grasses are extremely beautiful and very different from ours; the rivers and harbors are so abundant and of such extreme excellence when compared to those of Christian lands that it is a marvel. All these islands are densely populated with the best people under the sun; they have neither ill-will nor treachery. All of them, women and men alike, go about naked as their mothers bore them, although some of the women wear a small piece of cotton or a patch of grass with which they cover themselves. They have neither iron nor weapons, except for canes on the end of which they place a thin sharp stick. Everything they make is done with [stone tools]. And I have not learned that any of them have any private property, because while I was spending a few days with this king in the village of La Navidad, I saw that all of the people, and the women in particular, would bring him *agís* [hot red pepper], which is the food they eat, and he would order them to be distributed. . . .

Nowhere in these islands have I known the inhabitants to have a religion, or idolatry, or much diversity of language among them, but rather they all understand one another. I learned that they know that all powers reside in heaven. And, generally, in whatever lands I traveled, they believed and believe that I, together with these ships and people, came from heaven, and they greeted me with such veneration. And today, this very day, they are of the same mind, nor have they strayed from it. . . . And then, upon arriving at whatever settlement, the men, women, and children go from house to house calling out, "Come, come and see the people from heaven!" Everything they have or had they gave for whatever one gave them in exchange, even taking a piece of glass or broken crockery or some such thing, for gold or some other thing of whatever value.

One sailor got more than two and a half *castellanos* [in gold] for the ends of leather latchets. There are ten thousand like occurrences to tell.

The islands are all very flat and low-lying, except for Juana and Española. These two are very high lands, and there are mountain chains and very high peaks, much higher than those of the island of Tenerife. The mountains are of a thousand different shapes and all [are] most beautiful, and fertile and walkable and full of trees; it seems they touch the sky. And both the one and the other of the said islands are very large. . . . Juana has many rivers, and great mountains, and very large valleys and meadows and fields, and it is all full of trees and huge palms of a thousand varieties, such as to make one marvel. [Española] has the advantage in every respect; the trees are not so tall or of the same kind, but rather very fruitful and broad; and [they are] delectable lands for all things, and for sowing and planting and raising livestock, of which I have not seen any kind on any of these islands. This island has marvelously temperate breezes, and marvelous meadows and fields incomparable to those of Castile; and the same can be said of the rivers of great and good waters, most of which are gold-bearing. There are so many and such good sea harbors that it has to be seen to be believed. I have not tarried in these islands or the others for many reasons, as I said above, but especially because it was winter when I sailed these coasts, which did not allow me to go south because I was on their north side and the [winds] were almost always easterly, which were contrary to continuing my navigation. Then I did not understand those people nor they me, except for what common sense dictated, although they were saddened and I much more so, because I wanted to have good information concerning everything. And what I did to remedy this was the Indians I had with me, for they learned our language and we theirs, and the next voyage will tell. So, there was no reason for me to tarry at any harbor wasting time when the opportunity came to set sail. Moreover, as I have said, these vessels I brought with me were too large and heavy for such a purpose, especially the [larger and heavier *Santa Maria*], about which I was quite troubled before leaving Castile. I would much have preferred taking small caravels, but since this was the first voyage and the people I brought were afraid of running into high seas and uncertain about the voyage, and there was and has been so much opposition, and anybody dared to contradict this route and ascribe to it a thousand dangers without being able to give me any reasons, they caused me to act against my own judgment and do everything that those who were to go with me wanted, in order to get the voyage finally under way and find the land. But Our Lord, who is the light and strength of all those who seek to do good and makes them victorious in deeds that seem impossible, wished to ordain that I should find and was to find gold and mines and spicery and innumerable peoples . . . I left in [Española], in possession of the village of La Navidad, the people I brought on the [*Santa Maria*] and some from the caravels, stocked with provisions to last over a year, [with] much artillery and quite without danger from anyone, but rather with much friendship from the king of that place, who prided himself in calling me and having me for a brother; who [also] appeared to accept everything as the greatest boon in the world, as I said. And the others [feel] just as the king does, so that the people I left there suffice to subjugate the entire island without danger. This island is in a place, as I have said, signaled by the hand of Our Lord, where I hope His Majesty will give Your Highnesses as much gold as you need, spicery of a certain pepper [to fill] as many ships as Your Highnesses may order to be loaded, and as much mastic[1] as you may order to load, which today can be found only on the island of Chios, in Greece. . . . And . . . as much cotton as you may order to be loaded, and so many slaves that they are innumerable; and they will come from the idolaters. And I believe there are rhubarb and cinnamon. All this I found on this hasty trip, but I have faith in God that upon my return the people I left there will have found a thousand other things of importance, because that is the charge I left them with. And I left them a boat and its equipment and [the tools] to make boats, and masters in all the nautical arts. And above all I consider all the above-mentioned islands as belonging to Your Highnesses and you may command them as you do the kingdoms of Castile, and even more completely, especially this one of Española.

I conclude here: that through the divine grace of Him who is the origin of all good and virtuous things, who favors and gives victory to all those who walk in His path, in seven years from today I will be able to pay Your Highnesses for five thousand cavalry and fifty thousand foot soldiers for the war and conquest of Jerusalem, for which purpose this enterprise was undertaken. And in another five years another five thousand cavalry and fifty thousand foot soldiers, which will total ten thousand cavalry and one hundred thousand foot soldiers; and all of this with very little investment now on Your Highnesses' part in this beginning of the taking of the Indies and all that they contain, as I will tell Your Highnesses in person later. And I have reason for this [claim] and do not speak uncertainly, and one should not delay in it, as was the case with the execution of this enterprise, may God forgive whoever has been the cause of it.

Most powerful sovereigns: all of Christendom should hold great celebrations, and especially God's Church, for the finding of such a multitude of such friendly peoples, which with very little effort will be converted to our Holy Faith, and so many lands filled with so many goods very necessary to us in which all Christians will have comfort and profits, all of which was unknown nor did anyone speak of it except in fables. . . . Your Highnesses should order that [many] praises should be given to the Holy Trinity . . . because of the great love [the Holy Trinity] has shown you, more than to any other prince.

Now, most serene sovereigns, remember that I left my woman and children behind and came from my homeland to serve you, in which [service] I spent what I had. And I spent seven years of my time and put up with a thousand indignities and disgrace and I suffered much hardship. I did not wish to deal with other princes who solicited me, although Your Highnesses' giving of your protection to this voyage has owed more to my importuning [you] than to anything else. And not only has no favor been shown to me, but moreover nothing of what was promised me has been fulfilled. I do not ask favors of Your Highnesses in order to amass treasure, for I have no purpose other than to serve God and Your Highnesses and to bring this business of the Indies to perfection, as time will be my witness. And therefore I beseech you that honor be bestowed upon me according to [the quality of] my service.

The Church of God should also work for this: providing prelates and devout and wise religious; and because the matter is so great and of such a charac-

---

1. **mastic:** tree resin used in making varnish.

ter, there is reason for the Holy Father to provide prelates who are very free of greed for temporal possessions and very true to the service of God and of Your Highnesses. And therefore I beseech you to ask the Church, in the letter you write regarding this victory, for a cardinalate for my son, and that it be granted him although he may not yet be of sufficient age, for there is little difference in his age and that of the son of the Medicis of Florence, to whom a cardinal's hat was granted without his having served or having had a purpose so honorable to Christianity, and that you give me the letter pertaining to this matter so that I [myself] may solicit it.

Furthermore, most serene sovereigns, because the sin of ungratefulness was the first one to be punished, I realize that since I am not guilty of it I must at all times try to gain from Your Highnesses the following [favor], because, without a doubt, were it not for [my friend and crew member] Villacorta, who every time it was necessary persuaded and worked on [the enterprise's] behalf, because I was already sick of it and everyone who had been and was involved in the matter was tired, [the enterprise would not have succeeded]. Therefore, I beseech Your Highnesses that you do me the favor of making him paymaster of the Indies, for I vouch that he will do it well.

Wherefore Your Highnesses should know that the first island of the Indies, closest to Spain, is populated entirely by women, without a single man, and their comportment is not feminine, but rather they use weapons and other masculine practices. They carry bows and arrows and take their adornments from the copper mines, which metal they have in very large quantity. They call this island Matenino. . . . Here are found those people which all those of the other islands of the Indies fear; they eat human flesh, are great bowmen, have many [large] canoes . . . in which they travel all over the islands of the Indies, and they are so feared that they have no equal. They go about naked like the others, except that they wear their hair very full, like women. I think the great cowardice . . . [of the] peoples of the other islands, for which there is no remedy, makes them say that these of Caribe are brave, but I think the same of them as of the rest. And when Your Highnesses give the order for me to send slaves, I hope to bring or send [you] these for the most part; these are the ones who have intercourse with the women of Matenino, who if they bear a female child they keep her with them, and if it is a male child, they raise him until he can feed himself and then they send him to Cardo. Between the islands of Cardo and Española there is another island they call Borinque, all of it is a short distance from the other region of the island of Juana that they call Cuba. In the westernmost part [of Cuba], in one of the two provinces I did not cover, which is called Faba, everyone is born with a tail. Beyond this island of Juana, still within sight, there is another that these Indians assured me was larger than Juana, which they call Jamaica, where all the people are bald. On this one there is gold in immeasurable quantities; and now I have Indians with me who have been on these [islands] as well as the others and they know the language and customs. Nothing further, except that may the Holy Trinity guard and make Your Highnesses' royal estate prosper in Its service. Written in the Sea of Spain, on the fourth day of March in the year fourteen ninety-three. At sea.

4

Description of Virginia

John Smith

Before he became one of the original settlers of Jamestown in 1607, Captain John Smith (1580–1631) was already experienced as a soldier and diplomat, fighting the Spanish in the Netherlands and the Turks in Hungary. At Jamestown he took part in governing the colony—leading it from 1608 to 1609—and in managing relations with the Native Americans. His story, told years later, of being saved from death by the friendly intervention of Pocahontas, the daughter of Chief Powhatan, has a secure place in American legend. Historians and ethnographers disagree about whether the incident happened and, if it did, whether Smith correctly understood its meaning in the context of the native culture. Many suspect that it was part of a ritual inducting Smith into the tribe rather than a rescue.

Smith returned to England in 1609. His later years were given over to promoting both himself and the settlement of the New World he had helped to colonize. His descriptions in numerous writings both of British America and of its Native American inhabitants set patterns that continued for centuries.

BEFORE YOU READ

1. How would you describe Smith's account of the New World? What kind of modern writing or communication does it suggest?

2. What adjectives would you apply to Smith's description of the Native Americans? How reliable does his account of the Indians seem to you?

THE COMMODITIES IN VIRGINIA
OR THAT MAY BE HAD BY INDUSTRY

The mildness of the air, the fertility of the soil, and the situation of the rivers are so propitious to the nature and use of man as no place is more convenient for pleasure, profit, and man's sustenance. Under that latitude or climate, here will live any beasts, as horses, goats, sheep, asses, hens, etc. The waters, islands, and shoals are full of safe harbors for ships of war or merchandise, for boats of all sorts, for transportation or fishing, etc.

The Bay and rivers have much marketable fish and places fit for salt works, building of ships, making of iron, etc.

Captain John Smith of Willoughby by Alford, Lincolnshire; President of Virginia and Admiral of New England. Works: 1608–1631, ed. Edward Arber, The English Scholar's Library, No. 16 (Birmingham, 1884), pp. 63–67. The text has been modernized by Elizabeth Marcus.

Muscovia and Polonia yearly receive many thousands for pitch, tar, soap ashes, rosin, flax, cordage, sturgeon, masts, yards, wainscot, furs, glass, and suchlike; also Swethland[1] for iron and copper. France, in like manner, for wine, canvas, and salt, Spain as much for iron, steel, figs, raisins and sherry. Italy with silks and velvets, consumes our chief commodities. Holland maintains itself by fishing and trading at our own doors. All these temporize with others for necessities, but all as uncertain as to peace or war, and besides the charge, travel and danger in transporting them, by seas, lands, storms and pirates. Then how much has Virginia the prerogative of all those flourishing kingdoms for the benefit of our lands, when as within one hundred miles all those are to be had, either ready provided by nature or else to be prepared, were there but industrious men to labor. Only copper might be lacking, but there is good probability that both copper and better minerals are there to be had if they are worked for. Their countries have it. So then here is a place a nurse for soldiers, a practice for mariners, a trade for merchants, a reward for the good, and that which is most of all, a business (most acceptable to God) to bring such poor infidels to the true knowledge of God and his holy Gospel.

OF THE NATURAL INHABITANTS
OF VIRGINIA

The land is not populous, for the men be few, their far greater number is of women and children. Within 60 miles of Jamestown there are about some 5,000 people, but of able men fit for their wars scarce 1,500. To nourish so many together they have yet no means, because they make so small a benefit of their land, be it never so fertile.

Six or seven hundred have been the most that have been seen together, when they gathered themselves to have surprised Captain Smyth at Pamaunke, having but 15 to withstand the worst of their fury. As small as the proportion of ground that has yet been discovered, is in comparison of that yet unknown. The people differ very much in stature, especially in language, as before is expressed.

Since being very great as the Sesquaesahamocks, others very little as the Wighcocomocoes: but generally tall and straight, of a comely proportion, and of a color brown, when they are of any age, but they are born white. Their hair is generally black, but few have any beards. The men wear half their heads shaven, the other half long. For barbers they use their women, who with 2 shells will grate away the hair in any fashion they please. The women are cut in many fashions agreeable to their years, but ever some part remain long.

They are very strong, of an able body and full of agility, able to endure, to lie in the woods under a tree by the fire, in the worst of winter, or in the weeds and grass, in ambush in the summer.

They are inconstant in everything, but what fear constrains them to keep. Crafty, timorous, quick of apprehension and very ingenious. Some are of disposition fearful, some bold, most cautious, all savage. Generally covetous of cop-

---

1. **Swethland:** Sweden.

per, beads and such like trash. They are soon moved to anger, and so malicious, that they seldom forget an injury: they seldom steal from one another, lest their conjurors should reveal it, and so they be pursued and punished. That they are thus feared is certain, but that any can reveal their offenses by conjuration I am doubtful. Their women are careful not to be suspected of dishonesty without leave of their husbands.

Each household knows their own lands and gardens, and most live off their own labors.

For their apparel, they are some time covered with the skins of wild beasts, which in winter are dressed with the hair but in summer without. The better sort use large mantles of deerskin not much different in fashion from the Irish mantles. Some embroidered them with beads, some with copper, others painted after their manner. But the common sort have scarce to cover their nakedness but with grass, the leaves of trees or suchlike. We have seen some use mantles that nothing could be discerned but the feathers, that was exceedingly warm and handsome. But the women are always covered about their middles with a skin and are ashamed to be seen bare.

They adorn themselves most with copper beads and paintings. Their women have their legs, hands, breasts and face cunningly embroidered with diverse works, as beasts, serpents, artificially wrought into their flesh with black spots. In each ear commonly they have three great holes, from which they hang chains, bracelets or copper. Some of their men wear in those holes a small green and yellow colored snake, near half a yard in length, which crawling and lapping herself around his neck oftentimes familiarly would kiss his lips. Others wear a dead rat tied by the tail. Some on their heads wear the wing of a bird or some large feather, with a rattle; those rattles are somewhat like the chape of a rapier, but less, which they take from the tails of a snake. Many have the whole skin of a hawk or some strange fowl, stuffed with the wings abroad. Others a broad piece of copper, and some the hand of their enemy dried. Their heads and shoulders are painted red with the root Pocone pounded to a powder mixed with oil; this they hold in summer to preserve them from the heat and in winter from the cold. Many other forms of paintings they use, but he is the most gallant that is the most monstrous to behold.

Their buildings and habitations are for the most part by the rivers or not far distant from some fresh spring. Their houses are built like our arbors of small young springs bowed and tied, and so close covered with mats or the barks of trees very handsomely, that notwithstanding either wind, rain or weather, they are as warm as stoves, but very smokey; yet at the top of the house there is a hole made for the smoke to go into right over the fire.

Against the fire they lie on little mounds of reeds covered with a mat, borne from the ground a foot and more by a mound of wood. On these round about the house, they lie heads and points one by the other against the fire, some covered with mats, some with skins, and some stark naked lie on the ground, from 6 to 20 in a house.

Their houses are in the midst of their fields or gardens; which are small plots of ground, some 20, some 40, some 100, some 200, some more, some less.

Sometimes from 2 to 100 of these houses are together, or but a little separated by groves of trees. Near their habitations is a little small wood, or old trees on the ground, by reason of their burning of them for fire. So that a man may gallop a horse among these woods anyway, but where the creeks or rivers shall hinder.

Men, women and children have their several names according to the particular whim of their parents. Their women (they say) are easily delivered of child, yet do they love children dearly. To make them hardy, in the coldest mornings they wash them in the rivers, and by painting and ointments so tan their skins that after a year or two no weather will hurt them.

The men bestow their times in fishing, hunting, wars, and such manlike exercises, scorning to be seen in any woman like exercise, which is the cause that the women be very painful and the men often idle. The women and children do the rest of the work. They make mats, baskets, pots, mortars, pound their corn, make their bread, prepare their victuals, plant their corn, gather their corn, bear all kinds of burdens and suchlike.

5

Testimony of Pueblo Indians
Pedro Naranjo and Josephe

Once Cortés conquered Tenochtitlán in 1521, the Spanish quickly gained control over the entire Aztec empire. Indians accustomed to tribute and forced labor simply adapted to new masters. But as Spanish soldiers, settlers, and missionaries moved northward in search of precious metals and outposts to secure their empire from European and Indian enemies, they found that the methods that had worked farther south failed among the more independent tribes that had never been conquered by their Aztec predecessors. Franciscan and Jesuit missionaries struggled mightily to convert Native Americans as settlement inched northward; by 1670, about twenty-eight hundred Spaniards populated the valley of the Rio Grande.

The country was generally poor, punctuated only by an occasional silver mine; the population lived largely by farming and raising livestock. Needed supplies from Mexico arrived infrequently and at great cost. Governors and missionaries battled for preeminence, while settlers, there at the king's command, were disgruntled. And the Indians, however sincere their conversion to Catholicism, were at the bottom of society bearing the brunt of these harsh circumstances. Nor were the old religions dead. The valley was a true frontier with Apache, Hopi, and Navaho, all beyond Spanish power, threatening the Pueblo Indians while providing a powerful example of freedom.

The uprising of the Pueblo Indians in 1680 drove the Spanish out of Santa Fe and all the surrounding settlements. Four hundred Spaniards died during the conflict, and the rest retreated south to El Paso. Efforts at reconquest in 1681 had only temporary success. A number of the converted Indians who made peace at La Isleta moved south for Spanish protection against their tribal enemies. But others remained independent and returned to the practice of their native religions. In the 1690s, a new Spanish commander, Don Diego de Vargas, through skillful diplomacy and a few carefully limited military campaigns, brought most of the Pueblo tribes back under Spanish rule. In the meantime, however, the Indian capture of Spanish horses had begun a momentous transformation. Within a generation, this super-weapon of the age had spread far northward among the Indians. When it met the other super-weapon—the rifle—carried westward by English and French frontiersmen and traders, the plains Indian brave who has dominated the American imagination was born.

Pedro Naranjo and Josephe were captured by the Spanish during the Pueblo rebellion and brought before a royal court in 1681. While Pedro was quite contrite in his testimony to the court regarding his admitted role in the revolt, Josephe seized the opportunity to tell of the colonists' cruelty.

Charles Wilson Hackett, *Revolt of the Pueblo Indians of New Mexico and Otermín's Attempted Reconquest, 1680–1682* (Albuquerque: University of New Mexico Press, 1942), pp. 238–42, 245–49.

BEFORE YOU READ

1. How did Pedro Naranjo explain the revolt? To what extent do you think he was tailoring his answer to his Spanish questioners?

2. How did Josephe explain the revolt? What differences do you notice between his account and Pedro Naranjo's?

3. What according to Josephe were the strategic objectives of the leaders of the revolt? How did they inspire the Pueblo Indians to revolt?

DECLARATION OF PEDRO NARANJO OF THE QUERES NATION

December 19, 1681

In the said plaza de armas on the said day, month, and year, for the prosecution of the judicial proceedings of this case his lordship caused to appear before him an Indian prisoner named Pedro Naranjo, a native of the pueblo of San Felipe, of the Queres nation, who was captured in the advance and attack upon the pueblo of La Isleta. He makes himself understood very well in the Castilian language and speaks his mother tongue and the Tegua. He took the oath in due legal form in the name of God, our Lord, and a sign of the cross. . . .

Asked whether he knows the reason or motives which the Indians of this kingdom had for rebelling, forsaking the law of God and obedience to his Majesty, and committing such grave and atrocious crimes, and who were the leaders and principal movers, and by whom and how it was ordered; and why they burned the images, temples, crosses, rosaries, and things of divine worship, committing such atrocities as killing priests, Spaniards, women, and children, and the rest that he might know touching the question, he said that since the government of Señor General Hernando Ugarte y la Concha they have planned to rebel on various occasions through conspiracies of the Indian sorcerers, and that although in some pueblos the messages were accepted, in other parts they would not agree to it; and that it is true that during the government of the said señor general seven or eight Indians were hanged for this same cause, whereupon the unrest subsided. Some time thereafter they [the conspirators] sent from the pueblo of Los Taos through the pueblos of the custodia two deerskins with some pictures on them signifying conspiracy after their manner, in order to convoke the people to a new rebellion, and the said deerskins passed to the province of Moqui, where they refused to accept them. The pact which they had been forming ceased for the time being, but they always kept in their hearts the desire to carry it out, so as to live as they are living to-day. Finally, in the past years, at the summons of an Indian named Popé, who is said to have communication with the devil, it happened that in an estufa of the pueblo of Los Taos there appeared to the said Popé three figures of Indians who never came out of the estufa. They gave the said Popé to understand that they were going underground to the lake of Copala. He saw these figures emit fire from all the extremities of their bodies, and that one of them was called Caudi, another Tilini, and the other Tleume; and these three beings spoke to the said Popé, who was in hiding from the secretary, Francisco Xavier, who wished to punish him as a sorcerer. They told him to make a cord of maguey fiber and tie some knots in it which would signify the number of days that they must wait before the rebellion. He said that the cord was passed through all the pueblos of the kingdom so that the ones which agreed to it [the rebellion] might untie one knot in a sign of obedience, and by the other knots they would know the days which were lacking; and this was to be done on pain of death to those who refused to agree to it. As a sign of agreement and notice of having concurred in the treason and perfidy they were to send up smoke signals to that effect in each one of the pueblos singly. The said cord was taken from pueblo to pueblo by the swiftest youths under the penalty of death if they revealed the secret. Everything being thus arranged, two days before the time set for its execution, because his lordship had learned of it and had imprisoned two Indian accomplices from the pueblo of Tesuque, it was carried out prematurely that night, because it seemed to them that they were now discovered; and they killed religious, Spaniards, women, and children. This being done, it was proclaimed in all the pueblos that everyone in common should obey the commands of their father whom they did not know, which would be given through El Caydi or El Popé. This was heard by Alonso Catití, who came to the pueblo of this declarant to say that everyone must unite to go to the villa to kill the governor and the Spaniards who had remained with him, and that he who did not obey would, on their return, be beheaded; and in fear of this they agreed to it. Finally the señor governor and those who were with him escaped from the siege, and later this declarant saw that as soon as the Spaniards had left the kingdom an order came from the said Indian, Popé, in which he commanded all the Indians to break the lands and enlarge their cultivated fields, saying that now they were as they had been in ancient times, free from the labor they had performed for the religious and the Spaniards, who could not now be alive. He said that this is the legitimate cause and the reason they had for rebelling, because they had always desired to live as they had when they came out of the lake of Copala. Thus he replies to the question.

Asked for what reason they so blindly burned the images, temples, crosses, and other things of divine worship, he stated that the said Indian, Popé, came down in person, and with him El Saca and El Chato from the pueblo of Los Taos, and other captains and leaders and many people who were in his train, and he ordered in all the pueblos through which he passed that they instantly break up and burn the images of the holy Christ, the Virgin Mary and the other saints, the crosses, and everything pertaining to Christianity, and that they burn the temples, break up the bells, and separate from the wives whom God had given them in marriage and take those whom they desired. In order to take away their baptismal names, the water, and the holy oils, they were to plunge into the rivers and wash themselves with amole, which is a root native to the country, washing even their clothing, with the understanding that there would thus be taken from them the character of the holy sacraments. They did this, and also many other things which he does not recall, given to understand that this mandate had come from the Caydi and the other two who emitted fire from their extremities in the said estufa of Taos, and that they thereby returned to the state of their antiquity, as when they came from the lake of Copala; that this was the better life and the one they desired, because the God of the Spaniards was worth nothing and theirs was very strong, the Spaniards' God being rotten wood. These things were observed and obeyed by all except some who, moved by the zeal of Christians, opposed it, and such persons the said Popé caused to be killed immediately. He saw to it that they at once erected and rebuilt their houses of idolatry which they call estufas, and made very ugly masks in imitation of the devil in order to dance the dance of the cacina; and he said likewise that the devil had given them to understand that living thus in accordance with the law of their ancestors, they would harvest a great deal of maize, many beans, a great abundance of cotton, calabashes, and very large watermelons and cantaloupes; and that they could erect their houses and enjoy abundant health and leisure. As he has said, the people were very much pleased, living at their ease in this life of their antiquity, which was the chief cause of their falling into such laxity. Following what has already been stated, in order to terrorize them further and cause them to observe the diabolical commands, there came to them a pronouncement from the three demons already described, and from El Popé, to the effect that he who might still keep in his heart a regard for the priests, the governor, and the Spaniards would be known from his unclean face and clothes, and would be punished. And he stated that the said four persons stopped at nothing to have their commands obeyed. Thus he replies to the question.

Asked what arrangements and plans they had made for the contingency of the Spaniards' return, he said that what he knows concerning the question is that they were always saying they would have to fight to the death, for they do not wish to live in any other way than they are living at present; and the demons in the estufa of Taos had given them to understand that as soon as the Spaniards began to move toward this kingdom they would warn them so that they might unite, and none of them would be caught. He having been questioned further and repeatedly touching the case, he said that he has nothing more to say. . . . His declaration being read to him, he affirmed and ratified all of it. He declared himself to be eighty years of age, and he signed it with his lordship and the interpreters and assisting witnesses. . . .

DECLARATION OF JOSEPHE, SPANISH-SPEAKING INDIAN

December 19, 1681

In this said place and plaza de armas of this army on the 19th day of the month of December, 1681, for the said judicial proceedings of this case, his lordship caused to appear before him an Indian prisoner named Josephe, able to speak the Castilian language, a servant of Sargento Mayor Sebastián de Herrera who fled from him and went among the apostates. . . . Being asked why he fled from his master, the said Sargento Mayor Sebastián de Herrera, and went to live with the treacherous Indian apostates of New Mexico, where he has been until he came among us on the present occasion, he said that the reason why he left was that he was suffering hunger in the plaza de armas of La Toma [del Río del Norte], and a companion of his named Domingo urged this declarant to go to New Mexico for a while, so as to find out how matters stood with the Indians and to give warning to the Spaniards of any treason. They did not come with the intention of remaining always with the apostate traitors and rebels, and after they arrived they [the Indians] killed the said Domingo, his companion, because of the Pecos Indians having seen him fighting in the villa along with the Spaniards. He said that because his comrade was gone he had remained until now, when he saw the Spaniards and came to them, warning them not to be careless with the horses, because he had heard the traitors say that although the Spaniards might conclude peace with them, they would come to attack them by night and take away the horses. Thus he responds to this question.

Asked what causes or motives the said Indian rebels had for renouncing the law of God and obedience to his Majesty, and for committing so many kinds of crimes, and who were the instigators of the rebellion, and what he had heard while he was among the apostates, he said that the prime movers of the rebellion were two Indians of San Juan, one named El Popé and the other El Taqu, and another from Taos named Saca, and another from San Ildefonso named Francisco. He knows that these were the principals, and the causes they gave were alleged ill treatment and injuries received from the present secretary, Francisco Xavier, and the maestre de campo, Alonso García, and from the sargentos mayores, Luis de Quintana and Diego López, because they beat them, took away what they had, and made them work without pay. Thus he replies.

Asked why, since the said rebels had been of different minds, some believing that they should give themselves up peacefully and others opposing it, when the Spaniards arrived at the sierra of La Cieneguilla de Cochití, where the leaders of the uprising and people from all the nations were assembled, they had not attempted to give themselves up and return to the holy faith and to obedience to his Majesty—for while they had made some signs, they had done nothing definite—he said that although it is true that as soon as the Spaniards arrived some said that it was better to give up peaceably than to have war, the young men were unwilling to agree, saying that they wished to fight. In particular one Spanish-speaking Indian or coyote named Francisco, commonly called El Ollita, said that no one should surrender in peace, that all must fight, and that although some of his brothers were coming with the Spaniards, if they fought on the side of the Spaniards he would kill them, and if they came over to the side of the Indians he would not harm them. Whereupon everyone was disturbed, and there having arrived at this juncture Don Luis Tupatú, governor of the pueblo of Los Pecuríes, while they were thus consulting, news came to the place where the junta was being held from another Indian named Alonso Catití, a leader of the uprising, believed to be a coyote, in which he sent to notify the people that he had already planned to deceive the Spaniards with feigned peace. He had arranged to send to the pueblo of Cochití all the prettiest, most pleasing, and neatest Indian women so that, under pretense of coming down to prepare food for the Spaniards, they could provoke them to lewdness, and that night while they were with them, the said coyote Catití would come down with all the men of the Queres and Jemez nations, only the said Catití attempting to speak with the said Spaniards, and at a shout from him they would all rush down to kill the said Spaniards; and he gave orders that all the rest who were in the other junta where the said Don Luis and El Ollita were present, should at the same time attack the horse drove, so as to finish that too. This declarant being present during all these proceedings, and feeling compassion because of the treason they were plotting, he determined to come to warn the Spaniards, as he did, whereupon they put themselves under arms and the said Indians again went up to the heights of the sierra, and the Spaniards withdrew. Thus he replies to the question. . . .

. . . He said that what he has stated in his declaration is the truth and what he knows, under charge of his oath, which he affirms and ratifies, this, his said declaration, being read to him. He did not sign because of not knowing how, nor does he know his age. Apparently he is about twenty years old. . . .

6

Encounter with the Indians
Father Paul Le Jeune

In the sixteenth and seventeenth centuries, France's Society of Jesus of the Roman Catholic Church, more commonly known as the Jesuits, energetically proselytized in virtually every Portuguese, Spanish, and French colony. The first Jesuit missionaries arrived in French Canada in 1632 determined to bring Christianity to the Indians by living with them, learning their languages, educating their children, and demonstrating (sometimes at the cost of their lives) that they were as brave as the Native American warriors. The French, though haughty and arrogant at times, were much less authoritarian than the Spanish in dealing with natives—and far more successful. The Jesuits played a major role in cementing French alliances with many Native American nations across Canada and into the Ohio Valley. This gave France a strategic position in the New World, hemming the colonies of British North America against the eastern seaboard until French power was destroyed in the mid–eighteenth century. The Jesuits in Canada reported regularly on their ministry. These reports form an important account of American Indian life and greatly influenced the European perception of the New World. (It is regrettable that no Indian accounts survive to portray the surly nature of many of the French Jesuits.)

Father Paul Le Jeune, born in France in 1591, became a Jesuit in 1613. He had been a professor of rhetoric as well as Superior of the Jesuit House at Dieppe before he radically changed his activities by going to French North America in 1632. Le Jeune found much to admire in the Native Americans, as well as much that he could neither understand nor accept. The report included here was written from Quebec in August 1634. Le Jeune worked among the Indians until 1649. He died in Paris in 1664.

BEFORE YOU READ

1. What were Father Le Jeune's impressions and assessment of Native American religion?
2. What did he consider the Indians' virtues?
3. What did he consider their main vices?

CHAPTER IV. ON THE BELIEF, SUPERSTITIONS, AND ERRORS OF THE MONTAGNAIS SAVAGES

I have already reported that the Savages believe that a certain one named Atahocam had created the world, and that one named Messou had restored it. I

Reuben Gold Thwaites, ed., *The Jesuit Relations and Allied Documents: Travels and Explorations of the Jesuit Missionaries in New France* (Cleveland: Burrows Brothers, 1987).

have questioned upon this subject the famous Sorcerer and the old man with whom I passed the Winter; they answered that they did not know who was the first Author of the world,—that it was perhaps Atahocam, but that was not certain; that they only spoke of Atahocam as one speaks of a thing so far distant that nothing sure can be known about it. . . .

As to the Messou, they hold that he restored the world, which was destroyed in the flood; whence it appears that they have some tradition of that great universal deluge which happened in the time of Noë. . . .

They also say that all animals, of every species, have an elder brother, who is, as it were, the source and origin of all individuals, and this elder brother is wonderfully great and powerful. . . . Now these elders of all the animals are the juniors of the Messou. Behold him well related, this worthy restorer of the Universe, he is elder brother to all beasts. If any one, when asleep, sees the elder or progenitor of some animals, he will have a fortunate chase; if he sees the elder of the Beavers, he will take Beavers; if he sees the elder of the Elks, he will take Elks, possessing the juniors through the favor of their senior whom he has seen in the dream. . . .

Their Religion, or rather their superstition, consists besides in praying; but O, my God, what prayers they make! In the morning, when the little children come out from their Cabins, they shout, *Cacouakhi, Pakhais Amiscouakhi, Pakhais Mousouakhi, Pakhais,* "Come, Porcupines; come, Beavers; come, Elk;" and this is all of their prayers.

When the Savages sneeze, and sometimes even at other times, during the Winter, they cry out in a loud voice, *Etouctaian miraounam an Mirouscamikhi,* "I shall be very glad to see the Spring."

At other times, I have heard them pray for the Spring, or for deliverance from evils and other similar things; and they express all these things in the form of desires, crying out as loudly as they can, "I would be very glad if this day would continue, if the wind would change," etc. I could not say to whom these wishes are addressed, for they themselves do not know, at least those whom I have asked have not been able to enlighten me. . . .

These are some of their superstitions. How much dust there is in their eyes, and how much trouble there will be to remove it that they may see the beautiful light of truth! I believe, nevertheless, that anyone who knew their language perfectly, in order to give them good reasons promptly, would soon make them laugh at their own stupidity; for sometimes I have made them ashamed and confused, although I speak almost entirely by my hands, I mean by signs. . . .

CHAPTER V. ON THE GOOD THINGS
WHICH ARE FOUND AMONG THE SAVAGES

If we begin with physical advantages, I will say that they possess these in abundance. They are tall, erect, strong, well proportioned, agile; and there is nothing effeminate in their appearance. Those little Fops that are seen elsewhere are only caricatures of men, compared with our Savages. I almost believed, heretofore, that the Pictures of the Roman Emperors represented the ideal of the painters rather than men who had ever existed, so strong and powerful are their heads; but I see here upon the shoulders of these people the heads of Julius Caesar, of Pompey, of Augustus, of Otho, and of others, that I have seen in France, drawn upon paper, or in relief on medallions.

As to the mind of the Savage, it is of good quality. I believe that souls are all made from the same stock, and that they do not materially differ; hence, these barbarians having well formed bodies, and organs well regulated and well arranged, their minds ought to work with ease. Education and instruction alone are lacking. Their soul is a soil which is naturally good, but loaded down with all the evils that a land abandoned since the birth of the world can produce. I naturally compare our Savages with certain villagers, because both are usually without education, though our Peasants are superior in this regard; and yet I have not seen any one thus far, of those who have come to this country, who does not confess and frankly admit that the Savages are more intelligent than our ordinary peasants.

Moreover, if it is a great blessing to be free from a great evil, our Savages are happy; for the two tyrants who provide hell and torture for many of our Europeans, do not reign in their great forests,—I mean ambition and avarice. As they have neither political organization, nor offices, nor dignities, nor any authority, for they only obey their Chief through good will toward him, therefore they never kill each other to acquire these honors. Also, as they are contented with a mere living, not one of them gives himself to the Devil to acquire wealth.

They make a pretence of never getting angry, not because of the beauty of this virtue, for which they have not even a name, but for their own contentment and happiness, I mean, to avoid the bitterness caused by anger. The Sorcerer said to me one day, speaking of one of our Frenchmen, "He has no sense, he gets angry; as for me, nothing can disturb me; let hunger oppress me, let my nearest relation pass to the other life, let the Hiroquois, our enemies, massacré our people, I never get angry." What he says is not an article of faith; for, as he is more haughty than any other Savage, so I have seen him oftener out of humor than any of them; it is true also that he often restrains and governs himself by force, especially when I expose his foolishness. I have only heard one Savage pronounce this word, *Ninichcatihin*, "I am angry," and he only said it once. But I noticed that they kept their eyes on him, for when these Barbarians are angry, they are dangerous and unrestrained.

Whoever professes not to get angry, ought also to make a profession of patience; the Savages surpass us to such an extent, in this respect, that we ought to be ashamed. I saw them, in their hardships and in their labors, suffer with cheerfulness. My host, wondering at the great number of people who I told him were in France, asked me if the men were good, if they did not become angry, if they were patient. I have never seen such patience as is shown by a sick Savage. You may yell, storm, jump, dance, and he will scarcely ever complain. I found myself, with them, threatened with great suffering; they said to me, "We shall be sometimes two days, sometimes three, without eating, for lack of food; take courage, *Chihiné*, let thy soul be strong to endure suffering and hardship; keep thyself from being sad, otherwise thou wilt be sick; see how we do not cease to laugh, although we have little to eat." One thing alone casts them down,—it is when they see death, for they fear this beyond measure; take away this apprehension from the Savages, and they will endure all kinds of degradation and discomfort, and all kinds of trials and suffering very patiently. . . .

They are very much attached to each other, and agree admirably. You do not see any disputes, quarrels, enmities, or reproaches among them. Men leave the arrangement of the household to the women, without interfering with them; they cut, and decide, and give away as they please, without making the husband angry. . . .

CHAPTER VI. ON THEIR VICES
AND THEIR IMPERFECTIONS

The Savages, being filled with errors, are also haughty and proud. Humility is born of truth, vanity of error and falsehood. They are void of the knowledge of truth, and are in consequence, mainly occupied with thought of themselves. They imagine that they ought by right of birth, to enjoy the liberty of Wild ass colts, rendering no homage to any one whomsoever, except when they like. They have reproached me a hundred times because we fear our Captains, while they laugh at and make sport of theirs. All the authority of their chief is in his tongue's end; for he is powerful in so far as he is eloquent; and, even if he kills himself talking and haranguing, he will not be obeyed unless he pleases the Savages. . . .

I have shown in my former letters how vindictive the Savages are toward their enemies, with what fury and cruelty they treat them, eating them after they have made them suffer all that an incarnate fiend could invent. This fury is common to the women as well as to the men, and they even surpass the latter in this respect. I have said that they eat the lice they find upon themselves, not that they like the taste of them, but because they want to bite those that bite them.

These people are very little moved by compassion. When any one is sick in their Cabins, they ordinarily do not cease to cry and storm, and make as much noise as if everybody were in good health. They do not know what it is to take care of a poor invalid, and to give him the food which is good for him; if he asks for something to drink, it is given to him, if he asks for something to eat, it is given to him, but otherwise he is neglected; to coax him with love and gentleness, is a language which they do not understand. As long as a patient can eat, they will carry or drag him with them; if he stops eating, they believe that it is all over with him and kill him, as much to free him from the sufferings that he is enduring, as to relieve themselves of the trouble of taking him with them when they go to some other place. I have both admired and pitied the patience of the invalids whom I have seen among them.

The Savages are slanderous beyond all belief; I say, also among themselves, for they do not even spare their nearest relations, and with it all they are deceitful. For, if one speaks ill of another, they all jeer with loud laughter; if the other appears upon the scene, the first one will show him as much affection and treat him with as much love, as if he had elevated him to the third heaven by his praise. The reason of this is, it seems to me, that their slanders and derision do not come from malicious hearts or from infected mouths, but from a mind

which says what it thinks in order to give itself free scope, and which seeks grat-
ification from everything, even from slander and mockery. Hence they are not
troubled even if they are told that others are making sport of them, or have injured their reputation. All they usually answer to such talk is, *mama irinisiou*,
"He has no sense, he does not know what he is talking about"; and at the first
opportunity they will pay their slanderer in the same coin, returning him the
like.

Lying is as natural to Savages as talking, not among themselves, but to
strangers. Hence it can be said that fear and hope, in one word, interest, is the
measure of their fidelity. I would not be willing to trust them, except as they
would fear to be punished if they had failed in their duty, or hoped to be rewarded if they were faithful to it. They do not know what it is to keep a secret,
to keep their word, and to love with constancy,—especially those who are not
of their nation, for they are harmonious among themselves, and their slanders
and raillery do not disturb their peace and friendly intercourse. . . .

CHAPTER XII. WHAT ONE MUST SUFFER
IN WINTERING WITH THE SAVAGES

In order to have some conception of the beauty of this edifice, its construction
must be described. I shall speak from knowledge, for I have often helped to
build it. Now, when we arrived at the place where we were to camp, the
women, armed with axes, went here and there in the great forests, cutting the
framework of the hostelry where we were to lodge; meantime the men, having
drawn the plan thereof, cleared away the snow with their snowshoes, or with
shovels which they make and carry expressly for this purpose. Imagine now a
great ring or square in the snow, two, three or four feet deep, according to the
weather or the place where they encamp. This depth of snow makes a white
wall for us, which surrounds us on all sides, except the end where it is broken
through to form the door. The framework having been brought, which consists
of twenty or thirty poles, more or less, according to the size of the cabin, it is
planted, not upon the ground but upon the snow; then they throw upon these
poles, which converge a little at the top, two or three rolls of bark sewed together, beginning at the bottom, and behold, the house is made. The ground
inside, as well as the wall of snow which extends all around the cabin, is covered
with little branches of fir; and, as a finishing touch, a wretched skin is fastened
to two poles to serve as a door, the doorposts being the snow itself. . . .

You cannot stand upright in this house, as much on account of its low roof
as the suffocating smoke; and consequently you must always lie down, or sit flat
upon the ground, the usual posture of the Savages. When you go out, the cold,
the snow, and the danger of getting lost in these great woods drive you in again
more quickly than the wind, and keep you a prisoner in a dungeon which has
neither lock nor key.

This prison, in addition to the uncomfortable position that one must occupy upon a bed of earth, has four other great discomforts,—cold, heat, smoke,
and dogs. As to the cold, you have the snow at your head with only a pine

branch between, often nothing but your hat, and the winds are free to enter in a thousand places. . . . When I lay down at night I could study through this opening both the Stars and the Moon as easily as if I had been in the open fields.

Nevertheless, the cold did not annoy me as much as the heat from the fire. A little place like their cabins is easily heated by a good fire, which sometimes roasted and broiled me on all sides, for the cabin was so narrow that I could not protect myself against the heat. You cannot move to right or left, for the Savages, your neighbors, are at your elbows; you cannot withdraw to the rear, for you encounter the wall of snow, or the bark of the cabin which shuts you in. I did not know what position to take. Had I stretched myself out, the place was so narrow that my legs would have been halfway in the fire; to roll myself up in a ball, and crouch down in their way, was a position I could not retain as long as they could; my clothes were all scorched and burned. You will ask me perhaps if the snow at our backs did not melt under so much heat. I answer, "no"; that if sometimes the heat softened it in the least, the cold immediately turned it into ice. I will say, however, that both the cold and the heat are endurable, and that some remedy may be found for these two evils.

But, as to the smoke, I confess to you that it is martyrdom. It almost killed me, and made me weep continually, although I had neither grief nor sadness in my heart. It sometimes grounded all of us who were in the cabin; that is, it caused us to place our mouths against the earth in order to breathe. For, although the Savages were accustomed to this torment, yet occasionally it became so dense that they, as well as I, were compelled to prostrate themselves, and as it were to eat the earth, so as not to drink the smoke. I have sometimes remained several hours in this position, especially during the most severe cold and when it snowed; for it was then the smoke assailed us with the greatest fury, seizing us by the throat, nose, and eyes. . . .

As to the dogs, which I have mentioned as one of the discomforts of the Savages' houses, I do not know that I ought to blame them, for they have sometimes rendered me good service. . . . These poor beasts, not being able to live outdoors, came and lay down sometimes upon my shoulders, sometimes upon my feet, and as I only had one blanket to serve both as covering and mattress, I was not sorry for this protection, willingly restoring to them a part of the heat which I drew from them. It is true that, as they were large and numerous, they occasionally crowded and annoyed me so much, that in giving me a little heat they robbed me of my sleep, so that I very often drove them away. . . .

7

Captured by Indians

Mary Jemison

"Captivity narratives"—stories about white women taken captive by Indians—were popular during the entire period in which Native Americans were thought to constitute a danger to settlers on the frontier. Mary Jemison's Narrative *is one of the most famous, having gone through dozens of printings since its initial publication in 1824. That she fell in love with an Indian man and remained a member of the Seneca tribe all her life obviously added spice to her life story.*

Although it is written in the first person, the Narrative *is not really an autobiography. Jemison was eighty years old and illiterate when James E. Seaver interviewed her and wrote it. By then she was long famous in western New York as the "white woman of the Genesee" who since her abduction, probably in 1758 at the age of fifteen, had lived among the Senecas. The* Narrative *is an important source description of Seneca life and culture as well as a fascinating account of a white Anglo-American woman's assimilation into that culture.*

BEFORE YOU READ

1. What was the Seneca custom of adoption as Jemison explained it?
2. How did Jemison explain the Indians' famous cruelty?
3. Why do you think captivity narratives were such popular reading?
4. What do you think Jemison meant when she said "Indians must and will be Indians, in spite of all the means that can be used to instruct them in the arts and sciences"?

CHAPTER III

The night was spent in gloomy forebodings. What the result of our captivity would be, it was out of our power to determine, or even imagine. At times, we could almost realize the approach of our masters to butcher and scalp us; again, we could nearly see the pile of wood kindled on which we were to be roasted; and then we could imagine ourselves at liberty, alone and defenseless in the forest, surrounded by wild beasts that were ready to devour us. The anxiety of our minds drove sleep from our eyelids; and it was with a dreadful hope and painful impatience that we waited for the morning to determine our fate.

James E. Seaver, *A Narrative of the Life of Mary Jemison: Deh-He-Wä-Mis*, 4th ed. (New York: Miller, Orton, and Mulligan, 1856), pp. 52, 53–63, 67–70, 72–74.

The morning at length arrived, and our masters came early and let us out of the house, and gave the young man and boy to the French, who immediately took them away. Their fate I never learned, as I have not seen nor heard of them since.

I was now left alone in the fort, deprived of my former companions, and of every thing that was near or dear to me but life. But it was not long before I was in some measure relieved by the appearance of two pleasant-looking squaws, of the Seneca tribe, who came and examined me attentively for a short time, and then went out. After a few minutes' absence, they returned in company with my former masters, who gave me to the squaws to dispose of as they pleased.

The Indians by whom I was taken were a party of Shawnees, if I remember right, that lived, when at home, a long distance down the Ohio.

My former Indian masters and the two squaws were soon ready to leave the fort, and accordingly embarked—the Indians in a large canoe, and the two squaws and myself in a small one—and went down the Ohio. When we set off, an Indian in the forward canoe took the scalps of my former friends, strung them on a pole that he placed upon his shoulder, and in that manner carried them, standing in the stern of the canoe directly before us, as we sailed down the river, to the town where the two squaws resided.

On the way we passed a Shawnee town, where I saw a number of heads, arms, legs, and other fragments of the bodies of some white people who had just been burned. The parts that remained were hanging on a pole, which was supported at each end by a crotch stuck in the ground, and were roasted or burnt black as a coal. The fire was yet burning; and the whole appearance afforded a spectacle so shocking that even to this day the blood almost curdles in my veins when I think of them.

At night we arrived at a small Seneca Indian town, at the mouth of a small river that was called by the Indians, in the Seneca language, She-nan-jee, about eighty miles by water from the fort, where the two squaws to whom I belonged resided. There we landed, and the Indians went on; which was the last I ever saw of them.

Having made fast to the shore, the squaws left me in the canoe while they went to their wigwam or house in the town, and returned with a suit of Indian clothing, all new, and very clean and nice. My clothes, though whole and good when I was taken, were now torn in pieces, so that I was almost naked. They first undressed me, and threw my rags into the river; then washed me clean and dressed me in the new suit they had just brought, in complete Indian style; and then led me home and seated me in the center of their wigwam.

I had been in that situation but a few minutes before all the squaws in the town came in to see me. I was soon surrounded by them, and they immediately set up a most dismal howling, crying bitterly, and wringing their hands in all the agonies of grief for a deceased relative.

Their tears flowed freely, and they exhibited all the signs of real mourning. At the commencement of this scene, one of their number began, in a voice somewhat between speaking and singing, to recite some words to the following purport, and continued the recitation till the ceremony was ended; the company at the same time varying the appearance of their countenances, gestures, and tone of voice, so as to correspond with the sentiments expressed by their leader.

"Oh, our brother! alas! he is dead—he has gone; he will never return! Friendless he died on the field of the slain, where his bones are yet lying unburied! Oh! who will not mourn his sad fate? No tears dropped around him: oh, no! No tears of his sisters were there! He fell in his prime, when his arm was most needed to keep us from danger! Alas! he has gone, and left us in sorrow, his loss to bewail! Oh, where is his spirit? His spirit went naked, and hungry it wanders, and thirsty and wounded, it groans to return! Oh, helpless and wretched, our brother has gone! No blanket nor food to nourish and warm him; nor candles to light him, nor weapons of war! Oh, none of those comforts had he! But well we remember his deeds! The deer he could take on the chase! The panther shrunk back at the sight of his strength! His enemies fell at his feet! He was brave and courageous in war! As the fawn, he was harmless; his friendship was ardent; his temper was gentle; his pity was great! Oh! our friend, our companion, is dead! Our brother, our brother! alas, he is gone! But why do we grieve for his loss? In the strength of a warrior, undaunted he left us, to fight by the side of the chiefs! His warwhoop was shrill! His rifle well aimed laid his enemies low: his tomahawk drank of their blood: and his knife flayed their scalps while yet covered with gore! And why do we mourn? Though he fell on the field of the slain, with glory he fell; and his spirit went up to the land of his fathers in war! Then why do we mourn? With transports of joy, they received him, and fed him, and clothed him, and welcomed him there! Oh, friends, he is happy; then dry up your tears! His spirit has seen our distress, and sent us a helper whom with pleasure we greet. Deh-he-wä-mis has come: then let us receive her with joy!—she is handsome and pleasant! Oh! She is our sister, and gladly we welcome her here. In the place of our brother she stands in our tribe. With care we will guard her from trouble; and may she be happy till her spirit shall leave us."

In the course of that ceremony, from mourning they became serene,—joy sparkled in their countenances, and they seemed to rejoice over me as over a long-lost child. I was made welcome among them as a sister to the two squaws before mentioned, and was called Deh-he-wä-mis; which, being interpreted, signifies a pretty girl, a handsome girl, or a pleasant, good thing. That is the name by which I have ever since been called by the Indians.

I afterward learned that the ceremony I at that time passed through was that of adoption. The two squaws had lost a brother in Washington's war,[1] sometime in the year before, and in consequence of his death went up to Fort Du Quesne on the day on which I arrived there, in order to receive a prisoner, or an enemy's scalp, to supply their loss. It is a custom of the Indians, when one of their number is slain or taken prisoner in battle, to give to the nearest relative of the dead or absent a prisoner, if they have chanced to take one; and if not, to give him the scalp of an enemy. On the return of the Indians from the conquest, which is always announced by peculiar shoutings, demonstrations of joy, and the exhibition of some trophy of victory, the mourners come forward

---

1. **Washington's War:** the French and Indian War (1756–1763).

and make their claims. If they receive a prisoner, it is at their option either to satiate their vengeance by taking his life in the most cruel manner they can conceive of, or to receive and adopt him into the family, in the place of him whom they have lost. All the prisoners that are taken in battle and carried to the encampment or town by the Indians are given to the bereaved families, till their number is good. And unless the mourners have but just received the news of their bereavement, and are under the operation of a paroxysm of grief, anger, or revenge; or, unless the prisoner is very old, sickly, or homely, they generally save them, and treat them kindly. But if their mental wound is fresh, their loss so great that they deem it irreparable, or if their prisoner or prisoners do not meet their approbation, no torture, let it be ever so cruel, seems sufficient to make them satisfaction. It is family and not national sacrifices among the Indians, that has given them an indelible stamp as barbarians, and identified their character with the idea which is generally formed of unfeeling ferocity and the most barbarous cruelty.

It was my happy lot to be accepted for adoption. At the time of the ceremony I was received by the two squaws to supply the place of their brother in the family; and I was ever considered and treated by them as a real sister, the same as though I had been born of their mother.

During the ceremony of my adoption, I sat motionless, nearly terrified to death at the appearance and actions of the company, expecting every moment to feel their vengeance, and suffer death on the spot. I was, however, happily disappointed; when at the close of the ceremony the company retired, and my sisters commenced employing every means for my consolation and comfort.

Being now settled and provided with a home, I was employed in nursing the children, and doing light work about the house. Occasionally, I was sent out with the Indian hunters, when they went but a short distance, to help them carry their game. My situation was easy; I had no particular hardships to endure. But still, the recollection of my parents, my brothers and sisters, my home, and my own captivity, destroyed my happiness, and made me constantly solitary, lonesome, and gloomy.

My sisters would not allow me to speak English in their hearing; but remembering the charge that my dear mother gave me at the time I left her, whenever I chanced to be alone I made a business of repeating my prayer, catechism, or something I had learned, in order that I might not forget my own language. By practicing in that way, I retained it till I came to Genesee flats, where I soon became acquainted with English people, with whom I have been almost daily in the habit of conversing.

My sisters were very diligent in teaching me their language; and to their great satisfaction, I soon learned so that I could understand it readily, and speak it fluently. I was very fortunate in falling into their hands; for they were kind, good-natured women; peaceable and mild in their dispositions; temperate and decent in their habits, and very tender and gentle toward me. I have great reason to respect them, though they have been dead a great number of years.

In the second summer of my living at Wiishto, I had a child, at the time that the kernels of corn first appeared on the cob. When I was taken sick,

Sheninjee was absent, and I was sent to a small shed on the bank of the river, which was made of boughs, where I was obliged to stay till my husband returned. My two sisters, who were my only companions, attended me; and on the second day of my confinement my child was born; but it lived only two days. It was a girl; and notwithstanding the shortness of the time that I possessed it, it was a great grief to me to lose it.

After the birth of my child I was very sick, but was not allowed to go into the house for two weeks; when, to my great joy, Sheninjee returned, and I was taken in, and as comfortably provided for as our situation would admit. My disease continued to increase for a number of days; and I became so far reduced that my recovery was despaired of by my friends, and I concluded that my troubles would soon be finished. At length, however, my complaint took a favorable turn, and by the time the corn was ripe I was able to get about. I continued to gain my health, and in the fall was able to go to our winter quarters, on the Saratoga, with the Indians.

From that time nothing remarkable occurred to me till the fourth winter of my captivity, when I had a son born, while I was at Sciota. I had a quick recovery, and my child was healthy. To commemorate the name of my much-lamented father, I called my son Thomas Jemison.

CHAPTER IV

In the spring, when Thomas was three or four moons [months] old, we returned from Sciota to Wiishto, and soon after set out to go to Fort Pitt, to dispose of our furs and our skins that we had taken in the winter, and procure some necessary articles for the use of our family.

I had then been with the Indians four summers and four winters, and had become so far accustomed to their mode of living, habits, and dispositions, that my anxiety to get away, to be set at liberty and leave them, had almost subsided. With them was my home; my family was there, and there I had many friends to whom I was warmly attached in consideration of the favors, affection, and friendship with which they had uniformly treated me from the time of my adoption. Our labor was not severe; and that of one year was exactly similar in almost every respect to that of the others, without that endless variety that is to be observed in the common labor of the white people. Notwithstanding the Indian women have all the fuel and bread to procure, and the cooking to perform, their task is probably not harder than that of white women, who have those articles provided for them; and their cares certainly are not half as numerous, nor as great. In the summer season, we planted, tended, and harvested our corn, and generally had all our children with us; but had no master to oversee or drive us, so that we could work as leisurely as we pleased. We had no plows on the Ohio, but performed the whole process of planting and hoeing with a small tool that resembled, in some respect, a hoe with a very short handle.

Our cooking consisted in pounding our corn into samp or hominy, boiling the hominy, making now and then a cake and baking it in the ashes, and in boiling or roasting our venison. As our cooking and eating utensils consisted of a hominy block and pestle, a small kettle, a knife or two, and a few vessels of bark or wood, it required but little time to keep them in order for use.

Spinning, weaving, sewing, stocking knitting, and the like, are arts which have never been practiced in the Indian tribes generally. After the revolutionary war, I learned to sew, so that I could make my own clothing after a poor fashion; but I have been wholly ignorant of the application of the other domestic arts since my captivity. In the season of hunting, it was our business, in addition to our cooking, to bring home the game that was taken by the Indians, dress it, and carefully preserve the eatable meat, and prepare or dress the skins. Our clothing was fastened together with strings of deerskin, and tied on with the same.

In that manner we lived, without any of those jealousies, quarrels, and revengeful battles between families and individuals, which have been common in the Indian tribes since the introduction of ardent spirits among them.

The use of ardent spirits[2] among the Indians, and a majority of the attempts which have been made to civilize them by the white people, have constantly made them worse and worse; increased their vices, and robbed them of many of their virtues, and will ultimately produce their extermination. I have seen, in a number of instances, the effects of education upon some of our Indians, who were taken, when young, from their families, and placed at school before they had had an opportunity to contract many Indian habits, and there kept till they arrived to manhood; but I have never seen one of those but was an Indian in every respect after he returned.[3] Indians must and will be Indians, in spite of all the means that can be used to instruct them in the arts and sciences.

One thing only marred my happiness while I lived with them on the Ohio, and that was the recollection that I once had tender parents, and a home that I loved. Aside from that recollection, which could not have existed had I been taken in my infancy, I should have been contented in my situation. Notwithstanding all that has been said against the Indians, in consequence of their cruelties to their enemies—cruelties that I have witnessed and had abundant proof of—it is a fact that they are naturally kind, tender, and peaceable toward their friends, and strictly honest; and that those cruelties have been practiced only upon their enemies, according to their idea of justice.

2. **spirits:** alcohol.
3. Jemison is referring to the largely unsuccessful process of Americanizing Indians through a Western education, a policy implemented by the U.S. government.

New World Contact

Native Americans did not consider themselves collectively as one group of people or as a single nation before their encounter with Europeans and had no common term for themselves. Upon discovering the need to adopt a common name to differentiate themselves from the new strangers in their midst, Native Americans may have had little choice but to choose one that the whites had applied to them. In the end both sides adopted the term *Indian*, based on Christopher Columbus's geographical error in supposing he had arrived in Asia rather than in a new world.

The next most common term to describe these people was much less attractive. Medieval legend had depicted wild club-swinging men of the forest as hairy, naked links between humans and animals. Named in Latin *silvaticus*, "men of the woods," they became *sauvage* in French and *salvage* in English, a word that finally turned into *savage*.

These and other names bestowed on Native Americans by whites, such as *wild-men* and *barbarian*, propagated a belief among Europeans that Indians were essentially their opposites. Defined as "the other," Indians were heathens; they performed human sacrifices and were cannibals; they were dirty, warlike, superstitious, sexually promiscuous, and brutal to their captives and to their women. Evils observed anywhere among Indians, as well as evils not observed but imagined such as the Aztec practice of human sacrifice, were generalized to all Indians.

At the same time Europeans, troubled by what they regarded as the decadence and overly elaborate character of their own society, recognized positive traits in the Indian that Europeans lacked. In a vision always more popular among those who stayed in Europe than with those who migrated to the New World, Indians seemed direct, innocent, hospitable, courteous, handsome, and especially courageous. Their independence, pride, stamina, and endurance suggested a nobility that Europeans, undergoing capitalist transformation, seemed to be losing. From this image came a composite ideal called the "Noble Savage."

Both images contrasted sharply with European and later American notions of "civilization." Particularly in the United States, white civilization was expected to spread over the entire continent, dooming the Indians, however noble or ignoble an image they were accorded.

Plate 1. Unknown artist, "First European Attempt to Depict the Domestic Life of Native Americans," Germany, c. 1505

The first attempt by a European to depict the domestic lives of Native Americans can be seen in Plate 1, an anonymous German woodcut published around 1505 and based on explorer and geographer Amerigo Vespucci's account of his voyages to the New World. The inscription describes natives as: "naked, handsome, brown, well shaped in body; ... No one has anything, but all things are in common. And the men have as wives those who please them, be they mothers, sisters or friends. . . . They also fight with each other; and they eat each other. . . . They become a hundred and fifty years old and have no government." What perception of the inhabitants of the New World does this image present? How accurate do you think it is? How might Europeans have reacted to it?

Not all images of the time presented the Europeans and Native Americans as such opposites. Plate 2 shows a drawing of Cortés and his longtime lover and advisor, Malinche (Doña Marina). Malinche was born and raised an Aztec but was sold to the Maya as a slave and then passed on to another ethnic group in Tabasco, south of the Aztec empire. By the time Cortés arrived on the continent, Malinche spoke many local languages and found that she fit in with the Spanish as well as with any native group. This picture by an indigenous artist from around 1540 suggests a de-

Plate 2. Unknown artist, drawing of Cortés and Malinche, c. 1540

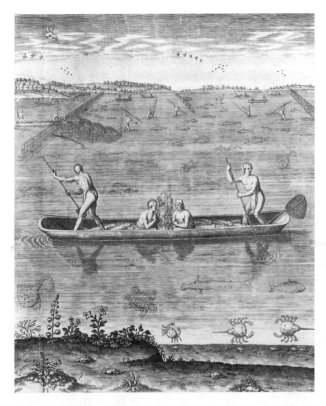

Plate 3. John White, "The Manner of Their Fishing," 1585

gree of understanding between Europeans and natives that is lacking in many of the more essentializing portraits of "barbarians" and "noble savages" by European artists, both earlier and later. How significant is it that this drawing was made by a Native American?

Plate 3 shows an engraving made from a drawing by John White, who from 1585 to 1586 lived in Roanoke, Virginia, part of the first English colony in North America. John White was commissioned to illustrate the first written account of that colony. Thomas Hariot's pamphlet, *A Brief and True Report of the New Found Land of Virginia*, published together with White's image in 1588, was "directed to the investors, farmers, and well-wishers of the project of colonizing and planting there" and emphasized the economic possibilities of the region. The caption to White's engraving reads in part:

> It is a pleasing picture to see these people wading and sailing in their shallow rivers. They are untroubled by the desire to pile up riches for their children, and live in perfect contentment with their present state, in friendship with each other, sharing all those things with which God has so bountifully provided them. Yet they do not render Him the thanks which His providence deserves, for they are savage and have no knowledge [of Christianity].

Why do you think White and Hariot's depiction of the Indian is so different from that in Plate 1? In which readings can you find images of Indians most like that of the German woodcut? In which readings can you find images of Indians similar to White's engraving?

Plate 4. Unknown artist, "Huron Woman," 1664

Plate 4 is another domestic scene of Indian life, this time from a French source, François de Creux's *Historia Canadensis*, published in 1664. How does it differ from the way Plate 1 depicts the Indian? Note that both figures in this image are Indian women. How might the absence of men in this engraving change the European view of the character of Indians? Are Indian men described in different terms from Indian women in the various readings?

Plate 5 depicts a conference between Colonel Henry Bouquet and some of the Indians he defeated at the battle of Bushy Run in 1766. Many tribes in the Ohio Valley led by Pontiac, a chief of the Ottawas, rose up against the British in 1763, laying to waste many white settlements in the Ohio Valley. The central focus of the engraving is the return of white captives taken during these raids. The theme of whites, and especially white women, captured by Indians greatly fascinated the colonists and their European counterparts. What attitude toward the Indians and what view of Indian-white relations are suggested by this image?

B. West inv.ᵗ   Canot sculp.

5. The Indians delivering up the English Captives to Colonel Bouquet,
near his Camp at the Forks of Muskingum in North America in Novʳ 1764.

Plate 5. Unknown artist, "Return of English Captives during a Conference between
Colonel Henry Bouquet and Indians on the Muskingum River," 1764

PART TWO

The Colonial Experience

A Rapidly Changing Society

The early seventeenth-century world of Massachusetts Puritans had a firmly fixed religious orientation that, for most settlers, faded as the century advanced. The Salem witchcraft trials of the 1690s demonstrated that early religious conviction certainly had been reduced to confusion. And the universe as envisioned by Benjamin Franklin a few generations later was yet further removed from Puritan roots. As adherence to orthodox Christianity declined so that it was no longer the encompassing view of the world, a number of colonists instead gradually embraced the Enlightenment confidence in science and human reason. And the physical, economic, and social circumstances of life in British America had undergone an equally great transformation. The entire white population of British America in 1660 would have fit into Yankee Stadium; by 1750 the colonists numbered over one million. Conflict with Indian neighbors initially threatened virtually all the early colonies; by midcentury whites firmly controlled the eastern seaboard. As colonial political life had reflected the instability of seventeenth-century England's Puritan revolution, so eighteenth-century colonial government mirrored a maturing if still clumsy empire that by 1763 dominated the world's diplomacy. And during the lengthy peace between the end of major European warfare in 1715 and the start of the French and Indian War in 1756, the depression of the late seventeenth century turned into a long economic boom.

African slaves, involuntary migrants to the New World, contributed enormously to the colonies' prosperity. Slaves imported through the trade in human beings that freedman Olaudah Equiano graphically describes became the critical labor force for the sugar plantations of the West Indies. Supplying these islands with fish, grain, lumber, livestock, and other goods enriched the economies of the middle colonies and New England. After about 1680 African slavery became an important part of Southern plantation agriculture on the mainland. In South Carolina by 1720, slaves outnumbered whites by about two to one.

News of opportunity in the new land brought an increasing number of European immigrants throughout the eighteenth century. Many thousands of

Germans came to the middle colonies. Like Gottlieb Mittelberger, most signed on as indentured servants to pay their passage. Harsh as their circumstances were, some eventually prospered in the New World. An even greater number of Scots-Irish—descendants of the Scottish Protestants who had settled in northern Ireland—followed to settle in the frontier valleys of Pennsylvania, Virginia, and the Carolinas.

Dutch settlers remained prominent in the East, the French continued to settle their Louisiana colony, and Spanish settlements dotted California and the Southwest. Rapid economic growth and immigration from Europe created a greater sense of permanence and led to the development of new cultures on the continent. This was reflected in American arts, letters, and architecture. The visual portfolio "Colonial Architecture" (page 89) demonstrates some of the ways people made use of local materials to erect versions of the buildings they remembered from their homelands and so altered the colonial landscape.

Prosperity, security, and political stability enabled a new leadership to emerge in the British colonies. Men like Benjamin Franklin (women—Abigail Bailey, for example—rarely had even remotely similar opportunities) became outstanding citizens of the British empire, moving comfortably between the colonies and the mother country and contributing to the life and culture of both. At the same time, they were planting deep roots in their local environments. Franklin's Philadelphia was the second-largest city in the English-speaking world—only London exceeded it. From such a combination of imperial interests and colonial pride came the Revolutionary War generation.

POINTS OF VIEW

The Salem Witchcraft Trials (1692)

8

The Case against George Burroughs

Ann Putnam et al.

In 1692 the perception of many people was that the devil assaulted the seaport town of Salem, Massachusetts—more specifically, Salem Village west of the port. Scores of warlocks and witches—men and women who had entered into a covenant with the devil to drive little children mad and to sicken and kill livestock and people—had seemingly in-

Paul S. Boyer and Stephen Nissenbaum, eds., *Salem-Village Witchcraft: A Documentary Record* (Belmont, CA: Wadsworth Pub. Co., 1972), pp. 67–68, 69, 72, 74, 77–78, 80, 84–85, 86–87; Charles W. Upham, *Salem Witchcraft*, vol. 2 (New York: Ungar, 1969), pp. 300–01.

vaded this village of a few hundred people. The jails bulged with over a hundred prisoners awaiting trial, including a four-year-old child bound for nine months in heavy iron chains. Twenty-seven people eventually came to trial; the court hanged nineteen—fourteen women and five men—as witches. One man, refusing to enter a plea, had heavy weights laid on his body until he was pressed to death.

Only three New Englanders had ever been hanged as witches before 1692, when nine adolescent girls in Salem suddenly appeared bewitched. Under intense questioning, the shrieking and contorting girls accused some of their neighbors and even some from outside Salem of witchcraft. Cotton Mather and other leading Puritan ministers carefully advised Puritan leaders that the young women's testimony was insufficient to support a conviction for witchcraft in the absence of "other, and more human, and most convincing testimonies" since the devil could assume what shape he pleased, even that of a leading divine like Mather himself.

The leader of all the New England witches, the afflicted girls alleged, was the Reverend George Burroughs, Salem's former minister. Burroughs had left Salem Village for Maine nearly twenty years earlier in the middle of controversies with several parishioners, chief among them John Putnam, whose twelve-year-old niece Ann was the first to identify Burroughs as the leader of all the witches and the murderer of at least three people by witchcraft. The magistrates issued a warrant, and he was seized and brought to Salem. His theology, local ministers discovered, had evolved in an unorthodox direction: he neither baptized infants nor celebrated communion. People remembered his boasting about his strength: though small and wiry, he was extraordinarily strong and agile and had been an outstanding athlete in his student days at Harvard. And some revived ancient gossip about mistreatment of his first two wives.

The court, well aware of its awesome responsibilities in trying a minister as a witch, nonetheless easily found Burroughs guilty. Faithful to the biblical injunction not to "suffer a witch to live," they sent him to Gallows Hill, where he protested his innocence, faultlessly recited the Lord's Prayer (which folklore said witches could not do), and stood to the snap of the rope.

BEFORE YOU READ

1. What evidence was presented to show that George Burroughs was a witch? Was it all "spectral evidence" (that is, evidence as to what his specter or apparition had done to the adolescent girls)? What was the nonspectral evidence (evidence of what Burroughs himself rather than his specter had done)? Did it justify convicting Burroughs in a society that accepted unquestioningly the existence of witchcraft?

2. How do you explain the young women's accusations?

3. How do you explain the belief of the elders of the community in the accusations? What does your textbook say on this issue?

TESTIMONY OF ANN PUTNAM

The deposition of Ann Putnam, who testifies and says that on 20th of April, 1692, at evening, she saw the apparition of a minister, at which she was grievously affrighted and cried out, oh, dreadful, dreadful, here is a minister come. What, are ministers witches, too? Whence come you, and what is your name? For I will complain of you, though you be a minister, if you be a wizard. And immediately I was tortured by him, being racked and almost choked by him. And he tempted me to write in his book, which I refused with loud outcries, and said I would not write in his book though he tore me all to pieces, but told him that it was a dreadful thing that he, which was a minister that should teach children to fear God, should come to persuade poor creatures to give their souls to the devil. Oh, dreadful, dreadful. Tell me your name that I may know who you are. Then again he tortured me and urged me to write in his book, which I refused.

And then presently he told me that his name was George Burroughs, and that he had had three wives, and that he had bewitched the first two of them to death, and that he killed Mistress Lawson because she was so unwilling to go from the village, and also killed Mr. Lawson's child because he went to the eastward with Sir Edmond [Andros] and preached so to the soldiers, and that he had bewitched a great many soldiers to death at the eastward when Sir Edmond was there, and that he had made Abigail Hobbs a witch, and several witches more. And he has continued ever since, by times tempting me to write in his book and grievously torturing me by beating, pinching, and almost choking me several times a day. And he also told me that he was above a witch, he was a conjurer.

TESTIMONY OF THOMAS PUTNAM, PETER PRESCOTT, ROBERT MORRELL, AND EZEKIEL CHEEVER

We whose names are underwritten, being present with Ann Putnam at the time above mentioned, heard her declare what is abovewritten, what she said she saw and heard from the apparition of Mr. George Burroughs, and also beheld her tortures and perceived her hellish temptations by her loud outcries, I will not, I will not write though you torment me all [the] days of my life. And, being conversant with her ever since, have seen her tortured and complaining that Mr. Burroughs hurt her and tempts her to write in his book.

Thomas Putnam
Peter Prescott
Robert Morrell

COMPLAINT AGAINST GEORGE BURROUGHS

Salem, April the 30th, 1692

There being complaint this day made (before us) by Captain Jonathan Walcot and Sergeant Thomas Putnam of Salem Village, in behalf of their Majesties, for themselves, and also for several of their neighbors, against George Burroughs, minister in Wells in the province of Maine, Lydia Dasting in Reading, widow Susanah Martin of Amesbury, widow Dorcas Hoar of Beverly, widow Sarah Murrell of Beverly, and Phillip English of Salem, merchant, for high suspicion of sundry acts of witchcraft done or committed by them upon the bodies of Mary Walcot, Marcy Lewis, Abigail Williams, Ann Putnam, and Eliz Hubert, and Susanah Sheldon *(viz.)* upon some or all of them, of Salem Village or farms, whereby great hurt and damage been done to the bodies of said persons above named, therefore craved justice.

Signed by both the

Complainers   { Jonathan Walcott

abovesaid   Thomas Putnam

The abovesaid complaint was exhibited before us this 30th April, 1692.

John Hathorne   }
Jonathan Corwin   } Assistants

SUMMARY OF THE EXAMINATION
OF GEORGE BURROUGHS

The examination of Geo. Burroughs, 9 May, 1692.

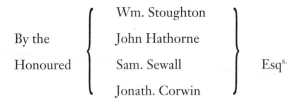

By the   Wm. Stoughton
                John Hathorne
Honoured   Sam. Sewall   Esq[s.]
                Jonath. Corwin

Being asked when he partook of the Lord's Supper, he being (as he said) in full communion at Roxbury, he answered it was so long since, he could not tell. Yet he owned he was at meeting one Sabbath at Boston part of the day, and the other at Charlestown part of a Sabbath, when that sacrament happened to be at both, yet did not partake of either. He denied that his house at Casco was haunted, yet he owned there were toads. He denied that he made his wife swear that she could not write to his father [-in-law] Ruck without his approbation of her letter to her father. He owned that none of his children but the eldest was baptized.

The above was in private, none of the bewitched being present. At his entry into the room, many, if not all, of the bewitched were grievously tortured.

1. Sus. Sheldon testified that Burroughs's two wives appeared in their winding sheets, and said that man killed them.

He was bid to look upon Sus. Sheldon.

He looked back and knocked down all (or most) of the afflicted who stood behind him. . . .

2. Mary Lewes deposition going to be read and he looked upon her, and she fell into a dreadful and tedious fit.

3. Mary Walcot

4. Eliz. Hubbard   Testimony going to be read and they all fell into
   Susan Sheldon   fits.

5. Susan Sheldon   Affirmed, each of them, that he brought the
   Ann Putnam jun^r.   book and would have them write.

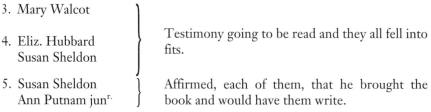

Being asked what he thought of these things, he answered it was an amazing and humbling providence, but he understood nothing of it. And he said, some of you may observe that when they begin to name my name, they cannot name it. . . .

INDICTMENT OF GEORGE BURROUGHS

Essex Ss. The jurors for our Sovereign Lord and Lady, the King and Queen, presents that George Burroughs, late of Falmouth within the province of the Massachusetts Bay in New England, clerk, the ninth day of May, [1692] . . . and divers other days and times as well, before and after, certain detestable arts called witchcraft and sorceries, wickedly and feloniously hath used, practiced, and exercised at and within the Township of Salem in the County of Essex and aforesaid, in, upon, and against one Ann Putnam of Salem in the County of Essex, singlewoman, by which said wicked arts the said Ann Putnam . . . was, and is, tortured, afflicted, pined, consumed, wasted and tormented. Also for sundry other acts of witchcrafts by said George Burroughs committed and done against the peace of our Sovereign Lord and Lady, the King and Queen, their crown and dignity, and against the form of the statute in that case made and provided.

TESTIMONY OF SAMUEL WEBBER

Samuel Webber, aged about 36 years, testifies and says that about seven or eight years ago, I lived at Casco Bay and George Burroughs was then minister there. And having heard much of the great strength of him, said Burroughs, he coming to our house, we were in discourse about the same, and he then told me that he had put his fingers into the bung of a barrel of molasses and lifted it up and carried it round him and set it down again.

Salem, August 2d, 1692.

Samuel Webber

TESTIMONY OF SIMON WILLARD

The deposition of Simon Willard, aged about forty two years, says, I being at the house of Mr. Robert Lawrence at Falmouth, in Casco Bay, in September 1689, said Mr. Lawrence was commenting [upon] Mr. George Borroughs's strength, saying that we, none of us, could do what he could do. For said Mr. Borroughs can hold out this gun with one hand. Mr. Borroughs, being there, said, I held my hand here behind the lock and took it up and held it out.

I, said deponent, saw Mr. Borroughs put his hand on the gun to show us how he held it and where he held his hand, and saying there he held his hand when he held said gun out. But I saw him not hold it out then. Said gun was about seven-foot barrel, and very heavy. I then tried to hold out said gun with both hands, but could not do it long enough to take sight.

Simon Willard

Simon Willard owned to the Jury of Inquest that the abovewritten evidence is the truth,
August 3, 1692

Capt. Wm. Wormall sworn to the above, and that he saw him raise it from the ground himself.

TESTIMONY OF THOMAS GREENSLIT

The deposition of Thomas Greenslit, aged about forty years, testifies that about the breaking out of this last Indian war, being at the house of Capt. Scottow's, at Black Point, he saw Mr. George Burroughs lift and hold out a gun of six foot barrel or thereabouts, putting the forefinger of his right hand into the muzzle of said gun, and so held it out at arm's end, only with that finger. And further this deponent testifies that at the same time he saw the said Burroughs take up a full barrel of molasses with but two fingers of one of his hands in the bung [handle], and carry it from the stage head to the door at the end of the stage, without letting it down, and that Lieut. Richard Hunniwell and John Greenslit and some other persons that are since dead were then present.

Salem, September 15, 1692. Thomas Greenslit appeared before their Majesties' Justices of Oyer and Terminer in open court and made oath that the above mentioned particulars, and every part of them, were true.

attest   Step. Sewall, Clerk

ROBERT CALEF'S ACCOUNT
OF GEORGE BURROUGHS'S EXECUTION

Mr. Burroughs was carried in a cart with the others, through the streets of Salem, to execution. When he was upon the ladder, he made a speech for the clearing of his innocency, with such solemn and serious expressions as were to the admiration of all present. His prayer (which he concluded by repeating the Lord's Prayer) was so well worded, and uttered with such composedness and such (at least seeming) fervency of spirit, as was very affecting, and drew tears from many, so that it seemed to some that the spectators would hinder the execution. The accusers said the black man stood and dictated to him. As soon as he was turned off, Mr. Cotton Mather, being mounted upon a horse, addressed himself to the people, partly to declare that he (Mr. Burroughs) was no ordained minister, and partly to possess the people of his guilt, saying that the Devil often had been transformed into an angel of light; and this somewhat appeased the people, and the executions went on. When he was cut down, he was dragged by a halter to a hole, or grave, between the rocks, about two feet deep; his shirt and breeches being pulled off, and an old pair of trousers of one executed put on his lower parts: he was so put in, together with Willard and Carrier, that one of his hands, and his chin, and a foot of one of them, was left uncovered.

9

Reconsidering the Verdict

Cotton Mather et al.

The witchcraft epidemic, so one interpretation has it, fed on local conflicts. In Salem, town and countryside were sharply diverging. Conservative back-country farmers struggled to cope with the demands of commerce. Sons coming of age—the potential marriage partners of the adolescent girls—needed land if they were to establish an independent family, but available reserves of land were shrinking. Puritan ministers lamented the "declension" from the piety of the colony's founders. Although ministers of every generation may be expected to denounce the decadence of their time, New England's preachers at the end of the seventeenth century had special reason to do so: the stern Puritanism of past generations was under threat from a growth in luxury and secular manners. No wonder the people of Salem found it easy to believe the rantings of hysterical adolescents and think so ill of their neighbors.

Nor could the colony of which Salem was part provide the stability the beleaguered village needed. Massachusetts Bay as a whole was passing through a time of troubles. Its charter voided in 1684, Massachusetts had no stable legal base until it received a new and radically different charter from the king in 1691. People worried whether the old land claims would be valid under the new charter and whether voting would be restricted to church members. At the same time, the devil in the form of Roman Catholic France and heathen Indians was at their door. The Maine and New Hampshire frontiers had collapsed during King William's War (1689–1697), and the colony's coun-

George L. Burr, ed., *Narratives of the Witchcraft Cases, 1648–1706* (New York: Charles Scribner's Sons, 1914), pp. 215–22; Paul S. Boyer and Stephen Nissenbaum, eds., *Salem-Village Witchcraft: A Documentary Record* (Belmont, CA: Wadsworth Pub. Co., 1972), pp. 118–22; Charles W. Upham, *Salem Witchcraft*, vol. 2 (New York: Ungar, 1969), p. 510; Harvey Wish, ed., *The Diary of Samuel Sewall* (New York: G. P. Putnam's Sons, 1967), pp. 80–81.

terattack had ended in disaster. *Massachusetts Bay was bankrupt and increased taxes to unprecedented levels. The birthrate declined, and refugees from the war, including Indians, were suddenly everywhere. Some of the bewitched teenagers were orphans of the war. During this time of political, religious, and social instability, how easy it must have been to believe that the devil had launched his greatest assault on New England. In fact, for a time the wider the net of accusations grew and the more people confessed to witchcraft, the easier it was to believe in the devil's conspiracy against the colony.*

Then the accusations went too far, extending to prominent members of Puritan society, including the governor's wife. The ministers' cautions concerning spectral evidence became more persuasive, and the governor finally halted the trials. The public mood changed. To the regret of some but to the relief of many, the world of spirits again became invisible, and the witches fled New England.

BEFORE YOU READ

1. Cotton Mather continued to defend the hanging of George Burroughs. What was his case against Burroughs? Does it depend on spectral evidence?

2. Why did Margaret Jacobs confess to being a witch? Do you consider her recantation sincere?

3. How did Governor Phips explain the witchcraft hysteria? Did he blame anyone for it?

4. Why did Samuel Sewall and Ann Putnam repent? What does it indicate about them?

COTTON MATHER EXPLAINS
THE DIFFICULTY OF WITCHCRAFT TRIALS

*Letter to John Foster, One of the Salem
Witchcraft Judges (August 17, 1692)*

Sir:

You would know whether I still retain my opinion about the horrible witchcrafts among us, and I acknowledge that I do.

I do still think that when there is no further evidence against a person but only this, that a specter in their shape does afflict a neighbor, that evidence is not enough to convict the [person] of witchcraft.

That the Devils have a natural power which makes them capable of exhibiting what shape they please I suppose nobody doubts, and I have no absolute promise of God that they shall not exhibit *mine.*

It is the opinion generally of all Protestant writers that the Devil may thus abuse the innocent; yea, 'tis the confession of some Popish[1] ones. And our honorable judges are so eminent for their justice, wisdom, and goodness, that whatever their own particular sense may be, yet they will not proceed capitally against any upon a principle contested with great odds on the other side in the learned and Godly world.

---

1. **Popish:** Roman Catholic.

Nevertheless, a very great use is to be made of the spectral impressions upon the sufferers. They justly introduce and determine an inquiry into the circumstances of the person accused, and they strengthen other presumptions.

When so much use is made of those things, I believe the use for which the great God intends them is made. And accordingly you see that the excellent judges have had such an encouraging presence of God with them as that scarce any, if at all any, have been tried before them against whom God has not strangely sent in other, and more human, and most convincing testimonies.

If any persons have been condemned about whom any of the judges are not easy in their minds that the evidence against them has been satisfactory, it would certainly be for the glory of the whole transaction to give that person a reprieve.

It would make all matters easier if at least bail were taken for people accused only by the invisible tormentors of the poor sufferers, and not blemished by any further grounds of suspicion against them.

The odd effects produced upon the sufferers by the look or touch of the accused are things wherein the Devils may as much impose upon some harmless people as by the representation of their shapes.

My notion of these matters is this. A suspected and unlawful communion with a familiar spirit is the thing inquired after. The communion on the Devil's part may be proved while, for aught I can say, the man may be innocent. The Devil may impudently impose his communion upon some that care not for his company. But if the communion on the man's part be proved, then the business is done.

I am suspicious lest the Devil may at some time or other serve us a trick by his constancy for a long while in one way of dealing. We may find the Devil using one constant course in nineteen several actions, and yet he be too hard for us at last, if we thence make a rule to form an infallible judgment of a twentieth. It is our singular happiness that we are blessed with judges who are aware of this danger. . . .

Our case is extraordinary. And so you and others will pardon the extraordinary liberty I take to address you on this occasion. But after all, I entreat you that whatever you do, you strengthen the hands of our honorable judges in the great work before them. They are persons for whom no man living has a greater veneration than

Sir,
Your servant
C. Mather

COTTON MATHER DEFENDS
THE CONVICTION OF GEORGE BURROUGHS

This G. B. [George Burroughs] was indicted for witchcraft, and in the prosecution of the charge against him, he was accused by five or six of the bewitched, as the author of their miseries; he was accused by eight of the confessing witches as being a head actor at some of their hellish rendez-vouses and one who had the promise of being a king in Satan's kingdom, now going to be erected; he was accused by nine persons for extraordinary lifting, and such feats of strength, as could not be done without a diabolical assistance. And for other such things he was accused, until about thirty testimonies were brought in against him; nor were these judged the half of what might have been considered for his conviction: however, they were enough to fix the character of a witch upon him. . . .

And now upon his trial, one of the bewitched persons [Ann Putnam] testified that in her agonies a little black haired man came to her, saying his name was B. and bidding her set her hand unto a book which he showed her; and bragging that he was a conjurer, above the ordinary rank of witches. That he often persecuted her with the offer of that book, saying she should be well and need fear nobody if she would but sign it; but he inflicted cruel pains and hurts upon her because of her denying so to do. The testimonies of the other sufferers concurred with these, and it was remarkable, that whereas biting was one of the ways which the witches used for the vexing of the sufferers, when they cried out of G. B. biting them, the print of the teeth would be seen on the flesh of the complainers, and just such a set of teeth as G. B.'s would then appear upon them, which could be distinguished from those of some other men. . . .

It cost the court a wonderful deal of trouble to hear the testimonies of the sufferers, for when they were going to give in their depositions, they would for a long time be taken with fits that made them incapable of saying anything. The chief judge asked the prisoner who he thought hindered these witnesses from giving their testimonies and he answered, he supposed it was the Devil. That honorable person then replied, how comes the Devil, so loathe to have any testimony born against you? Which cast him into very great confusion.

It has been a frequent thing for the bewitched people to be entertained with apparitions of ghosts of murdered people, at the same time that the specters of the witches trouble them. Accordingly, several of the bewitched had given in their testimony that they had been troubled with the apparitions of two women, who said that they were G. B.'s two wives, and that he had been the death of them, and that the magistrates must be told of it before whom if B. upon his trial denied it, they did not know but that they should appear again in the Court. Now, G. B. had been infamous for the barbarous usage of his two successive wives, all the country over. . . .

[O]ne of the bewitched persons was cast into horror at the ghosts of B.'s two deceased wives then appearing before him, and crying for vengeance against him. Hereupon, several of the bewitched persons were successively called in, who all not knowing what the former had seen and said, concurred in their horror of the apparition, which they affirmed that he had before him. . . .

Judicious writers have assigned it a great place in the conviction of witches when persons are impeached by other notorious witches, to be as [evil] as themselves; especially if the persons have been much noted for neglecting the worship of God. Now, as there might have been testimonies enough of G. B.'s antipathy to prayer, and the other ordinances of God, though by his profession singularly obliged thereunto; so, there now came in against the prisoner the testimonies of several persons who confessed their own having been horrible witches, and ever since their confessions had been themselves terribly tortured by the devils and other witches, even like the other sufferers. . . .

These now testified that G. B. had been at witch meetings with them, and that he was the person who had seduced and compelled them into the snares of witchcraft. That he promised them fine clothes for doing it, that he brought dolls to them and thorns to stick into those dolls, for the afflicting of other people, and that he exhorted them with the rest of the crew to bewitch all Salem Village, but be sure to do it gradually, if they would prevail in what they did. . . .

A famous Divine recites this among the convictions of a witch, the testimony of the party bewitched, whether pining or dying, together with the joint oaths of sufficient persons that have seen certain prodigious pranks or feats wrought by the party accused. Now God had been pleased so to leave this G. B. that he had ensnared himself by several instances, which he had formerly given of a preternatural strength and which were now produced against him. He was a very puny man, yet he had often done things beyond the strength of a giant. A gun of about seven foot barrel and so heavy that strong men could not steadily hold it out with both hands, there were several testimonies given in by persons of credit and honor, that he made nothing of taking up such a gun behind the lock, with but one hand and holding it out like a pistol at arms' end. G. B. in his vindication was so foolish as to say, that an Indian was there, and held it out at the same time: whereas none of the spectators ever saw any such Indian, but they supposed the black man (as the witches call the devil, and they generally say he resembles an Indian) might give him that assistance. . . .

Faltering, faulty, inconsistent, and contrary answers upon judicial and deliberate examination are counted some unlucky symptoms of guilt in all crimes, especially in witchcraft. Now, there was never a prisoner more eminent for them than G. B. both at his examination and on his trial. His evasions, contradictions and falsehoods were very sensible, he had little to say, but that he had heard some things that he could not prove, reflecting upon the reputation of some of the witnesses. Only he gave in a paper to the jury, wherein although he had many times before granted not only that there are witches but also that the present sufferings of the country are the effect of horrible witchcrafts, yet he now goes to show that there neither are nor ever were witches that, having made a compact with the Devil, can send a devil to torment other people at a distance. . . .

The jury brought him in guilty. But when he came to die, he utterly denied the fact, whereof he had been thus convicted.

DECLARATION OF MARGARET JACOBS TO THE SPECIAL WITCHCRAFT COURT APPOINTED BY THE GOVERNOR

The humble declaration of Margaret Jacobs to the honoured court now sitting at Salem, shows:

That whereas your poor and humble declarant being closely confined here in Salem jail for the crime of witchcraft, which crime, thanks be to the Lord, I am altogether ignorant of, as will appear at the great day of judgment. May it please the honoured court, I was cried out upon by some of the possessed persons, as afflicting of them; whereupon I was brought to my examination, which persons at the sight of me fell down, which did very much startle and affright me. The Lord above knows I knew nothing, in the least measure, how or who afflicted them; they told me, without doubt I did, or else they would not fall down at me; they told me if I would not confess, I should be put down into the dungeon and would be hanged, but if I would confess I should have my life; the which did so affright me, with my own vile wicked heart, to save my life made me make the confession I did, which confession, may it please the honoured court, is altogether false and untrue. The very first night after I had made my confession, I was in such horror of conscience that I could not sleep, for fear the Devil should carry me away for telling such horrid lies. I was, may it please the honoured court, sworn to my confession, as I understand since, but then, at that time, was ignorant of it, not knowing what an oath did mean. The Lord, I hope, in whom I trust, out of the abundance of his mercy, will forgive me my false forswearing myself.

What I said was altogether false, against my grandfather, and Mr. Burroughs, which I did to save my life and to have my liberty; but the Lord, charging it to my conscience, made me in so much horror, that I could not contain myself before I had denied my confession, which I did, though I saw nothing but death before me, choosing rather death with a quiet conscience, than to live in such horror, which I could not suffer. . . .

GOVERNOR WILLIAM PHIPS ENDS THE TRIALS

Letter to the Earl of Nottingham
(February 21, 1693)

Boston in New England Febry 21st, 1692–93

May it please your Lordship,

At my arrival here I found the prisons full of people committed upon suspicion of witchcraft, and that continual complaints were made to me that many persons were grievously tormented by witches, and that they cried out upon several persons by name, as the cause of their torments. The number of these complaints increasing every day, by advice of the Lieutenant Governor and the Council I gave a Commission of Oyer and Terminer to try the suspected witches and at that time the generality of the people represented the matter to me as real witchcraft and gave very strange instances of the same. The first in Commission was the Lieutenant Governor and the rest persons of the best prudence and figure that could then be pitched upon, and I depended upon the Court for a right method of proceeding in cases of witchcraft.

At that time I went to command the army at the eastern part of the Province, for the French and Indians had made an attack upon some of our frontier towns. I continued there for some time but when I returned I found people much dissatisfied at the proceedings of the Court, for about twenty

persons were condemned and executed of which number some were thought by
many persons to be innocent. The Court still proceeded in the same method
of trying them, which was by the evidence of the afflicted persons who, when
they were brought into the Court—as soon as the suspected witches looked
upon them, instantly fell to the ground in strange agonies and grievous
torments, but when touched by them upon the arm or some other part of
their flesh they immediately revived and came to themselves, upon [which]
they made oath that the prisoner at the bar did afflict them and that they
saw their shape or specter come from their bodies which put them to such
pains and torments. When I inquired into the matter I was informed by the
Judges that they began with this, but had human testimony against such as were
condemned and undoubted proof of their being witches. But at length I found
that the Devil did take upon him the shape of Innocent persons and some were
accused of whose innocency I was well assured and many considerable persons of unblameable life and conversation were cried out upon as witches and
wizards.

The Deputy Governor, notwithstanding, persisted vigorously in the same
method, to the great dissatisfaction and disturbance of the people, until I put an
end to the Court and stopped the proceedings, which I did because I saw many innocent persons might otherwise perish. . . . When I put an end to the Court there
were at least fifty persons in prison in great misery by reason of the extreme cold
and their poverty, most of them having only specter evidence against them, and
their *mittimusses* [warrants] being defective, I caused some of them to be let out
upon bail and put the Judges upon considering of a way to relieve others and prevent them from perishing in prison, upon which some of them were convinced
and acknowledged that their former proceedings were too violent and not
grounded upon a right foundation but that if they might sit again, they would proceed after another method, and whereas Mr. Increase Mathew [Mather] and several other Divines did give it as their Judgment that the Devil might afflict in the
shape of an innocent person and that the look and the touch of the suspected persons was not sufficient proof against them, these things had not the same stress
laid upon them as before. And upon this consideration I permitted a special Superior Court to be held at Salem in the County of Essex on the third day of January,
the Lieutenant Governor being Chief Judge. Their method of proceeding being
altered, all that were brought to trial, to the number of fifty two, were cleared saving [except] three, and I was informed by the King's Attorney General that some
of the cleared and the condemned were under the same circumstances or that
there was the same reason to clear the three condemned as the rest according to
his Judgment. The Deputy Governor signed a Warrant for their speedy execution
and also of five others who were condemned at the former Court of Oyer and
Terminer, but considering how the matter had been managed I sent a reprieve
whereby the execution was stopped until their Majesties' pleasure be signified and
declared. The Lieutenant Governor upon this occasion was enraged and filled
with passionate anger and refused to sit upon the bench in a Superior Court then
held at Charlestown, and indeed has from the beginning hurried on these matters
with great precipitancy and by his warrant has caused the estates, goods and chat-

tels of the executed to be seized and disposed of without my knowledge or consent.

The stop put to the first method of proceedings has dissipated the black cloud that threatened this Province with destruction; for whereas this delusion of the Devil did spread and its dismal effects touched the lives and estates of many of their Majesties' subjects and the reputation of some of the principal persons here, and indeed unhappily clogged and interrupted their Majesties' affairs which has been a great vexation to me, I have no new complaints but people's minds before divided and distracted by differing opinions concerning this matter are now well composed.

> I am
> Your Lordship's most faithful
> humble Servant
> William Phips

SAMUEL SEWALL'S CONFESSION (1697)

[January 1] On the 22nd of May I buried my abortive son; . . . The Lord pardon all my sins of omission and commission: and by his almighty power make me meet to be partaker of the inheritance with the Saints in Light. Second-day January 11, 1697 God helped me to pray more than ordinarily, that He would make up our loss in the burial of our little daughter and other children, and that would give us a child to serve Him, pleading with Him as the institutor of marriage, and the author of every good work.

[January 15, 1697] Copy of the Bill I put up on the Fast day; giving it to Mr. Willard as he pass'd by, and standing up at the reading of it, and bowing when finished; in the Afternoon.

> Samuel Sewall, sensible of the reiterated strokes of God upon himself and family; and being sensible, that as to the Guilt contracted upon the opening of the late Commission of Oyer and Terminer at Salem [the special witchcraft court] (to which the order for this Day relates) he is, upon many accounts, more concerned than any that he knows of, desires to take the blame and shame of it, Asking pardon of men, And especially desiring prayers that God, who has an Unlimited Authority, would pardon that sin and all other his sins; personal and relative: And according to his infinite benignity, and sovereignty, not visit the sin of him, or of any other, upon himself or any of his, nor upon the land: But that He would powerfully defend him against all temptations to sin, for the future; and vouchsafe him the efficacious, saving conduct of his word and spirit.

ANN PUTNAM'S CONFESSION (1706)

I desire to be humbled before God for that sad and humbling providence that befell my father's family in the year about '92; that I, then being in my childhood, should, by such a providence of God, be made an instrument for the accusing of several persons of a grievous crime, whereby their lives were taken away from them, whom now I have just grounds and good reason to believe they were innocent persons; and that it was a great delusion of Satan that deceived me in that sad time, whereby I justly fear I have been instrumental, with others, though ignorantly and unwittingly, to bring upon myself and this land the guilt of innocent blood; though what was said or done by me against any person I can truly and uprightly say, before God and man, I did it not out of any anger, malice, or ill-will to any person, for I had no such thing against one of them; but what I did was ignorant, being deluded by Satan. And particularly, as I was a chief instrument of accusing of Goodwife Nurse and her two sisters, I desire to lie in the dust, and to be humbled for it, in that I was a cause, with others, of so sad a calamity to them and their families; for which cause I desire to lie in the dust, and earnestly beg forgiveness of God, and from all those unto whom I have given just cause of sorrow and offence, whose relations were taken away or accused.

[Signed]

This confession was read before the congregation, together with her relation, Aug. 25, 1706; and she acknowledged it.

J. GREEN, *Pastor*

FOR CRITICAL THINKING

1. In what ways did the Salem witchcraft trials obscure rather than clarify the truth about the witchcraft threat? In what other trials did the process of adjudication seem to have worked against revealing the truth? Can you think of trials where the public response of the time affected the ability of a court to arrive at justice?

2. Imagine Cotton Mather interviewing Margaret Jacobs. Would this interview have raised questions for him about George Burroughs's guilt? How might Mather have explained why Jacobs changed her story?

3. When Ann Putnam recanted her testimony, among her listeners were the sons and daughters of Rebecca Nurse, one of the people Ann Putnam had accused and who was hanged for witchcraft. If they had entered into conversation about it, what kind of dialogue might they have had regarding Putnam's confession?

10

The African Slave Trade
Olaudah Equiano

The Life of Olaudah Equiano, or Gustavus Vassa, the African, Written by Himself *is one of the most important eyewitness accounts of the African slave trade. While scholars have long agreed on the horrors of the trade, they have argued for more than a century over how many people were involved. Estimates range from about nine and a half million to nearly fifteen million Africans imported into the Western Hemisphere. And this does not include those who were killed while resisting capture or who died during passage.*

Equiano's book is also the pioneering African American narrative of the journey from slavery to freedom, setting many of the conventions for the more than six thousand subsequent interviews, essays, and books by which former slaves told their dramatic stories. And the book, a best seller that has gone through many editions since it was first published in London in 1789, is also a remarkable adventure story recounting Equiano's travels in Africa, Europe, and America as well as his part in expeditions to the Arctic and Turkey and his service in the Seven Years' War.

Equiano (c. 1750–1797), an Ibo prince kidnapped into slavery when he was eleven years old, was brought first to Barbados and then sent to Virginia. After service in the British navy, he was at last sold to a Quaker merchant who allowed Equiano to purchase his freedom in 1766. In later years he worked to advance the Church of England, his adopted religion, and to abolish the slave trade.

BEFORE YOU READ

1. Describe the treatment of slaves in the slave trade.
2. What were Equiano's greatest fears during passage?
3. Equiano asks, "Learned you this from your God, who says unto you, Do unto all men as you would men should do unto you?" How would a slave trader have answered his question?

The first object which saluted my eyes when I arrived on the [Western Africa] coast, was the sea, and a slave ship, which was then riding at anchor, and waiting for its cargo. These filled me with astonishment, which was soon converted

Olaudah Equiano, *The Life of Olaudah Equiano, or Gustavus Vassa, the African, Written by Himself* (New York: Isaac Knapp, 1837), pp. 41–52.

into terror, when I was carried on board. I was immediately handled, and tossed up to see if I were sound, by some of the crew; and I was now persuaded that I had gotten into a world of bad spirits, and that they were going to kill me. Their complexions, too, differing so much from ours, their long hair, and the language they spoke, (which was very different from any I had ever heard) united to confirm me in this belief. Indeed, such were the horrors of my views and fears at the moment, that, if ten thousand worlds had been my own, I would have freely parted with them all to have exchanged my condition with that of the meanest slave in my own country. When I looked round the ship too, and saw a large furnace of copper boiling, and a multitude of black people of every description chained together, every one of their countenances expressing dejection and sorrow, I no longer doubted of my fate; and, quite overpowered with horror and anguish, I fell motionless on the deck and fainted. When I recovered a little, I found some black people about me, who I believed were some of those who had brought me on board, and had been receiving their pay; they talked to me in order to cheer me, but all in vain. I asked them if we were not to be eaten by those white men with horrible looks, red faces, and long hair. They told me I was not: and one of the crew brought me a small portion of spirituous liquor in a wine glass, but, being afraid of him, I would not take it out of his hand. One of the blacks, therefore, took it from him and gave it to me, and I took a little down my palate, which, instead of reviving me, as they thought it would, threw me into the greatest consternation at the strange feeling it produced, having never tasted any such liquor before. Soon after this, the blacks who brought me on board went off, and left me abandoned to despair.

I now saw myself deprived of all chance of returning to my native country, or even the least glimpse of hope of gaining the shore, which I now considered as friendly; and I even wished for my former slavery in preference to my present situation, which was filled with horrors of every kind, still heightened by my ignorance of what I was to undergo. I was not long suffered to indulge my grief; I was soon put down under the decks, and there I received such a salutation in my nostrils as I had never experienced in my life: so that, with the loathsomeness of the stench, and crying together, I became so sick and low that I was not able to eat, nor had I the least desire to taste any thing. I now wished for the last friend, death, to relieve me; but soon, to my grief, two of the white men offered me eatables; and, on my refusing to eat, one of them held me fast by the hands, and laid me across, I think the windlass, and tied my feet, while the other flogged me severely. I had never experienced any thing of this kind before, and although not being used to the water, I naturally feared that element the first time I saw it, yet, nevertheless, could I have got over the nettings, I would have jumped over the side, but I could not; and besides, the crew used to watch us very closely who were not chained down to the decks, lest we should leap into the water; and I have seen some of these poor African prisoners most severely cut, for attempting to do so, and hourly whipped for not eating. This indeed was often the case with myself. In a little time after, amongst the poor chained men, I found some of my own nation, which in a small degree gave ease to my mind. I inquired of these what was to be done with us? they gave me to understand, we were to be carried to these white people's country to work for them. I then was a little revived, and thought, if it were no worse than working, my situation was not so desperate; but still I feared I should be put to death, the white people looked and acted, as I thought, in so savage a manner; for I had never seen among any people such instances of brutal cruelty; and this not only shown towards us blacks, but also to some of the whites themselves. One white man in particular I saw, when we were permitted to be on deck, flogged so unmercifully with a large rope near the foremast, that he died in consequence of it; and they tossed him over the side as they would have done a brute. This made me fear these people the more; and I expected nothing less than to be treated in the same manner. I could not help expressing my fears and apprehensions to some of my countrymen; I asked them if these people had no country, but lived in this hollow place? (the ship) they told me they did not, but came from a distant one. "Then," said I, "how comes it in all our country we never heard of them?" They told me because they lived so very far off. I then asked where were their women? Had they any like themselves? I was told they had. "And why," said I, "do we not see them?" They answered, because they were left behind. I asked how the vessel could go? They told me they could not tell; but that there was cloth put upon the masts by the help of the ropes I saw, and then the vessel went on; and the white men had some spell or magic they put in the water when they liked, in order to stop the vessel. I was exceedingly amazed at this account, and really thought they were spirits. I therefore wished much to be from amongst them, for I expected they would sacrifice me; but my wishes were vain—for we were so quartered that it was impossible for any of us to make our escape.

While we stayed on the coast I was mostly on deck; and one day, to my great astonishment, I saw one of these vessels coming in with the sails up. As soon as the whites saw it, they gave a great shout, at which we were amazed; and the more so, as the vessel appeared larger by approaching nearer. At last, she came to an anchor in my sight, and when the anchor was let go, I and my countrymen who saw it, were lost in astonishment to observe the vessel stop—and were now convinced it was done by magic. Soon after this the other ship got her boats out, and they came on board of us, and the people of both ships seemed very glad to see each other.—Several of the strangers also shook hands with us black people, and made motions with their hands, signifying I suppose, we were to go to their country, but we did not understand them.

At last, when the ship we were in, had got in all her cargo, they made ready with many fearful noises, and we were all put under deck, so that we could not see how they managed the vessel. But this disappointment was the least of my sorrow. The stench of the hold while we were on the coast was so intolerably loathsome, that it was dangerous to remain there for any time, and some of us had been permitted to stay on the deck for the fresh air; but now that the whole ship's cargo were confined together, it became absolutely pestilential. The closeness of the place, and the heat of the climate, added to the number in the ship, which was so crowded that each had scarcely room to turn himself, almost suffocated us. This produced copious perspirations, so that the air soon became unfit for respiration, from a variety of loathsome smells, and brought on a sickness among the slaves, of which many died—thus falling victims to the improvident avarice, as I may call it, of their purchasers. This wretched situation was again aggravated by the galling of the chains, now became insupportable; and the filth of the necessary tubs, into which the children often fell, and were almost suffocated. The shrieks of the women, and the groans of the dying, rendered the whole a scene of horror almost inconceivable. Happily perhaps, for myself, I was soon reduced so low here that it was thought necessary to keep me almost always on deck; and from my extreme youth I was not put in fetters. In this situation I expected every hour to share the fate of my companions, some of whom were almost daily brought upon deck at the point of death, which I began to hope would soon put an end to my miseries. Often did I think many of the inhabitants of the deep much more happy than myself. I envied them the freedom they enjoyed, and as often wished I could change my condition for theirs. Every circumstance I met with, served only to render my state more painful, and heightened my apprehensions, and my opinion of the cruelty of the whites.

One day they had taken a number of fishes; and when they had killed and satisfied themselves with as many as they thought fit, to our astonishment who were on deck, rather than give any of them to us to eat, as we expected, they tossed the remaining fish into the sea again, although we begged and prayed for some as well as we could, but in vain; and some of my countrymen, being pressed by hunger, took an opportunity, when they thought no one saw them, of trying to get a little privately; but they were discovered, and the attempt procured them some very severe floggings. One day, when we had a smooth sea and moderate wind, two of my wearied countrymen who were chained together, (I was near them at the time,) preferring death to such a life of misery, somehow made through the nettings and jumped into the sea: immediately, another quite dejected fellow, who, on account of his illness, was suffered to be out of irons, also followed their example; and I believe many more would very soon have done the same, if they had not been prevented by the ship's crew, who were instantly alarmed. Those of us that were the most active, were in a moment put down under the deck, and there was such a noise and confusion amongst the people of the ship as I never heard before, to stop her, and get the boat out to go after the slaves. However, two of the wretches were drowned, but they got the other, and afterward flogged him unmercifully, for thus attempting to prefer death to slavery. In this manner we continued to undergo more hardships than I can now relate, hardships which are inseparable from this accursed trade. Many a time we were near suffocation from the want of fresh air, which we were often without for whole days together. This, and the stench of the necessary tubs, carried off many.

During our passage, I first saw flying fishes, which surprised me very much; they used frequently to fly across the ship, and many of them fell on the deck. I also now first saw the use of the quadrant; I had often with astonishment seen the mariners make observations with it, and I could not think what it meant. They at last took notice of my surprise; and one of them, willing to increase it, as well as to gratify my curiosity, made me one day look through it. The clouds appeared to me to be land, which disappeared as they passed along. This heightened my wonder; and I was now more persuaded than ever, that I was in another world, and that every thing about me was magic. At last, we came in sight of the island of Barbados, at which the whites on board gave a great shout, and made many signs of joy to us. We did not know what to think of this; but as the vessel drew nearer, we plainly saw the harbor, and other ships of different kinds and sizes, and we soon anchored amongst them, off Bridgetown. Many merchants and planters now came on board, though it was in the evening. They put us in separate parcels, and examined us attentively. They also made us jump, and pointed to the land, signifying we were to go there. We thought by this, we should be eaten by these ugly men, as they appeared to us; and, when soon after we were all put down under the deck again, there was much dread and trembling among us, and nothing but bitter cries to be heard all the night from these apprehensions, insomuch, that at last the white people got some old slaves from the land to pacify us. They told us we were not to be eaten, but to work, and were soon to go on land, where we should see many of our country people. This report eased us much. And sure enough, soon after we were landed, there came to us Africans of all languages.

We were conducted immediately to the merchant's yard, where we were all pent up together, like so many sheep in a fold, without regard to sex or age. As every object was new to me, every thing I saw filled me with surprise. What struck me first, was, that the houses were built with bricks and stories, and in every other respect different from those I had seen in Africa; but I was still more astonished on seeing people on horseback. I did not know what this could mean; and, indeed, I thought these people were full of nothing but magical arts. While I was in this astonishment, one of my fellow-prisoners spoke to a countryman of his, about the horses, who said they were the same kind they had in their country. I understood them, though they were from a distant part of Africa; and I thought it odd I had not seen any horses there; but afterwards, when I came to converse with different Africans, I found they had many horses amongst them, and much larger than those I then saw.

We were not many days in the merchant's custody before we were sold after their usual manner, which is this:—On a signal given, (as the beat of a drum,) the buyers rush at once into the yard where the slaves are confined, and make choice of that parcel they like best. The noise and clamor with which this is attended, and the eagerness visible in the countenances of the buyers, serve not a little to increase the apprehension of terrified Africans, who may well be supposed to consider them as the ministers of that destruction to which they think themselves devoted. In this manner, without scruple, are relations and friends separated, most of them never to see each other again. I remember, in the vessel in which I was brought over, in the men's apartment, there were several brothers, who, in the sale, were sold in different lots; and it was very moving on this occasion, to see and hear their cries at parting. O, ye nominal Christians! might not an African ask you—Learned you this from your God, who says unto you, Do unto all men as you would men should do unto you? Is it not enough that we are torn from our country and friends, to toil for your luxury and lust of gain? Must every tender feeling be likewise sacrificed to your avarice? Are the dearest friends and relations, now rendered more dear by their separation from their kindred, still to be parted from each other, and thus prevented from cheering the gloom of slavery, with the small comfort of being together, and mingling their sufferings and sorrows? Why are parents to lose their children, brothers their sisters, or husbands their wives? Surely, this is a new refinement in cruelty, which, while it has no advantage to atone for it, thus aggravates distress, and adds fresh horrors even to the wretchedness of slavery.

On the Misfortune
of Indentured Servants

Gottlieb Mittelberger

Indentured, or bonded, servants were an important source of labor in seventeenth- and eighteenth-century America. The term generally refers to immigrants who, in return for passage from Europe to America, bound themselves to work in America for a number of years, after which time they would become completely free. The practice was closely related to the tradition of apprenticeship, in which a youth was assigned to work for a master in a trade for a certain number of years and in return was taught the skills of that trade. Convicts were another important source of colonial labor; thousands of English criminals were sentenced to labor in the colonies for a specified period, after which they were freed.

Many indentured servants had valuable skills that they hoped to make better use of in the New World than they had been able to do at home. Some in fact did just that, while others, as Gottlieb Mittelberger describes, did not fare well. Mittelberger came to Pennsylvania from Germany in 1750. His own fortunes were not so bleak as those of his shipmates. He served as a schoolmaster and organist in Philadelphia for three years and then returned to Germany in 1754.

BEFORE YOU READ

1. Why do you think immigrants chose to endure the miseries of a transatlantic passage to come to the New World?

2. How did the treatment of indentured servants described by Mittelberger compare to the treatment of slaves in the slave trade described in the previous reading?

3. What happened to children whose parents died during the journey?

4. Why do you think Mittelberger returned to Germany?

Both in Rotterdam and in Amsterdam the people are packed densely, like herrings so to say, in the large sea-vessels. One person receives a place of scarcely 2 feet width and 6 feet length in the bedstead, while many a ship carries four to six hundred souls; not to mention the innumerable implements, tools, provisions, water-barrels and other things which likewise occupy much space.

Gottlieb Mittelberger, *Journey to Pennsylvania in the Year 1750 and Return to Germany in the Year 1754*, trans. Carl Theo (Philadelphia: John Joseph McVey, 1898), pp. 19–29.

On account of contrary winds it takes the ships sometimes 2, 3 and 4 weeks to make the trip from Holland to . . . England. But when the wind is good, they get there in 8 days or even sooner. Everything is examined there and the custom-duties paid, whence it comes that the ships ride there 8, 10 to 14 days and even longer at anchor, till they have taken in their full cargoes. During that time every one is compelled to spend his last remaining money and to consume his little stock of provisions which had been reserved for the sea; so that most passengers, finding themselves on the ocean where they would be in greater need of them, must greatly suffer from hunger and want. Many suffer want already on the water between Holland and Old England.

When the ships have for the last time weighed their anchors near the city of Kaupp [Cowes] in Old England, the real misery begins with the long voyage. For from there the ships, unless they have good wind, must often sail 8, 9, 10 to 12 weeks before they reach Philadelphia. But even with the best wind the voyage lasts 7 weeks.

But during the voyage there is on board these ships terrible misery, stench, fumes, horror, vomiting, many kinds of sea-sickness, fever, dysentery, headache, heat, constipation, boils, scurvy, cancer, mouth-rot, and the like, all of which come from old and sharply salted food and meat, also from very bad and foul water, so that many die miserably.

Add to this want of provisions, hunger, thirst, frost, heat, dampness, anxiety, want, afflictions and lamentations, together with other trouble, as . . . the lice abound so frightfully, especially on sick people, that they can be scraped off the body. The misery reaches the climax when a gale rages for 2 or 3 nights and days, so that every one believes that the ship will go to the bottom with all human beings on board. In such a visitation the people cry and pray most piteously.

When in such a gale the sea rages and surges, so that the waves rise often like high mountains one above the other, and often tumble over the ship, so that one fears to go down with the ship; when the ship is constantly tossed from side to side by the storm and waves, so that no one can either walk, or sit, or lie, and the closely packed people in the berths are thereby tumbled over each other, both the sick and the well—it will be readily understood that many of these people, none of whom had been prepared for hardships, suffer so terribly from them that they do not survive it.

I myself had to pass through a severe illness at sea, and I best know how I felt at the time. These poor people often long for consolation, and I often entertained and comforted them with singing, praying and exhorting; and whenever it was possible and the winds and waves permitted it, I kept daily prayer-meetings with them on deck. Besides, I baptized five children in distress, because we had no ordained minister on board. I also held divine service every Sunday by reading sermons to the people; and when the dead were sunk in the water, I commended them and our souls to the mercy of God.

Among the healthy, impatience sometimes grows so great and cruel that one curses the other, or himself and the day of his birth, and sometimes come near killing each other. Misery and malice join each other, so that they cheat and rob one another. One always reproaches the other with having persuaded him to undertake the journey. Frequently children cry out against their parents, husbands against their wives and wives against their husbands, brothers and sisters, friends and acquaintances against each other. But most against the soultraffickers.

Many sigh and cry: "Oh, that I were at home again, and if I had to lie in my pig-sty!" Or they say: "O God, if I only had a piece of good bread, or a good fresh drop of water." Many people whimper, sigh and cry piteously for their homes; most of them get home-sick. Many hundred people necessarily die and perish in such misery, and must be cast into the sea, which drives their relatives, or those who persuaded them to undertake the journey, to such despair that it is almost impossible to pacify and console them. . . .

No one can have an idea of the sufferings which women in confinement have to bear with their innocent children on board these ships. Few of this class escape with their lives; many a mother is cast into the water with her child as soon as she is dead. One day, just as we had a heavy gale, a woman in our ship, who was to give birth and could not give birth under the circumstances, was pushed through a loop-hole [port-hole] in the ship and dropped into the sea, because she was far in the rear of the ship and could not be brought forward.

Children from 1 to 7 years rarely survive the voyage. I witnessed . . . misery in no less than 32 children in our ship, all of whom were thrown into the sea. The parents grieve all the more since their children find no resting-place in the earth, but are devoured by the monsters of the sea.

That most of the people get sick is not surprising, because, in addition to all other trials and hardships, warm food is served only three times a week, the rations being very poor and very little. Such meals can hardly be eaten, on account of being so unclean. The water which is served out on the ships is often very black, thick and full of worms, so that one cannot drink it without loathing, even with the greatest thirst. Toward the end we were compelled to eat the ship's biscuit which had been spoiled long ago; though in a whole biscuit there was scarcely a piece the size of a dollar that had not been full of red worms and spiders' nests. . . .

At length, when, after a long and tedious voyage, the ships come in sight of land, so that the promontories can be seen, which the people were so eager and anxious to see, all creep from below on deck to see the land from afar, and they weep for joy, and pray and sing, thanking and praising God. The sight of the land makes the people on board the ship, especially the sick and the half dead, alive again, so that their hearts leap within them; they shout and rejoice, and are content to bear their misery in patience, in the hope that they may soon reach the land in safety. But alas!

When the ships have landed at Philadelphia after their long voyage, no one is permitted to leave them except those who pay for their passage or can give good security; the others, who cannot pay, must remain on board the ships till they are purchased, and are released from the ships by their purchasers. The sick always fare the worst, for the healthy are naturally preferred and purchased first; and so the sick and wretched must often remain on board in front of the city for 2 or 3 weeks, and frequently die, whereas many a one, if he could pay his debt and were permitted to leave the ship immediately, might recover and remain alive.

The sale of human beings in the market on board the ship is carried on thus: Every day Englishmen, Dutchmen, and High-German people come from the city of Philadelphia and other places, in part from a great distance, say 20, 30, or 40 hours away, and go on board the newly arrived ship that has brought and offers for sale passengers from Europe, and select among the healthy persons such as they deem suitable for their business, and bargain with them how long they will serve for their passage money, which most of them are still in debt for. When they have come to an agreement, it happens that adult persons bind themselves in writing to serve 3, 4, 5, or 6 years for the amount due by them, according to their age and strength. But very young people, from 10 to 15 years, must serve till they are 21 years old.

Many parents must sell and trade away their children like so many head of cattle; for if their children take the debt upon themselves, the parents can leave the ship free and unrestrained; but as the parents often do not know where and to what people their children are going, it often happens that such parents and children, after leaving the ship, do not see each other again for many years, perhaps no more in all their lives.

It often happens that whole families, husband, wife, and children, are separated by being sold to different purchasers, especially when they have not paid any part of their passage money.

When a husband or wife has died at sea, when the ship has made more than half of her trip, the survivor must pay or serve not only for himself or herself, but also for the deceased.

When both parents have died over half-way at sea, their children, especially when they are young and have nothing to pawn or to pay, must stand for their own and their parents' passage, and serve till they are 21 years old. When one has served his or her term, he or she is entitled to a new suit of clothes at parting; and if it has been so stipulated, a man gets in addition a horse, a woman, a cow.

When a serf has an opportunity to marry in this country, he or she must pay for each year which he or she would have yet to serve, 5 to 6 pounds. But many a one who has thus purchased and paid for his bride, has subsequently repented his bargain, so that he would gladly have returned his exorbitantly dear ware, and lost the money besides.

If some one in this country runs away from his master, who has treated him harshly, he cannot get far. Good provision has been made for such cases, so that a runaway is soon recovered. He who detains or returns a deserter receives a good reward.

If such a runaway has been away from his master one day, he must serve for it as a punishment a week, for a week a month, and for a month half a year.

A Man of the American Enlightenment
Benjamin Franklin

The new science of the Enlightenment, epitomized by Isaac Newton's Philosophiae
Naturalis Principia Mathematica *(1687), profoundly influenced the outlook of educated people in eighteenth-century Europe and North America alike, including many of
the leaders of the patriot cause in colonial America. Fundamental to the view of people
like Benjamin Franklin (1706–1790) was a belief in the power of human reason to
understand the laws of nature, to improve human life, and to establish rational governments and a code of moral conduct.*

*Franklin exemplified Enlightenment thinking in America. He was a scientist
studying the natural laws of electricity; an inventor improving human life through such
inventions as the lightning rod, the Franklin stove, and bifocals; a philanthropist organizing libraries and scientific societies to spread secular scientific knowledge; a journalist
advancing popular learning; a reformer improving fire prevention and other civic
needs; and the author of an autobiography unlike anything that had preceded it in its
didactic yet thoroughly secular account of his own remarkable moral development. His
autobiography was originally published in Paris in 1791, a year after his death; the
first English translation was published in London two years later.*

Before You Read

1. Why do you think Benjamin Franklin is considered the supreme representative
of the American Enlightenment?

2. Why did Franklin perform so many public services? What view of the world was
the basis of his activities?

3. Why did Franklin decide not to answer the criticisms of Abbé Nollet? What
does this decision indicate about his understanding of the importance of discussion and
debate regarding scientific experiments?

I should have mentioned before, that in the Autumn of the preceeding Year
[1727] I had formed most of my ingenious Acquaintance into a Club of mutual
Improvement, which we called the Junto. We met on Friday Evenings. The
Rules I drew up required that every member in his Turn should produce one or
more Queries on any Point of Morals, Politics or Natural Philosophy, to be dis-

Benjamin Franklin, "Autobiography," in Frank Luther Mott and Chester E. Jorgenson, eds., *Benjamin Franklin: Representative Selections* (New York: American Book Company, 1936), pp. 58, 68–70,
84–89, 92–95.

cussed by the Company, and once in three Months produce and read an Essay of his own Writing on any Subject he pleased. Our Debates were to be under the Direction of a President and to be conducted in the sincere Spirit of Enquiry after Truth, without Fondness for Dispute, or Desire of Victory; and to prevent Warmth, all Expressions of Positiveness in Opinions or direct Contradiction, were after some time made contraband and prohibited under small pecuniary Penalties. . . .

And now I sent on foot my first Project of a public Nature, [th]at for a Subscription Library. [I] drew up the Proposals, got them put into Form by our great Scrivener Brockden, and by the help of my Friends in the Junto, procur'd Fifty Subscribers . . . for 50 Years, the Term our Company was to continue. We afterwards obtain'd a Charter, the Company being increas'd to 100. This was the Mother of all the N American Subscription Libraries now so numerous, is become a great thing itself, and continually increasing. — These Libraries have improv'd the general Conversation of the Americans, made the common Tradesmen and Farmers as intelligent as most Gentlemen from other Countries, and perhaps have contributed in some degree to the Stand so generally made throughout the Colonies in Defence of their Privileges. . . .

I had been religiously educated as a Presbyterian; and tho' some of the dogmas of that persuasion, such as *the eternal decrees of God, election, reprobation, etc.*, appeared to me unintelligible, others doubtful, and I early absented myself from the public assemblies of the sect, Sunday being my studying day, I never was without some religious principles. I never doubted, for instance, the existence of the Deity; that he made the world, and govern'd it by his Providence; that the most acceptable service of God was the doing good to man; that our souls are immortal; and that all crime will be punished, and virtue rewarded, either here or hereafter. These I esteem'd the essentials of every religion; and, being to be found in all the religions we had in our country, I respected them all, tho' with different degrees of respect, as I found them more or less mix'd with other articles, which, without any tendency to inspire, promote, or confirm morality, serv'd principally to divide us, and make us unfriendly to one another. . . .

In 1732 I first publish'd my Almanack, under the name of *Richard Saunders;* it was continu'd by me about twenty-five years, commonly call'd *Poor Richard's Almanack.* I endeavour'd to make it both entertaining and useful, and it accordingly came to be in such demand, that I reap'd considerable profit from it, vending annually near ten thousand. And observing that it was generally read, scarce any neighborhood in the province being without it, I consider'd it as a proper vehicle for conveying instruction among the common people, who bought scarcely any other books; I therefore filled all the little spaces that occurr'd between the remarkable days in the calendar with proverbial sentences, chiefly such as inculcated industry and frugality, as the means of procuring wealth, and thereby securing virtue; it being more difficult for a man in want, to act always honestly, as, to use here one of those proverbs, *it is hard for an empty sack to stand upright.*

These proverbs, which contained the wisdom of many ages and nations, I assembled and form'd into a connected discourse prefix'd to the Almanack of 1757,

as the harangue of a wise old man to the people attending an auction. The bringing all these scatter'd counsels thus into a focus enabled them to make greater
impression. The piece, being universally approved, was copied in all the newspapers of the Continent; reprinted in Britain on a broad side, to be stuck up in
houses; two translations were made of it in French, and great numbers bought by
the clergy and gentry, to distribute gratis among their poor parishioners and tenants. In Pennsylvania, as it discouraged useless expense in foreign superfluities,
some thought it had its share of influence in producing that growing plenty of
money which was observable for several years after its publication.

    I considered my newspaper, also, as another means of communicating
instruction, and in that view frequently reprinted in it extracts from the Spectator,[1] and other moral writers; and sometimes publish'd little pieces of my own,
which had been first compos'd for reading in our Junto. . . .

    In the conduct of my newspaper, I carefully excluded all libelling and per-
sonal abuse, which is of late years become so disgraceful to our country. Whenever I was solicited to insert any thing of that kind, and the writers pleaded, as
they generally did, the liberty of the press, and that a newspaper was like a
stage-coach, in which any one who would pay had a right to a place, my answer
was, that I would print the piece separately if desired, and the author might
have as many copies as he pleased to distribute himself, but that I would not
take upon me to spread his detraction; and that, having contracted with my subscribers to furnish them with what might be either useful or entertaining, I
could not fill their papers with private altercation, in which they had no concern, without doing them manifest injustice. Now, many of our printers make
no scruple of gratifying the malice of individuals by false accusations of the
fairest characters among ourselves, augmenting animosity even to the producing of duels; and are, moreover, so indiscreet as to print scurrilous reflections
on the government of neighboring states, and even on the conduct of our best
national allies, which may be attended with the most pernicious consequences.
These things I mention as a caution to young printers, and that they may be encouraged not to pollute their presses and disgrace their profession by such infamous practices, but refuse steadily, as they may see by my example that such a
course of conduct will not, on the whole, be injurious to their interests. . . .

    Our club, the Junto, was found so useful, and afforded such satisfaction to
the members, that several were desirous of introducing their friends, which
could not well be done without exceeding what we had settled as a convenient
number, viz., twelve. We had from the beginning made it a rule to keep our institution a secret, which was pretty well observ'd; the intention was to avoid applications of improper persons for admittance, some of whom, perhaps, we
might find it difficult to refuse. I was one of those who were against any addition to our number, but, instead of it, made in writing a proposal, that every
member separately should endeavour to form a subordinate club, with the same
rules respecting queries, etc., and without informing them of the connection

---

    1. **the Spectator:** a London periodical, edited by Joseph Addison and Richard Steele, that
printed essays on social and cultural topics of the day.

with the Junto. The advantages proposed were, the improvement of so many more young citizens by the use of our institutions; our better acquaintance with the general sentiments of the inhabitants on any occasion, as the Junto member might propose what queries we should desire, and was to report to the Junto what pass'd in his separate club; the promotion of our particular interests in business by more extensive recommendation, and the increase of our influence in public affairs, and our power of doing good by spreading thro' the several clubs the sentiments of the Junto.

The project was approv'd, and every member undertook to form his club, but they did not all succeed. Five or six only were compleated, which were called by different names, as the Vine, the Union, the Band, etc. They were useful to themselves, and afforded us a good deal of amusement, information, and instruction, besides answering, in some considerable degree, our views of influencing the public opinion on particular occasions, of which I shall give some instances in course of time as they happened.

I began now to turn my thoughts a little to public affairs, beginning, however, with small matters. . . .

About this time I wrote a paper (first to be read in Junto, but it was afterward publish'd) on the different accidents and carelessnesses by which houses were set on fire, with cautions against them, and means proposed of avoiding them. This was much spoken of as a useful piece, and gave rise to a project, which soon followed it, of forming a company for the more ready extinguishing of fires, and mutual assistance in removing and securing of goods when in danger. Associates in this scheme were presently found, amounting to thirty. Our articles of agreement oblig'd every member to keep always in good order, and fit for use, a certain number of leather buckets, with strong bags and baskets (for packing and transporting of goods), which were to be brought to every fire; and we agreed to meet once a month and spend a social evening together, in discoursing and communicating such ideas as occurred to us upon the subject of fires, as might be useful in our conduct on such occasions.

The utility of this institution soon appeared, and many more desiring to be admitted than we thought convenient for one company, they were advised to form another, which was accordingly done; and this went on, one new company being formed after another, till they became so numerous as to include most of the inhabitants who were men of property; and now, at the time of my writing this, tho' upward of fifty years since its establishment, that which I first formed, called the Union Fire Company, still subsists and flourishes, tho' the first members are all deceas'd but myself and one, who is older by a year than I am. The small fines that have been paid by members for absence at the monthly meetings have been apply'd to the purchase of fire-engines, ladders, fire-hooks, and other useful implements for each company, so that I question whether there is a city in the world better provided with the means of putting a stop to beginning conflagrations; and, in fact, since these institutions, the city has never lost by fire more than one or two houses at a time, and the flames have often been extinguished before the house in which they began has been half consumed. . . .

I had, on the whole, abundant reason to be satisfied with my being established in Pennsylvania. There were, however, two things that I regretted, there
being no provision for defense, nor for a compleat education of youth; no militia, nor any college. . . .

The first step [toward establishing a college] I took was to associate in the
design a number of active friends, of whom the Junto furnished a good part; the
next was to write and publish a pamphlet, entitled *Proposals Relating to the Education of Youth in Pennsylvania*. This I distributed among the principal inhabitants
gratis, and as soon as I could suppose their minds a little prepared by the pe-
rusal of it, I set on foot a subscription for opening and supporting an academy;
it was to be paid in quotas yearly for five years; by so dividing it, I judg'd the
subscription might be larger, and I believe it was so, amounting to no less, if I
remember right, than five thousand pounds.

In the introduction to these proposals, I stated their publication, not as an
act of mine, but of some *publick-spirited gentlemen*, avoiding as much as I could,
according to my usual rule, the presenting myself to the publick as the author of
any scheme for their benefit.

The subscribers, to carry the project into immediate execution, chose out
of their number twenty-four trustees, and appointed Mr. Francis, then
attorney-general, and myself to draw up constitutions for the government of
the academy; which being done and signed, a house was hired, masters engag'd,
and the schools opened, I think, in the same year, 1749.

In 1746, being at Boston, I met there with a Dr. Spence, who was lately
arrived from Scotland, and show'd me some electric experiments. They were
imperfectly perform'd, as he was not very expert; but, being on a subject
quite new to me, they equally surpris'd and pleased me. Soon after my return
to Philadelphia, our library company receiv'd from Mr. P. Collinson, Fellow
of the Royal Society of London, a present of a glass tube, with some account
of the use of it in making such experiments. I eagerly seized the opportunity of
repeating what I had seen at Boston; and, by much practice, acquir'd
great readiness in performing those, also, which we had an account of from
England, adding a number of new ones. I say much practice, for my house was
continually full, for some time, with people who came to see these new
wonders.

To divide a little this incumbrance among my friends, I caused a number of
similar tubes to be blown at our glass-house, with which they furnish'd themselves, so that we had at length several performers. Among these, the principal
was Mr. Kinnersley, an ingenious neighbor, who, being out of business, I encouraged to undertake showing the experiments for money, and drew up for
him two lectures, in which the experiments were rang'd in such order, and accompanied with such explanations in such method, as that the foregoing should
assist in comprehending the following. He procur'd an elegant apparatus for
the purpose, in which all the little machines that I had roughly made for myself
were nicely form'd by instrument-makers. His lectures were well attended, and

gave great satisfaction; and after some time he went thro' the colonies, exhibiting them in every capital town, and pick'd up some money. In the West India Islands, indeed, it was with difficulty the experiments could be made, from the general moisture of the air.

Oblig'd as we were to Mr. Collinson for his present of the tube, etc., I thought it right he should be inform'd of our success in using it, and wrote him several letters containing accounts of our experiments. He got them read in the Royal Society, where they were not at first thought worth so much notice as to be printed in their Transactions. . . .

It was, however, some time before those papers were much taken notice of in England. A copy of them happening to fall into the hands of the Count de Buffon, a philosopher deservedly of great reputation in France, and, indeed, all over Europe, he prevailed with M. Dalibard to translate them into French, and they were printed at Paris. The publication offended the Abbé Nollet, preceptor in Natural Philosophy to the royal family, and an able experimenter, who had form'd and publish'd a theory of electricity, which then had the general vogue. He could not at first believe that such a work came from America, and said it must have been fabricated by his enemies at Paris, to decry his system. Afterwards, having been assur'd that there really existed such a person as Franklin at Philadelphia, which he had doubted, he wrote and published a volume of Letters, chiefly address'd to me, defending his theory, and denying the verity of my experiments, and of the positions deduc'd from them.

I once purpos'd answering the abbé, and actually began the answer; but, on consideration that my writings contain'd a description of experiments which any one might repeat and verify, and if not to be verifi'd, could not be defended; or of observations offer'd as conjectures, and not delivered dogmatically, therefore not laying me under any obligation to defend them; and reflecting that a dispute between two persons, writing in different languages, might be lengthened greatly by mistranslations, and thence misconceptions of one another's meaning, much of one of the abbé's letters being founded on an error in the translation, I concluded to let my papers shift for themselves, believing it was better to spend what time I could spare from public business in making new experiments, than in disputing about those already made. I therefore never answered M. Nollet, and the event gave me no cause to repent my silence; for my friend M. le Roy, of the Royal Academy of Sciences, took up my cause and refuted him; my book was translated into the Italian, German, and Latin languages; and the doctrine it contain'd was by degrees universally adopted by the philosophers of Europe, in preference to that of the abbé.

13

Leaving an Abusive Husband
Abigail Abbot Bailey

Memoirs of Mrs. Abigail Bailey, *originally published in 1815, is the first American autobiography detailing family violence and abuse. Abigail Abbot Bailey (1746–1815), a profoundly religious woman after her conversion to Christianity at the age of eighteen, claimed that "God gave me a heart to resolve never to be obstinate, or disobedient to my husband; but to be always kind, obedient, and obliging in all things not contrary to the word of God." However, her marriage to Asa Bailey, which lasted twenty-six years and included the birth of seventeen children, continuously and severely tested this belief. Within a month of the wedding, Asa began physically abusing Abigail so that at times she feared "that he wanted to kill" her. Then within three years he had committed adultery with a servant. A few years later he attempted to rape another servant girl but was repulsed and brought into court, only to be released for lack of evidence. After Asa committed incest with their sixteen-year-old daughter, Abigail finally began a painful effort to end the marriage. Seeking to avoid the attendant division of property, Asa persuaded Abigail to accompany him to upstate New York, where he abandoned her far from her family, church friends, and their children. She made a torturous journey back to their home in New Hampshire alone. Then her brothers accompanied her to a justice of the peace, enabling her to have Asa arrested and forcing him into a property settlement and an uncontested "bill of divorcement."*

Bailey based her Memoirs *in part on the diaries she kept throughout much of her marriage, writings largely given over to religious devotions and musings. The minister who edited the manuscript recommended it to "the intelligent reader" who would find "strikingly exhibited" there "the dreadful depravity of fallen man; the abomination of intrigue and deceit; the horrid cruelty, of which man is capable; the hardness of the way of transgressors; . . . and the wisdom of God in turning headlong the devices of the crafty." The modern reader will note as well how difficult it was for a woman of the late eighteenth century to achieve any control over a dreadful situation. As Ann Taves, a modern scholar of the* Memoirs, *writes: "Given the difficulty of obtaining a divorce in practice, if not in theory, in late-eighteenth-century New Hampshire, it is perhaps more surprising that Abigail extricated herself from her marriage at all than that it took her four and a half years to do so."*

BEFORE YOU READ

1. Given the laws and customs of the era, do you think that Abigail Abbot Bailey acted as assertively as she could in dealing with her husband's transgressions?

Ann Taves, ed., *Religion and Domestic Violence in Early New England: The Memoirs of Abigail Abbot Bailey* (Bloomington: Indiana University Press, 1989), pp. 56–58, 68–72, 75–83.

2. What role did religion play in Bailey's life, and how did it influence the way she responded to her domestic situation?

3. What similarities or differences do you see between the situation of the Bailey family and current examples of domestic violence and abuse?

I Abigail Bailey (daughter of Deacon James Abbot of Newbury, Coos, who moved thither from Concord, N.H. A.D. 1763) do now undertake to record some of the dealings of the allwise God with me, in events, which I am sure I ought solemnly to remember, as long as I live.

I shall first, in few words, record the merciful dealings of my heavenly Father, in casting my lot, not only under the gospel, but in a family, where I was ever treated with the greatest kindness by my tender parents; and particularly with the most religious attention from my very pious mother; and where I was ever treated with the greatest tenderness by my brothers and sisters. I can truly say, it was seldom that an angry word was ever spoken in my father's family— by parents, brothers, or sisters—against me, from my infancy, and during my continuance in my father's house. So that I passed the morning of my days in peace and contentment.

I was married to Asa Bailey, just after having entered the 22nd year of my age. I now left my dear parents;—hoping to find in my husband a true hearted and constant friend. My desires and hopes were, that we might live together in peace and friendship; seeking each other's true happiness till death. I did earnestly look to God for his blessing upon this solemn undertaking;—sensible, that "Except the Lord build the house, they labor in vain that build it." As, while I lived with my parents, I esteemed it my happiness to be in subjection to them; so now I thought it must be a still greater benefit to be under the aid of a judicious companion, who would rule well his own house. . . .

Relative to my new companion, though I had found no evidence that he was a subject of true religion; yet I did hope and expect, from my acquaintance with him, that he would wish for good regulations in his family, and would have its external order accord with the word of God. But I met with sore disappointment,—I soon found that my new friend was naturally of a hard, uneven, rash temper; and was capable of being very unreasonable. My conviction of this was indeed grievous, and caused me many a sorrowful hour. For such were my feelings and habits, that I knew not how to endure a hard word, or a frowning look from any one; much less from a companion. I now began to learn, with trembling, that it was the sovereign pleasure of the allwise God to try me with afflictions in that relation, from which I had hoped to receive the greatest of my earthly comforts. I had placed my highest worldly happiness in the love, tenderness, and peace of relatives and friends. But before one month, from my marriage day, had passed, I learned that I must expect hard and cruel treatment in my new habitation, and from my new friend. . . .

I think God gave me a heart to resolve never to be obstinate, or disobedient to my husband; but to be always kind, obedient, and obliging in all things not contrary to the word of God. I thought if Mr. B. were sometimes unreasonable, I would be reasonable, and would rather suffer wrong than do wrong. And as I hoped Mr. B. would kindly overlook my infirmities and failings, with which I was conscious I should abound; so I felt a forgiving spirit towards him. Many times his treatment would grieve my heart. But I never was suffered to my knowledge, to return any wickedness in my conduct towards him; nor ever to indulge a revengeful feeling or ill will. For some years I thought his repeated instances of hard treatment of me arose, — not from any settled ill will, or real want of kind affection toward me; — but from the usual depravity of the human heart; and from a want of self-government. I still confided in him, as my real friend, and loved him with increasing affection. . . .

[Her husband is on two occasions unfaithful with servants. He repents both times, but her confidence in him has been eroded.]

Now, alas! I must begin the sad detail of events, the most distressing; and which awfully verified my most fearful apprehensions; and convinced me, that all my trials of life hitherto, were as nothing. . . .

[Her husband concocts a pretext to go away for a lengthy period with a teenage daughter.]

But alas! words fail to set forth the things which followed! All this pretended *plan* was but a specious cover to infernal designs. . . .

I have already related that Mr. B. said he would take one of our sons, and one daughter, to wait on him in his distant tour, before he would take all the family. After he had talked of this for a few days, he said he had altered his plan; he would leave his son, and take only his daughter: he would hire what men's help he needed: his daughter must go and cook for him. He now commenced a new series of conduct in relation to this daughter, whom he selected to go with him, in order (as he pretended) to render himself pleasing and familiar to her; so that she might be willing to go with him, and feel happy: for though, as a father, he had a right to command her to go, yet (he said) he would so conduct toward her, as to make her cheerful and well pleased to go with him. A great part of the time he now spent in the room where she was spinning; and seemed shy of me, and of the rest of the family. He seemed to have forgotten his age, his honor, and all decency, as well as all virtue. He would spend his time with this daughter, in telling idle stories, and foolish riddles, and singing songs to her, and sometimes before the small children, when they were in that room. He thus pursued a course of conduct, which had the most direct tendency to corrupt young and tender minds, and lead them the greatest distance from every serious subject. He would try to make his daughter tell stories with him; wishing to make her free and sociable, and to erase from her mind all that fear and reserve, which he had ever taught his children to feel toward him. He had ever been sovereign, severe and hard with his children, and they stood in the greatest fear of him. His whole conduct, toward this daughter especially, was now changed, and became most disagreeable.

For a considerable time I was wholly at a loss what to think of his conduct, or what his wish or intentions could be. Had such conduct appeared toward any young woman beside his own young daughter, I should have had no question what he intended: but as it now was, I was loth to indulge the least suspicion of base design. His daily conduct forced a conviction upon my alarmed and tortured mind, that his designs were the most vile. All his tender affections were withdrawn from the wife of his youth, the mother of his children. My room was deserted, and left lonely. His care for the rest of his family seemed abandoned, as well as all his attention to his large circle of worldly business. Every thing must lie neglected, while this one daughter engrossed all his attention.

Though all the conduct of Mr. B. from day to day, seemed to demonstrate to my apprehension, that he was determined, and was continually plotting, to ruin this poor young daughter, yet it was so intolerably crossing to every feeling of my soul to admit such a thought, that I strove with all my might to banish it from my mind, and to disbelieve the possibility of such a thing. . . . And such were my infirmities, weakness and fears, (my circumstances being very difficult) that I did not dare to hint any thing of my fears to him, or to any creature. This may to some appear strange; but with me it was then a reality. I labored to divert his mind from his follies, and to turn his attention to things of the greatest importance. But I had the mortification to find that my endeavors were unsuccessful.

I soon perceived that his strange conduct toward this daughter was to her very disagreeable. And she shewed as much unwillingness to be in the room with him, as she dared. I often saw her cheeks bedewed with tears, on account of his new and astonishing behaviour. But as his will had ever been the law of the family, she saw no way to deliver herself from her cruel father. Such were her fears of him, that she did not dare to talk with me, or any other person, upon her situation: for he was exceedingly jealous of my conversing with her, and cautioning her. If I ever dropped words, which I hoped would put her upon her guard, or inquired the cause of her troubles, or what business her father had so much with her? if I was ever so cautious, he would find it out, and be very angry. He watched her and me most narrowly; and by his subtle questions with her, he would find out what I had said, during his absence. He would make her think I had informed him what I had said, and then would be very angry with me: so that at times I feared for my life. I queried with myself which way I could turn. How could I caution a young daughter in such a case? My thoughts flew to God for relief, that the Father of mercies would protect a poor helpless creature marked out for a prey; and turn the heart of a cruel father from every wicked purpose. . . .

The black cloud, rising like a storm of hail, had rolled on, and had gathered over my head. I clearly saw that Mr. B. entertained the most vile intentions relative to his own daughter. Whatever difficulty attended the obtaining of legal proof, yet no remaining doubt existed in my mind, relative to the existence of his wickedness: and I had no doubt remaining of the violence, which he had used; and that hence arose his rage against her. It must have drawn tears of anguish from the eyes of the hardest mortals, to see the barbarous corrections, which he, from time to time, inflicted on this poor young creature; and for no just cause. Sometimes he corrected her with a rod; and sometimes with a beach stick, large enough for the driving of a team; and with such sternness and anger sparkling in his eyes, that his visage seemed to resemble an infernal; declaring, that if she attempted to run from him again, she should never want but one correction more; for he would whip her to death! This his conduct could be for no common disobedience; for she had ever been most obedient to him in all lawful commands. It seemed as though the poor girl must now be destroyed under his furious hand. She was abashed, and could look no one in the face. . . .

None can describe the anguish of my heart on the beholding of such scenes. How pitiful must be the case of a poor young female, to be subjected to such barbarous treatment by her own father; so that she knew of no way of redress!

It may appear surprising that such wickedness was not checked by legal restraints. But great difficulties attend in such a case. While I was fully convinced of the wickedness, yet I knew not that I could make legal proof. I could not prevail upon this daughter to make known to me her troubles; or to testify against the author of them. Fear, shame, youthful inexperience, and the terrible peculiarities of her case, all conspired to close her mouth against affording me, or any one, proper information. My soul was moved with pity for her wretched case: and yet I cannot say I did not feel a degree of resentment, that she would not, as she ought, expose the wickedness of her father, that she might be relieved from him, and he brought to due punishment. But no doubt his intrigues, insinuations, commands, threats, and parental influence, led her to feel that it was in vain for her to seek redress.

My circumstances, and peculiar bodily infirmities [pregnancy], at that time, were such as to entitle a woman to the tenderest affection and sympathies of a companion. On this account, and as Mr. B. was exceeding stern, and angry with me for entertaining hard thoughts of him, I felt unable to do any thing more for the relief of my poor daughter. My hope in God was my only support. And I did abundantly and earnestly commit my cause to him. I felt confident that he would, in his own time, and as his infinite wisdom should determine, grant relief. . . .

. . . I took an opportunity with Mr. B. alone to have solemn conversation. My health being now restored, I thought it high time, and had determined, to adopt a new mode of treatment with Mr. B. I calmly introduced the subject, and told him, plainly and solemnly, all my views of his wicked conduct, in which he had long lived with his daughter. He flew into a passion, was high, and seemed to imagine, he could at once frighten me out of my object. But I was carried equally above fear, and above temper. Of this I soon convinced him, I let him know, that the business I now had taken in hand was of too serious a nature, and too interesting, to be thus disposed of, or dismissed with a few angry words. I told him I should no longer be turned off in this manner; but should pursue my object with firmness, and with whatever wisdom and ability God might give me; and that God would plead my cause, and prosper my present undertaking, as he should see best. I reminded Mr. B. of my long and unusually distressing illness; how he had treated me in it; how wicked and cruel he had been to the wife of his youth; how unable I had been to check him in that awful wickedness, which

I knew he had pursued; that all my inexpressible griefs and solemn entreaties had been by him trampled under foot.

I therefore had not known what to do better than to wait on God as I had done, to afford me strength and opportunity to introduce the means of his effectual control. This time I told him had arrived. And now, if God spared my life, (I told Mr. B.) he should find a new leaf turned over;—and that I would not suffer him to go on any longer as he had done. I would now soon adopt measures to put a stop to his abominable wickedness and cruelties. For this could and ought to be done. And if I did it not, I should be a partaker of his sins, and should aid in bringing down the curse of God upon our family.

By this time Mr. B. had become silent. He appeared struck with some degree of fear. He, by and by, asked me what I intended or expected to do, to bring about such a revolution as I had intimated? whether I knew what an awful crime I had laid to his charge? which he said could not be proved. He wished to know whether I had considered how difficult it would be for me to do any such thing against him? as I was under his legal control; and he could overrule all my plans as he pleased. I told him, I well knew I had been placed under his lawful government and authority, and likewise under his care and protection. And most delightful would it have been to me, to have been able quietly and safely to remain there as long as I lived. Gladly would I have remained a kind faithful, obedient wife to him, as I had ever been. But I told Mr. B. he *knew* he had violated his marriage covenant; and hence had forfeited all legal and just right and authority over me; and I should convince him that I well knew it. I told him I was not in any passion. I acted on principle, and from long and mature consideration. And though it had ever been my greatest care and pleasure (among my earthly comforts) to obey and please him; yet by his most wicked and cruel conduct, he had compelled me to undertake this most undesirable business—of stopping him in his mad career; and that I now felt strength, courage and zeal to pursue my resolution. And if my life was spared, he would find that I should bring something to pass, and probably more than he now apprehended.

As to what I could prove against him I told Mr. B. he knew not how much evidence I had of his unnatural crimes, of which I had accused him, and of which *he knew he was guilty.* I asked him why he should not expect that I should institute a process against him, for that most horrid conduct, which he had long allowed himself to pursue, and with the most indecent and astonishing boldness?

I told him I well knew that he was naturally a man of sense; and that his conscience now fully approved of my conduct.

Mr. B. seeing me thus bold and determinate, soon changed his countenance and conduct. He appeared panic-struck; and he soon became mild, sociable and pleasant. He now made an attempt, with all his usual subtlety, and flatteries to induce me to relinquish my design. He pretended to deny the charge of incest. But I told him I had no confidence in his denial of it; it was therefore in vain! Upon this he said, he really did not blame, or think hard of me, for believing him guilty of this sin. He said, he knew he had behaved foolishly; and had given me full reason to be jealous of him; and he repeated that he did not at all think hard of me for entertaining the views which I had of him. He then took the Bible, and said, he would lay his hand on it, and swear that he was not guilty of the crime laid to his charge. Knowing what I did, I was surprised and disgusted at this impious attempt. I stepped towards him, and in a resolute and solemn manner begged of him to forbear! assuring him, that such an oath could not undo or alter real facts, of which he was conscious. And this proceeding, I assured him, would be so far from giving me any satisfaction, that it would greatly increase the distress of my soul for him in his wickedness. Upon this he forbore, and laid his Bible aside.

Mr. B. now said, he was very sorry he had given me so much reason to think such things of him; and that he had so far destroyed my confidence in him as a man of truth. He then begged of me to forgive all that was past; and he promised that he would ever be kind and faithful to me in future, and never more give me reason to complain of him for any such conduct. I told him, if I had but evidence of his real reformation, I could readily forgive him as a fellow creature, and could plead with God to forgive him. But as to my living with him in the most endearing relation any longer, after such horrid crimes, I did not see that I *could*, or *ought* to do it! He then anxiously made some remarks upon the consequences of my refusing to remain his wife, and seeking a separation from him. These he seemed unable to endure. I remarked, that I well knew it was no small thing for a husband and wife to part, and their family of children to be broken up; that such a separation could not be rendered expedient or lawful, without great sin indeed: and that I would not be the cause of it, and of breaking up our family, for *all the world*. But, said I, you have done all in your power to bring about such a separation, and to ruin and destroy our family. And I meet it as my duty now to do all in my power to save them from further destruction. . . .

But God, in his infinite wisdom, did not see fit that my peculiar trials should end thus. A long and most insupportable series of afflictions still awaited me, to be occasioned by this most perfidious of men.

I again clearly perceived that the same wicked passions, as before, were in operation in Mr. B.'s heart. Alas, "Can the Ethiopian change his skin?" Upon a certain sabbath, I went to meeting. Mr. B. did not go. Before I reached home at night, I met with evidence, which convinced me, that the same horrid conduct had on this holy day been repeated in my family! I rode up to the door. Mr. B. stood waiting for me. He seemed very kind, and was coming to take me tenderly from my horse. I leaped from my saddle, before he had opportunity to reach me. My heart was disgusted at the proffer of his deceitful help. I said nothing upon the dreadful subject this day. Some broken stories of the children corroborated the information I had received. But Mr. B. probably pleased himself with the idea that all was concealed, and he was safe.

The next day, I took him alone, and told him of what he had again been guilty, even after all his vows, and fair promises of fidelity. He started, and seemed very angry, that I should think such a thing [of] him. I told him I charged him only with facts; and hence I was not worthy of his censure! He asked how I knew any such thing? I replied, that the thing was true; and he knew it! And I felt myself under no obligations to inform him how I came by the knowledge of it. If that God, who protects the innocent, and upon whom with his angels he (Mr. B.) had lately so solemnly called to witness his vows of fidelity, had sent an angel to inform me of this renewed perfidy, he had no right to object. But the truth of the thing he knew; and a holy Providence had unfolded it to me. I added, that as he was now renewing my most grievous afflictions, by his unnatural wickedness; and violating his most solemn appeals to God; so he had reason to expect that God (who regards the cry of the afflicted, and relieves those who trust in him) would bring to light his abominable deeds, and deliver an injured wife from such cruel hands. I added, your right hand, which so lately renewed the covenant, is a right hand of falsehood. And, though you did wish and hope to hide from me, and from every eye, that conduct, of which you now know not how to endure the mention; yet God, who seeth in secret, was determined to bring your deeds to light, after all your vain dreams of secrecy. . . .

Mr. B. said he believed there never before was any man, who was so great a fool as he had been! that after I had so kindly settled with him for his past offences, and upon such low and reasonable terms, that he should again move me to jealousy, and thus destroy all my confidence in him. He said he wished he could be set back on the ground he had left, or had remained on so favorable a footing, as that on which I had placed him, in our settlement. I replied, that I really thought too, that he was one of the most foolish of men; that I had long been constrained to view him not only extremely *wicked*, but extremely *foolish!*

I told him he had truly been a wonder to me[;] I had looked upon him with astonishment. He was naturally, I added, a man of sense; he was a man of much knowledge;—had acquired property; and had been a man of considerable note. And that he should thus degrade and ruin himself, soul and body, and destroy a large promising family, as he had done, it was indeed most astonishing! I reminded him that he had been much in good company; and many gentlemen had honored him with their friendly attention. I asked, if any sum of money would induce him to be willing that those gentlemen should know that of him, which I knew? And, that though he seemed to be too willing to throw himself away, as though he were of no worth, I assured him, I did yet set something more by myself, than to be viewed as capable of conniving at such detestable conduct.

Mr. B. replied, that if I had made up my mind no longer to live with him, I need not be at any trouble to obtain a legal separation. For he would depart to some distant country, where I should be troubled with him no more. I remarked, that when Abraham's wife was dead, he wished, however well he had loved her, to have her now buried out of his sight. And, though I could by no means compare him to the pious Sarah; yet, if true virtue and friendship in my husband were dead, I did truly wish him to be removed from my sight. And that true virtue and friendship were indeed dead in him, I thought I had the most melancholy and incontestable evidence.

Our unhappy daughter now became eighteen years of age, and thus legally free from her father. She immediately left us, and returned no more. As she was going, I had solemn conversation with her relative to her father's conduct. She gave me to understand that it had been most abominable. But I could not induce her to consent to become an evidence against him. I plead with her the honor and safety of our family; the safety of her young sisters; and her own duty; but she appeared overwhelmed with shame and grief; and nothing effectual could yet be done.

I hence saw, that in relation to commencing a legal process, God's time seemed not yet to have arrived. I must still wait and look to him to open the path of my duty.

Colonial Architecture

What does architecture reveal about a people? Despite its provincial reliance on English craftsmanship and books on English architecture, and despite the fact that an overwhelming number of settlers were English, American colonial architecture was immensely diverse. Yet it is puzzling to see coexisting the grand mansions of Southern planters that began to sprout in the mid–eighteenth century and the comparatively simple homes of New Englanders, aside from the stately homes of merchants in seaport cities. Adding to this diversity are the entirely different homes of the Dutch in New York and the huts where inhabitants of the Appalachian backcountry lived. The range of architectural styles complemented the ability of the colonists to adapt their European backgrounds to the fresh challenges of a new country, such as building on rocky or swampy terrain, dealing with dislocated Indians, or finding a varied subsistence. The result was prosperity and growing commerce in a world where peoples learned to live together in reasonable comfort with little troubling divisiveness.

This pictorial section shows the varying ways that the colonists expressed themselves through their buildings. The wealthy, particularly in the South but also in the Connecticut River valley and in major cities like Philadelphia and Boston, wished to establish a degree of superiority that would win them special entitlements in politics, commerce, and perhaps even the professions. Circular driveways, ornamented doors with intimidating figures above, wrought iron railings, grand staircases, foyers with elaborate moldings where some people were welcome and others not—such is the stuff of larger Southern buildings, which were made of brick rather than the wood used to construct ordinary peoples' homes. In contrast, slaves and poor whites in the South occupied small dwellings with shared rooms that lacked privacy, but this condition also prevailed in Europe at the time. Locally available building materials dictated construction styles in each colony. New England and South Carolina had plenty of lumber; the Hudson River valley and Virginia, an abundance of clay soil that could be used to make bricks; Pennsylvania and New England, stone and limestone that formed the mortar to hold the stones together, allowing for the construction of high walls that conserved heat, provided safety, conveyed beauty, and suggested material success.

Look at the pictures in the portfolio and decide what they tell about the colonists. Were they simple people? Do the buildings exhibit grace and symmetry? Do they suggest aristocracy or democracy or both? And in particular, how was social space used in these buildings? How did it signify class and status?

Plate 1. J. David Bohl, photograph of Eleazor Arnold House, Rhode Island

Not many buildings remain from the seventeenth century and none at all in the South. Homes were nearly always "earthfast," constructed almost entirely of wood placed directly on the soil; termites and weather conditions soon wore the structures away. The Eleazor Arnold House (c. 1687) of Lincoln, Rhode Island, shown in Plate 1, has been restored to its original appearance. Its distinctive features are the huge stone "end" chimney used for cooking and heating. Its fieldstone wall reflects the local availability of limestone, used to make mortar to hold the stones in place. Local carpenters came from the western counties of England, where building in stone was a tradition and a skill. The small case-ment windows with lead dividing grids reflect a concern for cost and security. What other functions might the windows have served? Place these possibilities in a ranking of importance: ventilation, cost, protection against the Indians, conservation of heat, scenic considerations, and a desire to impress neighbors. With increased wealth, the subsequent owners of such houses installed larger sash windows and made numerous additions.

Plate 2. Model of an eighteenth-century New England kitchen, in a previous installation at Winterthur Museum, Winterthur, Delaware

The kitchen in Plate 2 is based on one found in a house built in Oxford, Massachusetts, around 1740. The furniture (note the comfortable New England Windsor chairs) is both beautiful and practical. What is the opening in the wall, encased in bricks, to the left of the fireplace? Why is the pair of andirons so enormous? Why was wood used in New England more than in other regions? Is there any evidence of mechanical means, such as a jack, used to turn the spit above the fire? What are the purposes of the various tools? Is there any evidence of firearms? What is in the bin in the left foreground?

Plate 3. Mount Vernon, Virginia, home of George Washington

Mount Vernon, shown in Plate 3, is located in Virginia on the banks of the Potomac River and displays both the substantial wealth and the social aspirations of the Southern planter of the mid–eighteenth century. George Washington expanded the original, smaller house into a main block with two wings connected by a covered walkway. The general plan is based on illustrations in English books on architecture. Washington had the wood exterior carved to resemble expensive stone blocks. Note that, for all of Washington's efforts to create a classically correct symmetrical facade and plan, the front door—perhaps a remnant of the original house—is off center. To what extent do you suppose Washington constructed Mount Vernon to please himself and to what extent to impress his neighbors? Why is there a circular courtyard in front of the house? Is there any evidence in the picture that Washington owned slaves?

Plate 4. John Collier, photograph of Monticello, Virginia, home of Thomas Jefferson

Thomas Jefferson's Monticello (named for the "little hill" on which it was constructed in the 1780s), shown in Plate 4, was built and rebuilt over many years. The design draws on Virginia's customary use of brick—made in kilns from the clay soil of the South—and on books on English architecture. But to it is added a familiarity with French practices observed by Jefferson during his five years in Paris and his travels through France. The style is a forerunner of early-nineteenth-century Greek revival architecture. Inside the house are famous examples of Jefferson's inventiveness: the "grass green" color in the foyer, the pulley that emptied chamber pots into the cellar and brought up wine, his bed that could be collapsed into the wall. What are the classical characteristics in Jefferson's structure? Can you think of any Greek or Roman buildings it resembles? Was Jefferson's work derivative? What impression does Monticello leave the viewer with?

Plate 5. Jack Boucher, photograph of exterior of Touro Synagogue, Rhode Island, 1971

In 1759, Newport's Jewish community built one of the first synagogues in the New World, naming it Touro for its first rabbi, whose descendants lie buried near the building under graceful monuments, headstones, and gravestones like those found in the simplest Protestant graveyards. Plates 5 and 6 show the Touro Synagogue. The exterior is quite modest, while the interior reflects the ethnic diversity and wealth of colonial cities as well as finely honed artistic taste. Much of the grace of the structure comes from the craftsmanship found in the details, such as the simple Doric columns, candled chandeliers, and elegant woodwork.

The colonies also had Jewish communities in Charles Town (now Charleston), New York City, and elsewhere. Their very existence is a tribute to the religious diversity that would forever mark the American future. Has the nation been religiously tolerant throughout its subsequent history? What advantages accrued to the diverse ethnicity that characterized colonial America?

Fascinated by the Touro Synagogue, Henry Wadsworth Longfellow later wrote a poem imagining its worshipers:

> How strange it seems! These Hebrews in their graves,
> Close by the street of this fair seaport town. . . .
> The very names recorded here are strange,
> Of foreign accent, and of different climes;
> Alvares and Rivera interchange

Plate 6. Arthur W. LeBoeuf, photograph of interior of Touro Synagogue, Rhode Island, 1937

With Abraham and Jacob of old times.
How came they here? What burst of Christian hate,
What persecution, merciless and blind,
Drove o'er the sea—that desert desolate—
These Ishmaels and Hagars of mankind?

Slave cabins of the eighteenth century consisted of little more than log huts, resembling the poorest dwellings of the most backward Appalachian highland regions. One traveler in South Carolina, where the painting of Mulberry Plantation in Plate 7 was made in 1770, described slave dwellings as having "no windows—no opening at all, except the doorway, with a chimney of sticks and mud, with no trees about them, no porches or shade of any kind." The decaying cabins at Roseberry Plantation in Dinwiddie County, south of Richmond, Virginia, shown in Plate 8, look only slightly better than the cabins described in the quotation above. Slave masters provided the building specifications and organized the construction by gangs of laborers. Children generally lived in a loft area where the chimney would provide some warmth during winter. Floors were generally earthen, but if lumber was available, wide slats might be nailed together. Were the living conditions described by the traveler to South Carolina economical for the slave owners? Why or why not? Speculate on the similarities between slave cabins and the homes of European peasants of this time.

Cabins were cramped, insects were impossible to control, and with poultry and small animals virtually part of the household, clean, neat cabins required great effort to maintain. Many slave owners skimped on bedding and blankets. One eighteenth-century slave narrative tells of a bed consisting of twelve-inch planks with sticks for pillows. More humane owners provided slaves with lumber to build comfortable bedsteads, usually on legs with one side attached to a wall. Cotton and straw were sometimes available for mattresses. The major argument for improving slave quarters was that doing so protected the health and reproductive powers of the slave owners' chattels. What other advantages did some privacy in the cabins offer?

Above right: Plate 7. Thomas Coram, "View of Mulberry, House and Street," oil on paper, Gibbes Museum of Art, Carolina Art Association
Right: Plate 8. Slave cabins dating from the 1800s. Roseberry Plantation, Dinwiddie County, Virginia. Photograph by Beckstrom, 1936

PART THREE

Resistance and Revolution

Struggling for Liberty

The generation that guided the colonies through the revolutionary era was welded together, despite remarkable differences among the colonies and their peoples, by a common commitment to American nationality. That nationality was defined partly by placement in the new continent but also partly by a long-standing British political heritage, which ironically was a major ideological reason for the rupture with Great Britain.

When, after 1763, the English developed restrictive colonial policies to raise revenues for the administration of an enlarged empire that now included India and Canada, the colonists quickly perceived threats to their traditional liberties. Newspapers like the *Boston Gazette and Country Journal* and political leaders and pamphleteers like John Adams directly challenged Great Britain's right to legislate for the colonies. So did many English critics of the mother country's governance of her North American colonies, as is evidenced by the brisk market in England for Paul Revere's engraving of the Boston Massacre. Leaders such as Captain Thomas Preston discovered how the rules of order had changed. Plain people like shoemaker George R. T. Hewes, who took part in both the Boston Massacre and the Boston Tea Party, Joseph Plumb Martin, who fought throughout the long war, and Boston merchant John Tudor developed new visions of their position in society.

To other colonists, commitment to the British tradition meant adherence to Britain. Many white Americans remained loyal to the king, often at great personal cost, as Philip and Catherine Van Cortlandt's experience illustrated.

For many slaves and Native Americans, patriot success portended crushed expectations or even disaster. Slaves took desperate risks seeking freedom, often suffering when their gamble failed. Some, like Boston King, did gain their freedom by going over to the British side, but they found uncertainty and hardship after the war. Most Native American nations found their strength undermined by the long war and its freeing of the colonists from British restrictions.

The American Revolution challenged long-held convictions that denied the capacity of human beings to use their reason in creating a new form of government. Women like Abigail Adams and Eliza Pinckney reflected this new spirit as vividly as any founding father. Such were the high stakes in the argument raging throughout the colonies over Shays's Rebellion (1786), which offered a prelude to the debates over ratification of the Constitution of the United States. At issue in both was a vision of the American Revolution as one of the climactic events of human history—a demonstration that people of virtue and reason can deliberately establish order and justice.

POINTS OF VIEW

The Boston Massacre (1770)

14

A British Officer's Description

Thomas Preston

Some historians in recent years have stressed the role of the "crowd" in the coming of the American Revolution. Anonymous colonists taking to the streets in the years after 1763 were an important part of the dynamic of revolution.

Firsthand accounts of an event do not necessarily make it easy to determine precisely what occurred. In early 1770 British troops were quartered in Boston. Many townspeople resented their presence, and on March 5 a mob of about sixty attacked a small group of soldiers. In the ensuing disturbance, some soldiers, without orders, fired on the mob, killing five people and wounding eight. The incident was taken up by anti-British radicals—the "patriots"—in Boston, who called it the "Boston Massacre." This selection is the account of the British officer who was tried for murder along with several of his men. John Adams and Josiah Quincy Jr., convinced that anyone accused of a crime should have legal counsel, defended the men. Two of the soldiers were convicted of manslaughter, and the others, including Preston, were acquitted, but the "Massacre" served to inflame anti-British sentiment throughout the colonies.

BEFORE YOU READ

1. What was Captain Preston's view of the Boston crowd?
2. Do you think his soldiers were justified in using violence?
3. Do you think the outcome of the trial was fair?

Merrill Jensen, ed., *English Historical Documents*, vol. 9 (London: Eyre and Spottiswoode, 1955), pp. 750–53.

CAPTAIN THOMAS PRESTON'S ACCOUNT
OF THE BOSTON MASSACRE (MARCH 13, 1770)

It is [a] matter of too great notoriety to need any proofs that the arrival of his Majesty's troops in Boston was extremely obnoxious to its inhabitants. They have ever used all means in their power to weaken the regiments, and to bring them into contempt by promoting and aiding desertions, and with impunity, even where there has been the clearest evidence of the fact, and by grossly and falsely propagating untruths concerning them. On the arrival of the 64th and 65th their ardour seemingly began to abate; it being too expensive to buy off so many, and attempts of that kind rendered too dangerous from the numbers.

And [conflict in the streets of Boston] has ever since their departure been breaking out with greater violence after their embarkation. One of their justices, most thoroughly acquainted with the people and their intentions, on the trial of a man of the 14th Regiment, openly and publicly in the hearing of great numbers of people and from the seat of justice, declared "that the soldiers must now take care of themselves, *nor trust too much to their arms*, for they were but a handful; that the inhabitants carried weapons concealed under their clothes, and would destroy them in a moment, *if they pleased.*" This, considering the malicious temper of the people, was an alarming circumstance to the soldiery. Since which several disputes have happened between the townspeople and the soldiers of both regiments, the former being encouraged thereto by the countenance of even some of the magistrates, and by the protection of all the party against government. In general such disputes have been kept too secret from the officers. On the 2d instant two of the 29th going through one Gray's rope-walk, the rope-makers insultingly asked them if they would empty a vault. This unfortunately had the desired effect by provoking the soldiers, and from words they went to blows. Both parties suffered in this affray, and finally the soldiers retired to their quarters. The officers, on the first knowledge of this transaction, took every precaution in their power to prevent any ill consequence. Notwithstanding which, single quarrels could not be prevented, the inhabitants constantly provoking and abusing the soldiery. The insolence as well as utter hatred of the inhabitants to the troops increased daily, insomuch that Monday and Tuesday, the 5th and 6th instant, were privately agreed on for a general engagement, in consequence of which several of the militia came from the country armed to join their friends, menacing to destroy any who should oppose them. This plan has since been discovered.

On Monday night about 8 o'clock two soldiers were attacked and beat. But the party of the townspeople in order to carry matters to the utmost length, broke into two meeting houses and rang the alarm bells, which I supposed was for fire as usual, but was soon undeceived. About 9 some of the guard came to and informed me the town inhabitants were assembling to attack the troops, and that the bells were ringing as the signal for that purpose and not for fire, and the beacon intended to be fired to bring in the distant people of the country. This, as I was captain of the day, occasioned my repairing immediately to the main guard. On my way there I saw the people in great commotion, and heard them use the most cruel and horrid threats against the troops. In a few minutes after I reached the guard, about 100 people passed it and went towards the custom house where the king's money is lodged. They immediately surrounded the sentry posted there, and with clubs and other weapons threatened to execute their vengeance on him. I was soon informed by a townsman their intention was to carry off the soldier from his post and probably murder him. On which I desired him to return for further intelligence, and he soon came back and assured me he heard the mob declare they would murder him. This I feared might be a prelude to their plundering the king's chest. I immediately sent a non-commissioned officer and 12 men to protect both the sentry and the king's money, and very soon followed myself to prevent, if possible, all disorder, fearing lest the officer and soldiers, by the insults and provocations of the rioters, should be thrown off their guard and commit some rash act. They soon rushed through the people, and by charging their bayonets in half-circles, kept them at a little distance. Nay, so far was I from intending the death of any person that I suffered the troops to go to the spot where the unhappy affair took place without any loading in their pieces; nor did I ever give orders for loading them. This remiss conduct in me perhaps merits censure; yet it is evidence, resulting from the nature of things, which is the best and surest that can be offered, that my intention was not to act offensively, but the contrary part, and that not without compulsion. The mob still increased and were more outrageous, striking their clubs or bludgeons one against another, and calling out, come on you rascals, you bloody backs, you lobster scoundrels, fire if you dare, G—d damn you, fire and be damned, we know you dare not, and much more such language was used. At this time I was between the soldiers and the mob, parleying with, and endeavouring all in my power to persuade them to retire peaceably, but to no purpose. They advanced to the points of the bayonets, struck some of them and even the muzzles of the pieces, and seemed to be endeavoring to close with the soldiers. On which some well behaved persons asked me if the guns were charged. I replied yes. They then asked me if I intended to order the men to fire. I answered no, by no means, observing to them that I was advanced before the muzzles of the men's pieces, and must fall a sacrifice if they fired; that the soldiers were upon the half cock and charged bayonets, and my giving the word fire under those circumstances would prove me to be no officer. While I was thus speaking, one of the soldiers having received a severe blow with a stick, stepped a little on one side and instantly fired, on which turning to and asking him why he fired without orders, I was struck with a club on my arm, which for some time deprived me of the use of it, which blow had it been placed on my head, most probably would have destroyed me. On this a general attack was made on the men by a great number of heavy clubs and snowballs being thrown at them, by which all our lives were in imminent danger, some persons at the same time from behind calling out, damn your bloods—why don't you fire. Instantly three or four of the soldiers fired, one after another, and directly after three more in the same confusion and hurry. The mob then ran away, except three unhappy men who instantly expired, in which number was Mr. Gray at whose rope-walk the prior quarrels took place; one more is since dead, three others are dangerously, and four slightly wounded. The whole of this melancholy affair was transacted in almost 20 minutes. On my asking the soldiers why they fired without orders, they said they heard the word fire and supposed it came from me. This might be the case as many of the mob called out fire, fire, but I assured the men that I gave no such order; that my words were, don't fire, stop your firing. In short, it was scarcely possible for the soldiers to know who said fire, or don't fire, or stop your firing. On the people's assembling again to take away the dead bodies, the soldiers supposing them coming to attack them, were making ready to fire again, which I prevented by striking up their firelocks with my hand. Immediately after a townsman came and told me that 4 or 5,000 people were assembled in the next street, and had sworn to take my life with every man's with me. On which I judged it unsafe to remain there any longer, and therefore sent the party and sentry to the main guard, where the street is narrow and short, there telling them off into street firings, divided and planted them at each end of the street to secure their rear, momently expecting an attack, as there was a constant cry of the inhabitants to arms, to arms, turn out with your guns; and the town drums beating to arms, I ordered my drums to beat to arms, and being soon after joined by the different companies of the 29th regiment, I formed them as the guard into street firings. The 14th regiment also got under arms but remained at their barracks. I immediately sent a sergeant with a party to Colonel Dalrymple, the commanding officer, to acquaint him with every particular. Several officers going to join their regiment were knocked down by the mob, one very much wounded and his sword taken from him. The lieutenant-governor and Colonel Carr soon after met at the head of the 29th regiment and agreed that the regiment should retire to their barracks, and the people to their houses, but I kept the picket to strengthen the guard. It was with great difficulty that the lieutenant-governor prevailed on the people to be quiet and retire. At last they all went off, excepting about a hundred.

A Council was immediately called, on the breaking up of which three justices met and issued a warrant to apprehend me and eight soldiers. On hearing of this procedure I instantly went to the sheriff and surrendered myself, though for the space of 4 hours I had it in my power to have made my escape, which I most undoubtedly should have attempted and could have easily executed, had I been the least conscious of any guilt. On the examination before the justices, two witnesses swore that I gave the men orders to fire. The one testified he was within two feet of me; the other that I swore at the men for not firing at the first word. Others swore they heard me use the word "fire," but whether do or do not fire, they could not say; others that they heard the word fire, but could not say if it came from me. The next day they got 5 or 6 more to swear I gave the word to fire. So bitter and inveterate are many of the malcontents here that they are industriously using every method to fish out evidence to prove it was a concerted scheme to murder the inhabitants. Others are infusing the utmost malice and revenge into the minds of the people who are to be my jurors by false publications, votes of towns, and all other artifices. That so from a settled rancour against the officers and troops in general, the suddenness of my trial after the affair while the people's minds are all greatly inflamed, I am, though perfectly innocent, under most unhappy circumstances, having nothing in reason to expect but the loss of life in a very ignominious manner, without the interposition of his Majesty's royal goodness.

15

Colonial Accounts

George Robert Twelves Hewes, John Tudor, and the *Boston Gazette and Country Journal*

George Robert Twelves Hewes (1742–1840) was in his nineties in 1833 when he told James Hawkes the story of his experiences in revolutionary Boston. Hewes claimed not to have read any published account of the happenings there and could "therefore only give the information which I derived from the event[s] of the day." Careful checking by the distinguished labor historian Alfred F. Young has authenticated much of Hewes's account. His story provides a rare opportunity to see an ordinary citizen taking a direct part in a great historical event. Hewes also participated in the Boston Tea Party of December 16, 1773, dressing as an Indian and pitching casks of tea into the harbor. These experiences had a profound personal effect on Hewes. In the 1760s he had been an awkward young cobbler nervously deferring to his aristocratic customers. A decade later, with these experiences behind him, he would risk his employment and perhaps even a beating for his refusal to take off his hat "for any man." For Hewes, the American Revolution meant that the poor and the ordinary no longer owed the rich and powerful what in the eighteenth century was called "deference."

John Tudor (1709–1795), a Boston merchant, gives a simpler account of the massacre in his diary and captures some of the sentiment following the deaths of the colonists.

The Boston Gazette and Country Journal *was one of several struggling journals published in Boston. Ever since being threatened with taxation under the Stamp Act of 1763, colonial newspapers, particularly those in Boston, had tended to support the patriot perspective. Journalism was not yet a profession, as most newspapers were produced by printers or postmasters, and the tradition of impartial reporting was still far in the future.*

James Hawkes [supposed author], *A Retrospect of the Boston Tea-Party, with a Memoir of George R. T. Hewes, a Survivor of the Little Band of Patriots who Drowned the Tea in Boston Harbour in 1773, by a Citizen of New York* (New York, 1834), pp. 27–33, 36–41; John Tudor, *Deacon Tudor's diary; or, "Memorandoms from 1709"* (Boston: Press of W. Spooner, 1896), pp. 1, vi, 110, [vii]–xxxvii, [7]; *Boston Gazette and Country Journal*, March 12, 1770, reprinted in Merrill Jensen, ed., *English Historical Documents*, vol. 9 (London: Eyre and Spottiswoode, 1955), pp. 745–49.

BEFORE YOU READ

1. According to Hewes, what sparked the Boston Massacre?
2. What role did he play in the event and subsequent trial?
3. Tudor wrote his account at the time of the event while Hewes related his story to Hawkes six decades later. To what extent might this explain their different perspectives?
4. How does the account of the riot as reported in the *Boston Gazette and Country Journal* differ from Hewes's account?
5. What political points does the *Boston Gazette and Country Journal* make about the Boston Massacre?

ACCOUNT OF GEORGE ROBERT TWELVES HEWES AS TOLD TO JAMES HAWKES

[W]hen I was at the age of twenty-six, I married the daughter of Benjamin Sumner, of Boston. At the time of our intermarriage, the age of my wife was seventeen. We lived together very happily seventy years. She died at the age of eighty-seven.

At the time when the British troops were first stationed at Boston, we had several children, the exact number I do not recollect. By our industry and mutual efforts we were improving our condition.

An account of the massacre of the citizens of Boston, in the year 1770, on the 5th of March, by some of the British troops, has been committed to the record of our history, as one of those interesting events which lead to the revolutionary contest that resulted in our independence. . . . We have been informed by the historians of the revolution, that a series of provocations had excited strong prejudices, and inflamed the passion of the British soldiery against our citizens, previous to the commencement of open hostilities; and prepared their minds to burst out into acts of violence on the application of a single spark of additional excitement, and which finally resulted in the unfortunate massacre of a number of our citizens.

On my inquiring of Hewes what knowledge he had of that event, he replied, that he knew nothing from history, as he had never read any thing relating to it from any publication whatever, and can therefore only give the information which I derived from the event of the day upon which the catastrophe happened. On that day, one of the British officers applied to a barber, to be shaved and dressed; the master of the shop, whose name was Pemont, told his apprentice boy he might serve him, and receive the pay to himself, while Pemont left the shop. The boy accordingly served him, but the officer, for some reason unknown to me, went away from the shop without paying him for his service. After the officer had been gone some time, the boy went to the house where he was, with his account, to demand payment of his bill, but the sentinel, who was before the door, would not give him admittance, nor permit him to see the officer; and as some angry words were interchanged between the sentinel and the boy, a considerable number of the people from the vicinity, soon gathered at the place where they were, which was in King street, and I was soon on the ground among them. The violent agitation of the citizens, not only on account of the abuse offered to the boy, but other causes of excitement, then fresh in the recollection, was such that the sentinel began to be apprehensive of danger, and knocked at the door of the house, where the officers were, and told the servant who came to the door, that he was afraid of his life, and would quit his post unless he was protected. The officers in the house then sent a messenger to the guard-house, to require Captain Preston to come with a sufficient number of his soldiers to defend them from the threatened violence of the people. On receiving the message, he came immediately with a small guard of grenadiers, and paraded them before the custom-house, where the British officers were shut up. Captain Preston then ordered the people to disperse, but they said they would not, they were in the king's highway, and had as good a right to be there as he had. The captain of the guard then said to them, if you do not disperse, I will fire upon you, and then gave orders to his men to make ready, and immediately after gave them orders to fire. Three of our citizens fell dead on the spot, and two, who were wounded, died the next day; and nine others were also wounded. The persons who were killed I well recollect, said Hewes; they were, Gray, a rope maker, Marverick, a young man, Colwell, who was the mate of Captain Colton, Attuck[s], a mulatto, and Carr, who was an Irishman. Captain Preston then immediately fled with his grenadiers back to the guard-house. The people who were assembled on that occasion, then immediately chose a committee to report to the governor the result of Captain Preston's conduct, and to demand of him satisfaction. The governor told the committee, that if the people would be quiet that night he would give them satisfaction, so far as was in his power; the next morning Captain Preston, and those of his guard who were concerned in the massacre, were, accordingly, by order of the governor, given up, and taken into custody the next morning, and committed to prison.

It is not recollected that the offence given to the barber's boy is mentioned by the historians of the revolution; yet there can be no doubt of its correctness. The account of this single one of the exciting causes of the massacre, related by Hewes, at this time, was in answer to the question of his personal knowledge of that event.

A knowledge of the spirit of those times will easily lead us to conceive, that the manner of the British officers application to the barber, was a little too strongly tinctured with the dictatorial hauteur, to conciliate the views of equality, which at that period were supremely predominant in the minds of those of the whig party, even in his humble occupation; and that the disrespectful notice of his loyal customer, in consigning him to the attention of his apprentice boy, and abruptly leaving his shop, was intended to be treated by the officer with contempt, by so underrating the services of his apprentice, as to deem any reward for them beneath his attention. The boy too, may be supposed to have imbibed so much of the spirit which distinguished that period of our history, that he was willing to improve any occasion to contribute his share to the public excitement; to add an additional spark to the fire of political dissention which was enkindling.

When Hewes arrived at the spot where the massacre happened, it appears his attention was principally engaged by the clamours of those who were disposed to aid the boy in avenging the insult offered to him by the British officer, and probably heard nothing, at that time, of any other of the many exciting causes which lead to that disastrous event, though it appeared from his general conversation, his knowledge of them was extensive and accurate.

But to pursue the destiny of Captain Preston, and the guard who fired on the citizens; in about a fortnight after, said Hewes, they were brought to trial and indicted for the crime of murder.

The soldiers were tried first, and acquitted, on the ground, that in firing upon the citizens of Boston, they only acted in proper obedience to the captain's orders. When Preston, their captain, was tried, I was called as one of the witnesses, on the part of the government, and testified, that I believed it was the same man, Captain Preston, that ordered his soldiers to make ready, who also ordered them to fire. Mr. John Adams, former president of the United States, was advocate for the prisoners, and denied the fact, that Captain Preston gave orders to his men to fire; and on his cross examination of me asked whether my position was such, that I could see the captain's lips in motion when the order to fire was given; to which I answered, that I could not. Although the evidence of Preston's having given orders to the soldiers to fire, was thought by the jury sufficient to acquit them, it was not thought to be of weight enough to convict him of a capital offence; he also was acquitted.

Although the excitement which had been occasioned by the wanton massacre of our citizens, had in some measure abated, it was never extinguished until open hostilities commenced, and we had declared our independence. The citizens of Boston continued inflexible in their demand, that every British soldier should be withdrawn from the town, and within four days after the massacre, the whole army decamped. But the measures of the British parliament, which led the American colonies to a separation from that government, were not abandoned.

JOHN TUDOR DESCRIBES THE MASSACRE IN HIS DIARY[1]

On Monday Evening the 5th current, a few minutes after 9 O'Clock a most horrid murder was committed in King Street before the Customhouse Door by eight or nine Soldiers under the Command of Captain Thomas Preston drawn of from the Main Guard on the South side of the Townhouse.

This unhappy affair began by Some Boys and young fellows throwing Snow Balls at the sentry placed at the Customhouse Door. On which eight or nine Soldiers Came to his assistance. Soon after a Number of people collected, when the Captain commanded the Soldiers to fire, which they did and three Men were Kil'd on the Spot and several Mortally Wounded, one of which died next morning. The Captain soon drew off his Soldiers up to the Main Guard, or the Consequences might have been terrible, for on the Guns firing the people were alarmed and set the Bells a Ringing as if for Fire, which drew Multitudes to the place of action. Lieutenant Governor Hutchinson, who was commander in Chief, was sent for and Came to the Council Chamber, where some of the Magistrates attended. The Governor desired the Multitude about 10 O'Clock to separate and

---

1. Spelling and punctuation have been modernized.

go home peacable and he would do all in his power that Justice should be done &c. The 29 Regiment being ten under Arms on the south side of the Townhouse, but the people insisted that the Soldiers should be ordered to their Barracks first before they would separate, Which being done the people separated about 1 O'Clock.— Captain Preston was taken up by a warrant given to the high Sheriff by Justice Dania and Tudor and came under Examination about 2 O'Clock and we sent him to Gaol soon after 3, having Evidence sufficient, to commit him, on his ordering the soldiers to fire: So about 4 O'clock the Town became quiet. The next forenoon the 8 Soldiers that fired on the inhabitants was also sent to Gaol. Tuesday A.M. the inhabitants met at Faneuil Hall and after some pertinent speeches, chose a Committee of 15 Gentlemen to wait on the Lieutenant Governor in Council to request the immediate removal of the Troops. . . .

(Thursday) Agreeable to a general request of the Inhabitants, were follow'd to the Grave (for they were all Buried in one) in succession the four Bodies of Messer's Samuel Gray, Samuel Maverick, James Caldwell, and Crispus Attucks, the unhappy victims who fell in the Bloody Massacre. On this sorrowful Occasion most of the shops and stores in Town were shut, all the Bells were order'd to toll a solemn peal in Boston, Charlesto[w]n, Cambridge, and Roxb[u]ry. The several Hearses forming a junction in King Street, the Theatre of that inhuman Tragedy, proceeded from thence thro' the main street, lengthened by an immense Concourse of people, So numerous as to be obliged to follow in Ranks of 4 and 6 abreast and brought up by a long Train of Carriages. The sorrow Visible in the Countenances, together with the peculiar solemnity, Surpass description, it was suppos'd that the Spectators and those that follow'd the corps amounted to 15,000, some supposed 20,000. Note Captain Preston was tried for his Life on the affair of the above October 24, 1770. The Trial lasted five Days, but the Jury brought him in not Guilty.

ACCOUNT IN THE *BOSTON GAZETTE AND COUNTRY JOURNAL*

March 12, 1770

The town of Boston affords a recent and melancholy demonstration of the destructive consequences of quartering troops among citizens in a time of peace, under a pretence of supporting the laws and aiding civil authority; every considerate and unprejudiced person among us was deeply impressed with the apprehension of these consequences when it was known that a number of regiments were ordered to this town under such a pretext, but in reality to enforce oppressive measures; to awe and control the legislative as well as executive power of the province, and to quell a spirit of liberty, which however it may have been basely opposed and even ridiculed by some, would do honour to any age or country. A few persons amongst us had determined to use all their influence to procure so destructive a measure with a view to their securely enjoying the profits of an American revenue, and unhappily both for Britain and this country they found means to effect it.

It is to Governor Bernard, the commissioners, their confidants and coadjutors, that we are indebted as the procuring cause of a military power in this capital. The Boston Journal of Occurrences, as printed in Mr. Holt's *New York Gazette*, from time to time, afforded many striking instances of the distresses brought upon the inhabitants by this measure; and since those Journals have been discontinued, our troubles from that quarter have been growing upon us. We have known a party of soldiers in the face of day fire off a loaden musket upon the inhabitants, others have been pricked with bayonets, and even our magistrates assaulted and put in danger of their lives, when offenders brought before them have been rescued; and why those and other bold and base criminals have as yet escaped the punishment due to their crimes may be soon matter of enquiry by the representative body of this people. It is natural to suppose that when the inhabitants of this town saw those laws which had been enacted for their security, and which they were ambitious of holding up to the soldiery, eluded, they should more commonly resent for themselves; and accordingly it has so happened. Many have been the squabbles between them and the soldiery; but it seems their being often worsted by our youth in those rencounters, has only served to irritate the former. What passed at Mr. Gray's rope-walk has already been given the public and may be said to have led the way to the late catastrophe. That the rope-walk lads, when attacked by superior numbers, should defend themselves with so much spirit and success in the club-way, was too mortifying, and perhaps it may hereafter appear that even some of their officers were unhappily affected with this circumstance. Divers stories were propagated among the soldiery that served to agitate their spirits; particularly on the Sabbath that one Chambers, a sergeant, represented as a sober man, had been missing the preceding day and must therefore have been murdered by the townsmen. An officer of distinction so far credited this report that he entered Mr. Gray's rope-walk that Sabbath; and when required of by that gentleman as soon as he could meet him, the occasion of his so doing, the officer replied that it was to look if the sergeant said to be murdered had not been hid there. This sober sergeant was found on the Monday unhurt in a house of pleasure. The evidences already collected show that many threatenings had been thrown out by the soldiery, but we do not pretend to say that there was any preconcerted plan. When the evidences are published, the world will judge. We may, however, venture to declare that it appears too probable from their conduct that some of the soldiery aimed to draw and provoke the townsmen into squabbles, and that they then intended to make use of other weapons than canes, clubs, or bludgeons.

On the evening of Monday, being the fifth current, several soldiers of the 29th Regiment were seen parading the streets with their drawn cutlasses and bayonets, abusing and wounding numbers of the inhabitants.

A few minutes after nine o'clock four youths, named Edward Archbald, William Merchant, Francis Archbald, and John Leech, jun., came down Cornhill together, and separating at Doctor Loring's corner, the two former were passing the narrow alley leading to Murray's barrack in which was a soldier brandishing a broad sword of an uncommon size against the walls, out of which he struck fire plentifully. A person of mean countenance armed with a large cudgel bore him company. Edward Archbald admonished Mr. Merchant to take care of the sword, on which the soldier turned round and struck Archbald on the arm, then pushed at Merchant and pierced through his clothes inside the arm close to the armpit and grazed the skin. Merchant then struck the soldier with a short stick he had; and the other person ran to the barrack and brought with him two soldiers, one armed with a pair of tongs, the other with a shovel. He with the tongs pursued Archbald back through the alley, collared and laid him over the head with the tongs. The noise brought people together; and John Hicks, a young lad, coming up, knocked the soldier down but let him get up again; and more lads gathering, drove them back to the barrack where the boys stood some time as it were to keep them in. In less than a minute ten or twelve of them came out with drawn cutlasses, clubs, and bayonets and set upon the unarmed boys and young folk who stood them a little while but, finding the inequality of their equipment, dispersed. On hearing the noise, one Samuel Atwood came up to see what was the matter; and entering the alley from dock square, heard the latter part of the combat; and when the boys had dispersed he met the ten or twelve soldiers aforesaid rushing down the alley towards the square and asked them if they intended to murder people? They answered Yes, by G—d, root and branch! With that one of them struck Mr. Atwood with a club which was repeated by another; and being unarmed, he turned to go off and received a wound on the left shoulder which reached the bone and gave him much pain. Retreating a few steps, Mr. Atwood met two officers and said, gentlemen, what is the matter? They answered, you'll see by and by. Immediately after, those heroes appeared in the square, asking where were the boogers? where were the cowards? But notwithstanding their fierceness to naked men, one of them advanced towards a youth who had a split of a raw stave in his hand and said, damn them, here is one of them. But the young man seeing a person near him with a drawn sword and good cane ready to support him, held up his stave in defiance; and they quietly passed by him up the little alley by Mr. Silsby's to King Street where they attacked single and unarmed persons till they raised much clamour, and then turned down Cornhill Street, insulting all they met in like manner and pursuing some to their very doors. Thirty or forty persons, mostly lads, being by this means gathered in King Street, Capt. Preston with a party of men with charged bayonets, came from the main guard to the commissioner's house, the soldiers pushing their bayonets, crying, make way! They took place by the custom house and, continuing to push to drive the people off, pricked some in several places, on which they were clamorous and, it is said, threw snow balls. On this, the Captain commanded them to fire; and more snow balls coming, he again said, damn you, fire, be the consequence what it will! One soldier then fired, and a townsman with a cudgel struck him over the hands with such force that he dropped his firelock; and, rushing forward, aimed a blow at the Captain's head which grazed his hat and fell pretty heavy upon his arm. However, the soldiers continued the fire successively till seven or eight or, as some say, eleven guns were discharged.

By this fatal maneuver three men were laid dead on the spot and two more struggling for life; but what showed a degree of cruelty unknown to British troops, at least since the house of Hanover has directed their operations, was an attempt to fire upon or push with their bayonets the persons who undertook to remove the slain and wounded!

Mr. Benjamin Leigh, now undertaker in the Delph manufactory, came up; and after some conversation with Capt. Preston relative to his conduct in this affair, advised him to draw off his men, with which he complied.

The dead are Mr. Samuel Gray, killed on the spot, the ball entering his head and beating off a large portion of his skull.

A mulatto man named Crispus Attucks, who was born in Framingham, but lately belonged to New-Providence and was here in order to go for North Carolina, also killed instantly, two balls entering his breast, one of them in special goring the right lobe of the lungs and a great part of the liver most horribly.

Mr. James Caldwell, mate of Capt. Morton's vessel, in like manner killed by two balls entering his back.

Mr. Samuel Maverick, a promising youth of seventeen years of age, son of the widow Maverick, and an apprentice to Mr. Greenwood, ivory-turner, mortally wounded; a ball went through his belly and was cut out at his back. He died the next morning.

A lad named Christopher Monk, about seventeen years of age, an apprentice to Mr. Walker, shipwright, wounded; a ball entered his back about four inches above the left kidney near the spine and was cut out of the breast on the same side. Apprehended he will die.

A lad named John Clark, about seventeen years of age, whose parents live at Medford, and an apprentice to Capt. Samuel Howard of this town, wounded; a ball entered just above his groin and came out at his hip on the opposite side. Apprehended he will die.

Mr. Edward Payne of this town, merchant, standing at his entry door received a ball in his arm which shattered some of the bones.

Mr. John Green, tailor, coming up Leverett's Lane, received a ball just under his hip and lodged in the under part of his thigh, which was extracted.

Mr. Robert Patterson, a seafaring man, who was the person that had his trousers shot through in Richardson's affair, wounded; a ball went through his right arm, and he suffered a great loss of blood.

Mr. Patrick Carr, about thirty years of age, who worked with Mr. Field, leather breeches-maker in Queen Street, wounded; a ball entered near his hip and went out at his side.

A lad named David Parker, an apprentice to Mr. Eddy, the wheelwright, wounded; a ball entered in his thigh.

The people were immediately alarmed with the report of this horrid massacre, the bells were set a-ringing, and great numbers soon assembled at the place where this tragical scene had been acted. Their feelings may be better conceived than expressed; and while some were taking care of the dead and wounded, the rest were in consultation what to do in those dreadful circumstances. But so little intimidated were they, notwithstanding their being within a few yards of the main guard and seeing the 29th Regiment under arms and drawn up in King Street, that they kept their station and appeared, as an officer of rank expressed it, ready to run upon the very muzzles of their muskets. The lieutenant-governor soon came into the town house and there met some of his Majesty's Council and a number of civil magistrates. A considerable body of the people immediately entered the council chamber and expressed themselves to his honour with a freedom and warmth becoming the occasion. He used his utmost endeavours to pacify them, requesting that they would let the matter subside for the night and promising to do all in his power that justice should be done and the law have its course. Men of influence and weight with the people were not wanting on their part to procure their compliance with his Honour's request by representing the horrible consequences of a promiscuous and rash engagement in the night, and assuring them that such measures should be entered upon in the morning as would be agreeable to their dignity and a more likely way of obtaining the best satisfaction for the blood of their fellow townsmen. The inhabitants attended to these suggestions; and the regiment under arms being ordered to their barracks, which was insisted upon by the people, they then separated and returned to their dwellings by one o'clock. At three o'clock Capt. Preston was committed, as were the soldiers who fired, a few hours after him.

Tuesday morning presented a most shocking scene, the blood of our fellow citizens running like water through King Street and the Merchants' Exchange, the principal spot of the military parade for about eighteen months past. Our blood might also be tracked up to the head of Long Lane, and through divers other streets and passages.

At eleven o'clock the inhabitants met at Faneuil Hall; and after some animated speeches becoming the occasion, they chose a committee of fifteen respectable gentlemen to wait upon the lieutenant-governor in Council to request of him to issue his orders for the immediate removal of the troops.

FOR CRITICAL THINKING

1. If you were John Adams, determined to prove that British officers and soldiers could receive a fair trial in Boston, how would you defend Captain Preston?

2. Compare the Boston Massacre with later urban riots in American history. What similarities and differences do you find?

16

A Soldier's View of the Revolutionary War
Joseph Plumb Martin

Joseph Plumb Martin was born in western Massachusetts in 1760 and became a soldier in the Revolution before his sixteenth birthday. After serving with Connecticut troops in 1776, he enlisted as a regular in the Continental Army in April 1777 and persevered until the army was demobilized in 1783. During this period he fought with the Light Infantry as well as in the Corps of Sappers and Miners, who built fortifications and dug trenches. One of the few soldiers to serve for virtually the entire war, he repeatedly risked health and life: in the defense of New York City in 1776, at the Battle of Germantown in Pennsylvania in 1777, at Valley Forge in the winter of 1777–78, at the Battle of Monmouth in New Jersey in 1778, and at the climactic siege of Yorktown in 1781.

Published in Maine in 1830, Martin's A Narrative of Some of the Adventures, Dangers, and Sufferings of a Revolutionary Soldier *is a usually good-humored, unvarnished picture of an ordinary soldier whose major concern is often his next meal or keeping warm through a cold night. Yet he expresses sharply the widely shared resentment among common soldiers toward civilian patriots "sitting still and expecting the army to do notable things while fainting from sheer starvation." And he fundamentally objects to the way his generation remembered the history of the war: "great men get great praise, little men, nothing. But it always was so and always will be." In fact, historians in the present age have at last devoted energy to recapturing the contributions of men like Joseph Plumb Martin, whose narrative offers the only detailed account historians have discovered of the wartime experience of a common Revolutionary War soldier.*

BEFORE YOU READ

1. Why do you think Martin begins with an apology for writing his memoirs?
2. What does the account of the sergeant who was almost executed suggest about the discipline of the Continental Army and the relations between officers and soldiers?
3. How well did the people seem to support the soldiers of the Continental Army?

PREFACE

I have somewhere read of a limner, who, when he had daubed a representation of some animal, was always compelled, for the information of the observer, to write under it what he intended it to represent: As, "this is a goose, this is a dog," &c. So, many books, and mine in particular among the rest, would per-

James Kirby Martin, ed., *Ordinary Courage: The Revolutionary War Adventures of Joseph Plumb Martin*, rev. ed. (St. James, NY: Brandywine Press, 1999), pp. 1–2, 15–17, 29, 34–35, 61–64.

haps be quite unintelligible as to the drift of them, unless the reader was informed beforehand what the author intended.

I shall, therefore, by way of preface, inform the reader that my intention is
to give a succinct account of some of my adventures, dangers, and sufferings
during my several campaigns in the Revolutionary army. My readers (who, by
the by, will, I hope, none of them be beyond the pale of my own neighborhood)
must not expect any great transactions to be exhibited to their notice. "No
alpine wonders thunder through my tale," but they are here, once for all, requested to bear it in mind, that they are not the achievements of an officer of
high grade which they are perusing, but the common transactions of one of the
lowest in station in an army, a private soldier.

Should the reader chance to ask himself this question (and I think it
very natural for him to do so) how could any man of common sense ever spend
his precious time in writing such a rhapsody of nonsense? To satisfy his inquiring
mind, I would inform him, that, as the adage says, "every crow thinks her
own young the whitest," so every private soldier in an army thinks his particular services as essential to carry on the war he is engaged in, as the services of the most influential general: And why not? What could officers do without such men? Nothing
at all. Alexander never could have conquered the world without private soldiers.

But, says the reader, this is low; the author gives us nothing but everyday
occurrences; I could tell as good a story myself. Very true, Mr. Reader, everyone can tell what he has done in his lifetime, but everyone has not been a soldier, and consequently can know but little or nothing of the sufferings and
fatigues incident to an army. All know everyday occurrences, but few know the
hardships of the "tented field." I wish to have a better opinion of my readers,
whoever they may be, than even to think that any of them would wish me to
stretch the truth to furnish them with wonders that I never saw, or acts or deeds
I never performed. I can give them no more than I have to give, and if they are
dissatisfied after all, I must say I am sorry for them and myself too; for them,
that they expect more than I can do, and myself, that I am so unlucky as not to
have it in my power to please them. . . .

The critical grammarian may find enough to feed his spleen upon if he pe-
ruses the following pages; but I can inform him beforehand, I do not regard his
sneers; if I cannot write grammatically, I can think, talk, and feel like other
men. Besides, if the common readers can understand it, it is all I desire; and to
give them an idea, though but a faint one, of what the army suffered that gained
and secured our independence, is all I wish. I never studied grammar an hour in
my life. When I ought to have been doing that, I was forced to be studying the
rules and articles of war. . . .

A note of interrogation: Why we were made to suffer so much in so good and
just a cause; and a note of admiration to all the world, that an army voluntarily engaged to serve their country, when starved, and naked, and suffering everything
short of death (and thousands even that), should be able to persevere through an
eight years war, and come off conquerors at last!

But lest I should make my preface longer than my story, I will here bring it
to a close.

CAMPAIGN OF 1776

I remained in New York two or three months, in which time several things occurred, but so trifling that I shall not mention them; when, sometime in the latter part of the month of August, I was ordered upon a fatigue party. We had scarcely reached the grand parade when I saw our sergeant major directing his course up Broadway toward us in rather an unusual step for him. He soon arrived and informed us, and then the commanding officer of the party, that he had orders to take off all belonging to our regiment and march us to our quarters, as the regiment was ordered to Long Island, the British having landed in force there. Although this was not unexpected to me, yet it gave me rather a disagreeable feeling, as I was pretty well assured I should have to sniff a little gunpowder. However, I kept my cogitations to myself, went to my quarters, packed up my clothes, and got myself in readiness for the expedition as soon as possible. I then went to the top of the house where I had a full view of that part of the Island; I distinctly saw the smoke of the field artillery, but the distance and the unfavorableness of the wind prevented my hearing their report, at least but faintly. The horrors of battle then presented themselves to my mind in all their hideousness; I must come to it now, thought I. Well, I will endeavor to do my duty as well as I am able and leave the event with Providence.

We were soon ordered to our regimental parade, from which, as soon as the regiment was formed, we were marched off for the ferry. At the lower end of the street were placed several casks of sea bread, . . . nearly hard enough for musket flints; the casks were unheaded and each man was allowed to take as many as he could as he marched by. As my good luck would have it, there was a momentary halt made; I improved the opportunity thus offered me, as every good soldier should upon all important occasions, to get as many of the biscuits as I possibly could; no one said anything to me, and I filled my bosom and took as many as I could hold in my hand, a dozen or more in all, and when we arrived at the ferry stairs I stowed them away in my knapsack. We quickly embarked on board the boats. As each boat started, three cheers were given by those on board, which was returned by the numerous spectators who thronged the wharves; they all wished us good luck, apparently, although it was with most of them perhaps nothing more than ceremony.

We soon landed at Brooklyn, upon the Island, marched up the ascent from the ferry to the plain. We now began to meet the wounded men, another sight I was unacquainted with, some with broken arms, some with broken legs, and some with broken heads. The sight of these a little daunted me, and made me think of home, but the sight and thought vanished together. We marched a short distance, when we halted to refresh ourselves. Whether we had any other victuals besides the hard bread I do not remember, but I remember my gnawing at them; they were hard enough to break the teeth of a rat. One of the soldiers complaining of thirst to his officer, "Look at that man," said he, pointing to me, "he is not thirsty, I will warrant it." I felt a little elevated to be styled a man.

While resting here, which was not more than 20 minutes or half an hour, the Americans and British were warmly engaged within sight of us. What were the feelings of most or all the young soldiers at this time, I know not, but I know what were mine. But let mine or theirs be what they might, I saw a lieutenant who appeared to have feelings not very enviable; whether he was actuated by fear or the canteen I cannot determine now. I thought it fear at the time, for he ran round among the men of his company, sniveling and blubbering, praying each one if he had aught against him, or if *he* had injured anyone that they would forgive him, declaring at the same time that he, from his heart, forgave them if they had offended him, and I gave him full credit for his assertion; for had he been at the gallows with a halter about his neck, he could not have shown more fear or penitence. A fine soldier you are, I thought, a fine officer, an exemplary man for young soldiers! I would have then suffered anything short of death rather than have made such an exhibition of myself. . . .

Another affair . . . deserves to be recorded by me, as no one else has to my knowledge ever mentioned it. A sergeant belonging to the Connecticut forces, being sent by his officers in the heat of the action to procure ammunition, was met by a superior officer, an aide-de-camp to some general officer (I believe), who accused him of deserting his post in time of action. He remonstrated with the officer and informed him of the absolute necessity there was of his obeying the orders of his own officers; that the failure of his procuring a supply of ammunition might endanger the success of the day, but all to no purpose. The officer would not allow himself to believe him, but drew his sword and threatened to take his life on the spot if he did not immediately return to his corps. The sergeant, fired with just indignation at hearing and seeing his life threatened, cocked his musket, and stood in his own defense. He was, however, taken, confined and tried for mutiny, and condemned to be shot.

The sentence of the court martial was approved by the Commander in Chief, and the day for his execution set. When it arrived, an embankment was thrown up to prevent the shot fired at him from doing other damage, and all things requisite on such occasions were in readiness. The Connecticut troops were then drawn out and formed in a square, and the prisoner brought forth; after being blindfolded and pinioned, he knelt upon the ground. The corporal with his six executioners were then brought up before him, ready at the fatal word of command to send a brave soldier into the eternal world because he persisted in doing his duty and obeying the lawful and urgent orders of his superior officers, the failure of which might, for aught the officer who stopped him knew, have caused the loss of hundreds of lives. But the sergeant was reprieved, and I believe it was well that he was, for his blood would not have been the only blood that would have been spilt.[1]

---

1. Colonel Joseph Reed of Pennsylvania, Washington's talented but quirky adjutant general and the officer in question, demanded the court martial of the sergeant, Ebenezer Leffingwell of Colonel John Durkee's 20th Continental regiment, originally organized in Connecticut. On September 22 a hearing board condemned Leffingwell to die, but he won this dramatic reprieve because Reed, having mused about the incident, implored Washington to pardon the sergeant. [Editor's note.]

The troops were greatly exasperated, and they showed what their feelings were by their lively and repeated cheerings after the reprieve, but more so by their secret and open threats before it. The reprieve was read by one of the chaplains of the army after a long harangue to the soldiers setting forth the enormity of the crime charged upon the prisoner, repeatedly using this sentence, "crimes for which men ought to die," which did much to further the resentment of the troops already raised to a high pitch. But, as I said before, it was well that it ended as it did, both on account of the honor of the soldiers and the safety of some others. . . .

. . . A number of our sick were sent off to Norwalk in Connecticut to recruit [rest]. I was sent with them as a nurse. We were billeted among the inhabitants. I had in my ward seven or eight *sick soldiers,* who were (at least soon after their arrival there) as well in health as I was. All they wanted was a cook and something for a cook to exercise his functions upon. The inhabitants here were almost entirely what were in those days termed tories. An old lady, of whom I often procured milk, used always when I went to her house to give me a lecture on my opposition to our good King George. She had always said (she told me) that the regulars would make us fly like pigeons. . . .

The man of the house where I was quartered had a smart-looking Negro man, a great politician. I chanced one day to go into the barn where he was threshing. He quickly began to upbraid me with my opposition to the British. The king of England was a very powerful prince, he said—a very powerful prince; and it was a pity that the colonists had fallen out with him; but as we had, we must abide by the consequences. I had no inclination to waste the shafts of my rhetoric upon a Negro slave. I concluded he had heard his betters say so. As the old cock crows, so crows the young one; and I thought, as the white cock crows, so crows the black one. He ran away from his master before I left there, and went to Long Island to assist King George; but it seems the King of Terrors was more potent than King George, for his master had certain intelligence that poor Cuff was laid flat on his back.

This man had likewise a Negress who (as he was a widower) kept his house. She was as great a doctress as Cuff was a politician, and she wished to be a surgeon. There was an annual thanksgiving while we were here. The *sick* men of my ward had procured a fine roasting pig, and the old Negro woman having seen the syringe that I picked up in the retreat from Kip's Bay, fell violently in love with it and offered me a number of pies of one sort or other for it. Of the pig and the pies we made an excellent thanksgiving dinner, the best meal I had eaten since I left my grandsire's table.

Our surgeon came among us soon after this and packed us all off to camp, save two or three who were discharged. I arrived at camp with the rest, where we remained, moving from place to place as occasion required, undergoing hunger, cold, and fatigue until the 25th day of December, 1776, when I was discharged (my term of service having expired) at Philipse Manor, in the state of New York near Hudson's River.

Here ends my first campaign. I had learned something of a soldier's life, enough I thought to keep me at home for the future. Indeed, I was then fully determined to rest easy with the knowledge I had acquired in the affairs of the army. But the reader will find . . . that the ease of a winter spent at home caused me to alter my mind. I had several *kind* invitations to enlist into the standing army then about to be raised, especially a very pressing one to engage in a regiment of horse, but I concluded to try a short journey on foot first. Accordingly, I set off for my good old grandsire's, where I arrived, I think, on the 27th, two days after my discharge, and found my friends all alive and well. They appeared to be glad to see me, and I am sure I was *really* glad to see them.

CAMPAIGN OF 1777

. . . [W]e joined the grand army near Philadelphia, and the heavy baggage being sent back to the rear of the army, we were obliged to put us up huts by laying up poles and covering them with leaves, a capital shelter from winter storms. Here we continued to fast; indeed we kept a continual Lent as faithfully as ever any of the most rigorous of the Roman Catholics did. But there was this exception; we had no fish or eggs or any other substitute for our commons. Ours was a real fast and, depend upon it, we were sufficiently mortified.

About this time the whole British army left the city, came out, and encamped, or rather lay, on Chestnut Hill in our immediate neighborhood. We hourly expected an attack from them; we had a commanding position and were very sensible of it. We were kept constantly on the alert, and wished nothing more than to have them engage us, for we were sure of giving them a drubbing, being in excellent fighting trim, as we were starved and as cross and ill-natured as curs. The British, however, thought better of the matter, and, after several days maneuvering on the hill, very civilly walked off into Philadelphia again. . . .

Soon after the British had quit their position on Chestnut Hill, we left this place, and after marching and countermarching back and forward some days, we crossed the Schuylkill on a cold, rainy, and snowy night upon a bridge of wagons set end to end and joined together by boards and planks. And after a few days more maneuvering we at last settled down at a place called "the Gulf" (so named on account of a remarkable chasm in the hills); and here we encamped some time, and here we had liked to have encamped forever—for starvation here *rioted* in its glory. . . .

While we lay here, there was a Continental thanksgiving ordered by Congress; and as the army had all the cause in the world to be particularly thankful, if not for being well off, at least that it was no worse, we were ordered to participate in it. We had nothing to eat for two or three days previous, except what the trees of the fields and forests afforded us. But we must now have what Congress said—a sumptuous thanksgiving to close the year of high living we had now nearly seen brought to a close. Well, to add something extraordinary to our present stock of provisions, our country, ever mindful of its suffering army, opened her sympathizing heart so wide upon this occasion as to give us something to make the world stare. And what do you think it was, reader?

Guess. You cannot guess, be you as much of a Yankee as you will. I will tell you: It gave each and every man *half* a *gill* of rice and a *tablespoonful* of vinegar!!

After we had made sure of this extraordinary superabundant donation, we were ordered out to attend a meeting and hear a sermon delivered upon the happy occasion. We accordingly went, for we could not help it. . . . I remember the text, like an attentive lad at church. I can *still* remember that it was this, "And the soldiers said unto him, And what shall we do? And he said unto them, Do violence to no man, nor accuse anyone falsely." The preacher ought to have added the remainder of the sentence to have made it complete: "And be content with your wages." But that would not do, it would be too apropos; however, he heard it as soon as the service was over, it was shouted from a hundred tongues. . . .

The army was now not only starved but naked. The greatest part were not only shirtless and barefoot but destitute of all other clothing, especially blankets. I procured a small piece of raw cowhide and made myself a pair of moccasins, which kept my feet (while they lasted) from the frozen ground, although as I well remember the hard edges so galled my ankles while on a march that it was with much difficulty and pain that I could wear them afterwards; but the only alternative I had was to endure this inconvenience or to go barefoot, as hundreds of my companions had to, till they might be tracked by their blood upon the rough frozen ground. But hunger, nakedness, and sore shins were not the only difficulties we had at that time to encounter; we had hard duty to perform and little or no strength to perform it with.

The army continued at and near the Gulf for some days, after which we marched for the Valley Forge in order to take up our winter quarters. We were now in a truly forlorn condition—no clothing, no provisions, and as disheartened as need be. We arrived, however, at our destination a few days before Christmas. Our prospect was indeed dreary. In our miserable condition, to go into the wild woods and build us habitations to *stay* (not to *live*) in, in such a weak, starved, and naked condition, was appalling in the highest degree, especially to New Englanders, unaccustomed to such kind of hardships at home. However, there was no remedy, no alternative but this or dispersion; but dispersion, I believe, was not thought of—at least I did not think of it. We had engaged in the defense of our injured country and were willing, nay, we were determined to persevere as long as such hardships were not altogether intolerable. I had experienced what I thought sufficient of the hardships of a military life the year before (although nothing in comparison to what I had suffered the present campaign) . . . ; but we were now absolutely in danger of perishing, and that too in the midst of a plentiful country. We then had but little and often nothing to eat for days together; but now we had nothing and saw no likelihood of any betterment of our condition. Had there fallen deep snows (and it was the time of year to expect them) or even heavy and long rainstorms, the whole army must inevitably have perished. Or had the enemy, strong and well provided as he then was, thought fit to pursue us, our poor emaciated carcasses must have "strewed the plain." But a kind and holy Providence took more notice and better care of us than did the country in whose service we were wearing away our lives by piecemeal.

We arrived at the Valley Forge in the evening. It was dark; there was no water to be found, and I was perishing with thirst. I searched for water till I was weary and came to my tent without finding any; fatigue and thirst, joined with hunger, almost made me desperate. I felt at that instant as if I would have taken victuals or drink from the best friend I had on earth by force. I am not writing fiction, all are sober realities. Just after I arrived at my tent, two soldiers whom I did not know passed by; they had some water in their canteens which they told me they had found a good distance off, but could not direct me to the place as it was very dark. I tried to beg a draught of water from them, but they were as rigid as Arabs. At length I persuaded them to sell me a drink for three pence, Pennsylvania currency, which was every cent of property I could then call my own, so great was the necessity I was then reduced to.

I lay here two nights and one day and had not a morsel of anything to eat all the time, save half of a small pumpkin, which I cooked by placing it upon a rock, the skin side uppermost, and making a fire upon it. By the time it was heat[ed] through I devoured it with as keen an appetite as I should a pie made of it at some other time.

The second evening after our arrival here I was warned to be ready for a two days command. I never heard a summons to duty with so much disgust before or since as I did that; how I could endure two days more fatigue without nourishment of some sort I could not tell. . . . However, in the morning . . . I went to the parade where I found a considerable number ordered upon the same business, whatever it was. We were ordered to go to the quartermaster general and receive from him our final orders. We accordingly repaired to his quarters, which was about three miles from camp; here we understood that our destiny was to go into the country on a foraging expedition, which was nothing more nor less than to procure provisions from the inhabitants for the men in the army and forage for the poor perishing cattle belonging to it, at the point of the bayonet. We stayed at the quartermaster general's quarters till sometime in the afternoon, during which time a beef creature was butchered for us. I well remember what fine stuff it was. . . .

We were then divided into several parties and sent off upon our expedition. Our party consisted of a lieutenant, a sergeant, a corporal, and 18 privates. We marched till night when we halted, and . . . this day we arrived at Milltown, or Downingstown, a small village halfway between Philadelphia and Lancaster, which was to be our quarters for the winter. It was dark when we had finished our day's march. There was a commissary and a wagonmaster general stationed here, the commissary to take into custody the provisions and forage that we collected, and the wagonmaster general to regulate the conduct of the wagoners and direct their motions. The next day after our arrival at this place we were put into a small house in which was only one room, in the center of the village. We were immediately furnished with rations of good and wholesome beef and flour, built us up some berths to sleep in, and filled them with straw, and felt as happy as any other pigs that were no better off than ourselves. And now having got into winter quarters and ready to commence our foraging business, I shall here end my account of my second campaign.

17

Choosing Sides

Boston King

In Massachusetts and other centers of revolutionary activity, patriots enthusiastically confronted the British, young men enlisted in the Continental Army, and loyalists actively defended their king. For many, however, especially those who were uneducated or lived in the hinterlands, the decision over which side to support often hinged on such pedestrian concerns as which side of a river they lived on, who shared their property line, and where they were when war broke out. Boston King faced a more difficult choice. His decision was daunting because he was a black slave.

Both loyalists and patriots recognized the importance of blacks to the war effort. Most free blacks supported the revolutionaries, and Northern states such as Connecticut and Rhode Island, with little plantation slavery, raised all-black regiments and made widespread use of blacks in their militias. But Southern states such as Virginia, South Carolina, and Georgia were more circumspect about allowing blacks to serve in the military, fearing that it might undermine slavery.

Early in the war, the British actively encouraged slaves to desert revolutionary masters in order to expand the loyalist forces and to weaken the rebel economy. In 1775, the British governor of Virginia, Lord Dunmore, issued a proclamation promising freedom to any slave who escaped a rebel master and took up arms for the king. Many slaves heeded this call despite the dangers of escape and the terrifying threats of punishment against family and friends of runaways. In 1778, the Continental Army responded with its own policy of freeing loyalist slaves, although in practice slaves of captured masters were often resold for profit. In 1779, Sir Henry Clinton issued the Philipsburg Proclamation, extending freedom to any slave who escaped a rebel master, thereby including old and young, male and female, and able bodied and invalid in the emancipation. Boston King was one of the thousands of slaves who responded to the promises of freedom by escaping to the British lines and fighting for the crown.

Born on a plantation near Charles Town (now Charleston), South Carolina, around 1760, King was raised as a "privileged" house slave. Learning to read and write and apprenticing to a carpenter as an adolescent, he had valuable skills and a freedom of movement that was rare for slaves. His fear of severe punishment after a misdeed prompted his flight to the British in his late teens. In 1782, after serving in the

Boston King, "Memoirs of the Life of Boston King, a Black Preacher, Written by Himself, during his Residence at Kingswood-School," <http://collections.ic.gc.ca/blackloyalists/documents/diaries/king-memoirs.htm> (1 Dec. 2002); orig. published in *Arminian [or the Methodist] Magazine* XXI (March, April, May, June 1798), 105–11, 157–61, 209–13, 261–65.

British army and twice escaping reenslavement, King found himself in New York, the last British stronghold. There thousands of loyalist refugees awaited repatriation to Canada, West Florida, and Jamaica. He and his wife, Violet, an escaped slave from North Carolina, were among the three thousand blacks anxiously awaiting the conclusion of negotiations between General Washington and the British commander-in-chief over the fate of fugitive slaves.

All blacks who had come to the British lines before the signing of the provisional peace treaty of 1782 would be free, and all others would be returned to their masters. The British compiled the "Book of Negroes" listing all those who had obtained freedom by going over to the crown, and they issued certificates of freedom. Boston and Violet King were repatriated to Birchtown, Nova Scotia, where they joined the nucleus of Canada's first black community. Ten years later, they moved to Sierra Leone with nearly twelve thousand of their Birchtown neighbors; King started a school for natives there and became a Methodist minister. He wrote his memoirs in 1798, while studying and preaching for two years in England. King died in Sierra Leone in 1802, where he was working as a teacher and missionary.

Before You Read

1. If you had been a slave during the American Revolution, which side would you have supported?

2. What obstacles did Boston King face in his escape from slavery?

3. Why do you think King went to such lengths to explain that his decision to escape was based on his fear of severe punishment? Do you think he would have attempted escape anyway?

I was born in the Province of South Carolina, 28 miles from Charles Town. My father was stolen away from Africa when he was young. . . . My mother was employed chiefly in attending upon those that were sick, having some knowledge of the virtue of herbs, which she learned from the Indians. She likewise had the care of making the people's clothes, and on these accounts was indulged with many privileges which the rest of the slaves were not. . . .

. . . When 16 years old, I was bound apprentice to a trade. After being in the shop about two years, I had the charge of my master's[1] tools, which being very good, were often used by the men, if I happened to be out of the way: When this was the case, or any of them were lost, or misplaced, my master beat me severely, striking me upon my head, or any other part without mercy. . . . About eight months after, we were employed in building a storehouse, and nails were very dear at that time, it being in the American war, so that the workmen had their nails weighed out to them; on this account they made the younger apprentices watch the nails while they were at dinner. It being my lot one day to take care of them, which I did till an apprentice returned to his work, and then I

1. The master of his apprenticeship, who was paid by King's owner to teach King carpentry.

went to dine. In the mean time he took away all the nails belonging to one of the journeymen, and he being of very violent temper, accused me to the master with stealing of them. For this offense I was beat and tortured most cruelly, and was laid up three weeks before I was able to do any work. My proprietor,[2] hearing of the bad usage I received, came to town, and severely reprimanded my master for beating me in such a manner, threatening him, that if he ever heard the like again, he would take me away and put me to another master to finish my time, and make him pay for it. This had a good effect and he behaved much better to me, the two succeeding years, and I began to acquire a proper knowledge of my trade.

My master being apprehensive that Charles Town was in danger on account of the war, removed into the country, about 38 miles off. Here we built a large house for Mr. Waters, during which time the English took Charles Town. Having obtained leave one day to see my parents, who had lived about 12 miles off, and it being late before I could go, I was obliged to borrow one of Mr. Waters's horses; but a servant of my master's took the horse from me to go a little journey, and stayed two or three days longer than he ought. This involved me in the greatest perplexity, and I expected the severest punishment, because the gentleman to who the horse belonged was a very bad man, and knew not how to show mercy. To escape his cruelty, I determined to go [to] Charles Town, and throw myself into the hands of the English. They received me readily, and I began to feel the happiness, liberty, of which I knew nothing before, altho' I was grieved at first, to be obliged to leave my friends, and among strangers.

In this situation I was seized with the smallpox and suffered great hardships; for all the Blacks affected with that disease, were ordered to be carried a mile from the camp, lest the soldiers should be infected, and disabled from marching. This was a grievous circumstance to me and many others. We lay sometimes a whole day without any thing to eat or drink; but Providence sent a man, who belonged to the York volunteers whom I was acquainted with, to my relief. He brought me such things as I stood in need of; and by the blessing of the Lord I began to recover. . . .

Being recovered, I marched with the army to Chamblem. When we came to the headquarters, our regiment was 35 miles off. I stayed at the headquarters three weeks during which time our regiment had an engagement with the Americans, and the man who relieved me when I was ill of the smallpox, was wounded in the battle, and brought to the hospital. As soon as I heard of his misfortune, I went to see him, and tarried with him in the hospital six weeks, till he recovered; rejoicing that it was in my power to return him the kindness he had showed me.

From thence I went to a place about 35 miles off, where we stayed two months: at the expiration of which, an express came to the Colonel to decamp in fifteen minutes. When these orders arrived I was at a distance from the camp, catching some fish for the captain that I waited upon; upon returning to the

2. King's owner.

camp, to my great astonishment, I found all the English were gone, and had left only a few militia. I felt my mind greatly alarmed, but Captain Lewes, who commanded the militia, said, "You need not be uneasy, for you will see your regiment before 7 o'clock tonight." This satisfied me for the present, and in two hours we set off. As we were on the march, the Captain asked, "How will you like me to be your master?" I answered that I was Captain Grey's servant. "Yes," said he; "but I expect they are all taken prisoners before now; and I have been long enough in the English service, and am determined to leave them." These words roused my indignation, and I spoke some sharp things to him. But he calmly replied, "If you do not behave well, I will put you in irons, and give you a dozen stripes every morning." I now perceived that my case was desperate, and that I had nothing to trust to, but to wait the first opportunity for making my escape.

The next morning, I was sent with a little boy over the river to an island to fetch the Captain some horses. When we came to the Island we found about fifty of the English horses that Captain Lewes had stolen from them at different times while they were at Rockmount. Upon our return to the Captain with the horses we were sent for, he immediately set off by himself. I stayed till about 10 o'clock and then resolved to go to the English army. After traveling 24 miles, I . . . arrived at the headquarters, I informed my Captain that Mr. Lewes had deserted. I also told him of the horses which Lewes had conveyed to the Island. Three weeks after, our Light-horse went to the Island and burnt his house; they likewise brought back forty of the horses, but he escaped.

I tarried with Captain Grey about a year, and then left him, and came to Nelson's ferry. Here I entered into the service of the commanding officer of that place. But our situation was very precarious; and we expected to be made prisoners every day; for the Americans had 1,600 men, not far off; whereas our whole number amounted only to 250: But here were 1,200 English about 30 miles off; only we knew not how to inform them of our danger, as the Americans were in possession of the country. Our commander at length determined to send me with a letter, promising me great rewards, if I was successful in the business, I refused going on horseback, and set off on foot about 3 o'clock in the afternoon; I expected every moment to fall in with the enemy, whom I well knew would show me no mercy. I went on without interruption, till I got within six miles of my journey's end, and then was alarmed with a great noise a little before me. But I stepped out of the road, and fell flat upon my face till they were gone by. I then arose, and praised the Name of the Lord for his great mercy, and again pursued my journey, till I came to Mums-corner tavern. I knocked at the door, but they blew out the candle. I knocked again, and entreated the master to open the door. At last he came with a frightful countenance, and said "I thought it was the Americans; for they were here about an hour ago, and I thought they were returned again." I asked, how many were there? He answered, "about one hundred," I desired him to saddle his horse for me, which he did, and went with me himself. When we had gone about two miles, we were stopped by the picket-guard, till the Captain came out with 30 men: As soon as he knew that I had brought an express from Nelson's ferry, he received me with great kindness, and expressed his approbation of my courage and conduct in this dangerous business. Next morning, Colonel Small . . . sent 600 men to relieve the troops at Nelson's ferry.

Soon after I went to Charles Town, and entered on board a [man] of war. As we were going to Chesapeake Bay, we were at the taking of a rich prize. We stayed in the bay two days, and they sailed for New-York, where I went on shore. Here I endeavoured to follow my trade, but for want of tools was obliged to relinquish it, and enter into service. But the wages were so low that I was not able to keep myself in clothes, so that I was under the necessity of leaving my master and going to another. I stayed with him four months, but he never paid me, and I was obliged to leave him also, and work about the town until I was married.

A year after I was taken very ill, but the Lord raised me up again in about five weeks. I then went out in a pilotboat. We were at sea eight days, and had only provisions for five, so that we were in danger of starving. On the 9th day we were taken by an American whaleboat. I went on board them with a cheerful countenance, and asked for bread and water, and made very free with them. They carried me to Brunswick, and used me well. Notwithstanding which, my mind was fairly distressed at the thought of being again reduced to slavery, and separated from my wife and family; and at the same time it was exceeding difficult to escape from my bondage, because the river at Amboy was above a mile over, and likewise another to cross at Staten-Island.

I called to remembrance the many great deliverances the Lord had wrought for me, and besought him to save me this once, and I would serve him all the days of my life. While my mind was thus exercised, I went into the jail to see a lad whom I was acquainted with at New-York. He had been taken prisoner, and attempted to make his escape, but was caught 12 miles off: They tied him to the tail of a horse, and in this manner brought him back to Brunswick. When I saw him, his feet were fastened in the stocks, and at night both his hands. This was a terrifying sight to me, as I expected to meet with the same kind of treatment, if taken in the act of attempting to regain my liberty. I was thankful that I was not confined in a jail, and my master used me as well as I could expect; and indeed the slaves about Baltimore, Philadelphia, and New-York, have as good victuals as many of the English; for they have meat once a day, and milk for breakfast and supper; and what is better than all, many of the masters send their slaves to school at night, that they may learn to read the Scriptures. This is a privilege indeed. But alas, all these enjoyments could not satisfy me without liberty! Sometimes I thought, if it was the will of God that I should be a slave, I was ready to resign myself to his will; but at other times I could not find the least desire to content myself in slavery.

Being permitted to walk about when my work was done, I used to go to the ferry, and observed, that when it was low water the people waded across the river; tho' at the same time I saw there were guards posted at the place to prevent the escape of prisoners and slaves. As I was at prayer on Sunday evening, I thought the Lord heard me, and would mercifully deliver me. Therefore putting my confidence in him, about one o'clock in the morning I went down to the river side, and found the guards were either asleep or in the tavern. I instantly entered into the river, but when I was a little distance from the opposite shore, I heard the sentinels disputing among themselves: One said "I am sure I saw a man cross the river." Another replied, "There is no such thing." It seems they were afraid to fire at me, or make an alarm, lest they should be punished for their negligence. When I had got a little distance from the shore, I fell down upon my knees, and thanked God for the deliverance. I traveled till about five in the morning, and then concealed myself till seven o'clock at night, when I proceeded forward, thro' bushes and marshes, near the road, for fear of being discovered. When I came to the river, opposite Staten-Island, I found a boat; and altho' it was very near a whaleboat, yet I ventured into it, and cutting the rope, got safe over. The commanding officer, when informed of my case, gave me a passport, and I proceeded to New-York.

When I arrived at New-York, my friends rejoiced to see me once more restored to liberty, and joined me in praising the Lord for his mercy and goodness. But notwithstanding this great deliverance, and the promises I had made to serve God, yet my good resolutions soon vanished away like the morning dew: The love of this world extinguished my good desires, and stole away my heart from God, so that I rested in a mere form of religion for near three years. About which time, (in 1783) the horrors and devastation of war happily terminated and peace was restored between America and Great Britain, which diffused universal joy among all parties; except us, who had escaped from slavery and taken refuge in the English army; for a report prevailed at New-York, that all the slaves, in number 2000, were to be delivered up to their masters altho' some of them had been three or four years among the English. This dreadful rumour filled us all with inexpressible anguish and terror, especially when we saw our old masters coming from Virginia, North Carolina, and other parts, and seizing upon their slaves in the streets of New York, or even dragging them out of their beds. Many of the slaves had very cruel masters, so that the thoughts of returning home with them embittered life to us. For some days we lost our appetite for food, and sleep departed from our eyes.

The English had compassion upon us in the day of distress, and issued out a Proclamation, importing, That all slaves should be free, who had taken refuge in the British lines, and claimed the sanction and privileges of the Proclamations respecting the security and protection of Negroes. In consequence of this, each of us received a certificate from the commanding officer at New-York, which dispelled all our fears, and filled us with joy and gratitude. Soon after, ships were fitted out, and furnished with every necessary for conveying us to Nova Scotia. We arrived at Birch Town in the month of August, where we all safely landed. Every family had a lot of land, and we exerted all our strength in order to build comfortable huts before the cold weather set in.

18

Secret Correspondence of a Loyalist Wife
Catherine Van Cortlandt

The Revolution was also a civil war. While most white Americans favored the patriot cause, loyalists were strong in many areas and among many groups. The areas surrounding New York City and along the Hudson River were predominately Tory, as were the eastern shore of Maryland and much of what was then the western frontier, particularly the Carolinas and Georgia. Old loyalties died hard. While Eliza Pinckney stood with her sons in the patriot cause, Benjamin Franklin's son William, as governor of New Jersey, was a prominent loyalist. George Washington, already commanding the Continental Army, still drank to the king's health daily until January 1776, when Thomas Paine's Common Sense *convinced him that the day of monarchy had passed.*

Philip Van Cortlandt of Hanover, New Jersey, retained his allegiance to the king. He escaped arrest by a patriot party in December 1776 and entered military service on the British side, receiving his commission from William Franklin. In letters sent to him by secret messenger from the patriot stronghold in which she was living, his wife, Catherine Van Cortlandt, described the family's plight. Finally, George Washington took pity on the family and gave them a pass to join Van Cortlandt in New York. The Van Cortlandts never returned to New Jersey. Like many loyalists, they migrated first to Nova Scotia and then to England.

BEFORE YOU READ

1. Do you think that Revolutionary soldiers had the right to seize Catherine Van Cortlandt's provisions and destroy her property?

2. Why do you think George Washington gave the family a pass to rejoin Van Cortlandt in New York?

December 15, 1776, Hanover, New Jersey

My dearest love,

You had not left us ten minutes last Sunday when a party of Light Horsemen, headed by Joseph Morris, came to our once peaceful mansion all armed, who said they had positive orders to take you, my dear Philly, prisoner to Easton, and your favourite horse Sampson to be carried to Morristown for the use of General Lee from whom these cruel mandates were issued. What were my emotions on seeing these wretches alight and without ceremony enter the

H. O. H. Vernon-Jackson, ed., "A Loyalist's Wife: Letters of Mrs. Philip Van Cortlandt, December 1776–February 1777," *History Today* 14 (1964): 574–80.

doors you can only conceive, you who know their base characters and how their present errand must be received by your beloved family. When these bloody-minded men came into the dining room our little flock gathered around me and with anxious eyes watched my looks, whilst I was answering questions. . . . One of them (flourishing his sword) swore bitterly that, if you was to be found alive on earth, he would take you or have your heart's blood. This was too much. They fled into their nursery, bursting into tears; screams out, "Oh my dear Pappa, they will kill him, they will kill him." One of the inhuman men seemed touched and endeavoured an excuse by saying they were sent by their General and therefore were obliged to do their duty, even though against a person they formerly much esteemed, but had been represented to General Lee as one too dangerous to be permitted to stay in the country. Finding you was certainly gone . . . they went off and left me in a situation . . . scarce to be described. My first care was the nursery to comfort those innocent pledges of our mutual love. . . . Their sobbing and crying had almost overcome them; and they would not be persuaded from a belief that the wretches were gone to murder their dear Pappa. . . .

. . . The house is surrounded by eighteen or twenty armed men every night in expectation of intercepting you, as they observed that you was too much attached to your family to be long absent. Our dear children are again taken from school in consequence of the cruel insults they daily receive for the principles of their parents.

I now write in fear and trembling and venture this by an honest Dutch farmer who says he will deliver it into your hands.

January 20, 1777, Hanover, New Jersey

My beloved Philly,

. . . The arrival of the Rebel Troops in this neighbourhood has been severely felt by us. Parties continually passing this way were always directed by officious people to stop at our house to breakfast, dine, or stay the night; the horses from the teams were put into our barns to feed, without even the ceremony of asking liberty. During the stay of the officers of the hospital we had some protection. But immediately on their removal, several field officers from the New England line and a company of privates took possession. . . . They were the most disorderly of their species and their officers were from the dregs of the people. Indeed, two lieutenants messed and slept in the kitchen altogether, and would not be prevailed upon to leave their quarters. . . . A French general has also come on the hill at Dashwood, and daily draws his supply for his numerous cavalry from our granary and barrack.

Many of our female neighbours have been here, but I find their visits are only to gratify curiosity and to add insult to our unremitted distress. One of them who lives across the river, whose family we took so much pleasure in relieving when friendless . . . said that formerly she always respected you and loved the ground over which you walked, but now could with pleasure see your blood run down the road. . . . The pious, devout and Reverend Mr. Green is very industrious in promoting your ruin by declaring you an enemy to their cause. The farmers are forbid to sell me provisions, and the millers to grind our grain. Our woods are cut down for the use of their army, and that which you bought and left corded near the river my servants are forbid to touch, though we are in the greatest distress for the want of it. . . . Our dear children have been six weeks without any other covering to their tender feet but woollen rags sewed round them to keep them from freezing.

A few days ago, the colonel and other officers quartered here told me they expected some of their brother officers to dine and spend the evening with them. This I understood as a hint to provide accordingly, which I was determined to do to the utmost of my powers, *though from necessity*. . . . After removal of the cloth, I took the earliest opportunity . . . to absent myself; and then they set in for a drinking match, every few minutes calling aloud upon the *landlady* to replenish the decanters which were kept continually going. . . . At length, one of them [the children] observed that the Gentlemen who used to dine with Papa never did so; and if these were not his friends, why did Mamma treat them so well. . . .

A Servant came down and said the Gentlemen desired my company, as they were going to dance. This confounded me. . . . Though I was much distressed, my resolution supported me whilst I told him that the present situation of myself and children would sufficiently apologize for my refusing to partake of any scenes of mirth where my husband could not attend me. . . . Near ten o'clock . . . he returned and entreated me to honour the Company for a few minutes as a Spectator. . . . The Officers were dancing Reels with some tawdry dressed females I had never seen. . . .

February 12, 1777, Hanover, New Jersey

. . . The narrow escape of your last was something remarkable. I was sitting about the dusk of evening in my room, very disconsolate with our dear children around me, reflecting on our deplorable situation and the gloomy prospects before me, when I heard a sudden rap at the street door. . . . I went myself to see who it was, and lucky I did. A tall, thin man presented himself, and on my stooping to unbolt the door whispered, he had a letter for me. My heart fluttered. The sentry was walking before the door, and two of the Officers were coming towards me. I recollected myself and *"desired the good man to walk into my room until I could give him a little wine for the sick woman."* He took the hint, and as soon as he came to my fireside gave me a letter, the outside of which I just looked at and threw it under the head of my bed and immediately set about getting him some wine for his wife to prevent suspicion. . . . The honest man after taking a dram went away, being followed out of doors and questioned by the Officers, who had been venting, cursing, and swearing against the sentry for permitting anyone to approach the house or speak to me without their first being acquainted with it. . . . The frequent frolics of the Officers in the house, the Soldiers in the Nursery, and Cattle constantly fed here has reduced our late Stock of plenty to a miserable pittance. The other day was almost too much for me. We had been several days without bread and were subsisting upon a half bushel of Indian meal which had been given me by a Dutch farmer I did not know, who said he had heard of our situation and would take no pay. . . . Our stock of meal had been expended five days and the Soldiers not being about, our little Sally immediately went into the Nursery, and picking up a piece of dirty bread which had been trod under their feet came running up to me, wiping it with her frock, and with joy sparkling in her eyes presented it to me crying out, "Do eat it, Mamma. 'Tis good. 'Tis charming good bread. Indeed it is. I have tasted it." This was too much.

The next day Doctor Bond . . . came to the house, and passing me suddenly went into the back room and taking from under his coat a loaf of bread he gave it to the children and before I could thank him he ran past me with his handkerchief and hat before his face. . . .

A few days after, Doctor Bond came here and with a faltering voice told me he was sent by General Washington to inform me that it was his positive orders that our house should be taken as an Hospital to innoculate his Army with the smallpox, and if I chose he would innoculate my family at the same time. . . . He . . . promised to use his influence with the General to obtain the only favour I had now to ask of him; which was, to go to my husband with my children, servants, and such effects as I could take with me. . . .

February 19, 1777, Hoboken Ferry

My beloved husband,

Doctor Bond succeeded and with orders for my removal brought me General Washington's pass which I now enclose.

To describe the scene at parting with our few though sincere friends, the destruction of our property, the insulting looks and behaviour of those who had been accessory to our ruin . . . is more than I dare attempt. At four in the afternoon, a cold, disagreeable day, we bid adieu to our home to make room for the sick of General Washington's Army and, after an unpleasant and fatiguing journey, arrived at twelve o'clock at night at the Fork of the Rivers Rockaway, Pompton and Haakinsack. A Young Woman, whose father and brother were both in the Rebel service, was much affected with my situation and endeavoured to remove me into another room. The next evening, after a most distressing ride through snow and rain . . . we arrived at Campbell's Tavern at Haakinsack, the mistress of which refused me admittance when she was informed whose family it was, alleging as an excuse that she expected a number of Officers. . . .

The town was filled with Soldiers and the night advancing . . . a person came up to me, looked me in the face, and asked me to accompany him to his Uncle's house with my whole family. On entering a room with a large fire, it had an effect on the children, whose stomachs had been empty the greatest part of the day, that caused instant puking, and was near proving fatal to them.

The next morning early, we again set off in a most uncomfortable sleet and snow. . . . Our youngest children could not pass a farm yard where they were milking cows without wishing for some. My little Willing was almost in agonies, springing in my Arms and calling for milk. I therefore rode up and requested the good man to let me have some from one of his pails. . . . The man stopped, asked who we were, and . . . swore bitterly he would not give a drop to any Tory Bitch. I offered him money, my children screamed; and, as I could not prevail, I drove on.

. . . [T]he servants . . . had been obliged to leave me soon after setting off from Haakinsack, on account of the baggage and the badness of the roads. About two hours ago, they came in and inform me that, crossing the river on the ice at the ferry, they were stopped and fired upon by a party of armed Rebels, nearly killing several of them. . . . Upon being shewn a copy of General Washington's pass, . . . they damned the General "for giving the mistress a pass" and said they were sorry they had not come a little sooner as they would have stopped the whole . . . and immediately fell to plundering chests, trunks, boxes, etc., throwing the heavy Articles into a hole in the ice, and breaking a barrel of old fashioned China into a thousand pieces. . . .

. . . [B]e not surprised, my dear Pappa, if you see your Kitty altered. Indeed, I am much altered. But I know your heart, you will not love me less, but heal with redoubled affection and tenderness the wounds received in your behalf for those principles of loyalty which alone induced you to leave to the mercy of Rebels nine innocent children and your fond and ever affectionate Wife,

C.V.C.

Republican Motherhood
Eliza Pinckney and Abigail Adams

When George Washington insisted on serving as a pallbearer at Eliza Pinckney's funeral in 1793, he was recognizing a new ideal that both Pinckney and Abigail Adams exemplified, that of the "Republican mother." These women took an active role in affairs within the narrow bounds allowed by eighteenth-century marriage while inculcating the love of virtue and country in their children.

Eliza Pinckney, born Eliza Lucas in the West Indies in 1722, moved to South Carolina in 1737. Two years later, when her father returned to the Caribbean island of Antigua to become governor, seventeen-year-old Eliza remained in South Carolina to take charge of the family's three plantations. A remarkable agriculturalist, she pioneered the cultivation of several new crops, most notably indigo, a source for dye that became a staple exported from the Carolinas for decades. In 1744, she married Charles Pinckney, a prominent lawyer, political leader, and planter and had three children by him. After her husband died in 1758, Eliza again managed extensive properties. She constantly impressed on her children the family tradition of opposition to "wrong, oppression, or tyranny of any sort, public or private"—an injunction that in the eighteenth century did not prohibit slaveholding. Her two sons, Charles Cotesworth Pinckney and Thomas Pinckney, both rose to the rank of general in the Revolutionary War, were signers of the Constitution, and held major offices in the new federal government.

Abigail Adams (1744–1818) was born Abigail Smith in Weymouth, Massachusetts. Like most young women of the era, she was educated at home by her parents and relatives. John Adams, a serious young lawyer, began courting her in 1761, and three years later they wed. The couple had five children, four of whom survived into adulthood.

Abigail Adams's letters to her husband and her son John Quincy Adams illustrate the power of her personality and the sense of authority—different from the authority accorded eighteenth-century men—that she created from the role of wife and mother. Never forgetting the sharp distinction that society made between men's responsibilities and women's, she nonetheless took clear stands on the moral and political issues of her day and molded her son into a man of virtue and patriotism according to her definitions of those traits.

Harriott Horry Ravenel, *Eliza Pinckney* (New York: Charles Scribner's Sons, 1896), pp. 264–65, 275–76, 307–10; Charles Francis Adams, ed., *Letters of Mrs. Adams, the Wife of John Adams* (Boston: Wilkins, Carter, 1848), pp. 94–96, 152–55; Charles Francis Adams, ed., *Familiar Letters of John Adams and His Wife Abigail Adams, during the Revolution* (Boston: Houghton, Mifflin, 1875), pp. 148–50.

BEFORE YOU READ

1. What standards did Eliza Pinckney and Abigail Adams set for their sons?

2. What lessons did Eliza Pinckney and Abigail Adams expect their sons to learn from the American Revolution?

3. Compare the tone of Abigail Adams's letter to her son with that of the letter to her husband.

4. What does this famous letter ask of John Adams?

ELIZA PINCKNEY

August 1775

I see by these preparations of tents etc, that our soldiers are making ready for the field. I hope there will be little occasion for them. Heaven interests itself in favor of those who have Virtue to assert the birthright of mankind, Divine Liberty! and Britain surely will be shortly taught by our successes and continued unanimity, in spite of all their base arts to disunite us, that America determines to be free, and that it is beyond their force of arms to enslave so vast a Continent.

What shall we think of those few base souls among us, who, leaving penury and want in their own country have lived luxuriously in our land, and raised themselves a name; who now spurn at their benefactors, and betray the place that has been their asylum. From the misrepresentation of such wretches, do we doubtless owe much of our present calamity.

Tell Mr. Horry his friend G. threatened the Committee with an assault the other day, for which pretty performance . . . could they have caught him, [patriots] intended him a genteel souse in the River or perhaps a fashionable suit [of tar and feathers].

Hampton, Santee, May 1779

My Dear Tomm, — I have just received your letter with the account of my losses, and your almost ruined fortunes by the enemy. A severe blow! but I feel not for myself, but for you; 't is for your losses my greatly beloved child that I grieve; the loss of fortune could affect me little, but that it will deprive my dear Children of my assistance when they may stand most in need of it. . . . Your Brother's timely generous offer, to divide what little remains to him among us, is worthy of him. I am greatly affected, but not surprised at his Liberality.

I know his disinterestedness, his sensibility and affection. You say, I must be sensible you can't agree to this offer; indeed my dear Tomm I am very sensible of it, nor can I take a penny from his young helpless family. Independence is all I want and a little will make us that. Don't grieve for my child as I assure you I do not for myself. While I have such children dare I think my lot hard? God forbid! I pray the Almighty disposer of events to preserve them and my grandchildren to me, and for all the rest I hope I shall be able to say not only contentedly but cheerfully, God's Sacred will be done!

Undated [after 1783]

[To her grandson, Daniel Horry]

With the most resigned acquiescence in the Divine Will, I submit to the loss of Fortune, when I see my dear children, after being exposed to a variety of suffering, danger and Death, alive and well around me. And when I contemplate with what philosophick firmness and calmness they both of them supported pain, sickness and evils of various sorts, and withstood the utmost efforts of the ennemies' malice, and see with what greatness of mind they now generously conduct themselves to all; my heart overflows with gratitude to their great Preserver for continuing to me such children. Be assured, my dear Daniel, no pleasure can equal that which a mother feels when she knows her children have acted their part well through life, and when she sees them happy in the consciousness of having done so. May the Almighty in his infinite goodness and condescencion accept my prayer when I earnestly entreat that your dear and greatly beloved mother may enjoy the same comfort in seeing you and your sister answer her most sanguine hopes: for though I hope your Country will never want your aid in a Millitary capacity you may be guided by the same principles of true honour and real virtue that have always actuated them, and though not called exactly to the same exertion, your conduct in publick and private life may Emulate the Example they have set you, and give your mother a comfort which nothing else can. . . .

When I take a retrospective view of our past sufferings, so recent too, and compare them with our present prospects, the change is so great and sudden it appears like a dream, and I can hardly believe the pleasing reality, that peace, with all its train of blessings is returned, and that everyone may find Shelter under his own Vine and his own Fig-tree, and be happy. Blessed be God! the effusion of human blood is stopped. Truth may now also appear in its full force and native Lustre, without dread of the oppressive hand of power as heretofore, when the injured were not heard, or heard only to be treated with contempt and insult; when in justice to themselves they would disprove those horrid falsehoods and misrepresentations which natural malevolence or party rage inspired. How much has this unhappy land felt the insolence of power and wanton cruelty; there are but few here but can feelingly tell a tale of woe. Were I to enumerate the distresses that have come to my own knowledge I should distress you and myself beyond measure, for their sorrows were greater than mine, and I experienced a large share of the bitter portion dealt out at those evil times. Both my Sons, their wives and Infants were exiled. Wounded sick and emaciated with a very pittance to support them in a strange Land [Philadelphia] they imbarked. Their estates had been long before sequestrated and mine was shattered and ruined, which left me little power to assist them; nor had I in Country or Town a place to lay my head, all was taken out of my possession; my house I lived in, that in Colleton Square, and at Belmont, all was taken from me, nor was I able to hire a lodging. But let me forget as soon as I can their cruelties, I wish to forgive and will say no more on this subject, and hope our joy and gratitude for our great deliverance may equal our former anguish, and our contentment in mediocrity, and moderation in prosperity, equal the fortitude with which the greatest number even of our sex sustained the great reverse of fortune they experienced.

ABIGAIL ADAMS

Letters to John Quincy Adams

June, 1778

My Dear Son,

'Tis almost four months since you left your native land, and embarked upon the mighty waters, in quest of a foreign country. Although I have not particularly written to you since, yet you may be assured you have constantly been upon my heart and mind.

It is a very difficult task, my dear son, for a tender parent to bring her mind to part with a child of your years going to a distant land; nor could I have acquiesced in such a separation under any other care than that of the most excellent parent and guardian who accompanied you. You have arrived at years capable of improving under the advantages you will be likely to have, if you do but properly attend to them. They are talents put into your hands, of which an account will be required of you hereafter; and being possessed of one, two, or four, see to it that you double your numbers.

The most amiable and most useful disposition in a young mind is diffidence of itself; and this should lead you to seek advice and instruction from him, who is your natural guardian, and will always counsel and direct you in the best manner, both for your present and future happiness. You are in possession of a natural good understanding, and of spirits unbroken by adversity and untamed with care. Improve your understanding by acquiring useful knowledge and virtue, such as will render you an ornament to society, an honor to your country, and a blessing to your parents. Great learning and superior abilities, should you ever possess them, will be of little value and small estimation, unless virtue, honor, truth, and integrity are added to them. Adhere to those religious sentiments and principles which were early instilled into your mind, and remember that you are accountable to your Maker for all your words and actions.

You have entered early in life upon the great theatre of the world, which is full of temptations and vice of every kind. You are not wholly unacquainted with history, in which you have read of crimes which your inexperienced mind could scarcely believe credible. You have been taught to think of them with horror, and to view vice as

> a monster of so frightful mien,
> That, to be hated, needs but to be seen.

Yet you must keep a strict guard upon yourself, or the odious monster will soon lose its terror by becoming familiar to you. The modern history of our own times, furnishes as black a list of crimes, as can be paralleled in ancient times, even if we go back to Nero, Caligula, or Cæsar Borgia. Young as you are, the cruel war, into which we have been compelled by the haughty tyrant of Britain and the bloody emissaries of his vengeance, may stamp upon your mind this certain truth, that the welfare and prosperity of all countries, communities, and, I may add, individuals, depend upon their morals. That nation to which we were once united, as it has departed from justice, eluded and subverted the wise laws which formerly governed it, and suffered the worst of crimes to go unpunished, has lost its valor, wisdom and humanity, and, from being the dread and terror of Europe, has sunk into derision and infamy.

Be assured I am most affectionately yours,

———— .

12 January, 1780

My Dear Son,

. . . These are times in which a genius would wish to live. It is not in the still calm of life, or the repose of a pacific station, that great characters are formed. Would Cicero have shone so distinguished an orator if he had not been roused, kindled, and inflamed by the tyranny of Catiline, Verres, and Mark Anthony? The habits of a vigorous mind are formed in contending with difficulties. All history will convince you of this, and that wisdom and penetration are the fruit of experience, not the lessons of retirement and leisure. Great necessities call out great virtues. When a mind is raised and animated by scenes that engage the heart, then those qualities, which would otherwise lie dormant, wake into life and form the character of the hero and the statesman. War, tyranny, and desolation are the scourges of the Almighty, and ought no doubt to be deprecated. Yet it is your lot, my son, to be an eyewitness of these calamities in your own native land, and, at the same time, to owe your existence among a people who have made a glorious defence of their invaded liberties, and who, aided by a generous and powerful ally, with the blessing of Heaven, will transmit this inheritance to ages yet unborn.

Nor ought it to be one of the least of your incitements towards exerting every power and faculty of your mind, that you have a parent who has taken so large and active a share in this contest, and discharged the trust reposed in him with so much satisfaction as to be honored with the important embassy which at present calls him abroad.

The strict and inviolable regard you have ever paid to truth, gives me pleasing hopes that you will not swerve from her dictates, but add justice, fortitude, and every manly virtue which can adorn a good citizen, do honor to your country, and render your parents supremely happy, particularly your ever affectionate mother,

A. A.

Braintree, 26 December, 1783

My Dear Son,

The early age at which you went abroad gave you not an opportunity of becoming acquainted with your own country. Yet the revolution, in which we were engaged, held it up in so striking and important a light, that you could not avoid being in some measure irradiated with the view. The characters with which you were connected, and the conversation you continually heard, must have impressed your mind with a sense of the laws, the liberties, and the glorious privileges, which distinguish the free, sovereign, independent States of America.

Let your observations and comparisons produce in your mind an abhorrence of domination and power, the parent of slavery, ignorance, and barbarism, which places man upon a level with his fellow tenants of the woods;

> A day, an hour, of virtuous liberty
> Is worth a whole eternity of bondage.

You have seen power in its various forms,—a benign deity, when exercised in the suppression of fraud, injustice, and tyranny, but a demon, when united with unbounded ambition,—a wide-wasting fury, who has destroyed her thousands. Not an age of the world but has produced characters, to which whole human hecatombs have been sacrificed.

What is the history of mighty kingdoms and nations, but a detail of the ravages and cruelties of the powerful over the weak? Yet it is instructive to trace the various causes, which produced the strength of one nation, and the decline and weakness of another; to learn by what arts one man has been able to subjugate millions of his fellow creatures, the motives which have put him upon action, and the causes of his success;—sometimes driven by ambition and a lust of power; at other times, swallowed up by religious enthusiasm, blind bigotry, and ignorant zeal; sometimes enervated with luxury and debauched by pleasure, until the most powerful nations have become a prey and been subdued by these Sirens, when neither the number of their enemies, nor the prowess of their arms, could conquer them. . . .

The history of your own country and the late revolution are striking and recent instances of the mighty things achieved by a brave, enlightened, and hardy people, determined to be free; the very yeomanry of which, in many instances, have shown themselves superior to corruption, as Britain well knows, on more occasions than the loss of her André. Glory, my son, in a country which has given birth to characters, both in the civil and military departments, which may vie with the wisdom and valor of antiquity. As an immediate descendant of one of those characters, may you be led to an imitation of that disinterested patriotism and that noble love of your country, which will teach you to despise wealth, titles, pomp, and equipage, as mere external advantages, which cannot add to the internal excellence of your mind, or compensate for the want of integrity and virtue.

May your mind be thoroughly impressed with the absolute necessity of universal virtue and goodness, as the only sure road to happiness, and may you walk therein with undeviating steps,—is the sincere and most affectionate wish of

Your mother,
A. Adams

Letter to John Adams

Braintree, 31 March, 1776

I wish you would ever write me a letter half as long as I write you, and tell me, if you may, where your fleet are gone; what sort of defense Virginia can make against our common enemy; whether it is so situated as to make an able defense. Are not the gentry lords, and the common people vassals? Are they not like the uncivilized vassals Britain represents us to be? I hope their riflemen, who have shown themselves very savage and even blood-thirsty, are not a specimen of the generality of the people. I am willing to allow the colony great merit for having produced a Washington; but they have been shamefully duped by a Dunmore [British commander].

I have sometimes been ready to think that the passion for liberty cannot be equally strong in the breasts of those who have been accustomed to deprive their fellow-creatures of theirs. Of this I am certain, that it is not founded upon that generous and Christian principle of doing to others as we would that others should do unto us.

I long to hear that you have declared an independency. And, by the way, in the new code of laws which I suppose it will be necessary for you to make, I desire you would remember the ladies and be more generous and favorable to them than your ancestors. Do not put such unlimited power into the hands of the husbands. Remember, all men would be tyrants if they could. If particular care and attention is not paid to the ladies, we are determined to foment a rebellion, and will not hold ourselves bound by any laws in which we have no voice or representation.

That your sex are naturally tyrannical is a truth so thoroughly established as to admit of no dispute; but such of you as wish to be happy willingly give up the harsh title of master for the more tender and endearing one of friend. Why, then, not put it out of the power of the vicious and the lawless to use us with cruelty and indignity with impunity? Men of sense in all ages abhor those customs which treat us only as the vassals of your sex; regard us then as beings placed by Providence under your protection, and in imitation of the Supreme Being make use of that power only for our happiness.

20

Shays's Rebellion: Prelude to the Constitution
George Richards Minot

During the 1780s, political conflict splintered much of the country. For relief from the economic hardships that followed the war, farmers looked to local and state government to pass and enforce laws that favored debtors over creditors. Wealthier townspeople wanted strong government that would ensure sound money, promote trade, pay the public debt, and keep order.

Nowhere was this battle waged more fiercely than in Massachusetts. Poor harvests made it difficult for farmers to pay their debts to merchants and to meet the high taxes levied by the state to discharge its Revolutionary War obligations. Soon creditors and the state were dispossessing farmers of their land and livestock, and some were even thrown into jail for nonpayment of debt. Farmers began demanding legislation to improve their situation. They called for lower taxes, the issuance of paper money to make debt repayment easier, and "stay laws" to postpone payment to creditors. When these efforts failed, the farmers took more dramatic action. Adopting as their symbol the "sprig of green" on the soldiers' caps worn during the Revolutionary War, these men, many of them veterans of that conflict, formed paramilitary units. Their main target was the courts to which creditors and tax collectors repaired to exact what they were owed. In a careful, orderly, but plainly illegal manner they surrounded courthouses and stopped proceedings. Informally organized, they had few recognized leaders, but the former Revolutionary War officers among them, like Daniel Shays of Pelham, drilled the men and became at least nominal leaders of the movement.

Merchants, professionals, and government leaders were horrified by the court closings, describing the Shaysites as "the most idle, vicious and disorderly set of men" who would "plunge the community into anarchy." Boston lawyer George Richards Minot (1758–1802) shouted for "Daniel Shays's decapitation," although a year later, when he wrote the account excerpted here, he had moderated his opinion so that historians have praised the fairness of his judgments. Governor James Bowdoin called for "the most vigorous measures . . . to enforce obedience to the law," and the state legislature responded as Massachusetts organized an army under Revolutionary War general Benjamin Lincoln.

The Shaysite armies harassed merchants and tried to capture the federal arsenal at Springfield. In the end, though, General Lincoln's army of militiamen easily defeated them; the rebellion dissipated, and its leaders fled the state. By the following year the

George Richards Minot, *The History of the Insurrections in Massachusetts, in the Year Seventeen Hundred and Eighty Six, and the Rebellion Consequent Thereon*, 2nd ed. (Boston: Books for Libraries Press, 1810), pp. 108–25.

economy had swung upward, and the Massachusetts government, though firmly set against the Shaysites, eased the credit squeeze by a limited issuance of paper money.

The crisis was over, but its political effect was not. The rebellion had alarmed political leaders throughout the colonies and greatly strengthened the position of those who advocated a stronger central government to control such uprisings. Shays's Rebellion was extensively debated as the Constitution was drafted and approved. The arguments over ratification in Massachusetts followed quite closely the political divisions expressed in the insurrection. Only their superior organization enabled the Federalists to achieve victory in this pivotal state by the close vote of 187 to 168.

BEFORE YOU READ

1. What position on Shays's Rebellion does George Richards Minot take in his account?

2. What strategy did the Shaysites pursue? How aggressive do they seem? How determined were they to bring the issue to actual combat?

3. What strategy did General Benjamin Lincoln, who led the state's army, pursue? How aggressive does he seem? How determined was he to bring the issue to actual combat?

4. Why do you think Shays's Rebellion became an important issue throughout the colonies?

... General Shepard, about 4 o'clock in the afternoon of the 25th, perceived Shays advancing on the Boston road, towards the arsenal where the militia were posted, with his troops in open column. Possessed of the importance of that moment, in which the first blood should be drawn in the contest, the General sent one of his aids with two other gentlemen, several times, to know the intention of the enemy, and to warn them of their danger. The purport of their answer was, that they would have possession of the barracks; and they immediately marched onwards to within 250 yards of the arsenal. A message was again sent to inform them, that the militia were posted there by order of the Governour, and of Congress, and that if they approached nearer, they would be fired upon. To this, one of their leaders replied, that *that* was all they wanted; and they advanced one hundred yards further. Necessity now compelled General Shepard to fire, but his humanity did not desert him. He ordered the two first shot to be directed over their heads; this however, instead of retarding, quickened their approach; and the artillery was at last pointed at the centre of their column. This measures was not without its effect. A cry of murder arose from the rear of the insurgents, and their whole body was thrown into the utmost confusion. Shays attempted to display his column, but it was in vain. His troops retreated with precipitation to Ludlow, about ten miles from the place of action, leaving three of their men dead, and one wounded on the field.

The advantages which the militia had in their power, both from the disorder of this retreat, which was as injudicious as the mode of attack, and from the nature of the ground, would have enabled them to have killed the greater part of the insurgents, had a pursuit taken place. But, the object of the commander was rather to terrify, than to destroy the deluded fugitives. ...

Notwithstanding the fatigue of a march, performed in an uncommonly severe winter, the army were ordered under arms at half past three o'clock, the same day on which they arrived. Four regiments, with four pieces of artillery, and the horse, crossed the river upon the ice, while the Hampshire troops, under the command of General Shepard, moved up the river, as well to prevent a junction of the party under Shays, who were on the east side, with those under Day, on the west, as to cut off the retreat of the latter. It was also a great object by this manœuvre, to encircle Day, with a force so evidently superior, as to prevent his people from firing, and thereby to avoid the shedding of blood. Upon the appearance of the army on the river, the guard at the ferry house turned out, but forsook the pass; and after a small shew of opposition, near the meeting house, retired in the utmost confusion. This was attended with the flight of all Day's party, who escaped to Northampton, with the loss of a very small number, that were overtaken by the light horse. The insurgent forces under Shays, made no greater opposition, on the day following. When the army approached him, he immediately began a retreat, through South-Hadley to Amherst, supplying the hunger of his men by plunder. . . .

The appearance of things was exceedingly changed by the flight of the insurgents from Springfield. . . . The apprehensions of the inhabitants had been . . . greatly raised, from the various reports of the numbers and objects of the insurgents; and more than all, from the aid which they affected to rely on, from secret, but influential characters within the state, and the discontented of neighbouring governments. From such ideas, the meeting of the two armies in full force, at Springfield was dreaded by all, in whose minds the tranquillity of the country was the primary object. But these fears wholly vanished, by the dispersing of the insurgent forces, and a security naturally arose from the flattering view of their broken and forlorn condition. . . .

The pursuit of Shays and his party, which commenced at two o'clock in the morning, was continued till the army reached Amherst, through which place, however, he passed before their arrival, on his way to Pelham, with the main body of his men. General Lincoln, finding the enemy out of his reach, directed his march to Hadley, the nearest place which could be found to afford a cover for his troops. Upon an examination of the houses at Amherst, it was discovered, that most of the male inhabitants had quitted them to follow the insurgents; and that ten sleigh loads of provisions had gone forward from the county of Berkshire for their use. Under such appearances, a strict prohibition was laid upon the remaining inhabitants, against affording any supplies to their deluded neighbours.

The morning after the arrival of the army at Hadley, information was received that a small number of General Shepard's men had been captured at Southampton, and that the enemy's party still continued there. The Brookfield volunteers, consisting of fifty men, and commanded by Colonel Baldwin, were sent in sleighs, with 100 horse, under the command of Colonel Crafts, to pursue them. They were soon found to consist of eighty men with ten sleighs, and at twelve o'clock the same night were overtaken at Middlefield. They had quartered themselves in separate places; and about one half of them, with one Luddington their captain, being lodged in a house together, were first surrounded. It was a singular circumstance, that among the government's volunteers, happened to be General Tupper, who had lately commanded a continental regiment, in which Luddington had served as a Corporal. The General, ignorant of the character of his enemy, summoned the party to surrender. How astonished was the Corporal at receiving the summons, in a voice to which he had never dared to refuse obedience! A momentary explanation took place, which but heightened the General's commands. Resistance was no longer made, the doors were opened, and a surrender was agreed to. By this time, the rest of the party had paraded under arms, at the distance of 200 yards, where they were met by a number of men prepared for their reception. Both sides were on the point of firing, but, upon an artful representation of the strength of the government's troops, the insurgents laid down their arms, and fifty-nine prisoners, with nine sleigh loads of provisions, fell into the hands of the conquerors, who returned to the army on the day following.

The whole force of the insurgents having taken post on two high hills in Pelham, called east and west hills, which were rendered difficult of access by the depth of the snow around them, General Lincoln, on the 30th of January, sent a letter directed to Captain Shays, and the officers commanding the men in arms against the government of the Commonwealth, as follows:

> Whether you are convinced or not of your error in flying to arms, I am fully persuaded that before this hour, you must have the fullest conviction upon your own minds, that you are not able to execute your original purposes.
>
> Your resources are few, your force is inconsiderable, and hourly decreasing from the disaffection of your men; you are in a post where you have neither cover nor supplies, and in a situation in which you can neither give aid to your friends, nor discomfort to the supporters of good order and government. — Under these circumstances, you cannot hesitate a moment to disband your deluded followers. If you should not, I must approach, and apprehend the most influential characters among you. Should you attempt to fire upon the troops of government, the consequences must be fatal to many of your men, the least guilty. To prevent bloodshed, you will communicate to your privates, that if they will instantly lay down their arms, surrender themselves to government, and take and subscribe the oath of allegiance to this Commonwealth, they shall be recommended to the General Court for mercy. If you should either withhold this information from them, or suffer your people to fire upon our approach, you must be answerable for all the ills which may exist in consequence thereof.

To this letter the following Answer was received.

Pelham, January 30th, 1787

To General Lincoln, commanding the government troops at Hadley.

Sir,

> The people assembled in arms from the counties of Middlesex, Worcester, Hampshire and Berkshire, taking into serious consideration the purport of the flag just received, return for answer, that however unjustifiable the measures may be which the people have adopted, in having recourse to arms, various circumstances have induced them thereto. We are sensible of the embarrassments the people are under; but that virtue which truly characterizes the citizens of a

republican government, hath hitherto marked our paths with a degree of innocence; and we wish and trust it will still be the case. At the same time, the
people are willing to lay down their arms, on the condition of a general pardon,
and return to their respective homes, as they are unwilling to stain the land,
which we in the late war purchased at so dear a rate, with the blood of our
brethren and neighbours. Therefore, we pray that hostilities may cease, on
your part, until our united prayers may be presented to the General Court, and
we receive an answer, as a person is gone for that purpose. If this request may
be complied with, government shall meet with no interruption from the
people, but let each army occupy the post where they now are.

DANIEL SHAYS, *Captain*

On the next day, three of the insurgent leaders came to Head Quarters
with the following letter.

The Honourable General Lincoln.

Sir,

As the officers of the people, now convened in defence of their rights and
privileges, have sent a petition to the General Court, for the sole purpose of
accommodating our present unhappy affairs, we justly expect that hostilities
may cease on both sides, until we have a return from our legislature.

Your Honour will therefore be pleased to give us an answer.

Per order of the committee for reconciliation.

FRANCIS STONE, *Chairman*
DANIEL SHAYS, *Captain*
ADAM WHEELER

Pelham, January 31, 1787

To this the following Answer was sent.

Hadley, January 31st, 1787

Gentlemen,

Your request is totally inadmissible, as no powers are delegated to me which
would justify a delay of my operations. Hostilities I have not commenced.

I have again to warn the people in arms against government, immediately to
disband, as they would avoid the ill consequences which may ensue, should
they be inattentive to this caution.

B. LINCOLN

To FRANCIS STONE,
DANIEL SHAYS,
ADAM WHEELER

During these negotiations between the army and the insurgents, the time
arrived for the assembling of the legislature. . . . The Court then acquainted the
Governour, that they were prepared to receive his communications, and he ad-

dressed them by a speech from the chair, which contained a retrospective account of the malcontents, as to their views and proceedings, and of the measures which the government had adopted to oppose them. Vigour and energy
were strongly recommended, as the proper means of crushing so unprovoked
an insurrection, while a want of them might draw on the evils of a civil war. . . .

Affairs had been brought to such a crisis, that there was no room left for the
legislature to waver in their opinions, or to delay their measures. The whole
community were in an alarm, and the appeal to the sword was actually made.
One army or the other was to be supported, and there could be no hesitation in
the mind of any reasonable man, which it ought to be. On the next day, therefore, a declaration of Rebellion was unanimously passed in the Senate, and concurred by the lower House. This however was accompanied by a resolve,
approving of General Lincoln's offer of clemency to the privates among the insurgents, and empowering the Governour in the name of the General Court to
promise a pardon, under such disqualifications, as should afterwards be provided, to all privates and noncommissioned officers, that were in arms against
the Commonwealth, unless excepted by the general officer commanding the
troops, upon condition of their surrendering their arms, and taking and sub-
scribing the oath of allegiance, within a time to be prescribed by the Governour.

On the same day, an answer was also sent to the Governour's speech. In
this the Court informed his Excellency of their entire satisfaction, in the measures which he had been pleased to take for subduing a turbulent spirit, that had
too long insulted the Government of the Commonwealth; and congratulated
him on the success which had attended them. They earnestly intreated him still
to continue them, with such further constitutional measures, as he might think
necessary, to extirpate the spirit of rebellion; for the better enabling of him to
do which, they thought it necessary to declare that a rebellion existed. . . . They
subjoined that they would vigorously pursue every measure, which would be
calculated to support the constitution, and would continue to redress any real
grievances, if such should be found to exist.

PART FOUR

Defining America

The Expanding Nation

When the turmoil of the American Revolution and the ratification of the Constitution finally subsided in the 1790s, thirteen colonies had been forged into a new nation. Covering more than a thousand miles of the Atlantic coast from Maine to Georgia, the United States of America already was populated by millions of people who spoke over a dozen European languages and countless Native American tongues. Divided between the mercantile, agricultural-industrial North and the plantation South, the one bond that seemed to unite people was their shared desire for land and the opportunity for a better life.

For almost two hundred years, American society had been confined to the corridor between the Atlantic Ocean and the Appalachians. Mountains, Indians, and conflict among European powers discouraged Americans from pushing west. Then, after about 1795, with Native Americans having been defeated or assimilated during the Revolution and the price of good eastern land climbing, a sizable white migration began. Thomas Jefferson's purchase of the vast Louisiana Territory in 1803 and his sponsorship of the expedition by Meriwether Lewis and William Clark quickened this movement, as did rising world prices for agricultural products.

A transportation revolution further encouraged the migration: turnpikes began to replace stump-filled rutted paths; steamboats overtook sailing ships and river rafts; canals offered the first economical means of moving eastward the bulky products of western farms; and finally, railroads spread westward in the 1840s and 1850s, overshadowing all other forms of long-distance transportation. The land seemed to have tilted permanently, shaking its human burden westward in a long, rough tumble toward the Pacific. But the improved life people sought in the West was far more than one of simple economic gain: evangelical preachers such as James B. Finley and Peter Cartwright crisscrossed the Western territories, and believers such as Priscilla Merriman Evans and her husband trekked heroically to reach their Mormon Zion in the wilderness.

But the new Westerners were not entering empty territory. Native Americans had been forced west for generations by white settlement, but in 1838 the U.S. Army marched over fifteen thousand Cherokee Indians from Georgia to Oklahoma. John Ross's letter presents a Native view of these events. The relocation of the Cherokee put them into competition with other groups already living in the West, including other Native Americans in the Western territories, and the Spanish and their heirs, the Mexicanos, Californios, Tejanos, and Mestizos who owned much of those territories. Shifting political alliances, religious and cultural differences, and mutual suspicions were everyday realities for most Americans pushing westward, as described by an officer of the "Army of the West" in his account of the taking of New Mexican villages. When Mexico and the United States finally went to war over Texas and the Southwest in 1846, it was no surprise to most Mexicans, who like Ramón Alcaraz believed the Americans were so hungry for land that they might claim all of northern Mexico. In fact, the conflicts with Mexico determined the future of nearly a million square miles of what is now Texas, New Mexico, Arizona, Nevada, California, Utah, and parts of Colorado, Wyoming, Kansas, and Oklahoma. The discovery of gold in California in 1848 and the rush of miners from as far away as China accelerated the settlement of the West, forcing decisions about its future that soon led to the Civil War.

Everywhere people were in motion: seeking their fortunes, looking for second chances, trying to save souls, or simply searching for adventure. They moved not only within the continent but also continued to travel to and from other parts of the world. Some Americans, as Nathaniel W. Taylor describes, even risked sailing in treacherous waters as far away as Antarctica to harvest valuable oil from whales and to share in the profits from the burgeoning demand for products of luxury, utility, and industry.

POINTS OF VIEW

The Mexican-American War (1846–1848)

21

A View from the Other Side

Ramón Alcaraz

In February 1847, General Antonio López de Santa Anna rode across the plains of Mexico with twenty-five thousand exhausted soldiers to meet the American general Zachary Taylor and five thousand fresh U.S. soldiers at the Battle of Buena Vista, near Saltillo, Coahuila, in northern Mexico. One of the fiercest conflicts of the Mexican-

Ramón Alcaraz, *The Other Side: or Notes for the History of the War between Mexico and the United States,* Trans. and ed. Albert C. Ramsey (New York: J. Wiley, 1850), pp. 114–29.

American War, the fighting in this heavily fortified mountain village would prove to be a turning point. Santa Anna's forces could not dislodge the outnumbered Americans, and they soon retreated. Ultimately, this led to the occupation of the Mexican capital, the annexation of the current states of Texas, Arizona, New Mexico, California, Utah, Nevada, and Colorado by the "gringos," and the permanent shift of power in hemispheric affairs to the United States.

For most Americans, the war with Mexico is remembered as the almost inevitable victory of a strong and democratic nation, with a "manifest destiny" to stretch from the Atlantic to the Pacific Ocean, over a weak and corrupt country destined to live in the other's shadow. Mexicans, however, view the war as the harvest of 350 years of European colonialism that left Mexico unable to incorporate its northern territories or defend its citizens. To Mexicans, the war permanently dismembered the nation and left northern Mexicans second-class citizens in their own lands. Their loss is seen as proof of "the tragedy of being born important." In this view, the rich soils, high-yield indigenous agriculture, vast mineral and precious metal reserves, and large native populations made Mexico a wealthy prize that the Spanish crown jealously guarded by blocking industrial development, independent commerce, and self-rule. When Mexico finally achieved independence, its government was crippled by nearly five decades of French and Spanish attempts at reconquest. Accordingly, the Battle of Buena Vista was not decided by the glory of General Taylor, the arrogance of Santa Anna, or the virtues of Anglo-American democracy. Instead, it was determined by three centuries of colonialism that had left a weak and corrupt Mexican state vulnerable to a rising power to the north.

This account was written by Ramón Alcaraz, a Mexican journalist who long warned of the dangers of war with the United States. He believed that Mexico's northern neighbor was intent on dominating his whole country and that Santa Anna should give up Texas in order to safeguard Mexico's other northern territories.

BEFORE YOU READ

1. What does this account of the Battle of Buena Vista reveal about the Mexican perspectives on the war?

2. What were the greatest hardships that the soldiers faced? Do you think those difficulties affected the outcome of the battle?

3. What do you think Alcaraz believed was Mexico's biggest weakness in the battle?

THE MARCH OF THE ARMY
FROM SAN LUIS—BATTLE OF BUENA VISTA

General Santa Anna . . . determined to seek the enemy. . . . To carry out this resolution he sent the suitable orders. In the city [of San Luis] the movement was notice at once, and the consequent agitation of the march of the army. Everything was prepared for the departure, and the troops undertook it with a strong desire to fight anew with the invaders.

The infantry and artillery had not till then left San Luis, but the cavalry were away before this time, divided in 4 brigades, squadroned as follows—One, under the orders of General Torrejon, was stationed in Bocas; another of General Juvera was in the Venado; the third, of which General Andrade was in command, having been for some time in the Cedral, advanced soon to Encarnation;

and the fourth, under General Miñon, who after having surprised in the same Encarnation a detachment of more than 100 Americans, and making them prisoners, was now posted in the hacienda of Potosi.

The movement of the army commenced on the 28th of January, the day on which all the artillery, with their trains and the materiel of war, moved out, accompanied by a battalion of sappers and company of San Patricio.[1] The division of General Pacheco followed on the 29th, denominated the 1st; the 2d, commanded by General Lombardini, on the next day, and the 3d, under the orders of General Ortega, on the 31st. The headquarters were changed from San Luis on the 2d of February.

Sad was the aspect which [San Luis] presented, contrasting them its silence and solitude with the martial, animating, and peopled liveliness of the former days. The inhabitants had received among them a large number of military characters, who had there assembled from all directions, and many of them with their families. When the army departed, all did not then abandon the city, even if some followed, accompanying the 18,000 men of whom the army was composed. The absence of these alone was sufficient to give San Luis the appearance of a city that had lost of a sudden a considerable portion of its population.

The infantry advanced in the order designated, making their days' marches as follows:—to Peñasco, Bocas, the Hedionda, the Venado, Charcas, Laguna Seca, Solis, and the Presa. The sufferings of the army began on the day they withdrew from San Luis. The division of Ortega left in the Hedionda three dead with cold, a number which, though imperceptible, so to speak, was already an indication of what they should experience from the rigor of the season. Now, too, soldiers remained after some days on the road, wearied out. But these miseries springing up did not alter the minds of the troops going to encounter the enemy. Their enthusiasm increased when meeting, first in Bocas, and soon after in the Venado, the two sections in which came the Americans, captured by General Miñon. The presence of these conquered enemies was an event of happy augury; it seemed a prediction that announced that the same fate would overtake the whole army of General Taylor.

On the 3d of February it began to blow a strong norther, which lasted all day. A light rain fell, and the cold, sufficiently rigorous, was felt. On the 4th the weather continued, the rain did not cease, the cold came to freezing, and the troops now perceived, in a very sensible manner, the ravages of the unpropitious season.

The division of Ortega passed these two days in the Venado, that of Pacheco in Solis, and Lombardini in the Laguna Seca. This hacienda, composed of a limited number of tenements, could not lodge the 5,000 soldiers who had arrived. In each they had put in so many that they could hardly move. Deprived of fire to warm their benumbed limbs, they tried to communicate heat to

---

1. The company of San Patricio, Saint Patrick, was composed of deserters from the American army. They were all Europeans, and some of them deserters from the British army in Canada, who afterwards had enlisted in the United States, and thence passing over to the enemy at Matamoros and Monterey. [note in 1850 text]

one another by the contact of their bodies, with their breath, and with friction on the parts most affected by the cold.

Fortunately on the 5th the atmosphere changed. The dull weather disappeared, and the clouds broke. The sun in its splendor shone with brightness and with power, spreading its light and heat, so much desired. All nature revived, the suffering army returned to life; sensation reanimated their strength, and gave birth to contentment and cheerfulness. But in a few hours this relief was converted into a torture of another kind. The heat became as intolerable as had been the cold on the days before. The embracing rays of this luminary suffocated the soldiers, who in vain sought a protecting shade on these plains, where they only found, at great intervals, some clusters of palm-trees, isolated and parched in the midst of a desert. Upon the road there was not water to quench their thirst, and they saw very distant the end of their journey, in which they suffered so much, not only the soldiers, but the women who followed, dead with fatigue and with their killing burdens of wood.

The afflictions of the troops decided the General-in-chief to order the divisions to rest for one day in Matehuala, continuing their march on the next. This respite was necessary to give some alleviation to the evils which they now experienced, which still were nothing in comparison to others afterwards.

The brigade of General Parrodi, composed of 1,000 men, united with the army in Matehuala, and from thence formed a part of the division of Ortega.

Nothing particular occurred until the 10th, when it began to blow a norther. The skies covered with black clouds, and intercepting the rays of the sun, announced a heavy fall of rain, which was not long in coming. The wind swept with violence in front, and the sand which it raised blinded their eyes. . . .

General Santa Anna, informed of the stop, in the Cedral, of the division of Lombardini, was highly incensed, and ordered him to proceed on to Las Animas, which he did on the subsequent day.

On the 11th, the norther completely died away, the rain followed, the water congealing in the air produced a sensation of cold the most painful. In a short time the grass was covered with a white carpet on which the foot slipped. The cold was so intense that the parts of the body uncovered were becoming affected, and paralysing the circulation of the blood. The soldiers were dying, and many breathed their last. The spectacle of these misfortunes was horrible. The unfortunate victims shed tears at seeing themselves losing that life which should have terminated more nobly in a glorious contest against a foreign enemy. . . .

The march continued on the 14th, the sick list increasing, the dead not diminishing. A mail was brought from Mexico, in which came the first notice of the revolution that was then taking place. The army received with pleasure, in the midst of the desert, the letters from their families, their friends, and every one bound to them by any ties of affection. They read them with avidity. This was the last time they should have news from many loved, before the battle they were to fight, and having in the perspective a probable death, they considered them as a tender farewell. Many, indeed, fell in action, leaving without answer these dear letters; but, if their loss was a good cause of affliction, their names, exalted by glory, will be to them a source of comfort and a soothing consolation.

The sun, concealed till twelve o'clock, appeared, bringing with it hope and happiness from the sufferings undergone in its absence. It was now necessary to pass three days in the desert, in a thick mist, in heavy showers of rain, in cold, without the means to procure heat, save the taking of that which some solar ray was worth as it beamed on the countenances of our soldiers. It was received as a friend that was desired, and as a benefactor who had deferred his favor to the most critical moment. Vivas and acclamations of joy resounded in thankfulness. It seemed as though this luminary would retrieve the empire which it swayed in Peru, before the Spanish conquest, and that the soldiers of the north, imitating the subjects of the Incas, would bend the knee to adore it as a divinity.

The provisions which previously had been placed at points on the route, began to grow scarce from the 14th. The rations, sufficiently scant before, now became more reduced, leaving almost the hunger of the troops unsatisfied. On the subsequent days the misery continued the more frightful, so that their strength naturally failed, and their suffering increased, but borne with that patience worthy of soldiers who went forth to fight for their country. . . .

The whole army was concentrated in the Encarnation where the first troops had been halted until the others came up. Being now united the General-in-chief [Santa Anna] reviewed them on horseback, and in passing the ranks he was received with enthusiastic vivas. His presence in the midst of his staff indicated that the hour of danger was near, and that he was prepared courageously to close with it. According to a statement there made, there were at that time 14,000 men of all arms. Thus before meeting the enemy, there had been a loss of 4,000 from death, sickness, stragglers, and desertion. But those who remained, felt reanimated by the proximity of the enemy. They prepared their arms for action, they shouted to their leaders, and showed how courageously they would conduct themselves in battle. . . .

Although General Santa Anna gave orders that the women who followed the troops should not pass the Encarnation, they were not obeyed. In consequence the very great number of these pushed on, forming a new army.

The night was passed in the gate of the Carnero. There were the light corps, the Husares, and the other troops in the midst of a plantation of palm trees. "In the night," relates an eye-witness, in a periodical of the capital, "the cold was intense, beyond description, and the army shivering by an instinct almost of desperation set fire to different points in the grove of palms. The flame increased its volume, and an ocean of fire suddenly sprang up with its awful waves in the midst of the heavens. . . . The spectacle was imposing and sublime. By the light the soldiers were seen half-dead with cold, looking like an army of lifeless bodies."

On the 22d the march was resumed. General Santa Anna on horseback presented himself to the troops and aroused their spirits. He proceeded to the advance guard, whose enthusiasm was at the highest pitch. Information soon was received that the Ameircans, who it was believed would defend the post of Aguanueva, had abandoned that hacienda, after having given it to the flames.

As soon as Santa Anna had become certain of this fact, he rode hastily to Aguanueva with his staff and the Husares. Having come there, he resolved at once to follow up the enemy, and ordered the cavalry to the front. They immediately obeyed, and while the divisions of the infantry halted to provide themselves with water, the cavalry passed without one man stopping to drink a drop, although all were fatigued, without food, and burning with thirst. In passing the hacienda, they turned their wistful looks to the well, which re-animated with its crystal waters, but submissive to the voice of duty, they went on together without leaving the ranks.

A little further on, they came up with the enemy on the field of battle known by the name of the Angostura. The ground which had to be passed over was formed of extensive and broad plains, in which it would not have been possible to resist the vigorous shock of our troops, especially of our beautiful cavalry. But where the enemy had halted to give battle, two successive series of hills and barrancas began, which formed a position truly formidable. Each hill was fortified with a battery, and ready to deal its murderous fire upon any attempting to take it. The position presenting serious obstacles to an attack, manifested very plainly, that for the Mexicans to gain a victory they would have to sustain a heavy loss in men.

As soon as the cavalry arrived at the Encantada, where they came in presence of the enemy, the firing of light arms commenced. The General-in-chief immediately ordered the infantry to accelerate their speed by marching in double quick time. When this was effected, notwithstanding the troops being exhausted, they were pushed forward to the Angostura, which thus made the day's tramp in all some 12 leagues. The fatigue alone killed several soldiers, who remained stretched upon the road. When the infantry came up, the brigade of General Mejía took a position to the left in the cornfields, and was supported by a corps of cavalry. The remainder of the infantry being placed upon the right, formed in two lines, with sufficient reserves and batteries. The brigades of cavalry were halted in the rear.

The General-in-chief directed Ampudia to occupy with the light corps a mountain that had remained abandoned on our right, and which as extremely important to deciding the action. These troops moved towards this position, and General Taylor at the same instant perceived the mistake he had made. In order to retrieve his error, he sent a respectable force in the same direction, in hopes to anticipate our reaching the point. The two divisions approached each other, and knowing that the occupation of the mountain would not now be an easy undertaking, and that it would belong to the victor, they opened their fire and joined in a fierce struggle. Besides the opposition of the enemy, this eminence presented in itself weighty obstacles. The ascent was almost perpendicular, and consequently to take the park along there were painful difficulties, making it necessary to adopt a thousand expedients to overcome them.

The action was prolonged with animation, and when the night had completely closed in, the result was even then doubtful. The light corps fought courageously, and the other part of the army, simple spectators of the battle, followed with their eyes the direction of the fires, anxious between doubt and hope. "As soon as it was dark," continues the account before quoted, "the scene was magnificent. A cloud of fire was seen in fact floating in the skies, which increased or diminished as the enemy gained or lost ground." At last the Americans gave way, their soldiers retreated, and ours scaled a summit as desperately defended as intrepidly won.

For the balance of the night they bivouacked in front of the enemy. It had rained: the cold was intense: and to make fires was not proper, as all lights had been prohibited in the camp. The greater portion of the army awaited the action indifferent and tranquil, as if death was not ringing in sounds about their heads. Meanwhile some officers watched, oppressed with reflections which prevail on the eve of a great battle.

The 23d commenced, and the first dawn of that ever-memorable day was saluted by martial strains from all the corps. General Santa Anna was now on his horse, giving directions. The fire of the cannon opened, the troops took their positions, and the brigade of General Mejía passed from the left to the right of the road. The battle soon after became general, and as there was no time to prepare food, the soldiers fought all day without eating.

The action began at the mountain gained in the evening, where the enemy now contended with our light corps without success. Between seven and eight in the morning General-in-chief gave the order to charge. All the troops now advanced, moving in a parallel line of battle. By the road moved forward a column under the orders of General Blanco (D. Santiago), composed of the battalions of Sappers, the mixed of Tampico, and the Fijo de Mexico; their left being supported by the regiment of Husares. To the right of this column was the division of Lombardini, forming the center, and at his side was that of Pacheco. A little further back still to the right, serving as a reserve, followed that of General Ortega. General Ampudia, with the light corps, reinforced by the 4th of the line, continued fighting with the American force at the foot of the mountain.

The line of the enemy was oblique, wherefore when our army marched in line parallel as we have said the column on the road was received a destructive fire from cannon, while the other divisions were yet distant from the Americans. However, it was not disconcerted, and the soldiers fearlessly rushed forward, closing up the gaps which the balls opened in their ranks, with musket to the shoulder, and desiring to come to the bayonet to avenge their slain comrades, sacrificed with impunity. But General Santa Anna perceiving the slaughter ordered a halt, sheltering them behind a slight undulation which shut out the enemy's fire.

In the meanwhile the divisions of Lombardini and Pacheco had debouched[2] and were at the points contested. When the action began Lombardini received an honorable wound, which caused him to retire, and the command devolved upon General Perez. The troops of General Pacheco, almost entirely raw recruits, were shaken and soon disbanded, pressed by the unerring fire which they received in the front, and moreover even another in flank which effectually threw them into disorder. The dispersion was general. In vain Pacheco, with a valor worthy of eulogy, endeavored to hold his men, who never halted until they reached the last ranks. The enemy, desirous of improving their advantage,

2. **debouched:** marched out into open ground.

hastened to complete the victory and advanced with intrepidity. But the division of General Perez calmy and steadily made a change of front to the right, and obliged them to retire. This skillful movement was seconded by a battery of 8, which Captain Ballarta had charge of, and which Santa Anna had placed under the orders of the serene General Micheltorena. The fire from these pieces occasioned a considerable loss to the Americans. Each discharge was effective from the short distance at which they fought, being only that of a small hill. The enemy who had dreamed for a moment of victory retired, routed, leaving the field covered with bodies, the brave mixed up on both sides who had fallen in this bloody conflict.

The ardor had been great with all who had here been engaged. Now our soldiers ascending the hill charged with the bayonet, now descending the barranca closed with the enemy, and again climbing up without ceasing to fight, and again turned like an avalanche from above headlong to the bottom. Thus they gained and lost ground, thus appeared the most distinguished, and thus at last they remained masters of the place achieved by such heroic efforts. The triumph would at that instant have been complete if the cavalry had been at hand to dash upon the broken remains of the conquered forces. Unfortunately this was at a distance, and when it came up, it met them already reformed. . . .

In the first to which we have referred, the Mexicans had conquered. But the advantages which the ground afforded to the enemy, required continued efforts, and not one victory, but many. . . .

At this time there came on a heavy shower of rain, and the troops, dead with fatigue, halted. Taylor having tenaciously receded from hill to hill, and losing all, after an obstinate resistance, prepared to make his final stand before yielding the palm of victory. But the battle had ceased; the charge feebly made was the last stroke of our forces. The enemy did not believe themselves routed, for so well had they lost all their positions, except one, which was sufficient still to present a hostile attitude, that they feigned the glory of having conquered. . . .

The valor of the troops has extorted praise even from the very enemy, who have only spoken ill of some generals, alleging that if all had imitated the example of the subordinates, the issue of the battle would have been decided in our favor.

General Santa Anna has not been embraced in this accusation. Friends and enemies have recognized the valor with which he constantly braved the fire. It is to be regretted his combinations did not correspond with his gallantry, that his errors dim the splendor of his merits, and that while it is painful to blame his conduct as a general, it is also pleasing to praise his courage as a soldier.

22

How the West Was Won

An Officer of the "Army of the West"

The Mexican-American War of 1846–1848 was seen by many Americans as being part of what had been called "our manifest destiny to over spread and to possess the whole of the continent" in an 1845 editorial in John L. O'Sullivan's U.S. Magazine and Democratic Review. *Yet when the Mexican and U.S. governments signed the Treaty of Guadalupe Hidalgo in February 1848, few Americans had a strong understanding of what they had won in the West.*

The Southwest remained something of a mystery to most Americans before, during, and after the war. No one was sure who the eighty thousand former Mexicans inhabiting these lands were, how they felt about becoming Americans, and whether they could ever be fully assimilated. There had always been a smattering of English-speaking Protestants in the West, but most residents there spoke Spanish, adhered in various degrees to Catholicism, and saw themselves as Mexican. Neither the Spanish-colonial government nor the newly independent Mexican government had ever successfully tamed this northern frontier or fully integrated its settlers, who received little protection from the Native Americans who raided their towns and livestock and traded stolen animals to the Anglos for guns.

Despite their different language and religion, many Mexicans in the West were clearly amenable to the possibility that American rule might have benefits. Unlike the war being waged in the heart of Mexico by generals Taylor and Scott, the war of the West was won as much by diplomacy and persuasion as it was by military valor. Nevertheless, the conquest of the West had its share of conflicts, such as the rebellion at Taos, New Mexico, and the battles of Los Angeles and Sacramento. This account is by an unnamed officer who participated in the taking of Santa Fe by the U.S. Army. The village of San Miguel, which he mentions, is about one-third of the way from Las Vegas to Santa Fe.

BEFORE YOU READ

1. If you were a Spanish-speaking inhabitant of New Mexico, which side of the war would you have supported?

2. What do you think accounted for the different reactions by Spanish-speaking villagers to the arrival of the U.S. Army?

3. What stereotypes or assumptions did this author hold regarding the Spanish-speaking inhabitants?

"Diary of an Officer of the 'Army of the West'" in "War with Mexico," *Niles' National Register*, October 10, 1846, pp. 89–91.

Thursday, August 13.—Started at 12 M., Col. Doniphan's regiment in sight as we left the camp. We soon met the spy company, (Capt. Bent,) who, with his small party, had captured four Mexicans, well mounted and armed. They summoned him and his party to surrender, but the captain told them that he thought their safest plan was to surrender to him.—They prudently consented to do so. They acknowledged themselves sent to ascertain who we were.—They were made prisoners.

One of the Mexicans who was taken day before yesterday, was disarmed and sent forward to his village, distant twenty-four miles, with letters and proclamations. He promised to meet us to-morrow. At eight miles, we came to the establishment of a Mr. Wells, an American. He had an abundance of horses, mules, and cattle. With him was another American, who had been sent from Santa Fe by an American merchant of that place, to inform Gen. Kearney that the Mexicans were 10,000 strong and had determined to meet us fifteen miles this side of Santa Fe, at a deep ravine which they were fortifying. He stated, as his opinion, that not more than 2,000 would be well armed; and also, that they had four pieces of cannon.

The Americans at Santa Fe and other towns are very much alarmed for their safety. The Mexicans tell them, that if defeated, they will return to the towns and villages and take full vengeance on them. . . .

Saturday, Aug. 15.—. . . News reached the general late last night, that we would have a fight to-day in one of the mountain gorges, and our movement has been in a strict military manner. When passing through these narrow defiles, (where an enemy would be most formidable) the word, "draw sabre," was given and passed through at a fast trot. But no enemy has been seen. The infantry passed over the mountain to take them in rear. We passed through several other villages, where the general assembled the inhabitants and proceeded as with the first [telling them that he came by order of the government of the United States to take possession of New Mexico and to extend the laws of the United States over them]. The two last appeared to be happy to be recognized as citizens of the United States, and were seen to embrace each other in token of their joy at the change of government. At the last one, they brought forward their wives to receive the congratulations of the general, (whose manner on such occasions is most happy,) and it was evident that his words had gladdened their hearts, for they smiled upon him in a manner which woman alone knows how to do. We encamped at 4 P.M., in poor grass, having marched seventeen miles.—Captain Cook met us to-day, from Santa Fe, and says Governor Armijo[1] will meet us with an army. He had been kindly treated while in Santa Fe, and smoked a "segarito" from the fair lips of the ladies.

The villages we have passed to-day are built of sun-burnt bricks. The houses have flat roofs covered with earth, and are dry, and comfortable, from the absence of rain or moisture. Each one has a church, and a grave yard with high walls of sun-burnt brick. There is more intelligence among them than I expected to find, and with a good government and protection from the Indians, they will become a happy people.

1. General Manuel Armijo was the de facto governor (top official reporting to the governor of Chihuahua) of New Mexico from January 1824 to August 1846.

The Eutaws have recently stolen their stock and carried off several children. Well may they hail this revolution as a blessing. One of the Alcaldes said to-day, that God ruled the destinies of men, and that as we had come with a strong army among them to change their form of government, it must be right, and he submitted cheerfully. Major Swords and Lieutenant Gillman brought us the mail to the 19th of July, and many a heart was made glad by tidings from wives, mothers, children, and dearly beloved ones. There are plenty of cattle, sheep, and goats in the country, and we shall fare well enough.

Sunday, August 16. Started at the usual hour, and at seven miles came to the village of St. Miguel, built like the others, of sun-burned brick, and with flat roofs. After much delay the Alcalde and Padre were found, and presented to General Kearney, but it was evident that they did not relish an interview with him. This village contains a respectable church and about two or three hundred houses. The general expressed a wish to ascend one of the houses, with the priest and Alcalde, and to address the people of the town, informing them of the object of his mission. After many evasions, delays, and useless speeches, the Padre made a speech, stating that "he was a *Mexican*, but should obey the laws that were placed over him for *the time*, but if the general should point all his cannon at his breast, he could not consent to go up there and address the people."

The general very mildly told him, through the interpreter, Mr. Robideau, that he had not come to injure him, nor did he wish him to address the people. He only wished him to go up there and hear him (the general) address them. The Padre still fought shy, and commenced a long speech which the general interrupted, and told him, he had no time to listen to "useless remarks," and repeated that he only wanted him to go up and listen to his speech. He consented. The general made pretty much the same remarks to the Alcalde and people, that he had made to the people of the other villages. He assured them that he had an ample force and would have possession of the country against all opposition, but gave them assurances of the friendship and protection of the United States. He stated to them that this had never been given them by the government of Mexico, but the United States were able and would certainly protect them, not only in their persons, property, and religion, but against the cruel invasion of the Indians. That they saw but a small part of the force that was at his disposal. Many more troops were near him on another road (some of which he showed them a mile or two distant) and that another army would, probably, be through their village in three weeks. After this, he said, "Mr. Alcalde, are you willing to take the oath of allegiance to the United States." He replied that "he would prefer waiting till the general had taken possession of the capital." The general told him, "it was sufficient for him to know that he had possession of his village." He then consented and with the usual formalities, he said, "You swear that you will bear true allegiance to the government of the United States of America." The Alcalde said, "provided I can be protected in my religion." The general said, "I swear you shall be." He then continued, "and that you will defend her against all her enemies and opposers, in the name of the Father, Son, and Holy Ghost—Amen."

The general then said, "I continue you as the Alcalde of this village, and require you, the inhabitants of this village to obey him as such. Your laws will be

continued for the present, but as soon as I have time to examine them, if any change can be made that will be for your benefit, it shall be done." After shaking hands with them he left. The Padre then invited him to his house, and gave him and his staff refreshments; and after sundry hugs, jokes, and professions of friendship, with an expression from the general, that, "the better they became acquainted the better friends they would be," and an invitation to the Padre to visit him at Santa Fe (which he promised), we left the village. The Padre was evidently the ruling spirit of the village, and the Alcalde was under great restraint by his presence. The visit to the priest, and the frank and friendly manner of the general had the desired effect, and I believe they parted the best of friends, and have no doubt that the inhabitants of St. Miguel will soon be as good democrats as can be found in Missouri.

The Alcalde informed the general that 400 men left the village to join the Mexican army, but that two hundred had returned home.

Soon after leaving this village an express arrived from Santa Fe, informing the general that a large force would oppose his march 15 miles from that place, in a deep ravine. It was headed by an individual known as Salazar. That Gen. Armijo refused to command them, and said he would defend the town. The same information was soon after brought by Puebla Indians, who said there was a large force of their people among the Mexicans, armed with bows and arrows; that their people had been forced into the service, and their chiefs would not permit them to take their guns.

As it is not more than two days march to Santa Fe, if we have to fight it will probably be to-morrow.—Marched 17 miles.

Monday, Aug. 17.—Started at the usual time. Our picket guard took a prisoner, the son of the noted Salazar, well remembered by the Texan prisoners for his cruelties to them. He stated that the Mexican army had left the cannon and gone home. The general told him he would keep him a prisoner, and if he found that he had told him falsely, he would hang him. We soon met others from Santa Fe, who congratulated the general on his arrival in the country, and their deliverance from the tyrannical rule of Armijo.

They further said, that Armijo had taken one hundred dragoons and his cannon, and gone this morning towards Chihuahua. We passed to-day the ruins of the ancient town of Pecos. I visited it with some Mexicans, and an interpreter, who gave me a full account of it. It was said to have been built long before the conquest. It stands on an eminence. The dwellings were built of small stones and mud; some of the buildings are still so far perfect as to show three full stories. There were four rooms under ground, fifteen feet deep and twenty-five feet across in a circular form. In one of these rooms, burned the "holy fire," which was kindled many centuries before the conquest; and when the Pecos Indians were converted to the Catholic faith they still continued their own religious rites, and among them the "sacred fire," which never ceased to burn till seven years since, when the village was broken up. The population is probably one thousand. The church is large, and although in ruins, was evidently a fine building. It was built after the conquest. The eastern roof of the main building is still good—it is filled with birds. As we came in front of it the Mexicans took off their hats, and on entering the building we did the same.

The general learned to-day that Salazar had been in command at the cannon, and that he had passed around us and gone to St. Miguel, the town we passed yesterday. The general sent him word that he had his son a prisoner, and would treat him well, if the father remained peaceable, but if he took up arms, or excited the people to resistance, he would hang him.

We encamped at 3 P.M., on the Pecos creek, in excellent grass, where there was a beautiful farm well watered—distance to-day fifteen and three quarter miles.

An abundance of vegetables have been brought into camp this evening, and we have fared better than since we left Missouri. Bread, coffee, and bacon are excellent articles of food, when accompanied with other little "fixings" which ladies can only provide us with, but of themselves, after a few weeks, campaigners become a little tired.

An American gentleman has just arrived in camp from Santa Fe; he left at 12 M. to-day, and says that after the governor's abdication, the Alcaldes held a meeting, and *gravely* discussed the propriety of tearing down the churches to prevent their being converted into barracks, and that the American citizens interfered and assured them that they had nothing to fear on that subject; and thereby saved the churches. A lady also sent for him this morning, and asked him if he did not think it advisable for her to leave the town, with her daughters, to save them from dishonor. He advised her by all means to remain at home, and assured her that she and her daughters were in no danger from the approach of the army.

Most of the respectable people of the town have left, and many country people are going to town for protection.

Tuesday, August 18.—Started as usual and at six miles came to the cannon, where the Mexican army under Armijo had been assembled. There had been 3,000 troops there, but it seems that the nearer we approach them, the fewer they became, and when we passed through they had all gone. The position they chose was near the lower end, and it was one of great strength. The passage was not more than forty feet wide—in front they had made an obstruction with timber, and beyond this, at 300 yards distance, was an eminence in the road, on which their cannon had been placed; and it was thought by us, that their position was equal to 5,000 men. We reached the hill which overlooks Santa Fe at 5 P.M. Major Clark's artillery was put into line, and the mounted troops and infantry were marched through the town to the Palace (as it is called) on the public square, whether [*sic,* where] the general and his staff dismounted, and were received by the acting governor and other dignitaries and conducted to a large room.

FOR CRITICAL THINKING

1. Was the Mexican-American War a just war?

2. Why did Santa Anna fail to win the war even though his troops far outnumbered those of the Americans? Are the reasons given in the accounts adequate to explain what happened?

3. What do these documents suggest about the relationship between English-speaking and Spanish-speaking people of the region?

Crossing the Great Divide

Meriwether Lewis and William Clark

The most famous expedition in American history was the brainchild of Thomas Jefferson. For years Jefferson had dreamed that a party of explorers could search out a passage to the Pacific, win the allegiance of the Indians to the new Republic, and study the geography, plants, and minerals of a vast and unknown territory.

Meriwether Lewis (1774–1809) and William Clark (1770–1838) were two young men willing to follow Jefferson's dream. Their expedition from St. Louis to the mouth of the Columbia River and back is one of the great adventure stories of our history. The journals and notebooks that members of the party kept have been invaluable to historians, geographers, anthropologists, botanists, and zoologists.

The selections here present the expedition crossing the Great Divide—the peak of the Rocky Mountains where the rivers flow either to the east or the west—in one of the most difficult parts of their journey. The reader can see their careful search for information about the best route west and their close observation of Native American ways. Here also is the most famous single dramatic episode of the expedition: the extraordinary moment when Sacajawea, wife of one of their interpreters, meets a party of Shoshone, her native nation, headed by a chief who is the brother she has not seen since she was a small child. The first excerpt was written by Nicholas Biddle, who was not on the expedition. Biddle's descriptions are taken from the notes of various participants in the journey. They have sometimes been published—incorrectly—as part of the actual journals of Lewis and Clark.

BEFORE YOU READ

1. How did Lewis characterize the Indians and Indian life? What about them did he find fascinating, hard to understand, or admirable?
2. What did he offer Chief Cameahwait in return for his help and horses?
3. Why was crossing the Rocky Mountains so difficult?

NICHOLAS BIDDLE

Saturday, August 17th 1805.

Captain Lewis rose very early and despatched Drewyer and the Indian down the river in quest of the boats. Sheilds was sent out at the same time to hunt, while

Bernard DeVoto, *The Journals of Lewis and Clark* (Boston: Houghton Mifflin Co., 1953), pp. 202–6, 207–11, 213–14.

M'Neal prepared a breakfast out of the remainder of the meat. Drewyer had been gone about two hours, and the Indians were all anxiously waiting for some news, when an Indian who had straggled a short distance down the river, returned with a report that he had seen the white men, who were only a short distance below, and were coming on. The Indians were all transported with joy, and the chief in the warmth of his satisfaction renewed his embrace to Capt. Lewis. . . .

On setting out at seven o'clock, Captain Clarke with Chaboneau and his wife walked on shore, but they had not gone more than a mile before Clarke saw Sacajawea, who was with her husband 100 yards ahead, began to dance and show every mark of the most extravagant joy, turning round him and pointing to several Indians, whom he now saw advancing on horseback, sucking her fingers at the same time to indicate that they were of her native tribe. As they advanced, Captain Clarke discovered among them Drewyer dressed like an Indian, from whom he learnt the situation of the party. While the boats were performing the circuit, he went towards the forks with the Indians, who as they went along, sang aloud with the greatest appearance of delight.

We soon drew near to the camp, and just as we approached it a woman made her way through the crowd towards Sacajawea, and recognising each other, they embraced with the most tender affection. The meeting of these two young women had in it something peculiarly touching, not only in the ardent manner in which their feelings were expressed, but from the real interest of their situation. They had been companions in childhood, in the war with the Minetarees they had both been taken prisoners in the same battle, they had shared and softened the rigours of their captivity, till one of them had escaped from the Minetarees, with scarce a hope of ever seeing her friend relieved from the hands of her enemies. While Sacajawea was renewing among the women the friendships of former days, Captain Clarke went on, and was received by Captain Lewis and the chief, who after the first embraces and salutations were over, conducted him to a sort of circular tent or shade of willows. Here he was seated on a white robe; and the chief immediately tied in his hair six small shells resembling pearls, an ornament highly valued by these people, who procure them in the course of trade from the sea-coast. The moccasins of the whole party were then taken off, and after much ceremony the smoking began. After this the conference was to be opened, and glad of an opportunity of being able to converse more intelligibly, Sacajawea was sent for; she came into the tent, sat down, and was beginning to interpret, when in the person of Cameahwait she recognised her brother: She instantly jumped up, and ran and embraced him, throwing over him her blanket and weeping profusely: The chief was himself moved, though not in the same degree. After some conversation between them she resumed her seat, and attempted to interpret for us, but her new situation seemed to overpower her, and she was frequently interrupted by her tears. After the council was finished the unfortunate woman learnt that all her family were dead except two brothers, one of whom was absent, and a son of her eldest sister, a small boy, who was immediately adopted by her.

MERIWETHER LEWIS

Saturday August 17th 1805.

we made them [the Indians] sensible of their dependance on the will of our government for every species of merchandize as well for their defence & comfort; and apprized them of the strength of our government and it's friendly dispositions towards them. we also gave them as a reason why we wished to pe[ne]trate the country as far as the ocean to the west of them was to examine and find out a more direct way to bring merchandize to them. that as no trade could by carryed on with them before our return to our homes that it was mutually advantageous to them as well as to ourselves that they should render us such aids as they had in their power to furnish in order to haisten our voyage and of course our return home. that such were their horses to transport our baggage without which we could not subsist, and that a pilot to conduct us through the mountains was also necessary if we could not decend the river by water. but that we did not ask either their horses or their services without giving a satisfactory compensation in return. that at present we wished them to collect as many horses as were necessary to transport our baggage to their village on the Columbia where we would then trade with them at our leasure for such horses as they could spare us.

the chief thanked us for friendship towards himself and nation & declared his wish to serve us in every rispect. that he was sorry to find that it must yet be some time before they could be furnished with firearms but said they could live as they had done heretofore until we brought them as we had promised. he said they had not horses enough with them at present to remove our baggage to their village over the mountain, but that he would return tomorrow and encourage his people to come over with their horses and that he would bring his own and assist us. this was complying with all we wished at present.

we next enquired who were chiefs among them. Cameahwait pointed out two others whom he said were Chiefs. we gave him a medal of the small size with the likeness of Mr. Jefferson the President of the U' States in releif on one side and clasp hands with a pipe and tomahawk in the other, to the other Chiefs we gave each a small medal which were struck in the Presidency of George Washing[ton] Esqr. we also gave small medals of the last discription two young men whom the 1st Chief informed us were good young men and much rispected among them. we gave the 1st Chief an uniform coat shirt a pair of scarlet legings a carrot of tobacco and some small articles to each of the others we gave a shi[r]t leging[s] handkerchief a knife some tobacco and a few small articles we also distributed a good quantity paint mockerson awles knives beads looking-glasses &c among the other Indians and gave them a plentifull meal of lyed corn which was the first they had ever eaten in their lives. they were much pleased with it. every article about us appeared to excite astonishment in there minds; the appearance of the men, their arms, the canoes, our manner of working them, the b[l]ack man york and the sagacity of my dog were equally objects of admiration. I also shot my air-gun which was so perfectly incomprehensible that they immediately denominated it the great medicine.

Capt. Clark and myself now concerted measures for our future operations, and it was mutually agreed that he should set out tomorrow morning with eleven men furnished with axes and other necessary tools for making canoes, their arms accoutrements and as much of their baggage as they could carry. also to take the indians, C[h]arbono and the indian woman with him; that on his arrival at the Shoshone camp he was to leave Charbono and the Indian woman to haisten the return of the Indians with their horses to this place, and to proceede himself with the eleven men down the Columbia in order to examine the river and if he found it navigable and could obtain timber to set about making canoes immediately. In the mean time I was to bring the party and baggage to the Shoshone Camp, calculating that by the time I should reach that place that he would have sufficiently informed himself with rispect to the state of the river &c. as to determine us whether to prosicute our journey from thence by land or water. in the former case we should want all the horses which we could perchase, and in the latter only to hire the Indians to transport our baggage to the place at which we made the canoes.

Sunday August 18th 1805.

This morning while Capt. Clark was busily engaged in preparing for his rout, I exposed some articles to barter with the Indians for horses as I wished a few at this moment to releive the men who were going with Capt Clark from the labour of carrying their baggage, and also one to keep here in order to pack the meat to camp which the hunters might kill. I soon obtained three very good horses. for which I gave an uniform coat, a pair of legings, a few handkerchiefs, three knives and some other small articles the whole of which did not cost more than about 20$ in the U' States. the Indians seemed quite as well pleased with their bargin as I was. the men also purchased one for an old checked shirt a pair of old legings and a knife. two of those I purchased Capt. C. took on with him. at 10 A.M. Capt. Clark departed with his detachment and all the Indians except 2 men and 2 women who remained with us.

after there departure this morning I had all the stores and baggage of every discription opened and aired. and began the operation of forming the packages in proper parsels for the purpose of transporting them on horseback. the rain in the evening compelled me to desist from my operations. I had the raw hides put in the water in order to cut them in throngs proper for lashing the packages and forming the necessary geer for pack horses, a business which I fortunately had not to learn on this occasion. I had the net arranged and set this evening to catch some trout which we could see in great abundance at the bottom of the river.

Monday August 19th 1805.

The Shoshonees may be estimated at about 100 warriors, and about three times that number of women and children[1] they have more children among them than I expected to have seen among a people who procure subsistence with such difficulty. there are but few very old persons, nor did they appear to treat those

1. Lewis's figures refer to this band only.

with much tenderness or rispect. The man is the sole propryetor of his wives and daughters, and can barter or dispose of either as he thinks proper. a plurality of wives is common among them, but these are not generally sisters as with the Minnitares & Mandans but are purchased of different fathers. The father frequently disposes of his infant daughters in marriage to men who are grown or to men who have sons for whom they think proper to provide wives. the compensation given in such cases usually consists of horses or mules which the father receives at the time of contract and converts to his own uce. the girl remains with her parents untill she is conceived to have obtained the age of puberty which with them is considered to be about the age of 13 or 14 years. the female at this age is surrendered to her soveriegn lord and husband agreeably to contract, and with her is frequently restored by the father quite as much as he received in the first instance in payment for his daughter; but this is discretionary with the father. Sah-car-gar-we-ah had been thus disposed of before she was taken by the Minnetares, or had arrived to the years of puberty. the husband was yet living with this band. he was more than double her age and had two other wives. he claimed her as his wife but said that as she had had a child by another man, who was Charbono, that he did not want her.

They seldom correct their children particularly the boys who soon become masters of their own acts. they give as a reason that it cows and breaks the sperit of the boy to whip him, and that he never recovers his independence of mind after he is grown. They treat their women but with little rispect, and compel them to perform every species of drudgery. they collect the wild fruits and roots, attend to the horses or assist in that duty, cook, dress the skins and make all their apparel, collect wood and make their fires, arrange and form their lodges, and when they travel pack the horses and take charge of all the baggage; in short the man dose little else except attend his horses hunt and fish. the man considers himself degraded if he is compelled to walk any distance; and if he is so unfortunately poor as only to possess two horses he rides the best himself and leavs the woman or women if he has more than one, to transport their baggage and children on the other, and to walk if the horse is unable to carry the additional weight of their persons. the chastity of their women is not held in high estimation, and the husband will for a trifle barter the companion of his bead for a night or longer if he conceives the reward adiquate; tho' they are not so importunate that we should caress their women as the siouxs were. and some of their women appear to be held more sacred than in any nation we have seen. I have requested the men to give them no cause of jealousy by having connection with their women without their knowledge, which with them, strange as it may seem is considered as disgracefull to the husband as clandestine connections of a similar kind are among civilized nations. to prevent this mutual exchange of good officies altogether I know it impossible to effect, particularly on the part of our young men whom some months abstanence have made very polite to those tawney damsels. no evil has yet resulted and I hope will not from these connections.

notwithstanding the late loss of horses which this people sustained by the Minnetares the stock of the band may be very safely estimated at seven hundred of which they are perhaps about 40 coalts and half that number of mules. their arms offensive and defensive consist in the bow and arrows shield, some lances, and a weapon called by the Cippeways who formerly used it, the pog-gar'-mag-gon' [war club]. in fishing they employ wairs, gigs, and fishing hooks. the salmon is the principal object of their pursuit. they snair wolves and foxes.

I was anxious to learn whether these people had the venerial, and made the enquiry through the interpreter and his wife; the information was that they sometimes had it but I could not learn their remedy; they most usually die with it's effects. this seems a strong proof that these disorders bothe ganaraehah and Louis Venerae[2] are native disorders of America. tho' these people have suffered much by the small pox which is known to be imported and perhaps those other disorders might have been contracted from other indian tribes who by a round of communications might have obtained from the Europeans since it was introduced into that quarter of the globe. but so much detached on the other ha[n]d from all communication with the whites that I think it most probable that those disorders are original with them.

from the middle of May to the first of September these people reside on the waters of the Columbia where they consider themselves in perfect security from their enimies as they have not as yet ever found their way to this retreat; during this season the salmon furnish the principal part of their subsistence and as this fish either perishes or returns about the 1st of September they are compelled at this season in surch of subsistence to resort to the Missouri, in the vallies of which, there is more game even [than] within the mountains. here they move slowly down the river in order to collect and join other bands either of their own nation or the Flatheads, and having become sufficiently strong as they conceive venture on the Eastern side of the Rocky mountains into the plains, where the buffaloe abound. but they never leave the interior of the mountains while they can obtain a scanty subsistence, and always return as soon as they have acquired a good stock of dryed meat in the plains; when this stock is consumed they venture again into the plains; thus alternately obtaining their food at the risk of their lives and retiring to the mountains, while they consume it. These people are now on the eve of their departure for the Missouri, and inform us that they expect to be joined at or about the three forks by several bands of their own nation, and a band of the Flatheads.

Tuesday August 20th 1805.

I walked down the river about 3/4 of a mile and selected a place near the river bank unperceived by the Indians for a cash [cache], which I set three men to make, and directed the centinel to discharge his gun if he perceived any of the Indians going down in that direction which was to be the signal for the men at work on the cash to desist and seperate, least these people should discover our deposit and rob us of the baggage we intend leaving here. by evening the cash was completed unperceived by the Indians, and all our packages made up. the Pack-saddles and harness is not yet complete. in this operation we find ourselves at a loss for nails and boards; for the first we substitute throngs of raw hide which answer verry well, and for the last [had] to cut off the blades of our

---

2. **ganaraehah and Louis Venerae:** gonorrhea and syphilis.

oars and use the plank of some boxes which have heretofore held other articles and put those articles into sacks of raw hide which I have had made for the purpose. by this means I have obtained as many boards as will make 20 saddles which I suppose will be sufficient for our present exegencies. I made up a small assortment of medicines, together with the specemines of plants, minerals, seeds &c, which, I have collected between this place and the falls of the Missouri which I shall deposit here.

I now prevailed on the Chief to instruct me with rispect to the geography of his country. this he undertook very cheerfully, by delineating the rivers on the ground. but I soon found that his information fell far short of my expectation or wishes. he drew the river on which we now are [the Lemhi] to which he placed two branches just above us, which he shewed me from the openings of the mountains were in view; he next made it discharge itself into a large river which flowed from the S.W. about ten miles below us [the Salmon], then continued this joint stream in the same direction of this valley or N.W. for one days march and then enclined it to the West for 2 more days march. here we placed a number of heaps of sand on each side which he informed me represented the vast mountains of rock eternally covered with snow through which the river passed. that the perpendicular and even juting rocks so closely hemned in the river that there was no possibil[it]y of passing along the shore; that the bed of the river was obstructed by sharp pointed rocks and the rapidity of the stream such that the whole surface of the river was beat into perfect foam as far as the eye could reach. that the mountains were also inaccessible to man or horse. he said that this being the state of the country in that direction that himself nor none of his nation had ever been further down the river than these mountains.

in this manner I spend the day smoking with them and acquiring what information I could with respect to their country. they informed me that they could pass to the Spaniards by the way of the yellowstone river in 10 days. I can discover that these people are by no means friendly to the Spaniards. their complaint is, that the Spaniards will not let them have fire arms and ammunition, that they put them off by telling them that if they suffer them to have guns they will kill each other, thus leaving them defenceless and an easy prey to their bloodthirsty neighbours to the East of them, who being in possession of fire arms hunt them up and murder them without rispect to sex or age and plunder them of their horses on all occasions. they told me that to avoid their enemies who were eternally harrassing them that they were obliged to remain in the interior of these mountains at least two thirds of the year where the[y] suffered as we then saw great heardships for the want of food sometimes living for weeks without meat and only a little fish roots and berries. but this added Câmeahwait, with his ferce eyes and lank jaws grown meager for the want of food, would not be the case if we had guns, we could then live in the country of buffaloe and eat as our enimies do and not be compelled to hide ourselves in these mountains and live on roots and berries as the bear do. we do not fear our enimies when placed on an equal footing with them. I told them that the Minnetares Mandans . . . had promised us to desist from making war on them & that we would indevour to find the means of making the Minnetares of fort d[e] Prarie or as they call them Pahkees desist from waging war against them also. that after our finally returning to our homes towards the rising sun white-men would come to them with an abundance of guns and every other article necessary to their defence and comfort, and that they would be enabled to sup-ply themselves with these articles on reasonable terms in exchange for the skins of the beaver Otter and Ermin so abundant in their country. they expressed great pleasure at this information and said they had been long anxious to see the whitemen that traded guns; and that we might rest assured of their friendship and that they would do whatever we wished them.

24

The Great Revival of 1800

James B. Finley and Peter Cartwright

Evangelicalism, the highly emotional proselytizing religion so characteristic of American Protestantism, began in the 1730s and 1740s with the visits to the colonies of the English preacher, George Whitefield. The meetings Whitefield held triggered what became known as the Great Awakening. Thousands responded to the dynamic preaching of Whitefield and the ministers he inspired with dramatic experiences of religious conversion. The Revolutionary War and the rise of the Enlightenment greatly weakened enthusiastic religion, but at the turn of the nineteenth century revivalism once again burst forth, giving rise to a religious movement still vibrant in America today. To the surprise of religious leaders, who had worried about the religious state of the rude, unchurched Western frontier, the new inspiration came from the settlements that were farthest west — in Kentucky.

Ministers in Kentucky's Presbyterian and Methodist churches revolted against the "formality and deadness" of their churches and, encouraging direct displays of religious fervor, provoked emotional scenes in which, according to one observer, the floors of churches were "covered with the slain; their screams for mercy pierced the heavens." Word spread, and people traveled from considerable distances to gather at these services. With churches too small to hold them and distant travelers not wishing to return home after only a few hours of worship, services were held out of doors, and many camped out for several days. In this way the camp meeting was born. In 1801, a meeting was announced for August 6 at Cane Ridge, Kentucky. Word flew about the hollows and cabins, and a crowd estimated at over twenty thousand people (nearly ten percent of the state's population) gathered for the largest religious service ever experienced up to that time in the United States.

Western evangelists traveled endlessly across sparsely settled territory preaching their highly emotional and individualistic religion during the first decades of the nineteenth century. Their creeds emphasized the importance of personal morality, civic virtue, and education. Their contribution to the characteristic culture of the American Middle West soon provided a model for much of American life. In these readings you will see the great revivals through the eyes of James B. Finley (1781–1856), one of the preachers who conducted the early revivals, as well as share the experience of Peter Cartwright (1785–1872), whose conversion during one of these revivals led to a life spent as an itinerant preacher for the Methodist Church, riding across vast circuits of congregations in Kentucky, Indiana, Ohio, and Illinois.

Rev. James B. Finley, *Autobiography or, Pioneer Life in the West*, ed. W. P. Strickland (Cincinnati: Methodist Book Concern, 1853), pp. 362–69; Peter Cartwright, *Autobiography of Peter Cartwright, the Backwoods Preacher*, ed. W. P. Strickland (New York: Carlton & Porter, 1857), pp. 34–38.

BEFORE YOU READ

1. Why is James B. Finley writing this account of the revivals? Who is his audience, and what is he attempting to persuade them to do?

2. How do you explain the various physical states accompanying conversion, such as people going into trances or experiencing the jerks? How does Finley analyze and explain them?

3. What spurred Peter Cartwright's conversion?

JAMES B. FINLEY

Great Revival in the West

In the spring of 1800 one of the most astonishing and powerful revivals occurred that has ever been known in the western country. This was also the most extensive revival that perhaps ever was witnessed in this country. It was marked by some peculiarities which had not been known to characterize any revival in former times. The nearest approximation to it, of which I can form any conception, was the revival on the day of pentecost, when thousands were awakened and converted to God under the most exciting circumstances.

The commencement of the revival is traceable to the joint labors of two brothers in Cumberland county, Kentucky, one of whom was a Presbyterian and the other a Methodist preacher. They commenced laboring together, every Sabbath preaching, exhorting, and praying alternately. This union was regarded as quite singular, and excited the curiosity of vast multitudes, who came to the places of meeting to hear two men preach who held views in theology supposed to be entirely antagonistic. Nothing was discoverable in their preaching of a doctrinal character, except the doctrine of man's total depravity and ruin by sin, and his recovery therefrom by faith in Christ. All were exhorted to flee the wrath to come, and be saved from their sins. The word which they preached was attended with the power of God to the hearts of listening thousands. The multitudes who flocked from all parts of the country to hear them, became so vast that no church would hold them, and they were obliged to resort to the fields and woods. Every vehicle was put in requisition; carriages, wagons, carts and sleds. Many came on horseback, and larger crowds still came on foot.

As the excitement increased, and the work of conviction and conversion continued, several brought tents, which they pitched on the ground, and remained day and night for many days. The reader will here find the origin of camp meetings.

In the spring of 1801 Bishop M'Kendree was appointed presiding elder of the Kentucky district; and being thus brought in contact with this wonderful work, he was prepared to form a correct judgment of its character. That there were extravagances that constituted no part of religion, he was prepared to admit, but that it was all a wild, fanatical delusion, he was very far from conceding. Nay, he believed that it was the work of God's Spirit on the hearts of the people, and that thousands were genuinely converted to God.

These meetings began to follow one another in quick succession, and the numbers which attended were almost incredible. While the meetings lasted, crowds were to be seen in all directions, passing and repassing the roads and paths, while the woods seemed to be alive with people. Whole settlements appeared to be vacated, and only here and there could be found a house having an inhabitant. All ages, sexes, and conditions, pressed their way to the camp meeting. At these meetings the Presbyterians and Methodists united. They were held at different places. On the 22d of May, 1801, one was held at Cabin creek; the next was held at Concord, in one of my father's old congregations; the next was at Point Pleasant, and the succeeding one at Indian creek, in Harrison county. At these meetings thousands fell under the power of God, and cried for mercy. The scenes which successively occurred at these meetings were awfully sublime, and a general terror seemed to have pervaded the minds of all people within the reach of their influences.

The great general camp meeting was held at Cane Ridge meeting-house. This house was built for my father, and here was my old home. I have elsewhere described this meeting, or, rather, attempted to do so. Language is utterly impuissant to convey any thing like an adequate idea of the sublimity and grandeur of the scene. Twenty thousand persons tossed to and fro, like the tumultuous waves of the sea in a storm, or swept down like the trees of the forest under the blast of the wild tornado, was a sight which mine own eyes witnessed, but which neither my pen nor tongue can describe.

During the religious exercises within the encampment, all manner of wickedness was going on without. So deep and awful is man's depravity, that he will sport while the very fires of perdition are kindling around him. Men, furious with the effects of the maddening bowl, would outrage all decency by their conduct; and some, mounted on horses, would ride at full speed among the people. I saw one, who seemed to be a leader and champion of the party, on a large, white horse, ride furiously into the praying circle, uttering the most horrid imprecations. Suddenly, as if smitten by lightning, he fell from his horse. At this a shout went up from the religious multitude, as if Lucifer himself had fallen. I trembled, for I feared God had killed the bold and daring blasphemer. He exhibited no signs whatever of life; his limbs were rigid, his wrists pulseless, and his breath gone. Several of his comrades came to see him, but they did not gaze long till the power of God came upon them, and they fell like men slain in battle. I was much alarmed, but I had a great desire to see the issue. I watched him closely, while for thirty hours he lay, to all human appearance, dead. During this time the people kept up singing and praying. At last he exhibited signs of life, but they were fearful spasms, which seemed as if he were in a convulsive fit, attended by frightful groans, as if he were passing through the intensest agony. It was not long, however, till his convulsions ceased, and springing to his feet, his groans were converted into loud and joyous shouts of praise. The dark, fiend-like scowl which overspread his features, gave way to a happy smile, which lighted up his countenance.

A certain Dr. P., accompanied by a lady from Lexington, was induced, out of mere curiosity, to attend the meeting. As they had heard much about the involuntary jerkings and falling which attended the exercises, they entered into an agreement between themselves that, should either of them be thus strangely attacked or fall, the other was to stand by to the last. It was not long till the lady was brought down in all her pride, a poor sinner in the dust, before her God. The Doctor, agitated, came up and felt for her pulse; but, alas! her pulse was gone. At this he turned pale, and, staggering a few paces, he fell beneath the power of the same invisible hand. After remaining for some time in this state, they both obtained pardon and peace and went rejoicing home. They both lived and died happy Christians. Thousands were affected in the same way.

These camp meetings continued for some time, the Presbyterians and Methodists uniting together as one in the army of the Lord. Some ministers had serious doubts concerning the character of the work; but its genuineness was demonstrated by the fruits. Men of the most depraved hearts and vicious habits were made new creatures, and a whole life of virtue subsequently confirmed the conversion. To all but Methodists the work was entirely strange. Some of the peculiarities had been witnessed before by the preachers, and they were enabled to carry it on.

These meetings exhibited nothing to the spectator unacquainted with them but a scene of confusion, such as scarcely could be put into human language. They were generally opened with a sermon or exhortation, at the close of which there would be a universal cry for mercy, some bursting forth in loud ejaculations of prayer or thanksgiving for the truth; some breaking forth in strong and powerful exhortations, others flying to their careless friends with tears of compassion, entreating them to fly to Christ for mercy; some, struck with terror and conviction, hastening through the crowd to escape, or pulling away from their relations, others trembling, weeping, crying for mercy; some falling and swooning away, till every appearance of life was gone and the extremities of the body assumed the coldness of death. These were surrounded with a company of the pious, singing melodious songs adapted to the time, and praying for their conversion. But there were others collected in circles round this variegated scene, contending for and against the work.

Many circumstances transpired that are worthy of note in reference to this work. Children were often made the instruments through which the Lord wrought. At one of these powerful displays of Divine power, a boy about ten years old broke from the stand in time of preaching under very strong impressions, and having mounted a log at some distance, and raising his voice in a most affecting manner, cried out, "On the last day of the feast Jesus stood and cried, If any man thirst, let him come unto me and drink." He attracted the main body of the congregation, and, with streaming eyes, he warned the sinners of their danger, denouncing their doom, if they persevered in sin, and strongly expressed his love for the salvation of their souls, and the desire that they would turn to God and live. By this time the press was so great that he was taken up by two men and held above the crowd. He spoke for near an hour with that convincing eloquence that could be inspired only from heaven; and when exhausted, and language failed to describe the feelings of his soul, he raised his handkerchief, and dropping it, cried, "Thus, O sinner, will you drop into hell unless you forsake your sins and turn to God." At this moment the power of God fell upon the assembly, and sinners fell as men slain in mighty battle, and the cries for mercy seemed as though they would rend the heavens, and the work spread in a manner which human language can not describe.

We will now try to give something in reference to the manner and the exercise of mind of those who were the subjects of this work. Immediately before they became totally powerless, they were sometimes seized with a general tremor, and often uttered several piercing shrieks in the moment of falling. Men and women never fell when under this jerking exercise till they became exhausted. Some were unable to stand, and yet had the use of their hands and could converse with companions. Others were unable to speak. The pulse became weak, and they drew a difficult breath about once a minute. In many instances they became cold. Breathing, pulsation, and all signs of life forsook them for hours; yet I never heard of one who died in this condition, and I have conversed with persons who have laid in this situation for many hours, and they have uniformly testified that they had no bodily pain, and that they had the entire use of their reason and powers of mind. From this it appears that their falling was neither common fainting nor a nervous affection. Indeed, this strange work appears to have taken every possible turn to baffle the conjectures and philosophizing of those who were unwilling to acknowledge it was the work of God. Persons have fallen on their way home from meeting, some after they had arrived at home, others pursuing their common business on their farms, and others when they were attending to family or secret devotions. Numbers of thoughtless, careless sinners have fallen as suddenly as if struck by lightning. Professed infidels, and other vicious characters, have been arrested, and sometimes at the very moment when they were uttering their blasphemies against God and the work, and have, like Saul, declared that to be God's work which they so vehemently persecuted.

I trust I have said enough on this subject to enable my readers to judge how far the charge of enthusiasm and delusion is applicable to this work, unequaled for power and for the entire change of the hearts and lives of so many thousands of men and women. Lord Lyttleton, in his letter on the conversion of St. Paul, observes, and I think justly, that enthusiasm is a vain, self-righteous spirit, swelled with self-sufficiency and disposed to glory in its religious attainments. If this be a good definition, there was as little enthusiasm in this work as any other. Never were there more genuine marks of that humility which disclaims the merits of its own works, and looks to the Lord Jesus Christ as the only way of acceptance with God. Christ was all and in all in their exercises and religion, and their Gospel, and all believers in their highest attainments seemed most sensible of their entire dependence upon Divine grace; and it was truly affecting to hear with what anxiety awakened sinners inquired for Christ as the only Physician who could give them help. Those who call this enthusiasm ought to tell us what they understand by the spirit of Christianity. Upon the whole, this revival in the west was the most extraordinary that ever visited the Church of Christ, and was peculiarly adapted to the circumstances of the country. Infidelity was triumphant, and religion at the point of expiring. Something of an extraordinary nature was necessary to arrest the attention of a wicked and skeptical people, who were ready to conclude that Christianity was a fable and futurity a dream. This great work of God did do it. It confounded infidelity and vice into silence, and brought numbers beyond calculation under the influence of experimental religion and practical piety.

PETER CARTWRIGHT

Chapter IV. Conversion

In 1801, when I was in my sixteenth year, my father, my eldest half brother, and myself, attended a wedding about five miles from home, where there was a great deal of drinking and dancing, which was very common at marriages in those days. I drank little or nothing; my delight was in dancing. After a late hour in the night, we mounted our horses and started for home. I was riding my race-horse.

A few minutes after we had put up the horses, and were sitting by the fire, I began to reflect on the manner in which I had spent the day and evening. I felt guilty and condemned. I rose and walked the floor. My mother was in bed. It seemed to me, all of a sudden, my blood rushed to my head, my heart palpitated, in a few minutes I turned blind; an awful impression rested on my mind that death had come and I was unprepared to die. I fell on my knees and began to ask God to have mercy on me.

My mother sprang from her bed, and was soon on her knees by my side, praying for me, and exhorting me to look to Christ for mercy, and then and there I promised the Lord that if he would spare me, I would seek and serve him; and I never fully broke that promise. My mother prayed for me a long time. At length we lay down, but there was little sleep for me. Next morning I rose, feeling wretched beyond expression. I tried to read in the Testament, and retired many times to secret prayer through the day, but found no relief. I gave up my race-horse to my father, and requested him to sell him. I went and brought my pack of cards, and gave them to mother, who threw them into the fire, and they were consumed. I fasted, watched, and prayed, and engaged in regular reading of the Testament. I was so distressed and miserable, that I was incapable of any regular business.

My father was greatly distressed on my account, thinking I must die, and he would lose his only son. He bade me retire altogether from business, and take care of myself. . . .

In the spring of this year, Mr. M'Grady, a minister of the Presbyterian Church, who had a congregation and meeting-house, as we then called them, about three miles north of my father's house, appointed a sacramental meeting in this congregation, and invited the Methodist preachers to attend with them, and especially John Page, who was a powerful Gospel minister, and was very popular among the Presbyterians. Accordingly he came, and preached with great power and success.

There were no camp-meetings in regular form at this time, but as there was a great waking up among the Churches, from the revival that had broken out at Cane Ridge, before mentioned, many flocked to those sacramental meetings.

The church would not hold the tenth part of the congregation. Accordingly, the officers of the Church erected a stand in a contiguous shady grove, and prepared seats for a large congregation.

The people crowded to this meeting from far and near. They came in their large wagons, with victuals mostly prepared. The women slept in the wagons, and the men under them. Many stayed on the ground night and day for a number of nights and days together. Others were provided for among the neighbors around. The power of God was wonderfully displayed; scores of sinners fell under the preaching, like men slain in mighty battle; Christians shouted aloud for joy.

To this meeting I repaired, a guilty, wretched sinner. On the Saturday evening of said meeting, I went, with weeping multitudes, and bowed before the stand, and earnestly prayed for mercy. In the midst of a solemn struggle of soul, an impression was made on my mind, as though a voice said to me, "Thy sins are all forgiven thee." Divine light flashed all round me, unspeakable joy sprung up in my soul. I rose to my feet, opened my eyes, and it really seemed as if I was in heaven; the trees, the leaves on them, and everything seemed, and I really thought were, praising God. My mother raised the shout, my Christian friends crowded around me and joined me in praising God; and though I have been since then, in many instances, unfaithful, yet I have never, for one moment, doubted that the Lord did, then and there, forgive my sins and give me religion.

Our meeting lasted without intermission all night, and it was believed by those who had a very good right to know, that over eighty souls were converted to God during its continuance. I went on my way rejoicing for many days. This meeting was in the month of May. In June our preacher, John Page, attended at our little church, *Ebenezer*, and there in June, 1801, I joined the Methodist Episcopal Church, which I have never for one moment regretted. I have never for a moment been tempted to leave the Methodist Episcopal Church, and if they were to turn me out, I would knock at the door till taken in again.

25

The Trail of Tears
John Ross

John Ross (1790–1866), of mixed Cherokee and white ancestry, was exactly the phenomenon that led Georgians and their great ally, Andrew Jackson, to insist on the removal of the so-called civilized tribes. Ross epitomized the "civilized," literate, prosperous, politically astute Native American who successfully competed with whites. He had fought as an officer under Jackson against the Creek Indians at Horseshoe Bend. In the years after the War of 1812, he became a leader of the Cherokee as well as the successful owner of a three-hundred-acre plantation run with the labor of more than twenty slaves. As leader of the fight against the removal, Ross was the chief author of the Cherokee nation's Memorial and Petition *against Jackson's policy but took the bitter responsibility for managing his people's journey west in 1838—a forced migration known as the Trail of Tears—after all his efforts to prevent it had failed.*

Once relocated to Indian Territory, Ross developed a new cotton plantation, again using numerous slaves. He never ceased his service to the Cherokee, remaining as principal chief of the nation in Indian Territory until his death.

BEFORE YOU READ

1. How did John Ross argue the case against the removal of the Cherokees in the *Memorial and Petition* submitted to the Senate and House of Representatives? What are the chief points he made? How persuasive do you think his argument is?

2. What were the main problems facing Ross in carrying out the removal of his people to the West?

TO THE SENATE AND
HOUSE OF REPRESENTATIVES

Washington City February 22ed 1837

The memorial and petition of the undersigned, a delegation appointed by the Cherokee nation in full council respectfully showeth:

That the Cherokee Nation deeply sensible of the evils under which they are now laboring and the still more frightful miseries which they have too much reason to apprehend, have in the most formal and solemn manner known to

Gary E. Moulton, ed., *The Papers of Chief John Ross: Volume I, 1807–1839* (Tulsa: University of Oklahoma Press, 1985).

them, assembled in General Council to deliberate upon their existing relations with the Government of the United States, and to lay their case with respectful deference before your honorable bodies.

Invested with full powers to conclude an arrangement upon all the matters which interest them we have arrived at the seat of Government, and, in accordance with our usual forms of proceeding have notified the Honorable the Secretary of War [Benjamin F. Butler] that we had reached this place and, through him, solicited an interview with the Executive [Andrew Jackson]. This request has not yet been granted, nor has it to this day received an official answer, but we have reason to apprehend from circumstances which have reached us that we shall be denied this application, and are thus compelled in the discharge of our duty to our constituents, to submit to your Honorable bodies the memorial of which we are the bearers.

On former occasions we have in much detail laid before you the prominent facts of our case. We have reminded you of our long and intimate connexion with the United States, of the scenes of peril and difficulty which we have shared in common; of the friendship which had so long been generously proffered and affectionately and gratefully accepted; of the aids which were supplied us in promoting our advancement in the arts of civilized life, of the political principles which we had imbibed, of the religious faith we have been taught.

We have called your attention to the progress which under your auspices we have made, of the improvements which have marked our social and individual states; our lands brought into cultivation, our natural resources developed, our farms, workshops and factories, approximating in character and value to those of our brethren whose example we had diligently imitated.

A smooth and beautiful prospect of future advancement was opened before us. Our people had abandoned the pursuits, the habits and the tastes of the savage, and had put on the vestments of civilization, of intelligence and of a pure religion. The progress we had made furnished us with the most assured hopes of continued improvement, and we indulged in the anticipation that the time was not far distant when we should be recognised, on the footing of equality by the brethren from whom we had received all which we were now taught to prize.

This promise of golden sunshine is now overspread. Clouds and darkness have obscured its brilliancy. The winds are beginning to mutter their awful forebodings, the tempest is gathering thick and heavy over our heads, and threatens to burst upon us with terrific energy and overwhelming ruin.

In this season of calamity, where can we turn with hope or confidence? On all former occasions of peril or of doubt the Government of the United States spread over us its broad and paternal shield. It invited us to seek an asylum and a protection under its mighty arm. It assisted us with its encouragement and advice, it soothed us with its consoling assurances, it inspired us with hope and gave us a feeling of confidence and security.

But alas! this our long-cherished friend seems now to be alienated from us: this our father has raised his arm to inflict the hostile blow; this strength so long our protection is now exerted against us, and on the wide scene of existence no human aid is left us. Unless you avert your arm we are destroyed. Unless your feelings of affection and compassion are once more awakened towards your destitute and despairing children our annihilation is complete.

It is a natural inquiry among all who commiserate our situation what are the causes which have led to this disastrous revolution, to this entire change of relations? By what agency have such results been accomplished?

We have asked, and we reiterate the question how have we offended? Show us in what manner we have, however unwittingly, inflicted upon you a wrong, you shall yourselves be the judges of the extent and manner of compensation. Show us the offence which has awakened your feelings of justice against us and we will submit to that measure of punishment which you shall tell us we have merited. We cannot bring to our recollections anything we have done or anything we have omitted calculated to awaken your resentment against us.

But we are told a treaty has been made and all that is required at our hands is to comply with its stipulations. Will the faithful historian, who shall hereafter record our lamentable fate, say—the Cherokee Nation executed a treaty by which they freely and absolutely ceded the country in which they were born and educated, the property they had been industriously accumulating and improving, and, abandoning the high road to which they had been advancing from savagism had precipitated themselves into worse than their pristine degradation, will not the reader of such a narrative require the most ample proof before he will credit such a story? Will he not inquire where was the kind and parental guardian who had heretofore aided the weak, assisted the forlorn, instructed the ignorant and elevated the depressed? Where was the Government of the United States with its vigilant care over the Indian when such a bargain was made? How will he be surprised at hearing that the United States was a party to the transaction—that the authority of that Government, and the representatives of that people, which had for years been employed in leading the Cherokees from ignorance to light, from barbarism to civilization, from paganism to christianity, who had taught them new habits and new hopes was the very party which was about to appropriate to itself the fruits of the Indian's industry, the birth places of his children and the graves of his ancestors.

If such a recital could command credence must it not be on the ground that experience had shown the utter failure of all the efforts and the disappointment of all the hopes of the philanthropist and the Christian? That the natives of this favored spot of God's creation were incapable of improvement and unsusceptible of education and that they in wilful blindness, spurning the blessings which had been proffered and urged upon them would pertinaciously prefer the degradation from which it had been attempted to lead them and the barbarism from which it had been sought to elevate them?

How will his astonishment be augmented when he learns that the Cherokee people almost to a man denied the existence and the obligation of the alleged compact—that they proclaimed it to have been based in fraud and concocted in perfidy—that no authority was ever given to those who undertook in their names and on their behalf to negotiate it; that it was repudiated with unexampled unanimity when it was brought to their knowledge; that they denied that it conferred any rights or imposed any obligations.

Yet such must be the story which the faithful historian must record. In the name of the whole Cherokee people we protest against this unhallowed and unauthorized and unacknowledged compact. We deny its binding force. We recognise none of its stipulations. If contrary to every principle of justice it is to be enforced upon us, we shall at least be free from the disgrace of self humiliation. We hold the solemn disavowal of its provisions by eighteen thousand of our people.

We, the regularly commissioned delegation of the Cherokee Nation in the face of Heaven and appealing to the Searcher of all hearts for the truth of our statements ask you to listen to our remonstrances. We implore you to examine into the truth of our allegations. We refer you to your own records, to your own agents, to men deservedly enjoying your esteem and confidence as our witnesses, and we proffer ourselves ready if you will direct the inquiry to establish the truth of what we aver. If we fail to substantiate our statements overwhelm us with ignominy and disgrace. Cast us off from you forever. If however on the other hand every allegation we make shall be sustained by the most convincing and abundant proof, need we make further or stronger appeals than the simple facts of the case will themselves furnish, to secure your friendship, your sympathy and your justice.

We will not and we cannot believe after the long connexion that has subsisted between us, after all that has been done and all that has been promised that our whole nation will be forcibly ejected from their native land and from their social hearths without the pretence of crime, without charge, without evidence, without trial: that we shall be exiled from all that we hold dear and venerable and sacred, and driven into a remote, a strange and a sterile region, without even the imputation of guilt. We will not believe that this will be done by our ancient allies, our friends, our brethren. Yet between this and the abrogation to the pretended treaty there is no medium. Such an instrument so obtained, so contaminated cannot cover the real nature of the acts which it is invoked to sanction. If power is to be exerted let it come unveiled. We shall but submit and die.

Jno Ross

TO WINFIELD SCOTT[1]

Cherokee Agency East October 6th 1838

Sir

I had the honor to receive your communication of the 3rd inst. on the subject of my requisition of the 2ed and the state of the emigration generally. In reply, I beg leave to say, that although those detachments, only, which are in the greatest state of forwardness, are formally announced in my estimates and requisition; it ought to be borne in mind that, our efforts are directed, to carrying on the emigration with so much dispatch that, simultaneous preparations

---

1. **Winfield Scott:** Major General Scott was in overall charge of the Cherokee removal.

must be going on for the whole number of detachments by land, and even for the final clearing out of the sick, the infirm, the aged &c by water, who are unable to bear the fatigues of the journey by land. And that these preparations, may be made, with the least possible delay, I deemed it indispensable to have the necessary funds in readiness.

With regard to the number in some of the detachments, I would respectfully observe that the number one thousand, was understood by the Cherokees to be merely a common measure, assumed as the basis of the pecuniary calculations; and not as a precise, stipulated number which must absolutely be filled by each detachment; yet, their intention was, that each detachment should approximate that number as nearly as might be convenient. And it was expected that some would exceed and some come short of it.

In regard to Capt. [Hair] Conrad's detachment, I am sorry to say that it has been greatly diminished by causes beyond human control. That detachment was not, at first, expected to be large, and the amount of sickness with which it has been visited has greatly reduced its numbers, and even deprived it of the original conductor. I am happy to find, however, that a considerable number who have recovered are now on their way to join their friends in that detachment.

Mr. [George] Hicks's detachment was expected to number one thousand or more, but the same afflictive causes have operated extensively among them also, and a considerable number were unavoidably left behind. In addition to this it may not be improper to say that Mr. Hicks and some of the other conductors have had to contend with extraneous, counteracting influences which were used to frustrate their arrangements in particular, and to embarrass and retard the progress of the general arrangements, between yourself and the authorities of the nation. And here, Sir, permit me to say, that having secured your confidence in our good faith and integrity, on which we place the highest estimate; we should be extremely sorry that you should find the authority or the moral influence of the Nation inadequate to the prompt and faithful, discharge of its duties. I trust there does exist, in the Nation, a sufficient amount of energy, moral and official, for the performance of all its engagements. And here it may be proper to call your attention to the fact that certain individual Cherokees namely [John A.] Bell, [William] Boling & their associates under the assumed protection of the United States prompted and sustained, as I am assured, by individuals in official stations, of whose conduct I have more than once verbally complained; have been practising a course of interference, tending to retard the progress and disturb the arrangements of the detachments preparing for the road. We have refrained from exercising, the National Authority over those persons, from the feeling of uncertainty, whether, they were to be considered under the jurisdiction of the United States or that of the Cherokee Nation. If they are under the control of the Nation it would be desirable to have the fact known; but if they are under the control of the U. States we would respectfully call upon you to apply the corrective. In this connexion, it may not be out of place to add, that the continuing to issue rations, by the Govt. Agents at places from which the detachments have removed or after the regular organization of the detachments preparatory to their journey, as well as issuing, at the Agency, to little secluded parties, some of them many miles distant; is calculated to produce delay, in their being embodied with the detachments to which they properly belong, and more especially so, when this practice is connected with a systematic propagation of falsehoods and misrepresentations by the individuals alluded to and their emissaries.

The counteracting of these malign influences by prudent and gentle means, has, it is true, occasioned a little undesirable delay; but I have the pleasure to say, that our movements are now in a state of activity, which I trust will preclude all cause of complaint, with the assurance that our best efforts will be exerted to carry out our arrangements, with all reasonable dispatch. I remain with high respect, Sir, your obt. Servt.

Jno Ross

TO MATTHEW ARBUCKLE[2]

Illinois [Cherokee Nation] Apl 23rd 1839

Sir

From the many complaints which are daily made to me by Cherokees who have been recently removed into this country, of their sufferings, from the want of being properly subsisted with provisions, I am constrained to address you this hasty letter. It is reported that, apart from the scantiness of the ration allowed under the contract made on the part of the United States Government with [James] Glasgow & [James] Harrison, many inconveniences have been experienced by the Cherokee people, from the irregularity of proceedings on the part of those employed for carrying out the contract.

It has also been stated that the contractors were only required to furnish "one pound of fresh beef, three half pints of corn & four qts. of salt to every 100 lbs. of beef—or, if they (the contractors) choose they might furnish in lieu of the beef, 3/4 lb. salt pork or bacon provided the Indians will receive it." The beef being poor & not considered wholesome this season of the year, the Cherokees have generally objected to and refused receiving it and have insisted on being furnished with Salt Pork or Bacon in lieu of the beef, but it seems that the contractors do not choose and have refused to comply with the demand; saying that they were only bound to furnish Beef rations. Yet they would commute the ration by paying in money one dollar pr. month for the same. Thus the Cherokees are placed in a situation by compulsion to accept of either the beef or the money offered or to go unsupplied altogether. Here I must beg leave to remark, that previous to the removal of the Cherokees from the East to the West, the subject of providing subsistence for them after their arrival in this country was fully discussed with Major Genl. [Winfield] Scott who communicated with the War Deptmt. in reference to it. And we were afterwards informed by that distinguished officer that the Hon. Secry. of War [Joel R. Poinsett] had decided that the Cherokees should at least for

2. **Matthew Arbuckle:** Brigadier General Arbuckle was area commander in the Indian Territory.

a time be subsisted with provisions in kind, until they could provide for themselves, and then such an arrangement as would be most satisfactory to them should be made with them through Capt. Collins. Now Sir, it is evident from the exorbitant prices of meat and bread stuffs in this country that the Cherokees who have thus been forced to receive commutation in money from the contractors at the rate stated will soon be found in a starving condition — instead of being provided with subsistence as was anticipated and promised them. If the articles of agreement entered into with the contractors are to be construed so as to leave it wholly optional with them whether to furnish Salt Pork or Bacon in lieu of Beef, then it is obvious that there were no practical advantage for the interest of the Cherokees to have inserted any clause in that instrument in regard to Salt Pork or Bacon — for its effect has only been and will continue to be to mislead the mind of the people. And how it can be reconciled with the obligations imposed by the contract for the contractors to adopt the mode of commuting the subsistence rations they have engaged to furnish the Cherokees with and that too by a rate fixed by themselves, is a mystery which the Cherokees cannot understand — for it is not pretended that such a right or discretion has ever been given to them by the contract with the agents or the U.S. Govt. for subsisting the Cherokees. Nor can the sacred principle of justice sanction such a course under existing circumstances. Confiding however in the fair intentions of the Government towards them on this subject, the Cherokees still believe that the Hon. Secry. of War will when deemed expedient commute their rations at a rate at least equal to any sum fully ample to purchase provisions with for their comfortable subsistence — and that no sum less will be offered than what others would engage to supply the same for. I beg leave herewith to lay before you copies of sundry letters which I have just received from several leading men on behalf of the Cherokees on this very unpleasant subject. And in conclusion will further remark, that the health and existence of the whole Cherokee people who have recently been removed to this distant country demands a speedy remedy for the inconveniences and evils complained of, & unless a change of the quantity and the kind of rations as well as of the mode of issuing the same, be made from that which has heretofore been granted and observed, the Cherokees must inevitably suffer. Therefore to avoid hunger & starvation they are reduced to the necessity of calling upon you and other officers as the proper representatives of the U.S. Govt. in this matter, to take immediate steps as will ensure the immediate subsistence of the Cherokees who have recently been removed here, with ample and wholesome provisions, until such other arrangements, as may be most satisfactory to them, can be made for subsisting themselves &c. When every thing in reference to the late removal of the Cherokee nation from the East to the West is considered, and seen that it has been consummated through the military authority of the U.S. Govt. I trust you will pardon me for addressing this communication to you, especially when you are assured that the Cherokee people have been taught to expect that justice and protection would be extended to them through the Commanding General in this Hemisphere.

Jno Ross

26

Pulling a Handcart to the Mormon Zion
Priscilla Merriman Evans

Many of the men and women who settled the Far West often endured extraordinary physical hardships and dangers to reach their destinations. The Mormon pioneers who walked from Iowa City, Iowa, to Salt Lake City, Utah, pulling handcarts made of hickory were driven by both economic and religious motives. The handcart immigrants were poor: if they could have afforded to migrate any other way, they would have. They spoke one or more of several languages—German, Welsh, Danish, Swedish—as well as English. And they did not all have so successful a journey as the pregnant Mrs. Thomas D. Evans. With her one-legged husband, Priscilla Merriman Evans walked the one thousand miles in five months, arriving in Salt Lake City in October 1856, comfortably ahead of the winter weather. In two parties later that year, hundreds died in winter blizzards.

Nine more handcart companies reached the Mormon Zion in the five years after the Evanses' journey. All received rich welcomes with prayers and hymns. Priscilla Merriman Evans concluded her narrative by saying that she always "thanked the Lord for a contented mind, a home and something to eat."

BEFORE YOU READ

1. Why do you think Priscilla Merriman Evans became a Mormon and chose to emigrate?
2. What were the principal difficulties of the trip to Utah?
3. What rewards did Evans find in "Zion"?

I, Priscilla Merriman Evans, born May 4, 1835 at Mounton New Marbeth, Pembrokeshire, Wales, am the daughter of Joseph and Ann James Merriman. About 1839, father moved his family from Mounton up to Tenby, about ten miles distant. Our family consisted of father, mother, Sarah, aged six, and myself, aged four. Tenby was a beautiful place, as are all those Celtic Islands, with remains of old castles, vine- and moss-covered walls, gone to ruin since the time of the Conqueror. . . .

Besides reading, writing, spelling, and arithmetic, we were taught sewing and sampler making. The sampler work was done in cross stitch, worked in

Kate B. Carter, comp., *Heart Throbs of the West*, vol. 9 (Salt Lake City: International Society Daughters of Utah Pioneers), pp. 8–13.

bright colors, on canvas made for that purpose. . . . We were also taught the Bible. I was greatly interested in school, but was taken out at eleven years of age, owing to the illness in our family. I was a natural student, and greatly desired to continue my studies, but mother's health was very poor, so I was taken out to help with the work. My sister, Sarah, continued school, as she did not like housework and wished to learn a trade. She went to Mrs. Hentin and learned the millinery trade. Mother's health continued [to be] poor, and she died at the birth of her eighth child, Emma, when I was sixteen. I had many duties for a girl so young, caring for my sisters and brothers. While Sarah was learning millinery, she would sometimes wake me in the night to try on a hat—one she was practicing on. She learned the millinery business and then went up to London, opened a shop of her own and was very successful. She married a gentleman . . . who was devoted to her, and followed her to London. She died at the birth of her fourth child.

[When] Mother died on the eighth of November 1851 . . . the responsibility of the family rested on my young shoulders. . . . After the death of my mother we were very lonely, and one evening I accompanied my father to the house of a friend. When we reached there, we learned that they were holding a cottage meeting. Two Mormon Elders were the speakers, and I was very much interested in the principles they advocated. I could see that my father was very worried, and would have taken me away, had he known how. When he became aware that I believed in the Gospel as taught by the Elders, I asked him if he had ever heard of the restored Gospel. He replied, "Oh, yes, I have heard of Old Joe Smith, and his Golden Bible." When my father argued against the principles taught by the Elders, I said, "If the Bible is true, then Mormonism is true."

My father was very much opposed to my joining the Church . . . as he thought the Saints were too slow to associate with. . . . But I had found the truth and was baptized into the Church of Jesus Christ of Latter-day Saints in Tenby, February 26, 1852. My sister Sarah took turns with me going out every Sunday. She would go where she pleased on Sunday, while I would walk seven miles to Stepaside and attend the Mormon meeting. My father was very much displeased with me going out every Sunday. He forbade me to read the Church literature, and threatened to burn all I brought home. At the time I had a Book of Mormon borrowed from a friend, and when Father found out I had it, he began looking for it. It was in plain sight, among other books in the book case. I saw him handling it with the other books, and I sent up a silent prayer that he might not notice it, which he did not, although it was before him in plain sight. I do not think my father was as bitter against the principles of the Gospel as he seemed to be, for many times when the Elders were persecuted, he defended them, and gave them food and shelter. But he could not bear the idea of my joining them and leaving home.

About this time, Thomas D. Evans, a young Mormon Elder, was sent up from Merthyr Tydfil, Wales, as a missionary to Pembrokeshire. He was a fine speaker, and had a fine tenor voice, and I used to like to go around with the missionaries and help with the singing. Elder Evans and I seemed to be congenial from our first meeting, and we were soon engaged. He was traveling and preaching the restored Gospel without purse or script. Perhaps his mission will be better understood if I give a little account: [his father had died] and left his mother a widow with eight children, Thomas D. being four years old and the youngest. He was placed in a large forge of two-thousand men at the age of seven years to learn the profession of Iron Roller. At nine years of age, he had the misfortune to lose his left leg at the knee. He went through the courses and graduated as an Iron Roller. When I think of [when they met in 1852] it seems that we had put the world aside, and were not thinking of our worldly pleasures, and what our next dress would be. We had no dancing in those days, but we were happy in the enjoyment of the spirit of the Gospel. . . .

I was familiar with the Bible doctrine, and when I heard the Elders explain it, it seemed as though I had always known it, and it sounded like music in my ears. We had the spirit of gathering and were busy making preparations to emigrate.

About that time the Principle of Plurality of Wives was preached to the world, and it caused quite a commotion in our branch. One of the girls came to me with tears in her eyes and said, "Is it true that Brigham Young has nine wives? I can't stand that, Oh, I can't stand it!" I asked her how long it had been since I had heard her testify that she knew the Church was true, and I said if it was then, it is true now. I told her I did not see anything for her to cry about. After I talked to her awhile, she dried her eyes and completed her arrangements to get married and emigrate. She came with us. My promised husband and I went to Merthyr to visit his Mother, brothers, sisters, and friends, preparatory to emigrating. His family did all in their power to persuade him to remain with them. They were all well off, and his brothers said they would send him to school, support his wife, and pay all of his expenses but all to no avail. He bade them all goodbye, and returned to Tenby.

I think I would have had a harder time getting away, had it not been that my father was going to be married again, and I do not suppose the lady cared to have in the home, the grown daughter who had taken the place of the mother for so many years.

Elder Thomas D. Evans, my promised husband, and I walked the ten miles from Tenby to Pembroke, where we got our license and were married, and walked back to Tenby. We were married on the third of April, 1856. On our return from Pembroke we found a few of our friends awaiting us with supper ready. We visited our friends and relatives and made our preparations to emigrate to Zion. We took a tug from Pembroke to Liverpool, where we set sail on the 17th of April, 1856, on the sailing vessel S.S. *Curling.* Captain Curling said he would prefer to take a load of Saints than others, as he always felt safe with Saints on board. We learned that the next trip across the water that he was loaded with gentiles and his vessel sank with all on board. We were on the sea five weeks; we lived on the ship's rations. I was sick all the way. [Priscilla was then pregnant with their first child.]

We landed in Boston on May 23rd, then travelled in cattle cars . . . to Iowa City. We remained in Iowa City three weeks, waiting for our carts to be made. We were offered many inducements to stay there. My husband was offered ten dollars a day to work at his trade of Iron Roller, but money was no inducement to us, for we were anxious to get to Zion. We learned afterwards that many who stayed there apostatized or died of cholera.

When the carts were ready we started on a three-hundred-mile walk to Winterquarters on the Missouri River. There were a great many who made fun of us as we walked, pulling our carts, but the weather was fine and the roads were excellent and although I was sick and we were tired out at night, we still thought, "This is a glorious way to come to Zion."

We began our journey of one thousand miles on foot with a handcart for each family, some families consisting of man and wife, and some had quite large families. There were five mule teams to haul the tents and surplus flour. Each handcart had one hundred pounds of flour, that was to be divided and [more got] from the wagons as required. At first we had a little coffee and bacon, but that was soon gone and we had no use for any cooking utensils but a frying pan. The flour was self-raising and we took water and baked a little cake; that was all we had to eat.

After months of travelling we were put on half rations and at one time, before help came, we were out of flour for two days. We washed out the flour sacks to make a little gravy.

There were in our tent my husband with one leg, two blind men . . . a man with one arm, and a widow with five children. The widow, her children, and myself were the only ones who could not talk Welsh. My husband was commissary for our tent, and he cut his own rations short many times to help little children who had to walk and did not have enough to eat to keep up their strength.

The tent was our covering, and the overcoat spread on the bare ground with the shawl over us was our bed. My feather bed, and bedding, pillows, all our good clothing, my husband's church books, which he had collected through six years of missionary work, with some genealogy he had collected, all had to be left in a storehouse. We were promised that they would come to us with the next emigration in the spring, but we never did receive them. It was reported that the storehouse burned down, so that was a dreadful loss to us.

Edward Bunker was the Captain of our Company. His orders of the day were, "If any are sick among you, and are not able to walk, you must help them along, or pull them on your carts." No one rode in the wagons. Strong men would help the weaker ones, until they themselves were worn out, and some died from the struggle and want of food, and were buried along the wayside. It was heart rending for parents to move on and leave their loved ones to such a fate, as they were so helpless, and had no material for coffins. Children and young folks, too, had to move on and leave father or mother or both.

Sometimes a bunch of buffaloes would come and the carts would stop until they passed. Had we been prepared with guns and ammunition, like people who came in wagons, we might have had meat, and would not have come to near starving. President Young ordered extra cattle sent along to be killed to help the sick and weak, but they were never used for that purpose. One incident happened which came near being serious. Some Indians came to our camp and my husband told an Indian who admired me that he could have me for a pony. He was always getting off jokes. He thought no more about it, but in a day or two, here came the Indian with the pony, and wanted his pretty little squaw. It was no joke with him. I never was so frightened in all my life. There was no place to hide, and we did not know what to do. The Captain was called, and they had some difficulty in settling with the Indian without trouble.

In crossing rivers, the weak women and the children were carried over the deep places, and they waded the others. We were much more fortunate than those who came later, as they had snow and freezing weather. Many lost limbs, and many froze to death. President Young advised them to start earlier, but they got started too late. My husband, in walking from twenty to twenty-five miles per day [had pain] where the knee rested on the pad: the friction caused it to gather and break and was most painful. But he had to endure it, or remain behind, as he was never asked to ride in a wagon.

We reached Salt Lake City on October 2, 1856, tired, weary, with bleeding feet, our clothing worn out and so weak we were nearly starved, but thankful to our Heavenly Father for bringing us to Zion. William R. Jones met us on the Public Square in Salt Lake City and brought us to his home in Spanish Fork. I think we were over three days coming from Salt Lake City to Spanish Fork by ox team, but what a change to ride in a wagon after walking 1330 miles from Iowa City to Salt Lake City!

We stayed in the home of an ex-bishop, Stephen Markham. His home was a dugout. It was a very large room built half underground. His family consisted of three wives, and seven children. . . . There was a large fireplace in one end with bars, hooks, frying pans, and bake ovens, where they did the cooking for the large family, and boiled, fried, baked, and heated their water for washing.

There was a long table in one corner, and pole bedsteads fastened to the walls in the three other corners. They were laced back and forth with rawhide cut in strips, and made a nice springy bed. There were three trundle beds, made like shallow boxes, with wooden wheels, which rolled under the mother's bed in the daytime to utilize space. There was a dirt roof, and the dirt floor was kept hard and smooth by sprinkling and sweeping. The bed ticks were filled with straw. . . .

Aunt Mary [Markham] put her two children . . . in the foot of her bed and gave us the trundle bed. . . . How delightful to sleep on a bed again, after sleeping on the ground for so many months with our clothes on. We had not slept in a bed since we left the ship *Sam Curling.*

On the 31st of December, 1856, our first daughter was born. . . . My baby's wardrobe was rather meager: I made one night gown from her father's white shirt, another out of a factory lining of an oilcloth sack. Mrs. Markham gave me a square of homemade linsey for a shoulder blanket, and a neighbor gave me some old underwear, that I worked up into little things. They told me I could have an old pair of jean pants left at the adobe yard. I washed them and made them into petticoats. I walked down to the Indian farm and traded a gold pen for four yards of calico that made her two dresses.

One day my husband went down in the field to cut some willows to burn. The ax slipped and cut his good knee cap. It was with difficulty that he crawled to the house. He was very weak from the loss of blood. My baby was but a few days old, and the three of us had to occupy the trundle bed for awhile.

Wood and timber were about thirty miles up in the canyon, and when the men went after timber to burn, they went in crowds, armed, for they never knew when they would be attacked by Indians. Adobe houses were cheaper than log or frame, as timber was so far away. Many of the people who had lived in the dugouts after coming from Palmyra got into houses before the next winter. They exchanged work with each other, and in that way got along fine. Mr. Markham had an upright saw, run by water. The next spring they got timber from the canyon, and my husband helped Mr. Markham put up a three-roomed house and worked at farming.

He worked for William Markham a year, for which he received two acres of land. I helped in the house, for which, besides the land, we got our board and keep. The next Spring we went to work for ourselves. We saved our two acres of wheat, and made adobes for a two-roomed house, and paid a man in adobes for laying it up. It had a dirt roof. He got timber from Mr. Markham to finish the doors, windows, floors, shelves, and to make furniture. My husband made me a good big bedstead and laced it with rawhides. There were benches and the frames of chairs with the rawhide seat, with the hair left on; a table, shelves in the wall on either side of the fireplace, which was fitted with iron bars and hooks to hang kettles on to boil, frying pans and bake oven. A tick for a bed had to be pieced out of all kinds of scraps, as there were no stores, and everything was on a trade basis.

If one neighbor had something they could get along without, they would exchange it for something they could use. We were lucky to get factory, or sheeting to put up to the windows instead of glass. We raised a good crop of wheat that fall, for which we traded one bushel for two bushels of potatoes. We also exchanged for molasses and vegetables. We had no tea, coffee, meat, or grease of any kind for seasoning. No sugar, milk, or butter. In 1855–1856 the grasshoppers and crickets took the crops and the cattle nearly all died. They were dragged down in the field west [and left to die].

We bought a lot on Main Street, and my husband gave his parents our first little home with five acres of land. They had a good ox team, two cows, a new wagon, and they soon got pigs, chickens and a few sheep. It wasn't long before they were well off. . . .

It was indeed comfortable to be in a good house with a shingled roof and good floors. He set out an orchard of all kinds of fruit; also currents and goose-berries, planted lucern . . . in a patch by itself for cows and pigs. We had a nice garden spot, and we soon had butter, milk, eggs, and meat. We raised our bread, potatoes, and vegetables. While our fruit trees were growing is when the saleratus[1] helped. When I had the babies all about the same size, I could not get

---

1. **saleratus:** a form of baking soda.

out to gather saleratus as others did; so we went with team and wagon, pans, buckets, old brooms, and sacks down on the alkali land, between Spanish Fork and Springville. The smallest children were put under the wagon on a quilt, and the rest of us swept and filled the sacks, and the happiest time was when we were headed for home. The canyon wind seemed always to blow and our faces, hands and eyes were sore for some time after. We took our saleratus over to Provo, where they had some kind of refining machinery where it was made into soda for bread. It was also used extensively in soap making. We got our pay in merchandise.

Most people who had land kept a few sheep which furnished them meat, light and clothing. We had no sheep, but I, and my oldest daughter, learned to spin and we did spinning on shares to get our yarn for stockings and socks, which we knitted for the family. Before this time my sister, Sarah, had sent me a black silk dress pattern, with other things, which I sold [and] I bought a cow and a pair of blankets. Before the building of the Provo factory, the people had wool-picking bees. The wool was greased and the trash picked out of it; then it was carded into rolls. We made our own cloth, which was mostly gray in color, for dresses, by mixing the black and white wool. If a light gray was wanted, more white than black was put in, and dark was added if a darker gray was wanted. The dresses for grown people were three widths, and for younger women two widths, one yard wide. There was a row of bright colors—red, blue, green—about half way up the skirt, which was hemmed and pleated onto a plain waist with coat sleeves. When our dresses wore thin in front, they could be turned back to front and upside down, and have a new lease on life. With madder, Indigo, logwood, copperas, and other roots, I have colored beautiful fast colors. We were kept busy in those days carding, spinning, knitting, and doing all of our own sewing by hand.

After getting settled in our new home, my husband went over to Camp Floyd, where he worked quite a bit. He found a friend who was selling out prior to leaving for California. He bought quite a number of articles, which greatly helped us. One thing was a door knob and lock. He also bought me a stepstove. Stoves were very scarce at that time in Spanish Fork. I had never cooked on a stove in my life, and I burned my first batch of bread. Where I came from people mixed their dough and had it baked in the public oven, and at home we had a gate with an oven at the side. When the soldier camp broke up, they left many useful things which helped the people.

. . . My husband had poor luck farming. His farm was in the low land, near the river where the sugar factory now stands. Sometimes it would be high water, sometimes grasshoppers or crickets would take his crop; so he got discouraged with farming, sold his farm and put up a store. We had just got well started in the business and had got a bill of goods, when in the spring of 1875 my husband was called on another mission to England.

Before starting on his mission he sold his team and all available property, also mortgaged our home, for although he was called to travel without purse or scrip, he had to raise enough money to pay his passage and his expenses to his field of labor in Europe. He had too tender a heart for a merchant; he simply could not say no when people came to him with pitiful stories of sickness and privation. He would give them credit, and the consequence was that when he was suddenly called on a mission, the goods were gone and there were hundreds of dollars coming to us from the people, some of which we never got. Everything was left in my hands.

On the 24th of October 1875, after my husband's departure, our daughter Ada was born. . . . I nursed her, along with my little granddaughter Maud, as twins, kept all the books and accounts . . . and was sustained as President and Secretary of the Relief Society Teachers, which office I held through many reorganizations.

During my husband's absence, we had considerable sickness. My little daughter, Mary, came near dying with scarlet fever. To help out, our eldest daughter, Emma, got a position as clerk in the Co-op store. I appreciated that action of the Board very much, as before that time they had not been employing lady clerks and she was the first girl to work in the store. . . .

In 1877, my twelfth child was born. . . . I have had seven daughters and five sons. . . .

My husband's health was not good after his return from his mission. He had pneumonia twice. We sold our home on Main Street, paid off the mortgage and put up a little house on the five acres of land we had given his parents. They had left it to us when they died. We have some of our children as near neighbors and are quite comfortable in our new home.

27

Life on a Whaler
Nathaniel W. Taylor

The nineteenth century was a time of movement and migration. Throughout the world, political change and agricultural crisis drove people to cross continents and oceans looking for higher wages and new economic opportunities. Most were driven by necessity, but some, like Nathaniel W. Taylor (1823–1875), were largely in pursuit of adventure. In 1851, at the age of twenty-eight, he joined a whaling crew in New London, Connecticut, and served as ship's physician for twenty-one months, traveling over twenty-three thousand miles and passing two summers and a winter in the southern Indian Ocean near Antarctica. Although Taylor, an affluent New England doctor and the son of a Yale theology professor, was not typical of the men who went to sea on whaling ships, he paints a picture of the hard lives of some who were forced to leave their homes to make a living.

Among the many jobs that required people to travel, none was more difficult, dangerous, and time consuming than whaling. Few nineteenth-century businesses, however, were as profitable. The oil rendered from the blubber of sperm whales and elephant seals was the primary illuminant in oil lamps and a crucial lubricant for machinery, and it had dozens of other industrial and household applications. Every year ships would leave New England coastal cities for distant icy corners of the globe carrying whaling crews and their captains, many of whom spent so much of their lives at sea that they brought their entire families with them. The risky months on the sea punctuated by short breaks at remote whaling stations like South Georgia Island, Tristan de Cunha, and Fowler's Bay made it a hard and isolated life.

Taylor's ship, the Julius Caesar, *was one of the many New London whalers that gave the city a near monopoly on the rich whaling grounds near Desolation and Heard Islands in the southern Indian Ocean, midway between Australia and Africa. During the 1850s, these ships slaughtered many thousands of sperm whales and elephant seals, spurring the expansion of Connecticut shipbuilding and helping to make New London a wealthy center of commerce and industry. The whaling industry would go into decline with the maritime disruptions of the Civil War and the development of the petroleum industry in the 1860s, which provided more efficient, safer, and less costly illuminants and lubricants. Connecticut, however, would continue to dominate the American shipbuilding industry, producing vast fleets of steamships, naval vessels, and the celebrated nuclear submarines of the cold war.*

Nathaniel W. Taylor, *Life on a Whaler, or Antarctic Adventures in the Isle of Desolation*, in Howard Palmer, ed., *Occasional Publications*, vol. II (New London, CT: New London County Historical Society, 1929), pp. 58–64, 111–17.

BEFORE YOU READ

1. Why would an affluent New England doctor embark on such a long and dangerous journey?

2. What does Taylor's account add to our understanding of work in the nineteenth century?

3. Do you think Taylor and his crewmates ever considered the environmental impact of their profession? Why or why not?

4. How important do you think the whaling industry was in shaping the New England economy and culture?

I

The object of pursuit at the present time was about an eighth of a mile distant and blowing at intervals of two minutes. One of the boats soon went on and was fast with the first harpoon. This is fastened to a pole eight or ten feet in length to give it momentum when thrown, and to this is attached a line eight hundred or one thousand feet in length, coiled in a tub with the most exact precision. No sooner had the enormous creature felt the iron penetrate its body than, throwing its flukes upwards, it disappeared in the depths, carrying about sixty fathoms of the line.

As soon as the harpooner has thus fastened to a whale, he changes place with the boat-header or officer in command of the boat. It is the latter's task to take the post of honor and finish the work. This he does, after again coming up with the whale, by thrusts from a long and slender lance. While the officer is seeking to pierce some vital part, the crew sit ready to "Stern all" away from the animal's flukes, or from any manoeuvers which it may make upon feeling the pointed spear. Sometimes they peak their oars, or fasten the handles in places made to receive them, thus elevating the blades some distance above the surface of the water, but still ready for instant use. With their backs turned towards the whale and their hands free, they sit quietly, prepared alike for duty or danger.

It often happens that a whale, after being struck, sounds so quickly that it carries out all of the line from the tub before another can be fastened to it. If this happens the boat has then lost its hold of the whale, and any boat has the privilege of getting fast if it can. When fast, however, the men often have the pleasure of a "sleighride," as they call it when drawn through the water at great speed by a whale. Often this speed becomes so great that they are obliged to cut the line, and give up the whale. If its motion becomes slower, or it stops to rest, the boat is pulled up to it by means of the line, and while it lies tamely under its smart, the lance is thrust into its side, the men alternately sterning off and pulling on till the blood from its blowholes crimsons the sea for rods around. This is a sure sign of death and the order is hurriedly given, "Stern all for your lives."

The flurry or dying agonies are tremendous, quite in proportion to the creature's size. Woe to the boat that is within its reach as it rolls and thrashes about in the bloody waters. Life being ended, the whale rolls upon its back, and, to use the common expression, is "turned up." The danger is now past unless it happens that in the excitement of the chase the boats have attained a great distance from the ship, or have become enveloped in a fog. If all is well, a rope is easily passed around the tail of the inanimate body and the task of towing to the ship commenced.

II

The process of cutting in a whale, flensing or removing the blubber from the carcass, is simple in its details, though one requiring much hard labor and great perseverance. The time which is occupied varies from three to eight hours, according to the size of the fish, the state of the wind, and the number of men on duty. All things being favorable, our crew can cut in a sixty-barrel whale in three hours and a half.

The moment that the line attached to a whale is thrown on board, the forward sails of the ship are reserved and the helm is put down and secured in its place. This checks her motion by bringing her into the wind, as it is called. Were it otherwise, the tow-line, with a whale of fifty tons weight as a drag, would instantly be broken. A large and heavy chain is passed through a hawser-hole on the bows and fastened around the flukes of the whale. The boats are now hoisted to their places, cables, stages, etc., are gotten up from below, spades and knives sharpened, the windlass manned and the labor of cutting is begun.

The position of the officers is upon stages slung outside of the ship on each side of the waist or gangway. Both have a broad belt passing in front of them, the ends of which are secured to the ship. This is for protection against falling overboard when leaning forward. Thus secured and provided with cutting spades fastened to poles from fifteen to twenty feet in length, they anatomize the animal with considerable physiological precision.

A vessel in the situation thus described rolls and pitches badly. The fluke chain at one moment taut and at another slack, the dead weight of the fish acting against the buoyancy of the ship, the blubber to be cut varying in thickness from eight to twelve inches with a toughness peculiar to gristle—all render this task laborious and perilous, and demand the greatest strength and dexterity.

In case, as is generally the fact, the whale lies upon its back, the lips and tongue are first, and most easily, removed. The right whale has properly but one jaw, which constitutes the roof of the mouth and from which the slabs of whalebone depend. Upon either side of these the lips overlap. Two large cables of six or eight inches in circumference pass around the windlass and through huge tackle blocks, suspended from the mast at the main-top, over the ship's side, having attached to their ends a massive iron hook, a block, a strap and "toggle," or other appurtenances for fastening to the blubber.

After the lips and tongue have been removed, hoisted on deck, and lowered into the blubber room, one of the hooks is again fastened into the blubber of the fish, and as spiral incisions are made through it (the men heaving on the windlass), the body rolls slowly over till the top of the head appears on the surface of the water. The revolutions of the windlass are now stopped; and amid loud cries for the "monkey," a boat-steerer in his stocking feet and stripped to the waist makes his appearance.

A rope is fastened around his body and with an axe in his hands double the size of one used by wood choppers, he is lowered upon the slimy creature's back. In this slippery position, often immersed to his shoulders in the sea by the rising and falling of the whale, he severs the bony connection of the head with the body by vigorous and oft-repeated blows. There is danger during this operation of the loss of a toe or a foot from the approach of the greedy shark, and equal hazard of the "monkey's" taking cold in his half-nude state; but a scantiness of clothing is necessary to allow full play to his muscles and to enable him to swim with greater ease in case the rope should break or be twitched from the hands of the assistants.

The head is hoisted on board, and if you choose, dear reader, you can walk into it with me in imagination and admire the beautifully arched roof of delicate pink, while you wonder into how many hundred hoops its ebony colored clapboards can be manufactured. The laminae of bone vary from five to fifteen feet in length, and are about one inch thick at their insertion into the gum, where they are a foot wide. They taper gradually to a point. They are removed with spades and axes from the skull, and must undergo several processes of cleaning and drying before they are fit for use.

The work goes on systematically and without intermission till all the blubber is stowed on board and the carcass is turned adrift, a noble feast for the thousand birds of prey which hover near.

Mincing and trying out constitute no inconsiderable portion of the work on a whaleship. All hands are on duty during the labor of capture and cutting in; whereas in mincing and boiling the watches are alternately occupied for a space of six hours each. The blanket pieces, as the large masses of blubber now on board are called, are cut up by men between decks into pieces about two feet square called horse pieces; these are hoisted by others on deck and passed over to the mincers.

The mincer is a man selected from the crew as possessing the important qualifications of great muscular strength and power of endurance. The necessity of these qualities will be recognized when it is stated that during the six hours watch a sufficient quantity of minced blubber is to be supplied for the "try-pots" to yield twenty barrels of oil. This is the allowance usually made when trying out in good weather; if rainy or foggy, and the sea runs high, a much less quantity is the result, while the difficulty of working is greatly increased. The mincer has his assistant, who supplies the horse or mincing-tub with blubber, which he holds in a firm position with an iron hook while it is cut by the former into slices an inch in thickness by drawing the long two-handled knife through it with a steady and regular motion.

In the meantime one of the mates or a harpooner superintends the trying out, feeding the fires and alternately filling the pots with fresh blubber and bailing out the hot oil into a large copper cooler from which it slowly runs into the deck pot. From this vessel the casks are filled by still another person, who officiates in any other capacity the occasion may require. The oil is not thoroughly cold when poured into the cask. As it cools, the cask shrinks, especially if it is a new one, requiring the immediate services of the cooper. When filled, six or eight hands are needed to roll it from the cooler and end it up that the hoops may be tightened. It is no boy's play to handle a six, eight, or ten-barrel cask filled with oil upon the deck of a ship covered with grease, rolling and pitching in the rough seas of the southern ocean; but on the contrary a difficult and often very dangerous task. Unless the weather is exceedingly stormy the fires are kept burning night and day till the blubber is all converted into oil. . . .

III

It was nearly noon before the welcome shout was heard and echoed through the vessel. The mate's boat . . . was fast to a whale, which was coming down the bay at headlong speed, galled into fury by the barbed harpoon in its side. Could you, dear reader, have seen the sight, that mere egg-shell of a boat, with its hardy and daring, but then almost breathless, crew, so swiftly borne along by the angry monster of the deep that it seemed barely to touch the top of each successive wave. . . .

On they came, eager only for their prey. The great speed at which the whale was moving would have rendered it necessary for the harpooner to cut the line and let it escape had it not been for the fortunate position of the . . . boats, which had been instantly lowered and rowed off to different points upon either side of the course which the whale was pursuing. Should both our boats succeed in getting fast, there was even then but a chance that the weight of three boats and their crews would much retard it in its fright. Once out of the bay, the ocean was too rough to pursue the game. A whale once frightened, or gallied, as sailors say, if it seeks escape by flight is rarely taken; while one that sounds or goes down the moment it is struck by the harpoon becomes a more sure victim, as it usually rises to the surface again not far away.

The cause of this difference in the actions of whales seems to lie in the penetration of the iron to a deeper and more sensitive part of the body in the one instance than in the other. Unattacked, the whale is a meek, peaceful and sluggish animal, but when suffering under wounds inflicted by human ingenuity it becomes a dreadful and often a deadly enemy. The two loose boats had a fair chance; they pulled bravely on, and both got fast. The rage of the whale now received a new impulse from the torture of the instruments, and its attention was diverted from flight by the sight of the boats and the schooner. Turning in its course, it came head-on for the latter.

I had read of ships being sunk by whales, and for the instant I would gladly have transferred my situation to one in the boats, but there were braver hearts there than mine. Mr. Niles' boat, having been the last one fast, was consequently nearest the whale, and by the powerful lever force exerted with his steering oar nearly thirty feet in length, he just succeeded in getting out of the way; but as soon as he perceived that he should escape the shock from the head, he at once ordered his men to "pull three stern two." This manoeuver brought him upon the whale's side, and with a large flensing spade carried in the bow of the boat he succeeded in inflicting several severe wounds upon the small of the monster's back where the large tendons are given off which direct the motions of the tail.

This new attack caused the whale to go down, but the impulse given by the oarsmen to the boat could not be checked, and its enormous flukes, at first rising high out of the water, descended upon the bow of the boat from which Mr. Niles safely escaped by a vigorous leap overboard. His was the victory, however, and the injury to the boat and the cold ducking were trifles to men of his hardihood. He was immediately rescued, and his crew, getting into another boat, the one which had been broken by the whale's flukes was towed to the schooner. The whale reappeared on the surface in about twenty minutes, but so much disabled that capture was rendered comparatively easy. The death wound was inflicted by Captain Morgan. With a few convulsive struggles the whale reared its tail on high and, whirling it with a noise resembling the discharge of a cannon, rolled over its body and expired. A rope was passed around its tail, and with loud hurras the body was towed to the vessel, which now made sail for the head of the bay.

. . . The remainder of the day was spent in stripping the whale of its blubber and cutting it into pieces suitable for mincing. During the progress of this labor, we were witnesses of a most exciting chase of a large whale by all the boats from the other schooners. For nearly four hours ten boats vied with each other for his capture with singular success. The whale did not get frightened, but seemed to be playing the game of "catch me if you can," enjoying its power of dodging and diving to avoid the harpoons. Many an unsuccessful harpoon was darted from the bows of the boats, while from their sterns many a half-uttered curse broke forth.

A boat from one of our schooners was the first which succeeded in getting fast. The whale immediately sounded and the rival boats prepared to withdraw from the contest. However, as all for the moment rested upon their oars, the whale unexpectedly and sooner than is the habit appeared upon the surface, moving slowly and evidently not at all alarmed. The men in the boat which was fast began to draw themselves up to it by means of the line, when suddenly the harpoon was drawn out of the body and the whale was again, by the rules of our fleet, a lawful object of pursuit by all.

Every boat was instantly in motion, each officer urging on his crew in an excited but low tone of voice, and each man straining every muscle to its utmost power. The loud whisperings of the men as they urged each other to exertions and the beseeching and promising tones of one officer or the profane and threatening mutterings of another were heard above the stifled sounds of the oars in their muffled rowlocks as the boats swept readily past . . . ; above all was heard the hoarse noise, like the rumbling of distant thunder, as the whale, pursuing its lazy course, threw volumes of water from the blowholes high in the air. It was for a time a scene of breathless suspense and well worthy of description by an abler pen than mine. One of the rival boats got the lead, and the first harpoon thrown by its boatsteerer penetrated the animal's side, causing it again to seek the depths below. Then came a pause and rest for all. With their oars peaked and in perfect silence, the crews awaited the reappearance for the whale for half an hour. A second time it rose to the surface, unagitated and blowing at regular intervals, but at such a distance from the place where it went down as to render it manifest to all that it was yet an unclaimed prize. The last harpoon thrown had been broken off in its side. While the discomfited crew of the boat which was a moment before the happy claimant of the prize now hauled in their slackened line, the others were fast fading from our view in a rapid pursuit.

"We've got it at last," said Bill as two hours after dark the dead whale was made fast. . . . "He fought like a tiger, but we were too much for him. We closed with him right and left and buried five harpoons in his blubber before he woke up; then we gave it to him fore and aft with lance and fluke-spade. Ha! he squirmed worse than any angleworm you ever cut in two with a hoe, I reckon, but he's a noble fellow; get a few more like him, and it won't be long 'fore we'll see the gal in Connecticut, hip hurra!" In the excitement of the moment he threw his cap overboard, a sacrifice to Neptune for our remarkably good luck. Bill was the harpooner in Han Woodcock's boat, which had been in first at the death. The loud laugh of the latter could be heard for a mile across the water as he exulted in his success. He was now rapidly rising in our skipper's good graces. It seemed already a settled matter that he should be promoted to a captaincy on his return home.

All were happy in the fullest signification of the word. The more whales taken, the sooner came freedom from hard work and inclement weather. Of course we looked with compassion on our rivals; they had not captured any whales, while in two days we had killed three. Although we had three schooners and they but two, each of theirs carried three boats, while ours carried but two, and during the last chase the . . . boats [of one of our schooners] were not lowered. Their loss of the whale by the breaking of an iron, as whalemen call the harpoon, was an accident which happened to them frequently, for many of their weapons were of an inferior quality. Their success as whalemen, however, when they substituted other irons, became equal to our own, and was accompanied by many hazardous and exciting adventures. It is not our purpose to narrate these in this work, for, given in detail, they would lengthen our story too much and lose their interest by resemblance to those already described. It may be well to add, however, that the labor on these occasions was often fatiguing and excessive, and more frequently without than with success.

. . . The lean meat of the whale was a common dish and highly esteemed. Whenever opportunity offered, large quantities were cut from the whale and hung over the stern of the schooner, where, owing to the cold weather, it not only kept well, but improved in flavor and tenderness. Portions of this it was customary to broil in the form of steaks or to cut up in a hash with pork and potatoes, the latter only an occasional luxury in [our] cabin. . . .

Early on the morning of the tenth the *Marcia* made her appearance with the body of the sunken whale. Its blubber was soon transferred to our deck, and with a double reef breeze we started for Pot Harbor. The Sabbath had not only lost all character as a day of rest, but even the clean shirt, which for some time had been the only thing which marked it, ceased to be seen. To "remember the Sabbath day" was considered of far less importance than to obtain a few gallons of oil. The representations made to us by the owners of the ship before leaving home respecting the reverence paid to the Sabbath by its officers could now only be regarded in the same light as the tempting bait of light work and plenty to eat held out by ship agents to green hands.

It was consolation when starting on our long voyage, as the lofty spires faded from view, to think that, though there was no temple erected on the wilderness of waters to the Giver of all good, the sailor could still, on that hallowed and appointed day, bow the knee in humble adoration to the God of the sea and land. Indeed, our religious exercises, so long as they were continued, constituted some of the happiest features of the voyage. The crew at first so regarded them, and the scene of the ship itself on a Sabbath morning with its clean deck and the marked quiet which prevailed was one well calculated to awaken feelings of devotion; but the first Sunday on whaling ground orders were given to man the mastheads.

PART FIVE

An Age of Reform

Rearranging Social Patterns

During the second quarter of the nineteenth century, new social forces swept through the American villages, farms, and regions that had once existed in near isolation, disrupting traditional ways of work and life. The transportation revolution overcame barriers of distance, as highways, canals, steamships, and railroads linked and transformed established communities and existing markets. Farmers and craftsmen, inventors and factory owners, learned new ways to shape and dominate the physical world. Enterprises like the Lowell Mills introduced new methods of work as well as novel forms of social organization that changed the lives of workers like Harriet Hanson Robinson. The growing public school system inculcated common ideas and goals in young American minds, while evangelical Protestantism labored to purify souls.

The numerous reform movements of the time also represented a determination to perfect the republic of the founding fathers and, if possible, the lands beyond the nation's borders. In their search for social perfection, a few reformers questioned the foundations of capitalism. Some turned to religious or social experiments designed to reshape society. Most aimed at correcting specific problems. Reformers sometimes disagreed on goals and methods because they responded to contradictory moods: some feared what they saw as disorder in society, loss of community, and declining morality; others acted on an optimistic faith in the ultimate perfectibility of the world in general and American society in particular.

As the nation slid toward Civil War, however, the crusade against slavery came to dominate American reform. Slaves themselves generated much of the heat that ignited the fierce controversy. Nat Turner's rebellion in 1831 ushered in an angrier era. Charles Ball, Josiah Henson, Francis Henderson, Jacob Stroyer, and Henry "Box" Brown were slaves who, after running away or purchasing their freedom, wrote accounts of their lives under slavery. Henry Brown also organized and performed in a traveling show that documented his escape from slavery. Such testimonies provided the growing abolition movement with support for its arguments against the institution of slavery. White reformers like William Lloyd Garrison, whose newspaper *The Liberator* began publication in the same year as Nat Turner's rebellion, made Southern leaders fearful of economic disaster by insisting on immediate abolition. As antislavery sentiment grew in the North, images of slaves and of the institution of slavery assumed an increasingly stark character, as the visual portfolio "Slavery and Freedom" (page 253) illustrates. By 1856, when Thomas Henry Tibbles fought with the abolitionist John Brown in Kansas, Americans were already taking up arms over the question of slavery and freedom. And most of the early leaders of the women's rights movement had their first taste of organizing, petitioning, and public speaking in the antislavery movement. From this beginning, Elizabeth Cady Stanton, Susan B. Anthony, and others pioneered a women's rights movement that over many years would markedly affect the lives of American women.

POINTS OF VIEW
Nat Turner's Rebellion (1831)

28

A Slave Insurrection

Nat Turner

Slaveowners, especially those in areas with large slave populations, lived in dread of uprisings. Rebellions in 1739 in South Carolina, in 1800 in Virginia, in 1811 in Louisiana, and in 1822 in South Carolina kept such fears alive. Nat Turner (1800–1831), a slave in Southampton County, Virginia, led the most sensational rebellion in 1831. Beginning on August 21, Turner's rebellion lasted only five days, but it claimed the lives of at least fifty whites. In response, terrified white Southerners gunned down slaves and free blacks and increased restrictions on slaves' education, marriage, and right to assemble. The rebellion also dealt a serious blow to any chance of the South's voluntarily emancipating its slaves.

The Confessions of Nat Turner was published in 1832 by Thomas R. Gray, who interviewed Turner shortly before he was tried and executed. How much of the language of these confessions is Turner's and how much is Gray's is impossible to determine. Gray's account was widely read throughout the South.

The Confessions of Nat Turner, Leader of the Late Insurrection in Southampton, Virginia, as Fully and Voluntarily Made to Thomas R. Gray (1832; New York, 1964), pp. 5–17.

BEFORE YOU READ

1. What was Nat Turner's revelation? What purpose did he consider himself destined to fulfill?

2. How well planned was the rebellion?

3. What do you think Turner and his compatriots expected to achieve by their rebellion?

Agreeable to his own appointment, on the evening he was committed to prison, with permission of the jailer, I visited Nat on Tuesday the first of November, when, without being questioned at all, he commenced his narrative in the following words:

Sir,

You have asked me to give a history of the motives which induced me to undertake the late insurrection, as you call it. To do so I must go back to the days of my infancy, and even before I was born. I was thirty-one years of age the second of October last, and born the property of Benjamin Turner, of this county. In my childhood a circumstance occurred which made an indelible impression on my mind, and laid the groundwork of that enthusiasm which has terminated so fatally to many both white and black, and for which I am about to atone at the gallows. It is here necessary to relate this circumstance—trifling as it may seem, it was the commencement of that belief which has grown with time, and even now, sir, in this dungeon, helpless and forsaken as I am, I cannot divest myself of. Being at play with other children, when three or four years old, I was telling them something, which my mother overhearing, said it had happened before I was born. I stuck to my story, however, and related some things which went in her opinion to confirm it. Others being called on were greatly astonished, knowing that these things had happened, and caused them to say in my hearing, I surely would be a prophet, as the Lord had shown me things that had happened before my birth. And my father and mother strengthened me in this my first impression, saying in my presence, I was intended for some great purpose, which they had always thought from certain marks on my head and breast.

My grandmother, who was very religious, and to whom I was much attached—my master, who belonged to the church, and other religious persons who visited the house, and whom I often saw at prayers, noticing the singularity of my manners, I suppose, and my uncommon intelligence for a child, remarked I had too much sense to be raised—and if I was, I would never be of any service to any one—as a slave. The manner in which I learned to read and write, not only had great influence on my own mind, as I acquired it with the most perfect ease, so much so that I have no recollection whatever of learning the alphabet—but to the astonishment of the family, one day, when a book was shown me to keep me from crying, I began spelling the names of different objects—this was a source of wonder to all in the neighborhood, particularly the blacks—and this learning was constantly improved at all opportunities. When I got large enough to go to work, while employed, I was reflecting on many things that would present themselves to my imagination. I was not addicted to stealing in my youth, nor have never been. Yet such was the confidence of the Negroes in the neighborhood, even at this early period of my life, in my superior judgment, that they would often carry me with them when they were going on any roguery, to plan for them. Growing up among them, with this confidence in my superior judgment, and when this, in their opinions, was perfected by divine inspiration, from the circumstances already alluded to in my infancy, and which belief was ever afterward zealously inculcated by the austerity of my life and manners, which became the subject of remark by white and black. By this time, having arrived to man's estate, and hearing the Scriptures commented on at meetings, I was struck with that particular passage which says: "Seek ye the kingdom of Heaven and all things shall be added unto you." I reflected much on this passage, and prayed daily for light on this subject. As I was praying one day at my plough, the spirit spoke to me, saying "Seek ye the kingdom of Heaven and all things shall be added unto you." *Question*—What do you mean by the Spirit? *Answer*—The Spirit that spoke to the prophets in former days—and I was greatly astonished, and for two years prayed continually, whenever my duty would permit—and then again I had the same revelation, which fully confirmed me in the impression that I was ordained for some great purpose in the hands of the Almighty. Several years rolled round, in which many events occurred to strengthen me in this my belief. At this time I reverted in my mind to the remarks made of me in my childhood, and the things that had been shown me. And as it had been said of me in my childhood by those whom I had been taught to pray, both white and black, and in whom I had the greatest confidence, that I had too much sense to be raised, and if I was I would never be of any use to anyone as a slave. Now finding I had arrived to man's estate, and was a slave, and these revelations being made known to me, I began to direct my attention to this great object, to fulfill the purpose for which, by this time, I felt assured I was intended. Knowing the influence I had obtained over the minds of my fellow servants, (not by the means of conjuring and such like tricks—for to them I always spoke of such things with contempt) but by the communion of the Spirit whose revelations I often communicated to them, and they believed and said my wisdom came from God.

And on the twelfth of May 1828, I heard a loud noise in the heavens, and the Spirit instantly appeared to me and said the Serpent was loosened, and Christ had laid down the yoke he had borne for the sins of men, and that I should take it on and fight against the Serpent, for the time was fast approaching, when the first should be last and the last should be first. *Question*—Do you not find yourself mistaken now? *Answer*—Was not Christ crucified? And by signs in the heavens that it would make known to me when I should commence the great work—and until the first sign appeared, I should conceal it from the knowledge of men—and on the appearance of the sign (the eclipse of the sun last February), I should arise and prepare myself, and slay my enemies with their own weapons. And immediately on the sign appearing in the heavens, the seal was removed from my lips, and I communicated the great work laid out for me to do, to four in whom I had the greatest confidence (Henry, Hark, Nelson, and Sam). It was intended by us to have begun the work of death on the fourth of July last. Many were the plans formed and rejected by us, and it affected my mind to such a degree that I fell sick, and the time passed without our coming to any determination how to commence — still forming new schemes and rejecting them when the sign appeared again, which determined me not to wait longer.

Since the commencement of 1830, I had been living with Mr. Joseph Travis, who was to me a kind master, and placed the greatest confidence in me; in fact, I had no cause to complain of his treatment to me. On Saturday evening, the twentieth of August, it was agreed between Henry, Hark, and myself to prepare a dinner the next day for the men we expected, and then to concert a plan, as we had not yet determined on any. Hark on the following morning brought a pig, and Henry brandy, and being joined by Sam, Nelson, Will, and Jack, they prepared in the woods a dinner, where, about three o'clock, I joined them. . . .

I saluted them on coming up, and asked Will how came he there; he answered his life was worth no more than others, and his liberty as dear to him. I asked him if he thought to obtain it? He said he would or lose his life. This was enough to put him in full confidence. Jack, I knew, was only a tool in the hands of Hark. It was quickly agreed we should commence at home (Mr. J. Travis') on that night, and until we had armed and equipped ourselves, and gathered sufficient force, neither age nor sex was to be spared (which was invariably adhered to). We remained at the feast until about two hours in the night, when we went to the house and found Austin; they all went to the cider press and drank, except myself. On returning to the house, Hark went to the door with an ax, for the purpose of breaking it open, as we knew we were strong enough to murder the family, if they were awakened by the noise; but reflecting that it might create an alarm in the neighborhood, we determined to enter the house secretly, and murder them while sleeping. Hark got a ladder and set it against the chimney, on which I ascended, and hoisting a window, entered and came down stairs, unbarred the door, and removed the guns from their places. It was then observed that I must spill the first blood. On which armed with a hatchet, and accompanied by Will, I entered my master's chamber; it being dark, I could not give a death blow, the hatchet glanced from his head, he sprang from the bed and called his wife, it was his last word. Will laid him dead, with a blow of his ax, and Mrs. Travis shared the same fate, as she lay in bed. The murder of this family, five in number, was the work of a moment, not one of them awoke; there was a little infant sleeping in a cradle, that was forgotten, until we had left the house and gone some distance, when Henry and Will returned and killed it. We got here four guns that would shoot, and several old muskets, with a pound or two of powder. We remained some time at the barn, where we paraded; I formed them in a line as soldiers, and after carrying them through all the maneuvers I was master of, marched them off to Mr. Salathul Francis', about six hundred yards distant. Sam and Will went to the door and knocked. Mr. Francis asked who was there, Sam replied it was him, and he had a letter for him, on which he got up and came to the door; they immediately seized him, and dragging him out a little from the door, he was dispatched by repeated blows on the head; there was no other white person in the family. We started from there for Mrs. Reese's, maintaining the most perfect silence on our march, where finding the door unlocked, we entered, and murdered Mrs. Reese in her bed, while sleeping; her son awoke, but it was only to sleep the sleep of death, he had only time to say who is that, and he was no more. From Mrs. Reese's we went to Mrs. Turner's, a mile distant, which we reached about sunrise on Monday morning. Henry, Austin, and Sam went to the still, where, finding Mr. Pebbles, Austin shot him, and the rest of us went to the house; as we approached, the family discovered us, and shut the door. Vain hope! Will, with one stroke of his ax, opened it, and we entered and found Mrs. Turner and Mrs. Newsome in the middle of a room almost frightened to death. Will immediately killed Mrs. Turner, with one blow of his ax. I took Mrs. Newsome by the hand, and with the sword I had when I was apprehended, I struck her several blows over the head, but not being able to kill her, as the sword was dull. Will turning around and discovering it, dispatched her also. A general destruction of property and search for money and ammunition always succeeded the murders. By this time my company amounted to fifteen, and nine men mounted, who started for Mrs. Whitehead's (the other six were to go through a byway to Mr. Bryant's and rejoin us at Mrs. Whitehead's). . . . As we pushed on to the house, I discovered someone running round the garden, and thinking it was some of the white family, I pursued them, but finding it was a servant girl belonging to the house, I returned to commence the work of death, but they whom I left had not been idle; all the family were already murdered, but Mrs. Whitehead and her daughter Margaret. As I came round to the door I saw Will pulling Mrs. Whitehead out of the house, and at the step he nearly severed her head from her body, with his broad ax. Miss Margaret, when I discovered her had concealed herself in the corner, formed by the projection of the cellar cap from the house; on my approach she fled, but was soon overtaken, and after repeated blows with a sword, I killed her by a blow on the head with a fence rail. By this time, the six who had gone by Mr. Bryant's rejoined us, and informed me they had done the work of death assigned them. We again divided, part going to Mr. Richard Porter's and from thence to Nathaniel Francis', the others to Mr. Howell Harris', and Mr. T. Doyle's. On my reaching Mr. Porter's, he had escaped with his family. I understood there that the alarm had already spread.

I proceeded to Mr. Levi Waller's, two or three miles distant. I took my station in the rear, and as it was my object to carry terror and devastation wherever we went, I placed fifteen or twenty of the best armed and most to be relied on in front, who generally approached the houses as fast as their horses could run; this was for two purposes, to prevent their escape and strike terror to the inhabitants — on this account I never got to the houses, after leaving Mrs. Whitehead's, until the murders were committed, except in one case. I sometimes got in sight in time to see the work of death completed, viewed the mangled bodies as they lay, in silent satisfaction, and immediately started in quest of other victims. Having murdered Mrs. Waller and ten children, we started for

Mr. William Williams'—having killed him and two little boys that were there; while engaged in this, Mrs. Williams fled and got some distance from the house, but she was pursued, overtaken, and compelled to get up behind one of the company, who brought her back, and after showing her the mangled body of her lifeless husband, she was told to get down and lay by his side, where she was shot dead. I then started for Mr. Jacob Williams', where the family were murdered. Here we found a young man named Drury, who had come on business with Mr. Williams. He was pursued, overtaken, and shot. Mrs. Vaughan's was the next place we visited—and after murdering the family here, I determined on starting for Jerusalem. Our number amounted now to fifty or sixty, all mounted and armed with guns, axes, swords, and clubs. On reaching Mr. James W. Parker's gate, immediately on the road leading to Jerusalem, and about three miles distant, it was proposed to me to call there, but I objected, as I knew he was gone to Jerusalem, and my object was to reach there as soon as possible; but some of the men having relations at Mr. Parker's it was agreed that they might call and get his people. I remained at the gate on the road, with seven or eight; the others going across the field to the house, about half a mile off. After waiting some time for them, I became impatient, and started to the house for them, and on our return we were met by a party of white men, who had pursued our blood-stained track and who had fired on those at the gate and dispersed them, which I knew nothing of, not having been at that time rejoined by any of them. Immediately on discovering the whites, I order my men to halt and form, as they appeared to be alarmed. The white men, eighteen in number, approached us in about one hundred yards, when one of them fired.

I then ordered my men to fire and rush on them; the few remaining stood their ground until we approached within fifty yards, when they fired and retreated. We pursued and overtook some of them who we thought we left dead; after pursuing them about two hundred yards, and rising a little hill, I discovered they were met by another party, and had halted, and were reloading their guns, thinking that those who retreated first, and the party who fired on us at fifty or sixty yards distant, had all only fallen back to meet others with ammunition. As I saw them reloading their guns, and more coming up than I saw at first, and several of my bravest men being wounded, the others became panic struck and squandered over the field; the white men pursued and fired on us several times. Hark had his horse shot under him, and I caught another for him as it was running by me; five or six of my men were wounded, but none left on the field; finding myself defeated here I instantly determined to go through a private way, and cross the Nottoway River at the Cypress Bridge, three miles below Jerusalem, and attack that place in the rear, as I expected they would look for me on the other road, and I had a great desire to get there to procure arms and ammunition. After going a short distance in this private way, accompanied by about twenty men, I overtook two or three who told me the others were dispersed in every direction. After trying in vain to collect a sufficient force to proceed to Jerusalem, I determined to return, as I was sure they would make back to their old neighborhood, where they would rejoin me, make new recruits, and come down again. On my way back, I called at Mrs. Thomas's, Mrs. Spencer's, and several other places. The white families having fled, we found no more victims to gratify our thirst for blood, we stopped at Major Ridley's quarter for the night, and being joined by four of his men, with the recruits made since my defeat, we mustered now about forty strong. After placing out sentinels, I laid down to sleep, but was quickly roused by a great racket. Starting up, I found some mounted, and others in great confusion; one of the sentinels having given the alarm that we were about to be attacked, I ordered some to ride round and reconnoiter, and on their return the others being more alarmed, not knowing who they were, fled in different ways, so that I was reduced to about twenty again; with this I determined to attempt to recruit, and proceed on to rally in the neighborhood I had left. Dr. Blunt's was the nearest house, which we reached just before day; on riding up the yard, Hark fired a gun. We expected Dr. Blunt and his family were at Major Ridley's, as I knew there was a company of men there; the gun was fired to ascertain if any of they family were at home; we were immediately fired upon and retreated leaving several of my men. I do not know what became of them, as I never saw them afterward. Pursuing our course back, and coming in sight of Captain Harris's, where we had been the day before, we discovered a party of white men at the house, on which all deserted me but two (Jacob and Nat), we concealed ourselves in the woods until near night, when I sent them in search of Henry, Sam, Nelson, and Hark, and directed them to rally all they could at the place we had had our dinner the Sunday before, where they would find me, and I accordingly returned there as soon as it was dark, and remained until Wednesday evening, when discovering white men riding around the place as though they were looking for someone, and none of my men joining me, I concluded Jacob and Nat had been taken, and compelled to betray me. On this I gave up all hope for the present; and on Thursday night, after having supplied myself with provisions from Mr. Travis's, I scratched a hole under a pile of fence rails in a field, where I concealed myself for six weeks, never leaving my hiding place but for a few minutes in the dead of night to get water, which was very near; thinking by this time I could venture out, I began to go about in the night and eavesdrop the houses in the neighborhood; pursuing this course for about a fortnight and gathering little or no intelligence, afraid of speaking to any human being, and returning every morning to my cave before the dawn of day. I know not how long I might have led this life, if accident had not betrayed me, a dog in the neighborhood passing by my hiding place one night while I was out was attracted by some meat I had in my cave, and crawled in and stole it, and was coming out just as I returned. A few nights after, two Negroes having started to go hunting with the same dog, and passed that way, the dog came again to the place, and having just gone out to walk about, discovered me and barked, on which, thinking myself discovered, I spoke to them to beg concealment. On making myself known, they fled from me. Knowing then they would betray me, I immediately left my hiding place, and was pursued almost incessantly until I was taken a fortnight afterward by Mr. Benjamin Phipps, in a little hole I had dug out with my sword, for the purpose of concealment, under the top of a fallen tree. On Mr. Phipps discovering the place of my concealment, he cocked his gun and aimed at me. I requested him not to shoot, and I would give up, upon which he demanded my sword. I delivered it to him, and he brought me to prison. During the time I was pursued, I had many hair breadth escapes, which your time will not permit you to relate. I am here loaded with chains, and willing to suffer the fate that awaits me.

[Gray:] I here proceeded to make some inquiries of him, after assuring him of the certain death that awaited him, and that concealment would only bring destruction of the innocent as well as guilty, of his own color, if he knew of any extensive or concerted plan. His answer was, I do not. When I questioned him as to the insurrection in North Carolina happening about the same time, he denied any knowledge of it.

29

Who Is to Blame?

William Lloyd Garrison et al.

Nat Turner's rebellion occurred just when slavery was under attack from other quarters. In 1829, a free black named David Walker published his incendiary Walker's Appeal in Four Articles, Together with a Preamble to the Colored Citizens of the World, But in Particular and Very Expressly to Those of the United States of America, *which quoted the Declaration of Independence in justification of a slave insurrection. Then William Lloyd Garrison (1805–1879), who would also cite the Declaration of Independence, broke with the tradition among white abolitionists of calling for gradual emancipation. From the first issue of the* Liberator, *published in Boston on January 1, 1831, Garrison demanded the immediate and unconditional abolition of slavery.*

The Southern states reacted viscerally to Nat Turner's rebellion. In the immediate hysteria, slaves and free blacks were gunned down. The ongoing debate in Virginia over gradual emancipation ended. Instead, the Southern states moved toward strengthening the slave system by restricting the rights of free blacks as well as the right of owners to free slaves, augmenting the patrols that constricted the mobility of the slave population, setting limits on black religious meetings, and ensuring that marriage did not restrict the slave trade. And they moved on many fronts to close the South to antislavery propaganda, even touching off a national debate by forbidding the federal post office to deliver such antislavery writings as the Liberator *in Southern states.*

BEFORE YOU READ

1. Did William Lloyd Garrison approve of Nat Turner's rebellion?
2. How did he explain its occurrence?
3. Did John Hampden Pleasants, editor of the Richmond *Constitutional Whig*, approve of the treatment of blacks in the wake of the rebellion?

William E. Cain, ed., *William Lloyd Garrison and the Fight against Slavery* (Boston: Bedford/ St. Martin's, 1995), p. 80; *Constitutional Whig*, Richmond, Virginia, September 3, 1831; the original of Floyd's letter to Hamilton can be found in the Manuscript Division of the Library of Congress.

4. How did he explain its occurrence?
5. How did Virginia governor John Floyd explain the rebellion?
6. What did he propose to avoid further uprisings?

WILLIAM LLOYD GARRISON

The Liberator, *September 3, 1831*

What we have so long predicted,—at the peril of being stigmatized as an alarmist and declaimer,—has commenced its fulfilment. The first step of the earthquake, which is ultimately to shake down the fabric of oppression, leaving not one stone upon another, has been made. The first drops of blood, which are but the prelude to a deluge from the gathering clouds, have fallen. The first flash of the lightning, which is to smite and consume, has been felt. The first wailings of a bereavement, which is to clothe the earth in sackcloth, have broken upon our ears.

In the first number of the *Liberator*, we alluded to the hour of vengeance in the following lines:

> Wo if it come with storm, and blood, and fire,
> When midnight darkness veils the earth and sky!
> *Wo to the innocent babe*—the guilty sire—
> *Mother and daughter*—friends of kindred tie!
> *Stranger and citizen alike shall die!*
> Red-handed Slaughter his revenge shall feed,
> And Havoc yell his ominous death-cry,
> And wild Despair in vain for mercy plead—
> While hell itself shall shrink and sicken at the deed!

Read the account of the insurrection in Virginia, and say whether our prophecy be not fulfilled. What was poetry—imagination—in January, is now a bloody reality. "Wo to the innocent babe—to mother and daughter!" Is it not true? Turn again to the record of slaughter! Whole families have been cut off—not a mother, not a daughter, not a babe left. Dreadful retaliation! "The dead bodies of white and black lying just as they were slain, unburied"—the oppressor and the oppressed equal at last in death—what a spectacle!

True, the rebellion is quelled. Those of the slaves who were not killed in combat, have been secured, and the prison is crowded with victims destined for the gallows!

> Yet laugh not in your carnival of crime
> Too proudly, ye oppressors!

You have seen, it is to be feared, but the beginning of sorrows. All the blood which has been shed will be required at your hands. At your hands alone? No—but at the hands of the people of New-England and of all the free states. The crime of oppression is national. The south is only the agent in this guilty traffic. But, remember! the same causes are at work which must inevitably produce the same effects; and when the contest shall have again begun, it must be again a war of extermination. In the present instance, no quarters have been asked or given.

But we have killed and routed them now—we can do it again and again—we are invincible! A dastardly triumph, well becoming a nation of oppressors. Detestable complacency, that can think, without emotion, of the extermination of the blacks! We have the power to kill *all*—let us, therefore, continue to apply the whip and forge new fetters!

In his fury against the revolters, who will remember their wrongs? What will it avail them, though the catalogue of their sufferings, dripping with warm blood fresh from their lacerated bodies, be held up to extenuate their conduct? It is enough that the victims were black—that circumstance makes them less precious than the dogs which have been slain in our streets! They were black—brutes, pretending to be men—legions of curses upon their memories! They were black—God made them to serve us!

Ye patriotic hypocrites! ye panegyrists[1] of Frenchmen, Greeks, and Poles! ye fustian[2] declaimers for liberty! ye valiant sticklers for equal rights among yourselves! ye haters of aristocracy! ye assailants of monarchies! ye republican nullifiers! ye treasonable disunionists! be dumb! Cast no reproach upon the conduct of the slaves, but let your lips and cheeks wear the blisters of condemnation!

Ye accuse the pacific friends of emancipation of instigating the slaves to revolt. Take back the charge as a foul slander. The slaves need no incentives at our hands. They will find them in their stripes—in their emaciated bodies—in their ceaseless toil—in their ignorant minds—in every field, in every valley, on every hill-top and mountain, wherever you and your fathers have fought for liberty—in your speeches, your conversations, your celebrations, your pamphlets, your newspapers—voices in the air, sounds from across the ocean, invitations to resistance above, below, around them! What more do they need? Surrounded by such influences, and smarting under their newly made wounds, is it wonderful that they should rise to contend—as other "heroes" have contended—for their lost rights? It is *not* wonderful.

In all that we have written, is there aught to justify the excesses of the slaves? No. Nevertheless, they deserve no more censure than the Greeks in destroying the Turks, or the Poles in exterminating the Russians, or our fathers in slaughtering the British. Dreadful, indeed, is the standard erected by worldly patriotism!

For ourselves, we are horror-struck at the late tidings. We have exerted our utmost efforts to avert the calamity. We have warned our countrymen of the danger of persisting in their unrighteous conduct. We have preached to the slaves the pacific precepts of Jesus Christ. We have appealed to christians, philanthropists and patriots, for their assistance to accomplish the great work of national redemption through the agency of moral power—of public opinion—

---

1. **panegyrists:** people who celebrate a person, group, or deed.
2. **fustian:** pretentious, pompous.

of individual duty. How have we been received? We have been threatened, pro-
scribed, vilified and imprisoned—a laughing-stock and a reproach. Do we fal-
ter, in view of these things? Let time answer. If we have been hitherto urgent,
and bold, and denunciatory in our efforts,—hereafter we shall grow vehement
and active with the increase of danger. We shall cry, in trumpet tones,
night and day,—Wo to this guilty land, unless she speedily repent of her evil
doings! The blood of millions of her sons cries aloud for redress! IMMEDI-
ATE EMANCIPATION can alone save her from the vengeance of Heaven,
and cancel the debt of ages!

JOHN HAMPDEN PLEASANTS

Constitutional Whig, *September 3, 1831*

We have been astonished since our return from Southampton (whither we went
with Capt. Harrison's Troop of Horse) in reading over the mass of exchange
papers accumulated in our absence, to see the number of false, absurd, and idle
rumors, circulated by the Press, touching the insurrection in that county. Editors seem to have applied themselves to the task of alarming the public mind as
much as possible by persuading the slaves to entertain a high opinion of their
strength and consequences. While truth is always the best policy, and best remedy, the exaggerations to which we have alluded are calculated to give the slaves
false conceptions of their numbers and capacity, by exhibiting the terror and
confusion of the whites, and to induce them to think that practicable, which
they see is so much feared by their superiors.

We have little to say of the Southampton Tragedy beyond what is already
known. The origin of the conspiracy, the prime agents, its extent and ultimate
direction, is matter of conjecture.—The universal opinion in that part of
the country is that Nat, a slave, a preacher, and a pretended prophet was the
first [blurred word], the actual leader, and the most remorseless of the executioners. According to the evidence of a negro boy whom they carried along
to hold their horses, Nat commenced the scene of murder at the first house
(Travis') with his own hand. Having called upon two others to make good
their valiant boasting, so often repeated, of what they would do, and these
shrinking from the requisition, Nat proceeded to dispatch one of the family
with his own hand. Animated by the example and exhortations of their leader,
having a taste of blood and convinced that they had now gone too far to recede,
his followers dismissed their doubts and became as ferocious as their leader
wished them. To follow the [blurred word] capture of Travis' house early
that day, to their dispersion at Parker's cornfield early in the afternoon, when
they had traversed near 20 miles, murdered 63 whites, and approached within
3 or 4 miles of the Village of Jerusalem; the immediate object of their movement—to describe the scenes at each house, the circumstances of the murders,
the hair breadth escapes of the few who were lucky enough to escape—would
prove as interesting as heart rending. Many of the details have reached us but

not in so authentic a shape as to justify their publication, nor have we the time or space. Let a few suffice. Of the event at Dr. Blount's we had a narrative from the gallant old gentleman himself, and his son, a lad about 15, distinguished for his gallantry and modesty, and whom we take leave to recommend to Gen. Jackson, for a warrant in the Navy or at West Point. The Doctor had received information of the insurrection, and that his house would be attacked a short time before the attack was made. Crippled with the gout, and indisposed to leave, he decided to defend his home. His force was his son, overseer and three other white men. Luckily there were six guns, and plenty of powder and shot in the house. These were barely loaded, his force posted, and the instructions given, when the negroes from 15 to 30 strong, rode up about day break. The Doctor's orders were that each man should be particular in his aim and should fire one at a time; he himself reserved one gun, resolved if the house was forced to sell his life as dearly as he could. The remaining five fired in succession upon the assailants, at the distance of fifteen or twenty steps. The blacks, upon the fifth fire, retreated, leaving one killed (we believe) and one wounded (a fellow named Hark,) and were pursued by the Doctor's negroes with shouts and execrations. Had the shot been larger, more execution doubtless would have been done.

Mrs. Vaughan's was among the last houses attacked. A venerable negro woman described the scene which she had witnessed with great emphasis: it was near noon and her mistress was making some preparations in the porch for dinner, when happening to look towards the road she discerned a dust and wondered what it could mean. In a second, the negroes mounted and armed, rushed into view, and making an exclamation indicative of her horror and agony, Mrs. Vaughan ran into the house. — The negroes dismounted and ran around the house, pointing their guns at the doors and windows. Mrs. Vaughan appeared at a window, and begged for her life, inviting them to take everything she had. The prayer was answered by one of them firing at her, which was followed by another, and a fatal, shot. In the meantime, Miss Vaughan, who was upstairs, and unappraised of the terrible advent until she heard the noise of the attack, rushed down, and begging for her life, was shot as she ran a few steps from the door. A son of Mrs. Vaughan, about 15, was at the still house, when hearing a gun and conjecturing, it is supposed, that his brother had come from Jerusalem, approached the house and was shot as he got over the fence. It is difficult for the imagination to conceive a situation so truly and horribly awful, as that in which these unfortunate ladies were placed. Alone, unprotected, and unconscious of danger, to find themselves without a moment's notice for escape or defence, in the power of a band of ruffians, from whom instant death was the least they could expect! In a most lively and picturesque manner, did the old negress describe the horrors of the scene; the blacks riding up with imprecations, the looks of her mistress, white as a sheet, her prayers for her life, and the actions of the scoundrels environing the house and pointing their guns at the doors and windows, ready to fire as occasion offered. When the work was done they called for drink, and food, and becoming nice, damned the brandy as vile stuff.

The scene at Vaughan's may suffice to give an idea of what was done at the other houses. A bloodier and more accursed tragedy was never acted, even by the agency of the tomahawk and scalping knife. Interesting details will no doubt be evolved in the progress of the trials and made known to the public.

It is with pain we speak of another feature of the Southampton Rebellion; for we have been most unwilling to have our sympathies for the sufferers diminished or affected by their misconduct. We allude to the slaughter of many blacks, without trial, and under circumstances of great barbarity. How many have thus been put into death (generally by decapitation or shooting) reports vary; probably however some five and twenty and from that to 40; possibly a yet larger number. To the great honor of General Eppes, he used every precaution in his power, and we hope and believe with success, to put a stop to the disgraceful procedure.—We met with one individual of intelligence, who stated that he himself had killed between 10 and 15. He justified himself on the grounds of the barbarities committed on the whites; and that he thought himself right is certain from the fact that he narrowly escaped losing his own life in an attempt to save a negro woman whom he thought innocent but who was shot by the multitude in despite of his exertions. We (the Richmond Troop) witnessed with surprise the sanguinary temper of the population who evinced a strong disposition to inflict immediate death on every prisoner. Not having witnessed the horrors committed by the blacks, or seen the unburried and disfigured remains of their wives and children, we were unprepared to understand their feelings, and could not at first admit of their extenuation, which a closer observation of the atrocities of the insurgents suggested. Now, however, we feel individually compelled to offer an apology for the people of Southampton, while we deeply deplore that human nature urged them to such extremities. Let the fact not be doubted by those whom it most concerns, that another such insurrection will be the signal for the extermination of the whole black population in the quarter of the state where it occurs.

The numbers engaged in the insurrection are variously reported. They probably did not exceed 40 or 50, and were fluctuating from desertions and new recruits. About fifty are in Southampton jail, some of them on suspicion only.—We trust and believe that the intelligent magistracy of the county, will have the firmness to oppose the popular passions, should it be disposed to involve the innocent with the guilty, and to take suspicion for proof.

The presence of the troops from Norfolk and Richmond alone prevented retaliation from being carried much farther.

At the date of Capt. Harrison's departure from Jerusalem, Gen. Nat had not been taken. On that morning, however, Dred, another insurgent chief, was brought prisoner to Jerusalem, having surrendered himself to his master, in the apprehension, no doubt, of starving in the swamps or being shot by the numerous parties of local militia, who were in pursuit. Nat had not certainly been heard from since the skirmish in Parker's cornfield, which was in fact, the termination of the insurrection; the negroes after that dispersing themselves, and making no further attempt. He is represented as a shrewd fellow, reads, writes, and preaches; and by various artifices had acquired great influence over the minds of the wretched beings whom he has led into destruction. It is supposed that he induced them to believe that there were only 80,000 whites in the country, who, being exterminated, the blacks might take possession. Various of his tricks to acquire and preserve influence had been mentioned, but they are not worth repeating. If there was any ulterior purpose, he probably alone knows it. For our own part, we still believe there was none; and if he be the intelligent man represented, we are incapable of conceiving the arguments by which he persuaded his own mind of the feasibility of his attempt, or how it could possibly end but in certain destruction. We therefore incline to the belief that he acted upon no higher principle than the impulse of revenge against the whites, as the enslavers of himself and his race; that, being a fanatic, he possibly persuaded himself that Heaven would interfere; and that he may have convinced himself, as he certainly did his deluded followers to some extent, that the appearance of the sun some weeks ago, prognosticated something favorable to their cause. We are inclined to think that the solar phenomenon exercised considerable influence in promoting the insurrection; calculated as it was to impress the imaginations of the ignorant.

A more important inquiry remains—whether the conspiracy was circumscribed to the neighborhood in which it broke out, or had its ramifications through other counties. We, at first, adopted the first opinion; but there are several circumstances which favor the latter. We understand that the confessions of all the prisoners go to show that the insurrection broke out too soon, as it is supposed, in consequence of the last day of July being a Sunday, and not, as the negroes in Southampton believed, the Saturday before. The report is that the rising was fixed for the fourth Sunday in August, and that they supposing Sunday, the 31st of July to be the first Sunday in August, they were betrayed into considering the 3d Sunday as the 4th. This is the popular impression founded upon confessions, upon the indications of an intention of the negroes in Nansemond and other places to unite, and upon the allegation that Gen. Nat extended his preaching excursions to Petersburg and this city; allegations which we, however, disbelieve. It is more than probable, nevertheless, that the mischief was concerted and concocted under the cloak of religion. The trials which are now proceeding in Southampton, Sussex, and elsewhere, will develop all the truth. We suspect the truth will turn out to be that the conspiracy was confined to Southampton, and that the idea of its extensiveness originated in the panic which seized upon the South East of Virginia.

GOVERNOR JOHN FLOYD OF VIRGINIA

Letter to Governor James Hamilton Jr. of South Carolina

Richmond
November 19, 1831

Sir:

I received your letter yesterday and with great pleasure will give you my impressions freely—

I will notice this affair in my annual message, but here only give a very careless history of it, as it appeared to the public—

I am fully persuaded, the spirit of insubordination which has, and still manifests itself in Virginia, had its origin among, and eminated from, the Yankee population, upon their *first* arrival amongst us, but mostly especially the Yankee pedlers and traders.

The course has been by no means a direct one—they began first, by making them religious—their conversations were of that character—telling the blacks, God was no respecter of persons—the black man was as good as the white—that all men were born free and equal—that they cannot serve two masters—that the white people rebelled against England to obtain freedom, so have the blacks a right to do.

In the mean time, I am sure without any purpose of this kind, the preachers, principally Northern—were very assiduous in operating upon our population, day and night, they were at work—and religion became, and is, the fashion of the times—finally our females and of the most respectable were persuaded that it was piety to teach negroes to read and write, to the end that they might read the *Scriptures*—many of them became tutoresses in Sunday schools and, pious distributors of tracts, from the New York Tract Society.

At this point, more active operations commenced—our magistrates and laws became more inactive—large assemblages of negroes were suffered to take place for religious purposes—Then commenced the efforts of the black preachers, often from the pulpits these pamphlets and papers were read—followed by the incendiary publications of Walker,[3] Garrison and Knapp[4] of Boston, these too with songs and hymns of a similar character were circulated, read and commented upon—We resting in apathetic security until the Southampton affair.

From all that has come to my knowledge during and since this affair—I am fully convinced that every black preacher in the whole country east of the Blue Ridge was in the secret, that the plans as published by those Northern presses were adopted and acted upon by them—that their congregations, as they were called knew nothing of this intended rebellion, except a few leading and intelligent men, who may have been head men in the Church—*the mass* were prepared by making them aspire to an equal station by such conversations as I have related as the first step.

I am informed that they had settled the form of government to be that of white people, whom they intended to cut off to a man—with the difference that the preachers were to be their Governors, Generals and Judges. I feel fully justified to myself, in believing the Northern incendiaries, tracts, Sunday Schools, religion and reading and writing has accomplished this end.

I shall in my annual message recommend that laws be passed—To confine the Slaves to the estates of their masters—prohibit negroes from preaching—

---

3. **Walker:** David Walker, a free black whose published writing justified slave insurrection.
4. **Knapp:** Isaac Knapp, abolitionist editor and associate of William Lloyd Garrison.

absolutely to drive from this State all free negroes—and to substitute the surplus revenue in our Treasury annually for slaves, to work for a time upon our Rail Roads etc etc and these sent out of the country, preparatory, or rather as the first step to emancipation—This last point will of course be tenderly and cautiously managed and will be urged or delayed as your State and Georgia may be disposed to co-operate.

In relation to the extent of this insurrection I think it greater than will ever appear—the facts will as now considered, appear to be these—It commenced with Nat and nine others on Sunday night—two o'clock, we date it, Monday morning before day and ceased by the dispersion of the negroes on Tuesday morning at ten o'clock—During this time the negroes had murdered sixty one persons, and traversed a distance of twenty miles, and increased to about seventy slave men—they spared but one family and that one was so wretched as to be in all respects upon a par with them—all died bravely indicating no reluctance to loose [*sic*] their lives in such a cause.

> I am Sir,
> with consideration and respect
> Your obt Sevnt
> John Floyd

His Excy
James Hamilton, Jr.
Governor of South Carolina

For Critical Thinking

1. Examine the language of *The Confessions of Nat Turner*. Can you identify parts that seem to be the language expected of a Virginia lawyer like Thomas Gray and parts that you might imagine to be Nat Turner's own words? Compose a defense of his actions as you think Nat Turner might have presented it.

2. Why do you think that many people linked Turner's rebellion with the writings of William Lloyd Garrison? What does that say about their view of the slaves? What was Garrison's response to this linking?

3. Compose a possible reply from South Carolina governor James Hamilton Jr. to Governor Floyd's letter.

30

The Lowell Textile Workers
Harriet Hanson Robinson

The transportation revolution made the movement of goods easier and cheaper, greatly expanding the potential market for manufactured products, particularly textiles. Incorporation, moreover, permitted manufacturing concerns and transportation projects to expand. But where would the workers come from?

One early answer was the Waltham system, the brainchild of the New England industrialist and reformer Francis Cabot Lowell. To recruit respectable young women from New England farms to work in his mills, he developed a highly organized paternal system. Lowell offered reasonable wages and working conditions as well as carefully chaperoned boarding houses. He even sponsored literary journals to create a genteel atmosphere. But within a few years, under the pressure of business competition, working and living conditions worsened, and eventually the farm girls were replaced by desperately poor Irish immigrant workers.

As a young girl in the 1830s, Harriet Hanson Robinson (1825–1911) worked in the Lowell mills. She became deeply troubled by the deteriorating conditions under which many young women labored. This led her into reform movements, including woman suffrage. In 1898, more than sixty years after she worked in the mills, she published Loom and Spindle, *telling of her experience.*

BEFORE YOU READ

1. Why did Harriet Hanson Robinson work in the mills?
2. What did she like about life at the mills?
3. How did she think working at the mills affected the status of women?
4. Why did the young women strike?

CHAPTER II. CHILD-LIFE
IN THE LOWELL COTTON-MILLS

In 1831, under the shadow of a great sorrow, which had made her four children fatherless,—the oldest but seven years of age,—my mother was left to struggle alone; and, although she tried to earn bread enough to fill our hungry mouths, she could not do it, even with the help of kind friends. And so it happened that one of her more wealthy neighbors, who had looked with longing eyes on the

Harriet Hanson Robinson, *Loom and Spindle or Life among the Early Mill Girls* (New York: Crowell, 1898), pp. 16–22, 37–43, 51–53.

one little daughter of the family, offered to adopt me. But my mother, who had had a hard experience in her youth in living amongst strangers, said, "No; while I have one meal of victuals a day, I will not part with my children." I always remembered this speech because of the word "victuals," and I wondered for a long time what this good old Bible word meant.

That was a hard, cold winter; and for warmth's sake my mother and her four children all slept in one bed, two at the foot and three at the head,—but her richer neighbor could not get the little daughter; and, contrary to all the modern notions about hygiene, we were a healthful and a robust brood.

Shortly after this my mother's widowed sister, Mrs. Angeline Cudworth, who kept a factory boarding-house in Lowell, advised her to come to that city.

I had been to school constantly until I was about ten years of age, when my mother, feeling obliged to have help in her work besides what I could give, and also needing the money which I could earn, allowed me, at my urgent request (for I wanted to earn *money* like the other little girls), to go to work in the mill. I worked first in the spinning-room as a "doffer." The doffers were the very youngest girls, whose work was to doff, or take off, the full bobbins, and replace them with the empty ones.

Some of us learned to embroider in crewels,[1] and I still have a lamb worked on cloth, a relic of those early days, when I was first taught to improve my time in the good old New England fashion. When not doffing, we were often allowed to go home, for a time, and thus we were able to help our mothers in their housework. We were paid two dollars a week; and how proud I was when my turn came to stand up on the bobbin-box, and write my name in the paymaster's book, and how indignant I was when he asked me if I could "write." "Of course I can," said I, and he smiled as he looked down on me.

The working-hours of all the girls extended from five o'clock in the morning until seven in the evening, with one-half hour for breakfast and for dinner. Even the doffers were forced to be on duty nearly fourteen hours a day, and this was the greatest hardship in the lives of these children. For it was not until 1842 that the hours of labor for children under twelve years of age were limited to ten per day; but the "ten-hour law" itself was not passed until long after some of these little doffers were old enough to appear before the legislative committee on the subject, and plead, by their presence, for a reduction of the hours of labor.

I do not recall any particular hardship connected with this life, except getting up so early in the morning, and to this habit, I never was, and never shall be, reconciled, for it has taken nearly a lifetime for me to make up the sleep lost at that early age. But in every other respect it was a pleasant life. We were not hurried any more than was for our good, and no more work was required of us than we were able easily to do.

---

1. **crewels:** embroidery or embroidery yarns.

Most of us children lived at home, and we were well fed, drinking both tea and coffee, and eating substantial meals (besides luncheons) three times a day. We had very happy hours with the older girls, many of whom treated us like babies, or talked in a motherly way, and so had a good influence over us. And in the long winter evenings, when we could not run home between the doffings, we gathered in groups and told each other stories, and sung the old-time songs our mothers had sung, such as "Barbara Allen," "Lord Lovell," "Captain Kid," "Hull's Victory," and sometimes a hymn.

Among the ghost stories I remember some that would delight the hearts of the "Society for Psychical Research." The more imaginative ones told of what they had read in fairy books, or related tales of old castles and distressed maidens; and the scene of their adventures was sometimes laid among the foundation stones of the new mill, just building.

And we told each other of our little hopes and desires, and what we meant to do when we grew up. For we had our aspirations; and one of us, who danced the "shawl dance," as she called it, in the spinning-room alley, for the amusement of her admiring companions, discussed seriously with another little girl the scheme of their running away together, and joining the circus.

I cannot tell how it happened that some of us knew about the English factory children, who, it was said, were treated so badly, and were even whipped by their cruel overseers. But we did know of it, and used to sing, to a doleful little tune, some verses called, "The Factory Girl's Last Day." I do not remember it well enough to quote it as written, but have refreshed my memory by reading it lately in Robert Dale Owen's writings: —

The Factory Girl's Last Day

'Twas on a winter morning,
    The weather wet and wild,
Two hours before the dawning
    The father roused his child,
Her daily morsel bringing,
    The darksome room he paced,
And cried, 'The bell is ringing—
    My hapless darling, haste!'

The overlooker met her
    As to her frame she crept;
And with this thong he beat her,
    And cursed her when she wept.
It seemed as she grew weaker,
    The threads the oftener broke,
The rapid wheels ran quicker,
    And heavier fell the stroke.

The song goes on to tell the sad story of her death while her "pitying comrades" were carrying her home to die, and ends: —

That night a chariot passed her,
    While on the ground she lay;

The daughters of her master,
    An evening visit pay.
Their tender hearts were sighing,
    As negroes' wrongs were told,
While the white slave was dying
    Who gained her father's gold.

In contrast with this sad picture, we thought of ourselves as well off, in our cosey corner of the mill, enjoying ourselves in our own way, with our good mothers and our warm suppers awaiting us when the going-out bell should ring.

CHAPTER IV. THE CHARACTERISTICS
OF THE EARLY FACTORY GIRLS

When I look back into the factory life of fifty or sixty years ago, I do not see what is called "a class" of young men and women going to and from their daily work, like so many ants that cannot be distinguished one from another; I see them as individuals, with personalities of their own. This one has about her the atmosphere of her early home. That one is impelled by a strong and noble purpose. The other,—what she is, has been an influence for good to me and to all womankind.

Yet they were a class of factory operatives, and were spoken of (as the same class is spoken of now) as a set of persons who earned their daily bread, whose condition was fixed, and who must continue to spin and to weave to the end of their natural existence. Nothing but this was expected of them, and they were not supposed to be capable of social or mental improvement. That they could be educated and developed into something more than mere work-people, was an idea that had not yet entered the public mind. So little does one class of persons really know about the thoughts and aspirations of another! It was the good fortune of these early mill-girls to teach the people of that time that this sort of labor is not degrading; that the operative is not only "capable of virtue," but also capable of self-cultivation.

At the time the Lowell cotton-mills were started, the factory girl was the lowest among women. In England, and in France particularly, great injustice had been done to her real character; she was represented as subjected to influences that could not fail to destroy her purity and self-respect. In the eyes of her overseer she was but a brute, a slave, to be beaten, pinched, and pushed about. It was to overcome this prejudice that such high wages had been offered to women that they might be induced to become mill-girls, in spite of the opprobrium that still clung to this "degrading occupation." At first only a few came; for, though tempted by the high wages to be regularly paid in "cash," there were many who still preferred to go on working at some more *genteel* employment at seventy-five cents a week and their board.

But in a short time the prejudice against factory labor wore away, and the Lowell mills became filled with blooming and energetic New England women.

In 1831 Lowell was little more than a factory village. Several corporations were started, and the cotton-mills belonging to them were building. Help was in great demand; and stories were told all over the country of the new factory town, and the high wages that were offered to all classes of work-people,—stories that reached the ears of mechanics' and farmers' sons, and gave new life to lonely and dependent women in distant towns and farmhouses. Into this Yankee El Dorado, these needy people began to pour by the various modes of travel known to those slow old days. The stage-coach and the canal-boat came every day, always filled with new recruits for this army of useful people. The mechanic and machinist came, each with his homemade chest of tools, and often-times his wife and little ones. The widow came with her little flock and her scanty house-keeping goods to open a boarding-house or variety store, and so provided a home for her fatherless children. Many farmers' daughters came to earn money to complete their wedding outfit, or buy the bride's share of housekeeping articles.

Women with past histories came, to hide their griefs and their identity, and to earn an honest living in the "sweat of their brow." Single young men came, full of hope and life, to get money for an education, or to lift the mortgage from the home-farm. Troops of young girls came by stages and baggage-wagons, men often being employed to go to other States and to Canada, to collect them at so much a head, and deliver them at the factories.

[The] country girls had queer names, which added to the singularity of their appearance. Samantha, Triphena, Plumy, Kezia, Aseneth, Elgardy, Leafy, Ruhamah, Lovey, Almaretta, Sarepta, and Florilla were among them.

Their dialect was also very peculiar. On the broken English and Scotch of their ancestors was ingrafted the nasal Yankee twang; so that many of them, when they had just come *daown*, spoke a language almost unintelligible. But the severe discipline and ridicule which met them was as good as a school education, and they were soon taught the "city way of speaking."

Their dress was also peculiar, and was of the plainest of homespun, cut in such an old-fashioned style that each young girl looked as if she had borrowed her grandmother's gown. Their only head-covering was a shawl, which was pinned under the chin; but after the first payday, a "shaker" (or "scooter") sun-bonnet usually replaced this primitive headgear of their rural life.

But the early factory girls were not all country girls. There were others also, who had been taught that "work is no disgrace." There were some who came to Lowell solely on account of the social or literary advantages to be found there. They lived in secluded parts of New England, where books were scarce, and there was no cultivated society. They had comfortable homes, and did not perhaps need the *money* they would earn; but they longed to see this new "City of Spindles." . . .

The laws relating to women were such, that a husband could claim his wife wherever he found her, and also the children she was trying to shield from his influence; and I have seen more than one poor woman skulk behind her loom or her frame when visitors were approaching the end of the aisle where she worked. Some of these were known under assumed names, to prevent their husbands from trusteeing their wages. It was a very common thing for a male person of a certain kind to do this, thus depriving his wife of *all* her wages, perhaps, month after month. The wages of minor children could be trusteed, unless the children (being fourteen years of age) were given their time. Women's wages were also trusteed for the debts of their husbands, and children's for the debts of their parents.

It must be remembered that at this date woman had no property rights. A widow could be left without her share of her husband's (or the family) property, a legal "incumbrance" to his estate. A father could make his will without reference to his daughter's share of the inheritance. He usually left her a home on the farm as long as she remained single. A woman was not supposed to be capable of spending her own or of using other people's money. In Massachusetts, before 1840, a woman could not legally be treasurer of her own sewing-society, unless some man were responsible for her.

The law took no cognizance of woman as a money-spender. She was a ward, an appendage, a relict. Thus it happened, that if a woman did not choose to marry, or, when left a widow, to re-marry, she had no choice but to enter one of the few employments open to her, or to become a burden on the charity of some relative.

In almost every New England home could be found one or more of these women, sometimes welcome, more often unwelcome, and leading joyless, and in many instances unsatisfactory, lives. The cotton-factory was a great opening to these lonely and dependent women. From a condition approaching pauperism they were at once placed above want; they could earn money, and spend it as they pleased; and could gratify their tastes and desires without restraint, and without rendering an account to anybody. . . .

Among the older women who sought this new employment were very many lonely and dependent ones, such as used to be mentioned in old wills as "incumbrances" and "relicts," and to whom a chance of earning money was indeed a new revelation. How well I remember some of these solitary ones! As a child of eleven years, I often made fun of them—for children do not see the pathetic side of human life—and imitated their limp carriage and inelastic gait. I can see them now, even after sixty years, just as they looked,—depressed, modest, mincing, hardly daring to look one in the face, so shy and sylvan had been their lives. But after the first pay-day came, and they felt the jingle of silver in their pockets, and had begun to feel its mercurial influence, their bowed heads were lifted, their necks seemed braced with steel, they looked you in the face, sang blithely among their looms or frames, and walked with elastic step to and from their work. And when Sunday came, homespun was no longer their only wear; and how sedately gay in their new attire they walked to church, and how proudly they dropped their silver fourpences into the contribution-box! It seemed as if a great hope impelled them,—the harbinger of the new era that was about to dawn for them and for all women-kind.

CHAPTER V.
CHARACTERISTICS (CONTINUED)

One of the first strikes of cotton-factory operatives that ever took place in this country was that in Lowell, in October, 1836. When it was announced that the wages were to be cut down, great indignation was felt, and it was decided to strike, *en masse*. This was done. The mills were shut down, and the girls went in procession from their several corporations to the "grove" on Chapel Hill, and listened to "incendiary" speeches from early labor reformers.

One of the girls stood on a pump, and gave vent to the feelings of her companions in a neat speech, declaring that it was their duty to resist all attempts at cutting down the wages. This was the first time a woman had spoken in public in Lowell, and the event caused surprise and consternation among her audience.

Cutting down the wages was not their only grievance, nor the only cause of this strike. Hitherto the corporations had paid twenty-five cents a week towards the board of each operative, and now it was their purpose to have the girls pay the sum; and this, in addition to the cut in wages, would make a difference of at least one dollar a week. It was estimated that as many as twelve or fifteen hundred girls turned out, and walked in procession through the streets. They had neither flags nor music, but sang songs, a favorite (but rather inappropriate) one being a parody on "I won't be a nun."

> Oh! isn't it a pity, such a pretty girl as I—
>   Should be sent to the factory to pine away and die?
> Oh! I cannot be a slave,
>   I will not be a slave,
> For I'm so fond of liberty
>   That I cannot be a slave.

My own recollection of this first strike (or "turn out" as it was called) is very vivid. I worked in a lower room, where I had heard the proposed strike fully, if not vehemently, discussed; I had been an ardent listener to what was said against this attempt at "oppression" on the part of the corporation, and naturally I took sides with the strikers. When the day came on which the girls were to turn out, those in the upper rooms started first, and so many of them left that our mill was at once shut down. Then, when the girls in my room stood irresolute, uncertain what to do, asking each other, "Would you?" or "Shall we turn out?" and not one of them having the courage to lead off, I, who began to think they would not go out, after all their talk, became impatient, and started on ahead, saying, with childish bravado, "I don't care what you do, *I* am going to turn out, whether any one else does or not"; and I marched out, and was followed by the others.[2]

As I looked back at the long line that followed me, I was more proud than I have ever been since at any success I may have achieved, and more proud than I shall ever be again until my own beloved State gives to its women citizens the right of suffrage.

The agent of the corporation where I then worked took some small revenges on the supposed ringleaders; on the principle of sending the weaker to the wall, my mother was turned away from her boarding-house, that functionary saying, "Mrs. Hanson, you could not prevent the older girls from turning out, but your daughter is a child, and *her* you could control."

2. I was then eleven years and eight months old. [Robinson's note.]

It is hardly necessary to say that so far as results were concerned this strike did no good. The dissatisfaction of the operatives subsided, or burned itself out, and though the authorities did not accede to their demands, the majority returned to their work, and the corporation went on cutting down the wages.

And after a time, as the wages became more and more reduced, the best portion of the girls left and went to their homes, or to the other employments that were fast opening to women, until there were very few of the old guard left; and thus the *status* of the factory population of New England gradually became what we know it to be to-day.

31

Life under the Lash

Charles Ball et al.

One of the great efforts of the current generation of American historians has been to capture the African American experience of slavery directly rather than from sources written by whites. As a result of this work, not only have new documents been unearthed, but a new appreciation has developed for those slave writings that have been long known to historians but that required verification of their reliability.

The authors of the more than one hundred extant book-length accounts of slavery were by no means typical former slaves. Most of them succeeded in gaining their freedom by escape or purchase, which was not the lot of their less fortunate brothers and sisters. Most were highly literate. Some had help in writing their accounts from abolitionists and other ghost writers and editors. Nevertheless, historians in recent decades have discovered how generally accurate—in fact, how indispensable—their narratives are for any serious understanding of the institution of American slavery.

The sampling of the literature presented here provides insights into the work regimen of a plantation, living conditions of slaves, and limits on parental authority in the mid–nineteenth century. These accounts may be compared with some of the images in the visual portfolio "Slavery and Freedom" (page 253).

BEFORE YOU READ

1. How did Charles Ball explain the differences among the plantations on which he labored as a slave?
2. What, according to Josiah Henson and Francis Henderson, were living conditions under slavery?
3. What was Francis Henderson's view of white Southerners?
4. According to Jacob Stroyer, how did slavery affect family relations?

CHARLES BALL[1]

The Work Regimen of a Tobacco Plantation

In Maryland and Virginia, although the slaves are treated with so much rigour, and oftimes with so much cruelty, I have seen instances of the greatest tenderness of feeling on the part of their owners. I, myself, had three masters in Maryland,

---

1. Ball had been a slave in Maryland, South Carolina, and Georgia.

Steven Mintz, ed., *African American Voices: The Life Cycle of Slavery* (St. James, N.Y.: Brandywine Press, 1993), pp. 73–75, 78–79, 87–89, 111–13.

222

and I cannot say now, even after having resided so many years in a state where slavery is not tolerated, that either of them (except the last, who sold me to the Georgians, and was an unfeeling man,) used me worse than they had a moral right to do, regarding me merely as an article of property, and not entitled to any rights as a man, political or civil. My mistresses, in Maryland, were all good women; and the mistress of my wife, in whose kitchen I spent my Sundays and many of my nights, for several years, was a lady of most benevolent and kindly feelings. She was a true friend to me, and I shall always venerate her memory. . . .

If the proprietors of the soil in Maryland and Virginia, were skillful cultivators—had their lands in good condition—and kept no more slaves on each estate, than would be sufficient to work the soil in a proper manner, and kept up the repairs of the place—the condition of the coloured people would not be, by any means, a comparatively unhappy one. I am convinced, that in nine cases in ten, the hardships and suffering of the coloured population of lower Virginia, are attributable to the poverty and distress of its owners. In many instances, an estate scarcely yields enough to feed and clothe the slaves in a comfortable manner, without allowing anything for the support of the master and family; but it is obvious, that the family must first be supported, and the slaves must be content with the surplus—and this, on a poor, old, worn out tobacco plantation, is often very small, and wholly inadequate to the comfortable sustenance of the hands, as they are called. There, in many places, nothing is allowed to the poor Negro, but his peck of corn per week, without the sauce of a salt herring, or even a little salt itself. . . .

The general features of slavery are the same everywhere; but the utmost rigour of the system, is only to be met with, on the cotton plantations of Carolina and Georgia, or in the rice fields which skirt the deep swamps and morasses of the southern rivers. In the tobacco fields of Maryland and Virginia, great cruelties are practiced—not so frequently by the owners, as by the overseers of the slaves; but yet, the tasks are not so excessive as in the cotton region, nor is the press of labour so incessant throughout the year. It is true, that from the period when the tobacco plants are set in the field, there is no resting time until it is housed; but it is planted out about the first of May, and must be cut and taken out of the field before the frost comes. After it is hung and dried, the labor of stripping and preparing it for the hogshead in leaf, or of manufacturing it into twist, is comparatively a work of leisure and ease. Besides, on almost every plantation the hands are able to complete the work of preparing the tobacco by January, and sometimes earlier; so that the winter months, form some sort of respite from the toils of the year. The people are obliged, it is true, to occupy themselves in cutting wood for the house, making rails and repairing fences, and in clearing new land, to raise the tobacco plants for the next year; but as there is usually time enough, and to spare, for the completion of all this work, before the season arrives for setting the plants in the field; the men are seldom flogged much, unless they are very lazy or negligent, and the women are allowed to remain in the house, in the very cold, snowy, or rainy weather. . . .

In Maryland I never knew a mistress or a young mistress, who would not listen to the complaints of the slaves. It is true, we were always obliged to approach the door of the mansion, with our hats in our hands, and the most subdued and beseeching language in our mouths—but, in return, we generally received words of kindness, and very often a redress of our grievances; though I have known very great ladies, who would never grant any request from the plantation hands, but always referred them and their petitions to their master, under a pretence, that they could not meddle with things that did not belong to the house. The mistresses of the great families, generally gave mild language to the slaves; though they sometimes sent for the overseer and had them severely flogged; but I have never heard any mistress, in either Maryland or Virginia, indulge in the low, vulgar and profane vituperations, of which I was myself the object, in Georgia, for many years, whenever I came into the presence of my mistress. Flogging—though often severe and excruciating in Maryland, is not practiced with the order, regularity and system, to which it is often reduced in the South. On the Potomac, if a slave gives offence, he is generally chastised on the spot, in the field where he is at work, as the overseer always carried a whip—sometimes a twisted cow-hide, sometimes a kind of horse-whip, and very often a simple hickory switch or gad, cut in the adjoining woods. For stealing meat, or other provisions, or for any of the higher offences, the slaves are stripped, tied up by the hands—sometimes by the thumbs—and whipped at the quarter—but many times, on a large tobacco plantation, there is not more than one of these regular whippings in a week—though on others, where the master happens to be a bad man, or a drunkard—the back of the unhappy Maryland slaves, is seamed with scars from his neck to his hips.

JOSIAH HENSON[2]

"We Lodged in Log Huts"

My earliest employments were, to carry buckets of water to the men at work, and to hold a horse-plough, used for weeding between the rows of corn. As I grew older and taller, I was entrusted with the care of master's saddle-horse. Then a hoe was put into my hands, and I was soon required to do the day's work of a man; and it was not long before I could do it, at least as well as my associates in misery.

A description of the everyday life of a slave on a Southern plantation illustrates the character and habits of the slave and the slaveholder, created and perpetuated by their relative position. The principal food of those upon my master's plantation consisted of corn-meal and salt herrings; to which was added in summer a little buttermilk, and the few vegetables which each might raise for himself and his family, on the little piece of ground which was assigned to him for the purpose, called a truck-patch.

In ordinary times we had two regular meals in a day: breakfast at twelve o'clock, after laboring from daylight, and supper when the work of the remain-

2. Henson had been a slave in Maryland before he escaped.

der of the day was over. In harvest season we had three. Our dress was of tow-cloth; for the children, nothing but a shirt; for the older ones a pair of pan-taloons or a gown in addition, according to the sex. Besides these, in the winter a round jacket or overcoat, a wool-hat once in two or three years, for the males, and a pair of coarse shoes once a year.

We lodged in log huts, and on the bare ground. Wooden floors were an unknown luxury. In a single room were huddled, like cattle, ten or a dozen per-sons, men, women, and children. All ideas of refinement and decency were, of course, out of the question. We had neither bedsteads, nor furniture of any de-scription. Our beds were collections of straw and old rags, thrown down in the corners and boxed in with boards; a single blanket the only covering. Our favourite way of sleeping, however, was on a plank, our heads raised on an old jacket and our feet toasting before the smouldering fire. The wind whistled and the rain and snow blew in through the cracks, and the damp earth soaked in the moisture till the floor was miry as a pig-sty. Such were our houses. In these wretched hovels were we penned at night, and fed by day; here were the chil-dren born and the sick—neglected.

FRANCIS HENDERSON[3]

Living Conditions on the Plantation

Our houses were but log huts—the tops partly open—ground floor—rain would come through. My aunt was quite an old woman, and had been sick sev-eral years; in rains I have seen her moving from one part of the house to the other, and rolling her bedclothes about to try to keep dry—everything would be dirty and muddy. I lived in the house with my aunt. My bed and bedstead consisted of a board wide enough to sleep on—one end on a stool, the other placed near the fire. My pillow consisted of my jacket—my covering was what-ever I could get. My bedtick was the board itself. And this was the way the single men slept—but we were comfortable in this way of sleeping, being used to it. I only remember having but one blanket from my owners up to the age of nineteen, when I ran away.

Our allowance was given weekly—a peck of sifted corn meal, a dozen and a half herrings, two and a half pounds of pork. Some of the boys would eat this up in three days—then they had to steal, or they could not perform their daily tasks. They would visit the hog-pen, sheep-pen, and granaries. I do not remem-ber one slave but who stole some things—they were driven to it as a matter of necessity. I myself did this—many a time have I, with others, run among the stumps in chase of a sheep, that we might have something to eat. . . . In regard to cooking, sometimes many have to cook at one fire, and before all could get to the fire to bake hoe cakes, the overseer's horn would sound: then they must go at any rate. Many a time I have gone along eating a piece of bread and meat, or

3. Henderson escaped from slavery at the age of nineteen.

herring broiled on the coals—I never sat down at a table to eat except at harvest time, all the time I was a slave. In harvest time, the cooking is done at the great house, as the hands they have are wanted in the field. This was more like people, and we liked it, for we sat down then at meals. In the summer we had one pair of linen trousers given us—nothing else; every fall, one pair of woolen pantaloons, one woolen jacket, and two cotton shirts.

My master had four sons in his family. They all left except one, who remained to be a driver. He would often come to the field and accuse the slave of having taken so and so. If we denied it, he would whip the grown-up ones to make them own it. Many a time, when we didn't know he was anywhere around, he would be in the woods watching us—first thing we would know, he would be sitting on the fence looking down upon us, and if any had been idle, the young master would visit him with blows. I have known him to kick my aunt, an old woman who had raised and nursed him, and I have seen him punish my sisters awfully with hickories from the woods.

The slaves are watched by the patrols, who ride about to try to catch them off the quarters, especially at the house of a free person of color. I have known the slaves to stretch clothes lines across the street, high enough to let the horse pass, but not the rider; then the boys would run, and the patrols in full chase would be thrown off by running against the lines. The patrols are poor white men, who live by plundering and stealing, getting rewards for runaways, and setting up little shops on the public roads. They will take whatever the slaves steal, paying in money, whiskey, or whatever the slaves want. They take pigs, sheep, wheat, corn—anything that's raised they encourage the slaves to steal: these they take to market next day. It's all speculation—all a matter of self-interest, and when the slaves run away, these same traders catch them if they can, to get the reward. If the slave threatens to expose his traffic, he does not care—for the slave's word is good for nothing—it would not be taken.

JACOB STROYER[4]

Parents and Children

Gilbert was a cruel [slave] boy. He used to strip his fellow Negroes while in the woods, and whip them two or three times a week, so that their backs were all scarred, and threatened them with severer punishments if they told; this state of things had been going on for quite a while. As I was a favorite with Gilbert, I always managed to escape a whipping, with the promise of keeping the secret of the punishment of the rest. . . . But finally, one day, Gilbert said to me, "Jake," as he used to call me, "you am a good boy, but I'm gwine to wip you some today, as I wip dem toder boys." Of course I was required to strip off my only garment, which was an Osnaburg linen shirt, worn by both sexes of the Negro children in the summer. As I stood trembling before my merciless superior, who had a switch in his hand, thousands of thoughts went through my little

4. Stroyer, who grew up a slave in several Southern states, wrote *My Life in the South* (Salem, MA: Newcomb & Gauss, 1898).

mind as to how to get rid of the whipping. I finally fell upon a plan which I hoped would save me from a punishment that was near at hand. . . . I commenced reluctantly to take off my shirt, at the same time pleading with Gilbert, who paid no attention to my prayer. . . . Having satisfied myself that no mercy was to be found with Gilbert, I drew my shirt off and threw it over his head, and bounded forward on a run in the direction of the sound of the [nearby] carpenters. By the time he got from the entanglement of my garment, I had quite a little start of him. . . . As I got near to the carpenters, one of them ran and met me, into whose arms I jumped. The man into whose arms I ran was Uncle Benjamin, my mother's uncle. . . . I told him that Gilbert had been in the habit of stripping the boys and whipping them two or three times a week, when we went into the woods, and threatened them with greater punishment if they told. . . . Gilbert was brought to trial, severely whipped, and they made him beg all the children to pardon him for his treatment to them.

[My] father . . . used to take care of horses and mules. I was around with him in the barn yard when but a very small boy; of course that gave me an early relish for the occupation of hostler,[5] and I soon made known my preference to Col. Singleton, who was a sportsman, and an owner of fine horses. And, although I was too small to work, the Colonel granted my request; hence I was allowed to be numbered among those who took care of the fine horses and learned to ride. But I soon found that my new occupation demanded a little more than I cared for. It was not long after I had entered my new work before they put me upon the back of a horse which threw me to the ground almost as soon as I had reached his back. It hurt me a little, but that was not the worst of it, for when I got up there was a man standing near with a switch in hand, and he immediately began to beat me. Although I was a very bad boy, this was the first time I had been whipped by anyone except father and mother, so I cried out in a tone of voice as if I would say, this is the first and last whipping you will give me when father gets hold of you.

When I had got away from him I ran to father with all my might, but soon found my expectation blasted, as father very coolly said to me, "Go back to your work and be a good boy, for I cannot do anything for you." But that did not satisfy me, so on I went to mother with my complaint and she came out to the man who had whipped me; he was a groom, a white man master had hired to train the horses. Mother and he began to talk, then he took a whip and started for her, and she ran from him, talking all the time. I ran back and forth between mother and him until he stopped beating her. After the fight between the groom and mother, he took me back to the stable yard and gave me a severe flogging. And, although mother failed to help me at first, still I had faith that when he had taken me back to the stable yard, and commenced whipping me, she would come and stop him, but I looked in vain, for she did not come.

Then the idea first came to me that I, with my dear father and mother and the rest of my fellow Negroes, were doomed to cruel treatment through life, and was defenseless. But when I found that father and mother could not save

---

5. **hostler:** a person who takes care of horses.

me from punishment, as they themselves had to submit to the same treatment, I concluded to appeal to the sympathy of the groom, who seemed to have full control over me; but my pitiful cries never touched his sympathy. . . .

One day, about two weeks after Boney Young [the white man who trained horses for Col. Singleton] and mother had the conflict, he called me to him. . . . When I got to him he said, "Go and bring me the switch, sir." I answered, "yes, sir," and off I went and brought him one . . . [and] . . . he gave me a first-class flogging. . . .

When I went home to father and mother, I said to them, "Mr. Young is whipping me too much now, I shall not stand it, I shall fight him." Father said to me, "You must not do that, because if you do he will say that your mother and I advised you to do it, and it will make it hard for your mother and me, as well as for yourself. You must do as I told you, my son: do your work the best you can, and do not say anything." I said to father, "But I don't know what I have done that he should whip me; he does not tell me what wrong I have done, he simply calls me to him and whips me when he gets ready." Father said, "I can do nothing more than to pray to the Lord to hasten the time when these things shall be done away; that is all I can do. . . ."

32

Escape from Slavery
Henry "Box" Brown

Henry "Box" Brown was born a slave on a plantation in Louisa County, Virginia, sometime around 1815. When Brown was fifteen, the death of his master broke up his family. He and his sister Martha were sent to Richmond where Henry worked for modest wages in his new master's tobacco factory while his sister became a house slave.

The urban world that Brown discovered in Richmond was very different from life on a rural plantation. Living in the city and working in a factory with 150 other blacks, some slave and some free, gave Brown a strong vision of the capriciousness of the slave system. The 1831 Nat Turner uprising occurred soon after Brown's arrival in Richmond. Brown witnessed whites fleeing in terror, while soldiers and armed mobs killed and tortured blacks. The next two decades were turbulent. African Americans formed their own antislavery newspapers, escaped slaves like Frederick Douglass and Sojourner Truth published best-selling books, and fearful slaveholders strengthened Southern militias. In 1849, after his master sold his wife and children away from him, Henry Brown climbed into a wooden box and, with the help of some friends, mailed himself to Philadelphia and freedom. Separation from his family was the last in a series of terrible setbacks to Brown's attempts to build an ordinary life within the "peculiar institution" of slavery.

In addition to planning and executing the most famous escape in the history of American slavery, Brown was a gifted self-promoter and entrepreneur. Claiming the name "Box," he wrote a narrative of his life and escape from slavery that was first published in 1851 and from which the following account is taken. He also went on the antislavery lecture circuit, giving speeches, writing and performing songs, and reenacting his escape, box and all. He toured the North with a giant painted canvas panorama called The Mirror of Slavery *depicting American history from a black perspective. Despite the content of his shows, Brown came under criticism from such antislavery activists as Frederick Douglass, who believed that Brown was putting his commercial interests ahead of the abolitionist movement. The basic events of Brown's narrative are not in doubt, but it is prudent to approach critically the accounts of individuals who make a business out of telling their life stories.*

In 1850, the United States government passed the Fugitive Slave Act, and Brown was almost captured in Rhode Island by bounty hunters. After this traumatic event, he fled to England where he had a brief but successful career as an antislavery entertainer:

Henry Box Brown, *Narrative of the Life of Henry Box Brown, Written by Himself,* 1999, <http://docsouth.unc.edu/neh/boxbrown/boxbrown.html> (1 Dec. 2002), 32–57.

singing, lecturing, selling lithographs of himself, and even having himself shipped in a
box from Bradford to Leeds. Little is known about Brown's later years, but it is believed
that he married an Englishwoman and moved to Wales.

BEFORE YOU READ

1. Was Henry Brown wrong to put his career before the antislavery struggle?
2. Why do you think Brown frequently mentions that the people who enslaved and betrayed him were Christians?
3. How honest do you think Brown is in telling the story of his life?
4. What does Brown's story add to our understanding of the personal relations between slaves and masters?

CHAPTER VI

I now began to think of entering the matrimonial state; and with that view I had formed an acquaintance with a young woman named Nancy, who was a slave belonging to a Mr. Leigh a clerk in the Bank, and, like many more slave-holders, professing to be a very pious man. We had made it up to get married, but it was necessary in the first place, to obtain our masters' permission, as we could do nothing without their consent. I therefore went to Mr. Leigh, and made known to him my wishes, when he told me he never meant to sell Nancy, and if my master would agree never to sell me, I might marry her. He promised faithfully that he would not sell her, and pretended to entertain an extreme horror of separating families. He gave me a note to my master, and after they had discussed the matter over, I was allowed to marry the object of my choice. . . .

We had not, however, been married above twelve months, when his conscientious scruples vanished, and [Mr. Leigh] sold my wife to a Mr. Joseph H. Colquitt, a saddler, living in the city of Richmond, and a member of Dr. Plummer's church there. This Mr. Colquitt was an exceedingly cruel man, and he had a wife who was, if possible, still more cruel. . . . At this time my wife had a child and this vexed Mrs. Colquitt very much; she could not bear to see her nursing her baby and used to wish some great calamity to happen to my wife. . . . [Mr. Colquitt] proceeded to sell my wife to one Samuel Cottrell, who wished to purchase her. Cottrell was a saddler and had a shop in Richmond. This man came to me one day and told me that Mr. Colquitt was going to sell my wife[,] and stated that he wanted a woman to wait upon his wife, and he thought my wife would precisely suit her; but he said her master asked 650 dollars for her and her children, and he had only 600 that he could conveniently spare but if I would let him have fifty, to make up the price, he would prevent her from being sold away from me. I was, however, a little suspicious about being fooled out of my money, and I asked him if I did advance the money what security I could have that he would not sell my wife as the others had done; but he said to me "do you think if you allow me to have that money, that I could have the heart to sell your wife to any other person but yourself, and particularly knowing that your wife is my sister and you my brother in the Lord; while all of us are members of the church? Oh! no, I never could have the heart to do such a deed as that." After he had shown off his religion in this manner, and lavished it upon me, I thought I would let him have the money. . . . And that very same day he came to me and told me, that my wife and children were now his property, and that I must hire a house for them and he would allow them to live there if I would furnish them with everything they wanted, and pay him 50 dollars, a year; "if you don't do this," he said, "I will sell her as soon as I can get a buyer for her."

I was struck with astonishment to think that this man, in one day, could exhibit himself in two such different characters. A few hours ago filled with expressions of love and kindness, and now a monster tyrant, making light of the most social ties and imposing such terms as he chose on those whom, but a little before, had begged to conform to his will[.] Now, being a slave, I had no power to hire a house, and what this might have resulted in I do not know, if I had not met with a friend in the time of need, in the person of James C. A. Smith, Jr. He was a free man and I went to him and told him my tale and asked him to go and hire a house for me, to put my wife and children into; which he immediately did. . . .

But Mr. S. Cottrell had not yet done with robbing us; . . . for one pleasant morning, in the month of August, 1848, when my wife and children, and myself, were sitting at table, about to eat our breakfast, Mr. Cottrell called, and said, he wanted some money to day, as he had a demand for a large amount. I said to him, you know I have no money to spare, because it takes nearly all that I make for myself, to pay my wife's hire, the rent of my house, my own ties to my master, and to keep ourselves in meat and clothes; and if at any time, I have made anything more than that, I have paid it to you in advance, and what more can I do? Mr. Cottrell, however said, "I want money, and money I will have." I could make him no answer; he then went away. I then said to my wife, "I wonder what Mr. Cottrell means by saying I want money and money I will have," my poor wife burst into tears and said perhaps he will sell one of our little children, and our hearts were so full that neither of us could eat any breakfast, and after mutually embracing each other, as it might be our last meeting, and fondly pressing our little darlings to our bosoms, I left the house and went off to my daily labour followed by my little children who called after me to come back soon. . . .

I had not been many hours at my work, when I was informed that my wife and children were taken from their home, sent to the auction mart and sold, and then lay in prison ready to start away the next day for North Carolina with the man who had purchased them. I cannot express, in language, what were my feelings on this occasion. . . .

. . . I went to my *christian* master and informed him how I was served, but he shoved me away from him as if I was not human. I could not rest with this however, I went to him a second time and implored him to be kind enough to buy my wife and to save me from so much trouble of mind; still he was inexorable and only answered me by telling me to go to my work and not bother him any more. I went to him a *third* time, which would be about ten o'clock and told him how Cottrell had robbed me, as this scoundrel was not satisfied with selling my wife and children, but he had no sooner got them out of the town than he took everything which he could find in my house and carried it off to be sold; the things which he then took had cost me nearly three hundred dollars. I begged master to write Cottrell and make him give me up my things, but his answer was Mr. Cottrell is a gentleman I am afraid to meddle with his business.

So having satisfied myself that the master would do nothing for me, I left him and went to two young gentlemen with whom I was acquainted to try if I could induce them to buy my wife; but when I had stated my case to them they gave me to understand that they did not deal in slaves so they could not do that, but they expressed their willingness to do anything else that I might desire of them; so finding myself unsuccessful here, I went sorrowfully back to my own deserted home, and found that what I had heard was quite true; not only had my wife and children been taken away[,] but every article of furniture had also been removed to the auction mart to be sold. . . .

My agony was now complete, she with whom I had travelled the journey of life *in chains*, for the space of twelve years, and the dear little pledges God had given us I could see plainly must now be separated from me for ever, and I must continue, desolate and alone, to drag my chains through the world. . . . While I was thus musing I received a message, that if I wished to see my wife and children, and bid them the last farewell, I could do so, by taking my stand on the street where they were all to pass on their way for North Carolina. I quickly availed myself of this information, and placed myself by the side of a street, and soon had the melancholy satisfaction of witnessing the approach of a gang of slaves, amounting to three hundred and fifty in number, marching under the direction of a methodist minister, by whom they were purchased, and amongst which slaves were my wife and children. I stood in the midst of many who, like myself, were mourning the loss of friends and relations and had come there to obtain one parting look at those whose company they but a short time before had imagined they should always enjoy, but who were, without any regard to their own wills, now driven by the tyrant's voice and the smart of the whip on their way to another scene of toil, and, to them, another land of sorrow in a far off southern country[.]

These beings were marched with ropes about their necks, and staples on their arms, and, although in that respect the scene was no very novel one to me, yet the peculiarity of my own circumstances made it assume the appearance of unusual horror. This train of beings was accompanied by a number of waggons loaded with little children of many different families, which as they appeared rent the air with their shrieks and cries and vain endeavours to resist the separation which was thus forced upon them, and the cords with which they were thus bound; but what should I now see in the very foremost waggon but a little child looking towards me and pitifully calling, father! father! This was my eldest child, and I was obliged to look upon it for the last time that I should, perhaps, ever see it again in life; if it had been going to the grave and this gloomy procession had been about to return its body to the dust from whence it sprang, whence its soul had taken its departure for the land of spirits, my grief would

have been nothing in comparison to what I then felt; for then I could have reflected that its sufferings were over and that it would never again require nor
look for a father's care. . . . Thus passed my child from my presence—it was my
own child—I loved it with all the fondness of a father; but things were so ordered that I could only say, farewell, and leave it to pass in its chains while I
looked for the approach of another gang in which my wife was also loaded with
chains. My eye soon caught her precious face, but, gracious heavens! that glance
of agony may God spare me from ever again enduring! My wife, under the influence of her feelings, jumped aside; I seized hold of her hand while my mind
felt unutterable things, and my tongue was only able to say, we shall meet in
heaven! I went with her for about four miles hand in hand, but both our hearts
were so overpowered with feeling that we could say nothing, and when at last
we were obliged to part, the look of mutual love which we exchanged was all
the token which we could give each other that we should yet meet in heaven.

CHAPTER VII

. . . I now began to get weary of my bonds; and earnestly panted after liberty. I
felt convinced that I should be acting in accordance with the will of God, if I
could snap in sunder those bonds by which I was held body and soul as the
property of a fellow man. . . . I was well acquainted with a store-keeper in the
city of Richmond, from whom I used to purchase my provisions; and having
formed a favourable opinion of his integrity, one day in the course of a little
conversation with him, I said to him if I were free I would be able to do business
such as he was doing; he then told me that my occupation (a tobacconist) was a
money-making one, and if I were free I had no need to change for another. I
then told him my circumstances in regard to my master, having to pay him 25
dollars per month, and yet that he refused to assist me in saving my wife from
being sold and taken away to the South. . . . I told him this took place about five
months ago, and I had been meditating my escape from slavery since, and asked
him, as no person was near us, if he could give me any information about how I
should proceed. I told him I had a little money and if he would assist me I
would pay him for so doing. The man asked me if I was not afraid to speak that
way to him; I said no, for I imagined he believed that every man had a right to
liberty. He said I was quite right, and asked me how much money I would give
him if he would assist me to get away. I told him that I had 166 dollars and that
I would give him the half; so we ultimately agreed that I should have his service
in the attempt for 86. Now I only wanted to fix upon a plan. He told me of several plans by which others had managed to effect their escape, but none of them
exactly suited my taste. . . .

   One day, while I was at work, and my thoughts were eagerly feasting upon
the idea of freedom, I felt my soul called out to heaven to breathe a prayer to
Almighty God. I prayed fervently that he who seeth in secret and knew the in-
most desires of my heart, would lend me his aid in bursting my fetters asunder,
and in restoring me to the possession of those rights, of which men had robbed

me; when the idea suddenly flashed across my mind of shutting myself *up in a box*, and getting myself conveyed as dry goods to a free state.

Being now satisfied that this was the plan for me, I went to my friend Dr. Smith and, having acquainted him with it, we agreed to have it put at once into execution not however without calculating the chances of danger with which it was attended; but buoyed up by the prospect of freedom and increased hatred to slavery I was willing to dare even death itself rather than endure any longer the clanking of those galling chains. It being still necessary to have the assistance of the store-keeper, to see that the box was kept in its right position on its passage, I then went to let him know my intention, but he said although he was willing to serve me in any way he could, he did not think I could live in a box for so long a time as would be necessary to convey me to Philadelphia, but as I had already made up my mind, he consented to accompany me and keep the box right all the way.

My next object was to procure a box, and with the assistance of a carpenter that was very soon accomplished, and taken to the place where the packing was to be performed. In the mean time the store-keeper had written to a friend in Philadelphia, but as no answer had arrived, we resolved to carry out our purpose as best we could. It was deemed necessary that I should get permission to be absent from my work for a few days, in order to keep down suspicion until I had once fairly started on the road to liberty; and as I had then a gathered finger I thought that would form a very good excuse for obtaining leave of absence; but when I showed it to one overseer, Mr. Allen, he told me it was not so bad as to prevent me from working, so with a view of making it bad enough, I got Dr. Smith to procure for me some oil of vitriol in order to drop a little of this on it, but in my hurry I dropped rather much and made it worse than there was any occasion for, in fact it was very soon eaten in to the bone, and on presenting it again to Mr. Allen I obtained the permission required, with the advice that I should go home and get a poultice of flax-meal to it, and keep it well poulticed until it got better. I took him instantly at his word and went off directly to the store-keeper who had by this time received an answer from his friend in Philadelphia, and had obtained permission to address the box to him, this friend in that city, arranging to call for it as soon as it should arrive. There being no time to be lost, the store-keeper, Dr. Smith, and myself, agreed to meet next morning at four o'clock, in order to get the box ready for the express train. The box which I had procured was three feet one inch wide, two feet six inches high, and two feet wide: and on the morning of the 29th day of March, 1849, I went into the box—having previously bored three gimlet holes opposite my face, for air, and provided myself with a bladder of water, both for the purpose of quenching my thirst and for wetting my face, should I feel getting faint. I took the gimlet also with me, in order that I might bore more holes if I found I had not sufficient air. Being thus equipped for the battle of liberty, my friends nailed down the lid and had me conveyed to the Express Office, which was about a mile distant from the place where I was packed. I had no sooner arrived at the office than I was turned heels up, while some person nailed something on the end of the box. I was then put upon a waggon and driven off to the depôt with my head down, and I had no sooner arrived at the depôt, than the man who drove the waggon tumbled me roughly into the baggage car, where, however, I happened to fall on my right side.

The next place we arrived at was Potomac Creek, where the baggage had to be removed from the cars, to be put on board the steamer; where I was again placed with my head down, and in this dreadful position had to remain nearly an hour and a half, which, from the sufferings I had thus to endure, seemed like an age to me, but I was forgetting the battle of liberty, and I was resolved to conquer or die. I felt my eyes swelling as if they would burst from their sockets; and the veins on my temples were dreadfully distended with pressure of blood upon my head. In this position I attempted to lift my hand to my face but I had no power to move it; I felt a cold sweat coming over me which seemed to be a warning that death was about to terminate my earthly miseries, but as I feared even that, less than slavery, I resolved to submit to the will of God, and under the influence of that impression, I lifted up my soul in prayer to God, who alone, was able to deliver me. My cry was soon heard, for I could hear a man saying to another, that he had travelled a long way and had been standing there two hours, and he would like to get somewhat to sit down; so perceiving my box, standing on end, he threw it down and then two sat upon it. I was thus relieved from a state of agony which may be more easily imagined than described. . . .

The next place at which we arrived was the city of Washington, where I was taken from the steam-boat, and again placed upon a waggon and carried to the depôt right side up with care; but when the driver arrived at the depôt I heard him call for some person to help to take the box off the waggon, and some one answered him to the effect that he might throw it off; but, says the driver, it is marked "this side up with care"; so if I throw it off I might break something, the other answered him that it did not matter if he broke all that was in it, the railway company were able enough to pay for it. No sooner were these words spoken than I began to tumble from the waggon, and falling on the end where my head was, I could bear my neck give a crack, as if it had been snapped asunder and I was knocked completely insensible. The first thing I heard after that, was some person saying, "there is no room for the box, it will have to remain and be sent through to-morrow with the luggage train"; but the Lord had not quite forsaken me, for in answer to my earnest prayer He so ordered affairs that I should not be left behind; and I now heard a man say that the box had come with the express, and it must be sent on. I was then tumbled into the car with my head downwards again, but the car had not proceeded far before, more luggage having to be taken in, my box got shifted about and so happened to turn upon its right side; and in this position I remained till I got to Philadelphia, of our arrival in which place I was informed by hearing some person say, "We are in port and at Philadelphia." My heart then leaped for joy, and I wondered if any person knew that such a box was there.

Here it may be proper to observe that the man who had promised to accompany my box failed to do what he promised; but, to prevent it remaining long at the station after its arrival, he sent a telegraphic message to his friend, and I was only twenty-seven hours in the box, though travelling a distance of three hundred and fifty miles.

I was now placed in the depôt amongst the other luggage, where I lay till seven o'clock, P.M., at which time a waggon drove up, and I heard a person inquire for such a box as that in which I was. I was then placed on a waggon and conveyed to the house where my friend in Richmond had arranged I should be received. A number of persons soon collected round the box after it was taken in to the house, but as I did not know what was going on I kept myself quiet. I heard a man say, "let us rap upon the box and see if he is alive"; and immediately a rap ensued and a voice said, tremblingly, "Is all right within?" to which I replied—"all right." The joy of the friends was very great; when they heard that I was alive they soon managed to break open the box, and then came my resurrection from the grave of slavery. I rose a freeman, but I was too weak, by reason of long confinement in that box, to be able to stand, so I immediately swooned away. After my recovery from the swoon the first thing, which arrested my attention, was the presence of a number of friends, every one seeming more anxious than another, to have an opportunity of rendering me their assistance, and of bidding me a hearty welcome to the possession of my natural rights, I had risen as it were from the dead. . . .

A Pioneer for Women's Rights
Elizabeth Cady Stanton

The women's movement before the Civil War was among the most intensely unpopular of all the reform efforts of that era. The ideal of domesticity, which assigned to women a separate and less-powerful role in the family, made the reformists' claims for equal rights, especially the right to vote, a violation of social convention and of the religious beliefs of many. Friendships were enormously important in providing the courage and emotional support women needed to oppose the sometimes oppressive family, religious, and political institutions. Elizabeth Cady Stanton (1815–1902) was inspired by Lucretia Mott, whose Quaker ministry had given her experience in public speaking that she applied to the antislavery cause. The two had met at an antislavery convention in London in 1840 and, as Stanton was to recall later, "resolved to hold a convention as soon as we returned home, and form a society to advocate the rights of women." Yet eight years elapsed before this resolve bore fruit in the Seneca Falls Woman's Rights Convention. In the interim, Stanton had settled in three different locations, bore three children (she would eventually have seven), and assumed all the other cares of a financially strapped, middle-class household.

Reflecting on the Seneca Falls convention in her autobiography, Eighty Years and More, *published in 1898 when she was eighty-three, Elizabeth Cady Stanton remained astonished at the avalanche of criticism and sarcasm provoked by the "Declaration of Sentiments." Commenting on the meeting, a Philadelphia newspaper asserted, "A pretty girl is equal to ten thousand men," and sneered, "The ladies of Philadelphia . . . are resolved to maintain their rights as Wives, Belles, Virgins and Mothers, and not as Women." But the women who met at Seneca Falls in upstate New York in 1848 had succeeded in launching a women's rights movement that would continue, mainly by following Stanton's strategy of making woman suffrage the major objective until that goal was achieved in 1920 with the ratification of the Nineteenth Amendment to the Constitution.*

BEFORE YOU READ

1. Describe the impact of Elizabeth Cady Stanton's attendance at the World's Anti-slavery Convention in 1840.

2. What did Stanton do in the years between the World's Anti-slavery Convention in 1840 and the Seneca Falls Convention of 1848?

Elizabeth Cady Stanton, *Eighty Years and More: Reminiscences, 1815–1897* (London: T. Fisher Unwin, 1898), pp. 79–83, 143–50; Copy of the Declaration of Sentiments, courtesy of the Seneca Falls Historical Society, Seneca Falls, N.Y.

3. What does Stanton mean when she says that "if I had had the slightest premonition of all that was to follow that convention, I fear I should not have had the courage to risk it"?

4. Viewed more than a century and a half later, what relevance do you see in the Declaration of Sentiments?

EIGHTY YEARS AND MORE

Our chief object in visiting England at this time was to attend the World's Anti-slavery Convention, to meet June 12, 1840, in Freemasons' Hall, London. Delegates from all the anti-slavery societies of civilized nations were invited, yet, when they arrived, those representing associations of women were rejected. Though women were members of the National Anti-slavery Society, accustomed to speak and vote in all its conventions, and to take an equally active part with men in the whole anti-slavery struggle, and were there as delegates from associations of men and women, as well as those distinctively of their own sex, yet all alike were rejected because they were women. Women, according to English prejudices at that time, were excluded by Scriptural texts from sharing equal dignity and authority with men in all reform associations; hence it was to English minds pre-eminently unfitting that women should be admitted as equal members to a World's Convention. The question was hotly debated through an entire day. My husband made a very eloquent speech in favor of admitting the women delegates.

When we consider . . . [the] many remarkable women . . . [who] were all compelled to listen in silence to the masculine platitudes on woman's sphere, one may form some idea of the indignation of unprejudiced friends, and especially that of such women as Lydia Maria Child, Maria Chapman, Deborah Weston, Angelina and Sarah Grimké, and Abby Kelly, who were impatiently waiting and watching on this side, in painful suspense, to hear how their delegates were received. Judging from my own feelings, the women on both sides of the Atlantic must have been humiliated and chagrined, except as these feelings were outweighed by contempt for the shallow reasoning of their opponents and their comical pose and gestures in some of the intensely earnest flights of their imagination.

The clerical portion of the convention was most violent in its opposition. The clergymen seemed to have God and his angels especially in their care and keeping, and were in agony lest the women should do or say something to shock the heavenly hosts. Their all-sustaining conceit gave them abundant assurance that their movements must necessarily be all-pleasing to the celestials whose ears were open to the proceedings of the World's Convention. . . .

One of our champions in the convention, George Bradburn, a tall thick-set man with a voice like thunder, standing head and shoulders above the clerical representatives, swept all their arguments aside by declaring with tremendous emphasis that, if they could prove to him that the Bible taught the entire subjection of one-half of the race to the other, he should consider that the best thing he could do for humanity would be to bring together every Bible in the universe and make a grand bonfire of them.

It was really pitiful to hear narrow-minded bigots, pretending to be teachers and leaders of men, so cruelly remanding their own mothers, with the rest of womankind, to absolute subjection to the ordinary masculine type of humanity. I always regretted that the women themselves had not taken part in the debate before the convention was fully organized and the question of delegates settled. It seemed to me then, and does now, that all delegates with credentials from recognized societies should have had a voice in the organization of the convention, though subject to exclusion afterward. However, the women sat in a low curtained seat like a church choir, and modestly listened to the French, British, and American Solons for twelve of the longest days in June, as did, also, our grand Garrison and Rogers[1] in the gallery. They scorned a convention that ignored the rights of the very women who had fought, side by side, with them in the anti-slavery conflict. "After battling so many long years," said Garrison, "for the liberties of African slaves, I can take no part in a convention that strikes down the most sacred rights of all women." After coming three thousand miles to speak on the subject nearest his heart, he nobly shared the enforced silence of the rejected delegates. It was a great act of self-sacrifice that should never be forgotten by women. . . .

As the convention adjourned, the remark was heard on all sides, "It is about time some demand was made for new liberties for women." As Mrs. Mott and I walked home, arm in arm, commenting on the incidents of the day, we resolved to hold a convention as soon as we returned home, and form a society to advocate the rights of women. At the lodging house on Queen Street, where a large number of delegates had apartments, the discussions were heated at every meal, and at times so bitter that, at last, Mr. Birney packed his valise and sought more peaceful quarters. Having strongly opposed the admission of women as delegates to the convention it was rather embarrassing to meet them, during the intervals between the various sessions, at the table and in the drawing room.

These were the first women I had ever met who believed in the equality of the sexes and who did not believe in the popular orthodox religion. The acquaintance of Lucretia Mott, who was a broad, liberal thinker on politics, religion, and all questions of reform, opened to me a new world of thought. As we walked about to see the sights of London, I embraced every opportunity to talk with her. It was intensely gratifying to hear all that, through years of doubt, I had dimly thought, so freely discussed by other women, some of them no older than myself—women, too, of rare intelligence, cultivation, and refinement. . . .

In the spring of 1847 we moved to Seneca Falls. Here we spent sixteen years of our married life, and here our other children—two sons and two daughters—were born. . . .

The house we were to occupy had been closed for some years and needed many repairs, and the grounds, comprising five acres, were overgrown with weeds. My father gave me a check and said, with a smile, "You believe in woman's capacity to do and dare; now go ahead and put your place in order."

---

1. **Garrison and Rogers:** abolitionists William Lloyd Garrison (see p. 206) and Nathaniel P. Rogers.

After a minute survey of the premises and due consultation with one or two sons of Adam, I set the carpenters, painters, paper-hangers, and gardeners at work, built a new kitchen and woodhouse, and in one month took possession. Having left my children with my mother, there were no impediments to a full display of my executive ability. In the purchase of brick, timber, paint, etc., and in making bargains with workmen, I was in frequent consultation with Judge Sackett and Mr. Bascom. The latter was a member of the Constitutional Convention, then in session in Albany, and as he used to walk down whenever he was at home, to see how my work progressed, we had long talks, sitting on boxes in the midst of tools and shavings, on the status of women. I urged him to propose an amendment to Article II, Section 3, of the State Constitution, striking out the word "male," which limits the suffrage to men. But, while he fully agreed with all I had to say on the political equality of women, he had not the courage to make himself the laughing-stock of the convention. Whenever I cornered him on this point, manlike he turned the conversation to the painters and carpenters. However, these conversations had the effect of bringing him into the first woman's convention, where he did us good service.

In Seneca Falls my life was comparatively solitary, and the change from Boston was somewhat depressing. There, all my immediate friends were reformers, I had near neighbors, a new home with all the modern conveniences, and well-trained servants. Here our residence was on the outskirts of the town, roads very often muddy and no sidewalks most of the way, Mr. Stanton was frequently from home, I had poor servants, and an increasing number of children. To keep a house and grounds in good order, purchase every article for daily use, keep the wardrobes of half a dozen human beings in proper trim, take the children to dentists, shoemakers, and different schools, or find teachers at home, altogether made sufficient work to keep one brain busy, as well as all the hands I could impress into the service. Then, too, the novelty of housekeeping had passed away, and much that was once attractive in domestic life was now irksome. I had so many cares that the company I needed for intellectual stimulus was a trial rather than a pleasure.

There was quite an Irish settlement at a short distance, and continual complaints were coming to me that my boys threw stones at their pigs, cows, and the roofs of their houses. This involved constant diplomatic relations in the settlement of various difficulties, in which I was so successful that, at length, they constituted me a kind of umpire in all their own quarrels. If a drunken husband was pounding his wife, the children would run for me. Hastening to the scene of action, I would take Patrick by the collar, and, much to his surprise and shame, make him sit down and promise to behave himself. I never had one of them offer the least resistance, and in time they all came to regard me as one having authority. I strengthened my influence by cultivating good feeling. I lent the men papers to read, and invited their children into our grounds; giving them fruit, of which we had abundance, and my children's old clothes, books, and toys. I was their physician, also—with my box of homeopathic medicines I took charge of the men, women, and children in sickness. Thus the most amicable relations were established, and, in any emergency, these poor neighbors were good friends and always ready to serve me.

But I found police duty rather irksome, especially when called out dark nights to prevent drunken fathers from disturbing their sleeping children, or to minister to poor mothers in the pangs of maternity. Alas! alas! who can measure the mountains of sorrow and suffering endured in unwelcome motherhood in the abodes of ignorance, poverty, and vice, where terror-stricken women and children are the victims of strong men frenzied with passion and intoxicating drink?

Up to this time life had glided by with comparative ease, but now the real struggle was upon me. My duties were too numerous and varied, and none sufficiently exhilarating or intellectual to bring into play my higher faculties. I suffered with mental hunger, which, like an empty stomach, is very depressing. I had books, but no stimulating companionship. To add to my general dissatisfaction at the change from Boston, I found that Seneca Falls was a malarial region, and in due time all the children were attacked with chills and fever which, under homeopathic treatment in those days, lasted three months. The servants were afflicted in the same way. Cleanliness, order, the love of the beautiful and artistic, all faded away in the struggle to accomplish what was absolutely necessary from hour to hour. Now I understood, as I never had before, how women could sit down and rest in the midst of general disorder. Housekeeping, under such conditions, was impossible, so I packed our clothes, locked up the house, and went to that harbor of safety, [my parents'] home, as I did ever after in stress of weather.

I now fully understood the practical difficulties most women had to contend with in the isolated household, and the impossibility of woman's best development if in contact, the chief part of her life, with servants and children. Fourier's phalansterie² community life and co-operative households had a new significance for me. Emerson says, "A healthy discontent is the first step to progress." The general discontent I felt with woman's portion as wife, mother, housekeeper, physician, and spiritual guide, the chaotic conditions into which everything fell without her constant supervision, and the wearied, anxious look of the majority of women impressed me with a strong feeling that some active measures should be taken to remedy the wrongs of society in general, and of women in particular. My experience at the World's Anti-slavery Convention, all I had read of the legal status of women, and the oppression I saw everywhere, together swept across my soul, intensified now by many personal experiences. It seemed as if all the elements had conspired to impel me to some onward step. I could not see what to do or where to begin—my only thought was a public meeting for protest and discussion.

In this tempest-tossed condition of mind I received an invitation to spend the day with Lucretia Mott, at Richard Hunt's, in Waterloo. There I met several members of different families of Friends, earnest, thoughtful women. I poured out, that day, the torrent of my long-accumulating discontent, with such vehemence and indignation that I stirred myself, as well as the rest of the party, to do and dare anything. My discontent, according to Emerson, must have been healthy, for it moved us all to prompt action, and we decided, then

---

2. **phalansterie:** a community of the followers of Charles Fourier, who advocated a society organized into small, self-sustaining communal groups.

and there, to call a "Woman's Rights Convention." We wrote the call that evening and published it in the *Seneca County Courier* the next day, the 14th of July, 1848, giving only five days' notice, as the convention was to be held on the 19th and 20th. The call was inserted without signatures,—in fact it was a mere announcement of a meeting,—but the chief movers and managers were Lucretia Mott, Mary Ann McClintock, Jane Hunt, Martha C. Wright, and myself. The convention, which was held two days in the Methodist Church, was in every way a grand success. The house was crowded at every session, the speaking good, and a religious earnestness dignified all the proceedings.

These were the hasty initiative steps of "the most momentous reform that had yet been launched on the world—the first organized protest against the injustice which had brooded for ages over the character and destiny of one-half the race." No words could express our astonishment on finding, a few days afterward, that what seemed to us so timely, so rational, and so sacred, should be a subject for sarcasm and ridicule to the entire press of the nation. With our Declaration of Rights and Resolutions for a text, it seemed as if every man who could wield a pen prepared a homily on "woman's sphere." All the journals from Maine to Texas seemed to strive with each other to see which could make our movement appear the most ridiculous. The anti-slavery papers stood by us manfully and so did Frederick Douglass, both in the convention and in his paper, *The North Star*, but so pronounced was the popular voice against us, in the parlor, press, and pulpit, that most of the ladies who had attended the convention and signed the declaration, one by one, withdrew their names and influence and joined our persecutors. Our friends gave us the cold shoulder and felt themselves disgraced by the whole proceeding.

If I had had the slightest premonition of all that was to follow that convention, I fear I should not have had the courage to risk it, and I must confess that it was with fear and trembling that I consented to attend another, one month afterward, in Rochester. Fortunately, the first one seemed to have drawn all the fire, and of the second but little was said. But we had set the ball in motion, and now, in quick succession, conventions were held in Ohio, Indiana, Massachusetts, Pennsylvania, and in the City of New York, and have been kept up nearly every year since.

DECLARATION OF SENTIMENTS, 1848

When, in the course of human events, it becomes necessary for one portion of the family of man to assume among the people of the earth a position different from that which they have hitherto occupied, but one to which the laws of nature and of nature's God entitle them, a decent respect to the opinions of mankind requires that they should declare the causes that impel them to such a course.

We hold these truths to be self-evident: that all men and women are created equal; that they are endowed by their Creator with certain inalienable rights; that among these are life, liberty, and the pursuit of happiness; that to secure these rights governments are instituted, deriving their just powers from the consent of the governed. Whenever any form of government becomes destructive of these ends, it is the right of those who suffer from it to refuse allegiance to it, and to insist upon the institution of a new government, laying its foundation on such principles, and organizing its powers in such form, as to them shall seem most likely to effect their safety and happiness. Prudence, indeed, will dictate that governments long established should not be changed for light and transient causes; and accordingly all experience hath shown that mankind are more disposed to suffer, while evils are sufferable, than to right themselves by abolishing the forms to which they were accustomed. But when a long train of abuses and usurpations, pursuing invariably the same object evinces a design to reduce them under absolute despotism, it is their duty to throw off such government, and to provide new guards for their future security. Such has been the patient sufferance of the women under this government, and such is now the necessity which constrains them to demand the equal station to which they are entitled.

The history of mankind is a history of repeated injuries and usurpations on the part of man toward woman, having in direct object the establishment of an absolute tyranny over her. To prove this, let facts be submitted to a candid world.

He has never permitted her to exercise her inalienable right to the elective franchise.

He has compelled her to submit to laws, in the formation of which she had no voice.

He has withheld from her rights which are given to the most ignorant and degraded men — both natives and foreigners.

Having deprived her of this first right of a citizen, the elective franchise, thereby leaving her without representation in the halls of legislation, he has oppressed her on all sides.

He has made her, if married, in the eye of the law, civilly dead.

He has taken from her all right in property, even to the wages she earns.

He has made her, morally, an irresponsible being, as she can commit many crimes with impunity, provided they be done in the presence of her husband. In the covenant of marriage, she is compelled to promise obedience to her husband, he becoming to all intents and purposes, her master — the law giving him power to deprive her of her liberty, and to administer chastisement.

He has so framed the laws of divorce, as to what shall be the proper causes of divorce, and in case of separation, to whom the guardianship of the children shall be given, as to be wholly regardless of the happiness of women — the law, in all cases, going upon a false supposition of the supremacy of man, and giving all power into his hands.

After depriving her of all rights as a married woman, if single and the owner of property, he has taxed her to support a government which recognizes her only when her property can be made profitable to it.

He has monopolized nearly all the profitable employments, and from those she is permitted to follow, she receives but a scanty remuneration.

He closes against her all the avenues to wealth and distinction, which he considers most honorable to himself. As a teacher of theology, medicine, or law, she is not known.

He has denied her the facilities for obtaining a thorough education—all colleges being closed against her.

He allows her in Church as well as State, but a subordinate position, claiming Apostolic authority for her exclusion from the ministry, and, with some exceptions, from any public participation in the affairs of the Church.

He has created a false public sentiment by giving to the world a different code of morals for men and women, by which moral delinquencies which exclude women from society, are not only tolerated, but deemed of little account in man.

He has usurped the prerogative of Jehovah himself, claiming it as his right to assign for her a sphere of action, when that belongs to her conscience and to her God.

He has endeavored, in every way that he could, to destroy her confidence in her own powers, to lessen her self-respect, and to make her willing to lead a dependent and abject life.

Now, in view of this entire disfranchisement of one-half the people of this country, their social and religious degradation,—in view of the unjust laws above mentioned, and because women do feel themselves aggrieved, oppressed, and fraudulently deprived of their most sacred rights, we insist that they have immediate admission to all the rights and privileges which belong to them as citizens of these United States.

In entering upon the great work before us, we anticipate no small amount of misconception, misrepresentation, and ridicule; but we shall use every instrumentality within our power to effect our object. We shall employ agents, circulate tracts, petition the State and national Legislatures, and endeavor to enlist the pulpit and the press in our behalf. We hope this Convention will be followed by a series of Conventions, embracing every part of the country.

Firmly relying upon the final triumph of the Right and the True, we do this day affix our signatures to this declaration.

34

With Old John Brown in Kansas
Thomas Henry Tibbles

Thomas Henry Tibbles (1840–1928) was only sixteen in 1856 when he fought in "Bleeding Kansas" in the war between pro- and antislavery settlers. Caught by proslavery forces, he was ordered hanged but then escaped. After capturing the man who had sentenced him to death, he joined the staff of General James H. Lane, who led the antislavery militia in Kansas. Then, in the incident he describes here, Tibbles briefly joined forces with John Brown, one of the most incendiary abolitionists in the United States. Brown planned to steal slaves in order to free them, and shortly after the incident recounted here, he hacked to death with broadswords five proslavery settlers near Pottawatomie Creek in retaliation for a raid on an antislavery settlement.

Tibbles later served in the Civil War and was a freelance writer and newspaperman, a circuit preacher, and a lecturer for the cause of Native Americans. He married a highly accomplished Native American woman in 1882. He became an important journalist and publisher of the Populist Party's national organ, The Independent. *In 1904, he ran for vice president of the United States on a ticket headed by Thomas E. Watson of Georgia in a forlorn and foredoomed People's Party campaign. Tibbles's career illustrates the remarkable links among reform movements in America during the nineteenth century.*

BEFORE YOU READ

1. Why would a sixteen-year-old like Thomas Henry Tibbles join a guerrilla war?

2. How does this document add to our understanding of John Brown's life and work?

3. People came from all across America to fight slavery in Kansas. What were Tibbles's captors fighting for? Were their concerns only self-interest?

[A] man came to tell me that Old John Brown wanted to see me. When I told Lane, he urged me to go and meet Brown, because he himself wanted to know "what that old lunatic intended to do next." It took me several hours to ride from Lawrence to the queer rendezvous Brown had appointed—the spot where he was encamped on the bank of a creek. The men in the group with him were queer too. Some of them were as high-minded and brave a lot of fanatics as ever fought for a cause, but I had then, as now, a suspicion that some were cutthroats

Thomas Henry Tibbles, *Buckskin and Blanket Days: Memoirs of a Friend of the Indians* (New York: Doubleday, 1957), pp. 46–55.

245

and murderers who followed him for the prey and booty they could get in those disturbed times.

Brown had in his camp a fine-looking Negro, who said that he had run away from his master in Platte County, Missouri, because the man was going to sell him and his wife to a dealer who would take them south to Louisiana sugar plantations. The average Missouri Negro looked upon being sold south as one or two degrees worse than being sent straight to hell. This viewpoint was fostered by the masters, who always threatened, when things went wrong, to sell them down the river. John Brown had planned a raid into Platte County to rescue this Negro's wife and as many more slaves as possible.

He asked me, "Do you want a part in this holy crusade to free some of God's black children?"

"I do," I answered, "but I must report first to General Lane and get permission."

"That is proper and right," he agreed. Then he directed me, if Lane allowed me, to meet him at a certain place on a certain day.

When I reported to Lane, he laughed at me.

"Why, my boy," he argued, "if you go across the Missouri River stealing niggers, those Missourians will hang you sure! And this time they won't take the trouble to assemble a drumhead court-martial. They'll swing you up to the first tree they come to."

"They'd have to catch me first," I insisted.

"Catch you! The whole county over there would be after you, and every man in it is a Border Ruffian."

Though I pressed my request further, it was no use. Lane positively refused to let me go, but that evening he sent for me again.

He questioned me for a long time about Brown and his company, urging me to describe each man personally as nearly as I could. He inquired exactly what the old man had said to me, at what point he expected to cross the river, what types of arms they had, the condition of their horses, and many other matters of that nature. Then he asked abruptly:

"Do you still want to go?"

"I do," I answered.

"You may go; but you must file a request in writing with me so that I could prove, if there was any trouble, that I never ordered you to go. I would not order any man to go over into Platte County, much less a boy. I hope that someone of that crowd may get back, but I very much doubt if even one will escape. You go and see Brown, and after you get orders from him report to me before you make the trip."

When I reached Brown again, he told me that each man of his party would try to cross the river alone, keep hidden in the brush and the woods during the daytime, and meet at a designated place on a certain night at nine o'clock to receive further orders.

I reported again to Lane, who gave me a lot of written orders which I was to study until I knew them by heart. Then I was to burn them. Their substance was that I was to ride out of Lawrence after ten o'clock at night. After the first day I was to travel only by night. I was given the names of two Free State men who furnished Lane with information. I was also given a description of their houses and a rough map of the two little towns in which they lived on the west bank of the Missouri River. These men were of vast importance to the Free State cause, and I must do nothing that would bring suspicion on them in the slightest degree. I was to call upon them only after midnight, obtain what information and assistance I could, and get away without letting anyone else learn that I had been there. Before I had read that document half through, I saw the importance of burning it. I committed it to memory, and then put it into my first campfire.

That first night out I spent in an Indian camp, and traded for "jerked meat" some of the tobacco with which our New England friends, who had the sense to know that a man out of tobacco "wouldn't fight worth a cent," kept us well supplied. I got from the Indians enough meat, which could be eaten cooked or uncooked, wet or dry, to last me about ten days. All the next day Old Titus and I stayed in the camp and then stole away at nightfall.

I tried for two days to get to the house of one of those two Free State men. He lived in a tiny town of only two or three log houses and a shanty or two, but a guard was always posted there. Failing in my effort, I went to the other town, which was farther up the river. With its map indelibly printed on my brain, I easily found the house and the man.

He gave me a great deal of information which he advised me to carry straight back to Lane.

"Let Old John Brown do his 'nigger stealing' himself," he urged me. "It's vitally important for Lane to know some of these facts I'm telling you immediately."

The most important fact of all was that a lot of Border Ruffians were congregating at Westport and Independence in Missouri, preparing to make a raid into Kansas. When I refused to go back, he advised me to ride up along the river for some distance to where there was a flatboat ferry. I had not a cent of money—in fact had had none for a long time. The man gave me ten dollars— did Beecher[1] send it out there?—all in silver, as there would be no way for me to get change to pay small charges in that country.

Just before daylight [of August 27] I started on my way up the river; just before sundown that afternoon I appeared at the ferry and was carried across. On the Missouri side I "took to the brush" until it grew quite dark. During the night I made my way toward the appointed meeting place.

Once that night I was fired at by one of the "nigger patrols" which the slaveholders had organized to protect their property by riding around nightly in turn to see that none of their "niggers" ran away or were stolen. Finally I found a safe waiting spot in a mass of willows on low ground by the river, not more

---

1. **Beecher:** Henry Ward Beecher (1813–1887), Congregational clergyman and a leading abolitionist.

than two miles from the place where we were to meet. At dawn I left my horse, made my way to the nearest high ground, climbed a tree, and verified my location. I could plainly see on a hill the landmark house, which stood one mile east of our assembling point. Near me was a corncrib from which I carried away enough corn to give Old Titus three good feeds. As I went toward him, I all but stumbled over a "nigger" who very evidently had been out chicken stealing. He dropped his loot and ran for his life. I pretended I had not seen him.

This Platte County, into which John Brown had invited me, was thickly settled. Though most of the houses were built of logs, there were a few fine frame residences. Also, behind these residences, there were always "nigger quarters," ramshackle stables, and loom-houses where Negro women wove the jeans and linsey-woolsey which formed the outer clothing of the whole population. The planters' wealth was made up of fine horses, "likely niggers," and a rich soil which produced immense crops of corn and hemp. Though many of the owners of this countryside could neither read nor write, they were proud and rich. How long John Brown had been secretly lingering there near his chosen rendezvous, or how many men he had with him, I never knew.

Night settled down dark and moonless. Clouds hung low in the west. I had difficulty in making my way to the appointed place, but there I found Brown and the Negro whom I had seen in his camp. There were eight or ten dismounted men there also, who had left their horses across the Missouri. I learned from conversation I overheard that there were other men, farther down the river, who were mounted. These had crossed the river on a captured flatboat, and expected to recross by the same means before daylight. I noticed that Brown seemed to know the name of every slaveholder in that region, the number of his slaves, and the exact location of the road that led from his plantation to the river.

Brown directed our group to go to a certain cabin belonging to a certain house and get the slaves who were expecting us. We all were to take them to the river by a road he described. Then the rest of our group were to take these Negroes over the river in skiffs that would be found at a designated place, but I was to make my way back to the same ferry by which I had come and to cross by it as soon after daybreak as the man in charge turned up to navigate it.

Brown said there was a regular road in front of the house where we were to get the Negroes, but that, as it was guarded by the planters' patrol, our party was to enter the farm from the rear and approach the slave quarters through a cornfield. He bade me go alone a mile up the direct front road to watch for the patrol and keep our main party informed of any danger from that source. Just where a dim side road led off down to the river where the skiffs were waiting, he said, there was a certain sharp bend in the road. My orders were to tie my horse in a patch of pawpaw bushes nearby and take my station there in the turn itself, so that I could see in both directions.

When I objected to dismounting and separating myself from my horse, Brown told me with a metallic ring in his voice: "You will obey orders."

Doubtless if there had been more light, I should have seen a peculiar gleam in his eye. Anyone who had anything to do with Brown in Kansas learned that it was death, after one joined his band, to disobey any order he issued.

I went with his men as he had ordered. Because the night was so very dark, we had difficulty in finding the right place. I took my post in the bend, while the other men crept up through the cornfield. Just then the wind blew furiously and the rain poured down. I could see nothing except when lightning flashed now and then. I stood in the road barely outside the bushes, impatiently waiting for our men and the Negroes to climb over the fence and follow with me that vague side road to the river. Without warning someone threw his arms around me from behind, pinioning my elbows to my sides. Instantly two more men leaped upon me, but before they could clap a hand over my mouth, I uttered the loudest yell that had ever come out of me. It was the only warning I could give my associates.

My captors tied my hands and feet; they put a rope around my neck and dragged me along the ground by it for some distance. Then they lifted me to my feet, threw the rope end over the limb of a tree, and demanded:

"Tell us where the rest of this low-down gang of nigger stealers are, or up you go."

Without waiting for a reply they pulled away on the rope. When they let me down, I was "pretty tolerable mad." I gave them my opinion as to what sort of scoundrels they were. They cut that discourse short by swinging me up again. When next they let me down, they spent a few minutes in giving me their opinion of "nigger stealers." They wound up by declaring most solemnly that if I would tell them where the rest of the gang was, they would let me go and would hang the others.

I was not in condition to make a very good speech in reply. Still, I started — but before I had forced out a dozen words, they pulled away on the rope. One of them chuckled:

"We'll give him enough this time to make him reasonable."

Just at that moment pistols flashed. Two of the men who had been holding the rope dropped to the ground; the other ran away. My "gang," who had succeeded in creeping up through the cornfield and bringing away two Negro men and one woman, had then overheard the rather loud talk of the patrol at my "hanging bee." Thanks to the black night and the rain, they had stolen up to us unnoticed.

They soon had me on my feet and helped me to find Old Titus and mount him — for in fact there was little energy left in me. They said they would take the Negroes over the river, and they urged me to strike for the woods and reach my ferry by daybreak if possible. I noticed then that both my revolvers were gone, though I still had my Sharp's rifle, which I had left strapped to Titus's saddle. Two of my companions went back to the tree where the Platte County slaveholders had been giving me their "necktie reception," and soon brought me two revolvers, but only one of them was mine.

One of the Negroes pulled down the fence for me and told me to follow the corn rows to the other side of the field. If I tore down the fence there and went straight on, I would soon come to a road that led up the river. I rode away feeling rather uncomfortable.

Long before daylight it became obvious that the entire district was out on the warpath. I heard shots in several directions; I caught the baying of hounds; I saw signal fires both ahead of me and behind me. Twice I hid in the brush until bodies of armed men had passed. Certainly John Brown's "nigger stealing" raid into Platte County had started a tremendous uproar. By now, however, probably all the rest of Brown's men were safely back across the river, and here was I, at sixteen, left alone to fight the whole county.

Traveling through an unknown region in the night, with the population of an entire countryside, bloodhounds and all, on your trail and every man of the lot bent on swinging you up on a tree, as soon as caught, may make interesting reading when transferred to the printed page; it produces quite different sensations in the person chased, especially if his neck already is a bit sore from a recent hanging. I realized plainly before daylight that every approach to the river, as well as every road which ran north and south, was being guarded. Once I decided to strike out into the district to the east, but I had hardly made up my mind to that when I caught from that very direction such a racket of hounds and horns that I gave up the plan.

Just as day broke, I reached a dim lane that led toward the river. From sounds behind me I knew that not much over a mile away a large party was on my trail. After following that lane for a mile or so, I saw that a fence had been built across it, though there was not a human being in sight. I could hear the mob behind me drawing closer. In a moment I made my decision. I put my bridle reins in my teeth, took a revolver in each hand, and dashed toward the fence, trusting Old Titus to get over it somehow. I heard two shots fired at me from ambush, and I banged away right and left with my revolvers—and dug my spurs into Old Titus's sides. He went over the obstruction without touching a rail of it.

We forded quite a large stream and pressed on. Just as I was beginning to think that I had got well to the north of that whole raging section, with an open approach to my ferry, I saw ahead of me, to my disgust, a large group on horseback, gathered near a house which had just come into view. Hoping to escape notice, I leaped a fence into a cornfield—but they had seen me. I have never heard a more fiendish yell than they loosed then and there. I think that afterward, toned down several degrees, it became the famous "rebel yell," the battle cry of the Confederate troops. As that gang gave tongue to it, it fully convinced me that there was blood on the moon.

I plunged across the cornfield and finally reached the bottom lands of the river, which were covered in some places with grass as high as a man on horseback and in others with a dense growth of willows. My pursuers evidently had wholly lost my trail. At various times during the day I could see a patrol on the road that ran by the foot of the hills a mile or two away, but no one searched the bottom land where I was hiding. I stole out once during the day, crossed the road, and brought Old Titus an armful of corn from a field. The "jerked meat" I had bought from the Indians now did me good service.

Toward night I held a one-man council of war. It was clear that every road up or down the river was now patrolled both night and day. If I left the shelter of these willows and got back into the inhabited country, I must expect another night like the last. My only way of escape was to swim the Missouri River with its rapid current, its rushing, mud-colored water, and its treacherous quicksands. After much thought I decided to take the risk.

When evening closed down, I stripped. After tying all my clothing and accouterments to the top of my saddle, I led Old Titus down to the bank. I had expected to have a hard time to get him under way, but he went down the slope into the water without trouble and struck out for the far shore. I took hold of his tail and swam behind him; thus I not only relieved him of my weight, but was able to steer him wherever I wished. We landed in a wild and desolate spot.

I dressed and mounted. By riding all night I reached my Indian friends again at ten o'clock the next day. They all noticed my swollen neck and were very inquisitive about it. I concocted a story of how a lariat had got tangled around it. This satisfied them—and was not so very far from the truth, either.

Slavery and Freedom

The visual representations of African Americans in the nineteenth century varied considerably over time according to the presuppositions of the beholder. The growing controversy over the institution of slavery fostered new images that first appeared before the public in the 1830s. With the advent of photography in 1839, stills and daguerreotypes of slaves as well as of free blacks were developed for personal and public use. Magazines such as *Harper's Weekly* illustrated their stories with wood engravings made from photographs. Next, several commercial forms of photography evolved for sale to a mass market. One was the stereo card, a format that offered the illusion of three dimensions when two side-by-side images were seen through a viewer and that remained popular from the 1850s well into the twentieth century. Another was the carte-de-visite. Originally a way to produce small portraits cheaply, it soon led to the extensive sale of pictures of celebrities. About the size of the visiting card used in social life—hence their name—cartes-de-visite consisted of an image on a thin piece of photographic paper that was pasted to thicker cardboard backing; messages could be inscribed on the back. Most of these texts were simple advertisements for the photographic studios, but some were used as conveyors of propaganda to represent people's political, moral, or aesthetic passions, much as we print messages on buttons, T-shirts, and bumper stickers today. People collected cartes-de-visite most commonly for celebrity worship, as hobbyists buy and sell sports-figure cards today.

Early photographic processes set certain limits and created specific conventions about the images produced in this era. Bulky equipment, the time required for preparation of a photosensitive surface, and lengthy exposure times gave nineteenth-century portraiture a solemn character. Movement produced a blur, so people had to set their faces into an expression that they could hold for about thirty seconds, which is actually a long time. Smiling and saying "cheese" belong to a much later era when cameras had become easier to use and the portrait had evolved into the "snapshot"—an image captured in an instant. Most photographs from the nineteenth century convey seriousness, with their subjects, even unwilling ones, striving for a dignified appearance.

Plate 1. Unknown artist, "United States: The South," from *Malte-Brun's School Geography*, 1836

Plate 3. Brady & Co., "Interior View of the Price, Birch & Co. Slave Dealership, Alexandria, Va.," 1865

The plates on these pages offer sharply divergent images of slavery. Children throughout the nation learned to view the American South from images like the woodcut shown in Plate 1, taken from a widely used school geography book of the 1830s. The photographs in Plates 2 and 3 were made near the end of the Civil War by men who sold their work in various formats to a mass market. Some of these photographers were interested in reproducing the photos as testimonials to the need for the end of slavery. Plate 3, made by a photographer working for Brady & Company, famous for its depictions of the Civil War, is half of a set of stereo viewing images. How did the image of slavery change from the schoolbook image of 1836 to the photographs from 1865?

Left: Plate 2. Andrew J. Russell, "Price, Birch & Co., Dealers in Slaves, Alexandria, Va.," 1865

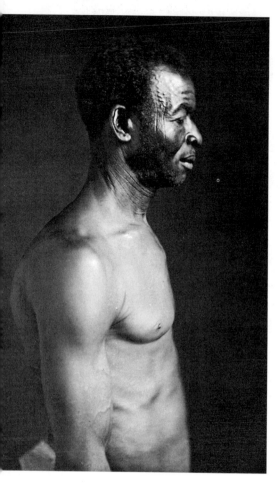 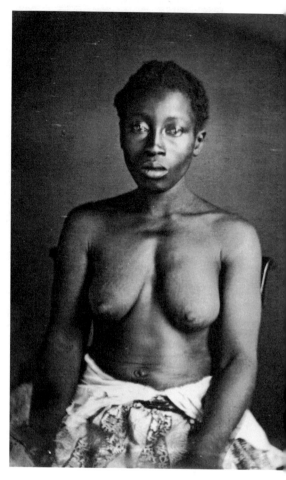

Plate 4. J. T. Zealy, "Jack (Driver), a Slave in Columbia, S.C., '. . . from the Guinea Coast,'" 1850

Plate 5. J. T. Zealy, "Delia, a Slave in Columbia, S.C., '. . . Country Born of African Parents,'" 1850

All the daguerreotypes on these pages were made for private enterprises or for personal reasons, not as public documents. One of the leading scientists in the United States, Louis Agassiz, used the images in Plates 4 and 5, which he instructed a South Carolina daguerreotypist to make, to demonstrate an anthropological theory of the "separate creation" of the different races. Plate 6 presents the image of a slaveholding family; note the position of the slave nanny within the picture. Plates 7 and 8 are representations of free African Americans choosing to be photographed at their own expense, just as middle-class whites of the period did. Plate 8, in fact, was made by Augustus Washington, an African American daguerreotypist who owned a studio in Hartford, Connecticut. What do these faces tell you about slavery and freedom?

Plate 6. Thomas M. Easterly, "Southern Man, His Two Daughters, and Nanny," St. Louis, Mo., 1848

Plate 7. Thomas M. Easterly, "Robert J. Wilkinson, Successful Businessman," St. Louis, Mo., c. 1860

Plate 8. Augustus Washington, "Portrait of an Unidentified Woman," Hartford, Conn., c. 1850

Plates 9 through 12 are all public representations of slaves from Northern sources. The photos were designed to make a particular point, as were the daguerreotypes that supposedly demonstrated racial theories for Agassiz. Plates 9 and 10 are from *Harper's Weekly*, a journal with a strong antislavery bias. What message does Plate 9 communicate? How do Plates 10 and 11 connect to what you know about the experiences of young female slaves? The message on the back of Plate 12, a carte-de-visite portrait of Gordon, a slave who entered Union territory in 1863 and became a Union soldier, reads:

> "The Peculiar Institution" Illustrated. Copy of a photograph taken from life at Baton Rouge, La. Ap. 2, '63; the lacerated body—months after the brutal flogging had been inflicted—having healed in the manner represented. The alleged offense was a trifling one. How noble and benignant the countenance of the victim!

What message about slavery was each of these images delivering? How did the public debate over slavery influence the way African Americans were visualized in these images?

Left: Plate 9. Unknown artist, "The Africans of the Slave Bark 'Wildfire,'" *Harper's Weekly*, June 2, 1860

Above right: Plate 10. Unknown artist, "Emancipated Slaves, White and Colored," *Harper's Weekly*, January 30, 1864

Right: Plate 11. Charles Payson, "Freedom's Banner. Charley, a Slave Boy from New Orleans," 1863

Far right: Plate 12. McPherson & Oliver, "'The Peculiar Institution.' Gordon, Escaped from Mississippi," 1863

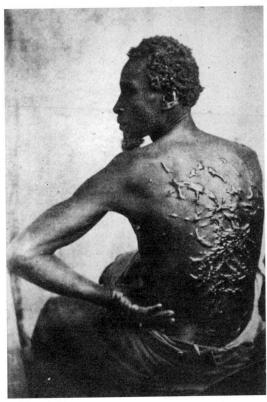

EX-SLAVES.   INQUIRING STRANGER.   EX-DOMINANT RACE.
"er, we's going to draw." "Draw what?" "Draw rations, Sir."   "Well, now the war is over, what are you people going to do for a living?"   "I reckon we'll run—" "Run!. After what?" "Of we'll run for offices of some sort—Congress, Legislature,
                                                                                                                                        or Notary Public, or any thing!"

Plates 13 through 15 are images from late in the Civil War and from the post-war Reconstruction era. What effect have these events had on photographers' perceptions of African Americans? Have the images become more positive? More realistic? More suggestive of people directing their own lives? Overall, in what ways did that generation of conflict over the question of slavery change the way African Americans were portrayed?

Above left: Plate 13. Timothy O'Sullivan, "'Contrabands.' Fugitive Slaves Crossing the Rappahannock River during Grant's Second Manassas Campaign," 1864

Left: Plate 14. Unknown artist, "Solution of the Labor Question in the South," *Harper's Weekly,* December 2, 1865

Below: Plate 15. Unknown artist, "The Ebony Bridal—The Wedding Ceremony," *Frank Leslie's Popular Monthly,* October 1877

PART SIX

Civil War and Reconstruction

The Price of War

During the thirty years leading to the Civil War, the United States' early nationalism gave way to antebellum sectionalism. Settlers from the North and from the South resolutely proceeded westward, but in economic and societal matters the rapidly growing Southwest, including Alabama, Mississippi, and Louisiana, differed greatly from the new Northwest of Ohio, Illinois, and Wisconsin. Though both regions were dominated by small farms, the South also cultivated large plantations. Slaves worked vast acreage in the South, while free labor developed the North. One society produced a rural gentry, and the other cities, entrepreneurs, and lawyers; one grew conservative and fearful of change, while the other spawned liberal religions and reforms. Beneath the expansion was a national antipathy to the black race that made Southerners fearful of the abolition of slavery and committed Northerners to halting the expansion of slavery in their own society, a commitment that in parts of the North coexisted with a moral abhorrence of the institution of slavery.

The readings in this section reflect the crises the nation faced at midcentury. Union nurse Cornelia Hancock's description of the battlefield and the accounts by Union soldier George Ward Nichols and Southern plantation mistress Pauline DeCaradeuc Heyward of the devastation wrought by William Tecumseh Sherman's march through Georgia and the Carolinas graphically illustrate the impact of war. Ellen Leonard's account of the New York antidraft riot in 1863 exposes the dilemma of conflicting visions of the goals of the war. African American war correspondent Thomas Morris Chester's description of the triumphant march of black soldiers into the Confederate capital suggests that the struggle for full civil rights was just beginning. Victory for the Union did not answer all the major questions posed by the antislavery debate and the war.

"I have vowed that if I should have children—the first ingredient of the first principle of their education shall be uncompromising hatred & contempt of the

Yankee," declared a white Southerner toward the end of the Civil War. You will read a similar response from another white Southerner, Caleb Forshey. "I'm free as a frog!" exulted one former slave, reacting like Felix Haywood and other black Southerners to the prospect of a future without slavery. Great hopes or extreme bitterness, more common than the philosophical resignation found in the journal of slave owner Henry Ravenel, promised a painful future for the South.

In the months following Lee's surrender to Grant at Appomattox, the South was a landscape of abandoned fields, twisted rails, burned buildings, white men hobbling about on one leg or dangling an empty sleeve, and former slaves exploring their new freedom or searching for food, shelter, and work. The visual portfolio "Civil War and Reconstruction" (page 325) demonstrates the extent of the destruction on many levels. Some things the war had settled: secession was impossible, slavery dead, and the South desperately impoverished, its prewar agricultural, slave-based economy gone with the wind. Other outcomes the region and the United States struggle with still. In particular, victory for the Union did not resolve questions about the role that African American men and women were to play in American life. The first attempts to secure rights for the former slaves, known as Reconstruction (1865–1876), produced the Thirteenth, Fourteenth, and Fifteenth Amendments to the Constitution, which provided the legal basis for a revolutionary change in American life. But determined opposition from white Southerners largely defeated Reconstruction. Emerging from the era of Civil War and Reconstruction neither slaves nor fully free, African Americans faced a civil rights struggle that would consume the next century and beyond.

POINTS OF VIEW

Sherman's "March to the Sea" (1863–1865)

35

Marching with Sherman's Army

George Ward Nichols

In 1864 the Union organized for final victory. General Ulysses S. Grant, in overall command of the Union Army, led his troops against Robert E. Lee in the East while his trusted subordinate William Tecumseh Sherman pressed into Georgia from the West. As Grant made his slow, bloody way through Virginia, Sherman was changing the rules of war.

George Ward Nichols, *The Story of the Great March from the Diary of a Staff Officer* (New York: Harper & Brothers, 1865).

Hacking a path through the lower South, slashing to bits much of what remained of the rebel heartland, Sherman's men burned and looted their way through Georgia and the Carolinas.

George Ward Nichols's The Story of the Great March *became one of the most popular accounts of Sherman's campaign. Within a year of its publication in 1865, the book sold sixty thousand copies, and it was reprinted in European newspapers. An aide-de-camp on the general's personal staff, Nichols depicted the public side of Sherman as he met with various groups—his field staff, his soldiers, and freed slaves. Nichols described as well Sherman's methods of warfare and the character of his famous "March to the Sea."*

Nichols (1831–1885), who had been active in the antislavery struggles in Kansas in the 1850s, settled in Cincinnati after the war and became a leading figure in developing that city's museum, art school, and orchestra.

BEFORE YOU READ

1. What did Nichols think of General Sherman and his strategy?
2. Why did the Union Army destroy Southern land and property?
3. What was Nichols's opinion of the Southerners he encountered?
4. How intense was the fighting during the march? How would you generally characterize it?

PREPARATIONS FOR THE SEAWARD MARCH— THE BURNING OF ATLANTA

General Sherman at once made preparations to abandon all the posts south of Dalton [Georgia]. From Gaylesville and Rome he issued his orders concerning the new movement. The sick and wounded, noncombatants, the machinery, extra baggage, tents, wagons, artillery, ammunition stores, every person and every thing not needed in the future campaigns, were sent back to Chattanooga. The army was stripped for fighting and marching.

Let us for a moment look at General Sherman as he appeared at Gaylesville, seated upon a camp-stool in front of his tent, with a map of the United States spread upon his knees. . . . General Sherman's finger runs swiftly down the map until it reaches Atlanta; then, with unerring accuracy, it follows the general direction to be taken by the right and left wings, until a halt is made at Milledgeville. "From here," the general says, "we have several alternatives; I am sure we can go to Savannah, or open communication with the sea somewhere in that direction." After studying the map a while, tracing upon the tangled maze of streams and towns a line from Savannah north and east, at Columbia, South Carolina, General Sherman looks up at General Howard with the remark, "Howard, I believe we can go there without any serious difficulty. If we can cross the Salkahatchie, we can capture Columbia. From Columbia"— passing his finger quickly over rivers, swamps, and cities to Goldsboro, North Carolina—"that point is a few days' march through a rich country. When we reach that important railroad junction—when I once plant this army at

Goldsboro—Lee must leave Virginia, or he will be defeated beyond hope of recovery. We can make this march, for General Grant assures me that Lee can not get away from Richmond without his knowledge, nor without serious loss to his army."

To those who gazed upon the map, and measured the great distance to be traversed, from this quiet village away up in the mountains of Northern Alabama down to the sea, and thence hundreds of miles through a strange and impassable country away to the south again, and over wide rivers and treacherous bogs, the whole scheme, in the hands of any man but he who conceived it, seemed weird, fatal, impossible. But it was at that moment in process of operation. General Sherman at once communicated the first part of his plan to General Grant, subsequently receiving his hearty approval, with entire freedom to act as he should deem best. The army was at once set in motion; the numerous threads spreading over a wide field of operations were gathered up; out of confusion came exquisite order. Detachments guarding various dépôts were sent to their commands, outposts were withdrawn, the cavalry were concentrated in one division, under the lead of a gallant soldier. Compact, confident, and cheerful, this well-appointed host, guided by that master mind, moved grandly on to the fulfillment of its high mission. The field of operations now entered upon belonged, as has been said, to the genius of strategy. Those who have written of this campaign always date its commencement as from Atlanta. Inasmuch as we trod upon hitherto unconquered soil when we went out from Atlanta, this statement is true; but the march really began at Rome and Kingston, and it is from this point that we take up the diary of events which occurred within the experience and knowledge of the writer.

November 13th.—Yesterday the last train of cars whirled rapidly past the troops moving south, speeding over bridges and into the woods as if they feared they might be left helpless in the deserted land. At Cartersville the last communications with the North were severed with the telegraph wire. It bore the message to General Thomas, "All is well." And so we have cut adrift from our base of operations, from our line of communications, launching out into uncertainty at the best, on a journey whose projected end only the General in command knows. Its real fate and destination he does not know, since that rests with the goodness of God and the brave hearts and strong limbs of our soldiers. The history of war bears no similar example, except that of Cortés burning his ships. It is a bold, hazardous undertaking. There is no backward step possible here. Thirty days' rations and a new base: that time and those supplies will be exhausted in the most rapid march ere we can arrive at the nearest sea-coast; arrived there, what then? I never heard that manna[1] grew on the sand-beaches or in the marshes, though we are sure that we can obtain forage on our way; and I have reason to know that General Sherman is in the highest degree sanguine and cheerful—sure even of success.

As for the soldiers, they do not stop to ask questions. Sherman says "Come," and that is the entire vocabulary to them. A most cheerful feature of

---

1. **manna:** food that, according to the Bible, was miraculously supplied to the Israelites during their escape from Egypt.

the situation is the fact that the men are healthful and jolly as men can be; hoping for the best, willing to dare the worst.

Behind us we leave a track of smoke and flame. Half of Marietta was burned up—not by orders, however; for the command is that proper details shall be made to destroy all property which can ever be of use to the Rebel armies. Stragglers will get into these places, and dwelling-houses are leveled to the ground. In nearly all cases these are the deserted habitations formerly owned by Rebels who are now refugees.

Yesterday, as some of our men were marching toward the Chattahoochee River, they saw in the distance pillars of smoke rising along its banks—the bridges were in flames. Said one, hitching his musket on his shoulder in a free and easy way: "I say, Charley, I believe Sherman has set the river on fire." "Reckon not," replied the other, with the same indifference; "if he has, it's all right." And so they pass along; obeying orders, not knowing what is before them, but believing in their leader.

From Kingston to Atlanta the rails have been taken up on the road, fires built about them, and the iron twisted into all sorts of curves; thus they are left, never to be straightened again. The Rebel inhabitants are in agony of wonder at all this queer manœuvring. It appears as if we intended evacuating Atlanta; but our troops are taking the wrong direction for the hopes and purposes of these people.

Atlanta is entirely deserted by human beings, excepting a few soldiers here and there. The houses are vacant; there is no trade or traffic of any kind; the streets are empty. Beautiful roses bloom in the gardens of fine houses, but a terrible stillness and solitude cover all, depressing the hearts even of those who are glad to destroy it. In the peaceful homes at the North there can be no conception how these people have suffered for their crimes.

Atlanta, Night of the 15th November. A grand and awful spectacle is presented to the beholder in this beautiful city, now in flames. By order, the chief engineer has destroyed by powder and fire all the store-houses, dépôt buildings, and machine-shops. The heaven is one expanse of lurid fire; the air is filled with flying, burning cinders; buildings covering two hundred acres are in ruins or in flames; every instant there is the sharp detonation or the smothered booming sound of exploding shells and powder concealed in the buildings, and then the sparks and flame shoot away up into the black and red roof, scattering cinders far and wide.

These are the machine-shops where have been forged and cast the Rebel cannon, shot and shell that have carried death to many a brave defender of our nation's honor. These warehouses have been the receptacle of munitions of war, stored to be used for our destruction. The city, which, next to Richmond, has furnished more material for prosecuting the war than any other in the South, exists no more as a means for injury to be used by the enemies of the Union.

A brigade of Massachusetts soldiers are the only troops now left in the town: they will be the last to leave it. To-night I heard the really fine band of the Thirty-third Massachusetts playing "John Brown's soul goes marching on," by the light of the burning buildings. I have never heard that noble anthem when it was so grand, so solemn, so inspiring.

News came from General Howard that the advance of the 17th Corps had arrived, at nine o'clock that morning, at a point thirteen miles from Cheraw, and had found the enemy intrenched in their front. It was said that Beauregard, Johnston, Hardee, and Hampton, with the garrisons of Charleston, Wilmington, and other points, were in Cheraw, and that a great battle was probable. The Rebels had certainly gathered an array of talent, in the way of generals, enough to appal this little army! The presence of all these men and any large force is doubtless an exaggeration, although there can be no question but the delays of the last few days have given the enemy an intimation of our plans, which they have improved by guarding the important outlet at Cheraw.

We were inclined to believe that the Rebels, not liking our society, would not interfere with our movements; indeed, that they would assist our passage through the country. The care with which they have laid in plentiful supplies of corn, fodder, hams, beef on the hoof, and other supplies, would have indicated this. Again, our infantry have hardly seen a Rebel soldier since we left Columbia until this morning. Our route from the Catawba crossed several creeks where there were valuable bridges uninjured, the destruction of any one of which would have delayed our column a day or more. Certainly we had every reason to suppose that the Rebels wished us a good riddance, and offered no objections to our speedy passage to the sea, or wherever we chose to go. Only one other hypothesis remained, and the presence of an enemy in our front to-night is a cogent argument in its favor. It is that the Rebel leaders did not divine the real movement until the last moment, and are now throwing obstacles in the way of our passage over the Pedee. We estimate that, without assistance from Virginia, they can not concentrate more than twenty-five thousand men in our front, and we will undertake to start that force in two or three days. Within that time we shall have brought up all our troops, and it will go hard with the Rebels, but we will have a pontoon floating quietly from either bank of the Pedee. Of course the hope of saving the bridge at Cheraw must be abandoned, and we must depend upon other resources.

Although for the last three days we have not seen the sun, and the rain has fallen now and then, the left wing has made some fine marches. The 14th Corps yesterday traveled over eighteen miles of the road which had already been used by the 20th Corps, and to-day the 20th Corps has marched twenty-one miles since daylight. Fortunately the route has led along the high ridges and through the pine barrens, where the soil is sandy, and better for the light fall of rain. Thus we were able to reach this place early in the afternoon, driving before us, at a good marching pace, Butler's, or rather Hampton's cavalry, who opposed the advance.

During the skirmishing, one of our men, a forager, was slightly wounded; but the most serious accident of the day occurred to a negro woman in a house where the Rebels had taken cover. When I saw this woman, who would not have been selected as the best type of South Carolina female beauty, the blood was streaming over her neck and bosom from a wound in the lobe of her ear, which the bullet had just clipped and passed by.

"What was it that struck you, aunty?" I asked.

"Lor bress me, massa, I dun know; I just fell right down."

"Didn't you feel any thing, nor hear any sound?"

"Yes, now I 'member, I heerd a s-z-z-z-z-z, and den I just knock down. I drap on de groun'. I'se so glad I not dead, for if I died den de Bad Man would git me, cos I dance lately a heap."

To-day is the first time within a week when I have seen a household where the women are neatly dressed and the children cleanly. The people who have inhabited the houses along the roads for fifty miles behind us are among the most degraded specimens of humanity I have ever seen. Many of the families I now refer to do not belong to the class known as the "poor whites" of the South, for these are large landowners, and holders of from ten to forty slaves.

The peasantry of France are uneducated, but they are usually cleanly in their habits. The serfs of Russia are ignorant, but they are semi-barbarous, and have, until lately, been slaves. A large proportion of the working classes in England are debased, but they work. But the people I have seen and talked to for several days past are not only disgustingly filthy in their houses and their persons, but are so provokingly lazy, or "shiftless," as Mrs. Stowe[2] has it, that they appear more like corpses recalled to a momentary existence than live human beings, and I have felt like applying a galvanic battery to see if they could be made to move. Even the inroads of our foragers do not start them into life; they loll about like sloths, and barely find energy enough to utter a whining lamentation that they will starve.

During this campaign I have seen terrible instances of the horrors of slavery. I have seen men and women as white as the purest type of the Anglo-Saxon race in our army, who had been bought and sold like animals. I have looked upon the mutilated forms of black men who had suffered torture at the caprice of their cruel masters, and I have heard tales of woe too horrible for belief; but in all these cases I have never been so impressed with the degrading, demoralizing influence of this curse of slavery as in the presence of these South Carolinians. The higher classes represent the scum, and the lower the dregs of civilization. They are South Carolinians, not Americans.

The clean people whom I met this afternoon were a refreshing spectacle. Several of the young ladies—the men ran away at our approach—were attending school at this place, where a seminary has been situated for many years. One of these girls, in reply to my question why she had not gone to her home, forty miles down the river, answered:

"What is the use? Your people go every where; you overrun the state; and I am as well off here as at my father's house."

I acknowledged the wisdom of her action, for there is no doubting the fact that our presence is quite sensibly felt.

---

2. **Mrs. Stowe:** Harriet Beecher Stowe, author of *Uncle Tom's Cabin.*

I happened to be present this afternoon at one of those interviews which so often occur between General Sherman and the negroes. The conversation was piquant and interesting; not only characteristic of both parties, but the more significant because, on the part of the General, I believe it a fair expression of his feelings on the slavery question.

A party of ten or fifteen negroes had just found their way through the lines from Cheraw. Their owners had carried them from the vicinity of Columbia to the other side of the Pedee, with the mules and horses which they were running away from our army. The negroes had escaped, and were on their way back to find their families. A more ragged set of human beings could not have been found out of the slave states, or, perhaps, Italy. The negroes were of all ages, and had stopped in front of the General's tent, which was pitched a few feet back from the sidewalk of the main street.

Several officers of the army, among them General Slocum, were gathered round, interested in the scene. General Sherman said to them:

"Well, men, what can I do for you—where are you from?"

"We's just come from Cheraw. Massa took us wid him to carry mules and horses away from youins."

"You thought we would get them; did you wish us to get the mules?"

"Oh yes, massa, dat's what I wanted. We knowed youins cumin, and I wanted you to hav dem mules; but no use; dey heard dat youins on de road, and nuthin would stop 'em. Why, as we cum along, de cavalry run away from de Yanks as if dey fright to deth. Dey jumped into de river, and some of dem lost dere hosses. Dey frightened at de berry name ob Sherman."

Some one at this point said: "That is General Sherman who is talking to you."

"God bress me! Is you Mr. Sherman?"

"Yes, I am Mr. Sherman."

"Dat's him, su' nuff," said one.

"Is dat de grre-aat Mr. Sherman dat we'se heard ob so long?" said another.

"Why, dey so frightened at your berry name dat dey run right away," shouted a third.

"It is not me that they are afraid of," said the General; "the name of another man would have the same effect with them if he had this army. It is these soldiers that they run away from."

"Oh no," they all exclaimed, "it's de name ob Sherman, su'; and we hab wanted to see you so long while you trabbel all roun' jis whar you like to go. Dey said dat dey wanted to git you a little furder on, and den dey whip all your soldiers; but, God bress me! you keep cumin' and a cumin', an' dey allers git out."

"Dey mighty 'fraid ob you, sar; dey say you kill de colored men too," said an old man, who had not heretofore taken part in the conversation.

With much earnestness, General Sherman replied:

"Old man, and all of you, understand me. I desire that bad men should fear me, and the enemies of the government which we are all fighting for. Now we are your friends; you are now free ('Tank you, Massa Sherman,' was ejaculated by the group). You can go where you please; you can come with us or go home to your children. Wherever you go you are no longer slaves. You ought to be able to take care of yourselves. ('We is; we will.') You must earn your freedom, then you will be entitled to it, sure; you have a right to be all that you can be, but you must be industrious, and earn the right to be men. If you go back to your families, and I tell you again you can go with us if you wish, you must do the best you can. When you get a chance, go to Beaufort or Charleston, where you will have a little farm to work for yourselves."

The poor negroes were filled with gratitude and hope by these kind words, which the General uttered in the kindest manner, and they went away with thanks and blessings on their lips.

36

A Southern Woman's Wartime Journal
Pauline DeCaradeuc Heyward

The journal of Pauline DeCaradeuc Heyward (1843–1914) offers a spirited narrative of a slaveholding family's experience of Sherman's march. Union soldiers, in Heyward's account, were determined to penalize South Carolina, the original seat of secession, for starting the Civil War. That the DeCaradeuc women managed to limit the damage done to their plantation and property indicates that even angry Union troops approaching the end of a terrible war continued to pay some homage to the code requiring gentlemen to treat ladies courteously.

The war cost the DeCaradeuc family the lives of two sons as well as most of its wealth. After the war Pauline married Geurard Heyward. When he failed as a planter, Geurard, Pauline, and their growing family moved to Savannah, Georgia, where they modestly prospered and continued to enlarge their family. Until her death in 1914, Pauline maintained the standards of gentility required of a Southern wife and mother.

BEFORE YOU READ

1. What were the Union soldiers seeking at the Heyward plantation?

2. How did the DeCaradeuc women manage to keep possessions they valued and avoid sexual assault?

3. Why was Pauline DeCaradeuc Heyward so afraid for her father?

Mary D. Robertson, ed., *A Confederate Lady Comes of Age: The Journal of Pauline DeCaradeuc Heyward, 1863–1888* (Charleston: University of South Carolina Press, 1992), pp. 36–37, 65–69.

Feb. 14th, 1864

Carrie and I went over to Augusta yesterday, and really in spite of everything had a very amusing time. We bought several photographs of our most illustrious Gen's. I got Lee, Davis & Kirby Smith. John Cochran sent me word the other day that he had sent out to Richmond for Stonewall Jackson's for me, so that I'll have that too. . . .

I met Lieut. Col. Croft who stopped me & talked awhile on the street, he is most dreadfully, *agonizingly*, wounded in his right hand & looks very badly.

When we finished our business we sauntered round to the church yard & sat there 'till time to meet the train. When we reached the depot there was such a concourse of soldiers there that I begged an old lady who was going too, to let us remain with her. I was very uneasy as I never was in a crowd of men without a protector before, however, a young & handsome soldier came up & introduced himself, Major Beaufort of Va. and begged us to allow him to remain near us until the car was opened. When the doors were unlocked we got in & obtained good seats, some twenty-five ladies had to stand up & as many had to be left, & such crowds of soldiers!! An officer in front of us spread his blanket on the seat & begged us to keep it for him, but 'twas impossible & he couldn't even get in the car again. After a little while I heard a plaintive voice outside under the window, say: "Oh, Miss Pauline, ain't there any room in there for me?" I looked out & saw Col. Croft, of course, he couldn't get in our car; he asked me to look for his cousin in our car who was wounded & on crutches, but I couldn't even move, after talking a while he went into the conductor's car then I heard another voice say: "Miss Pauline, can't you get me a seat in front of you? I want to get in your car so much." What could I do? He was a very handsome Capt. I felt assured I knew him, his face & voice were perfectly familiar, but I could not remember his name, he conversed for awhile just like some old friend, seemed to know me well, but I don't yet remember who he is. Anyhow *he* too had to go off. Then our Va. Major came under the window to chat, & I gave him some cake I bought for the children, they would not allow soldiers to come in our car, without a lady; meanwhile a soldier on crutches stood near us looking sick & weak, he *stood* of course, & Carrie, noble as she always is rose & insisted on his taking her seat, but he would not hear of it, he then introduced himself, Captain Croft, the cousin, the Lieut. Col. asked me to look for, he remained with us the rest of the time & proved to be most agreeable.

After awhile we looked up & there was our kind Virginia Major standing by us, he pretended to the conductor that he had to see us out, & thus got into our car from which he did not again move, he is really quite charming & entertained us very nicely, two more Captains spoke to us & offered to assist us in any way, but our Va. friend didn't give them a chance, he saw us to the carriage at Johnston's & all but cried when we got off the car. I think somehow we will hear of him again, he was 'mazin kind & attentive to us, should like to return it.

May 23, 1864

I have no heart to keep this Journal or tell of the dreadful, fatal battles in Va. Oh my God! my heart is too heavy, I am entirely miserable. Many whom I know are killed & wounded. Robert Taft and Col. Shooter are killed. Capt. Barnwell killed. George Lalane wounded. Wise's Brigade was subjected to a fearful firing from the enemy at Druery's Bluff. I suppose John Cochran is wounded, from the moment I saw him I felt that his life would be given to this devouring war; and I am assured that he is dead or wounded, for I *feel it.*

Feb. 18th, 1865

The Yankees have come & gone. On the 10th Feb. they encamped at Johnstons. The whole of Kilpatrick's forces, they were turned on the country for forage, plunder, & provisions. The first we saw of them was about a dozen of them, dashing thro the gate shouting: "Here come the Yankees, look out now you d——d rebels." A moment after they were in the house, Mother & Grandmother met them at the door, but they didn't listen to a word they tried to say, but said, "Come give us your keys, where is your liquor? get your gold, get your silver, you old women, hurry yourselves, I say." I had a belt on under my dress, with my revolver, and a bag of bullets, caps & powder in my pocket, they rushed into the room, where all of us ladies were sitting, saying, "Give me your revolvers, d——d you, if we find them, you'd better look out, where are your pistols, we know you've got 'em." I felt it wouldn't do for them to find mine on me, infuriated as they were, so I took Tante's arm, hurried upstairs & threw the revolver between her sheets, hardly I had finished when the door burst open & the room was filled with them, they pulled the bed to pieces, of course.

We all went into the parlor, and by this time there were hundreds of them, in the house, upstairs, in the garret, in every chamber, under the house, in the yard, garden, &c., &c., some singing, shouting, whistling, and Oh, my God, *such cursing.* Both pianos were going at the same time, with axes they broke open every door, drawer, trunk that was locked, smashed a large French mirror, broke pieces of furniture, and flung every piece of clothing, that they didn't carry off, all over the floors, they got some of Fa.'s prettiest paintings and broke bottles of catsup over them, they carried off every piece of silver, every knife, jewel, & particle of possessions in the house & negro houses, every paper, letter, receipt, &c., they flung to the winds, all the roads are strewn with them. Mother and G. M. went among them like brave women, trying to save some few things in vain, at one time a horrid looking ruffian came into the parlor, seeing only women there, he entered shut both doors, & said in an undertone, "You cursed rebels, now empty your pockets." Ah, mon Dieu, mine had my bag of ammunition in it, I rose, & while he was grabbing Miss Hessie's pocket book, I dropped my bag in a corner & flung an old bonnet over it, in my pocket, he found my watch. "Ah," said he, "This is a pretty little watch, now where is the key, & does it go good?" & the villain put his hand on my shoulder, I rose & stood before him, with all possible dignity & he turned away. Then after taking Tante's watch and everybody's money, he walked up to Mother, grinding his teeth & looking her full in the face, said: "Now, you've just *got* to tell me where your gold & silver is buried, I know you've got it, and if you know what's good for yourself & all in this room, you'll tell me where it is." "I have no gold, my silver you have all taken with every other valuable in the house." "That's a d——d lie, now I'll burn your house this minute, if you don't tell me." "I have nothing more to tell, do you think I'd tell a lie?" "I don't know." Then he walked up & down the room cursing, swearing, threatening, & spitting on every side, then finding he could do nothing with us, took Solomon out, put a pistol to his head, saying he would blow his brains out, if he didn't tell. Solomon is as true to us as steel, so are they all, all faithful & friends to us.

About sundown, on the 10th they left off coming here. I then went to ascertain the fate of my revolver, there it was still rolled in the sheets, thrown on the floor with the chaos of clothing. I of course, sent it off. They took every blanket & pillow case & towel, the cases for bags to carry off what they took, & towels for handkerchiefs, they even made the servants get our chemises & tear them up into pocket handkerchiefs for them.

Well the next day, which was Saturday, they came just the same, hundreds of them, one of our villianous neighbors told them that our boys fired the first gun on Sumter, so they said this house was the root of the rebellion & burn it they would, but our good servants & Mother and G. Mother entreated in such a way that they desisted, then they said that they had to arrest and shoot every influential citizen in S.C., every mover of secession, & from the accumulation of wealth, the quantities of food, books & clothes in this house, the finest they had seen in these parts, that they knew Father was wealthy, literary, & influential, & they had heard enough of him, to make an example of him & catch him they would. We have no less than five large libraries of refugees, here, besides our own, & the accumulated clothing & valuables of four separate families, no wonder they found us so rich, & came here so often.

As to provisions, 'tis true, few was so bountifully supplied. We had 7 barrels of fine flour, 300 bushels of corn, 1 barrel & 1 box of nice sugar, &c., &c.

Out of that we have 15 bushels corn, 1 bag flour, 3 hams, they took all the wine & brandy. They had scouts out in every direction looking for Father. Thus passed Saturday, on Sunday morning they burned Uncle & Daughter's home *everything* & every building on their place, even the well, they are here with nothing but their clothes on, in the world, they searched uncle's person. After breakfast, 500 Yankees came here in a body & dispersed over the house & place, carrying off everything they could, they attempted to get into Aiken Saturday morning but were repulsed by Wheeler.

Well, on Saturday night, Father who was encamped in the woods, with the mules, horses & some provisions & one or two of the servants, sent us word that he could not evade the scouts longer & he was going to give himself up to K.ptr. [Gen. Kilpatrick] & demand protection, as a Frenchman, for himself & household, I went down in the swamp to see him & when half way between there & the house saw four Yankees entering the gate, my goodness didn't I run, it was a regular tug between them & me to see who could get to the house first, but I beat in safety, but I never ran so in my life.

Well, after Father went, we were filled with anxiety about him, knowing their threats about him, Oh, we were so frightened for him, when the door opened & a Yankee rushed in with a lit candle, he looked all 'round then ran into every room in the house to look for "that d——d rebel," he then went out saying he'd return during the night to fire the house, — pleasant intelligence — then he & two others asked the servants if there were any young ladies in the house, how old they were & where they slept, during all this I had on blue spectacles & my face muffled up, Carrie too.

When I heard of their questions to the servants I thought that burning the house was nothing; I was almost frantic, I sat up in a corner, without moving or closing my eyes once the whole night. My God! I suffered agony, I trembled *unceasingly* till morning; about eleven o'clock that night, two men went up the back stairs, we heard them walking over head, they went into the room over the parlour (we were in the parlour, of course, all together) and went to bed there, they stayed there all night.

Well, none of us undressed or went to bed for six nights. On Sunday, Mother & Grandmother determined to go out to the camp, to Kilpatrick & ask for protection & for Father's release, they went in the cart with a little blind mule, the only animal they left us, with pieces of yarn for bridle, as they carried off all the harness, &c., during their absence, quantities of Yankees came here, and walked in *every direction* sticking the ground with their swords, feeling for buried things. Wherever the ground was soft they dug, they found all Tante's silver, bonds & jewels, a quantity of provisions, — barrel of wine, one of china, a box of Confederate money & bonds, &c.

Fortunately, the bulk of our silver was sent off.

Mother returned from the camp, bringing Father and William whom they had captured.

Monday morning only a few Yankees came, about ten, I suppose, and then the entire force fell back, not wishing to engage our troops, the R.R., of course, cut & we knew nothing more of them.

Our own soldiers have been coming here constantly, these last two or three days. My goodness, how different they are to the Yankees, the commonest one is as gentle & respectful to us as can be. . . .

FOR CRITICAL THINKING

1. Was Sherman's policy of total war against the Confederacy justified? Compare the picture of the South's circumstances presented by George Ward Nichols with that presented by Pauline DeCaradeuc Heyward, and argue for one side or the other.

2. How sympathetic are you to Heyward's moral outrage over the treatment her household received from Union soldiers? Should the soldiers have left the family's property alone? Argue for either side.

3. How effectively do George N. Barnard's images in the visual portfolio "Civil War and Reconstruction" (page 325) capture the scenes and emotions presented in the writings of Nichols and Heyward?

Three Days of Terror
Ellen Leonard

Rioting was an all too regular part of mid-nineteenth-century New York City life. Six-teen major and many lesser riots erupted in the city between 1834 and 1874. Almost any reason sufficed to bring out the clubs, guns, and paving stones: Protestants attacked Catholics, Irish Catholics fought Irish Protestants, slavery-supporting mobs roughed up abolitionists, partisans of one actor attacked the fans of another (in the infamous Astor Place riot of 1849), rival fire companies and gangs started violence that simply spread. Sometimes drunken brawls erupted into large-scale rioting with participants not quite knowing the reason for their fighting. But mobs had made their feelings known this way since the revolutionary era. In addition, municipal government was ineffective and corrupt; the weak and unprofessional New York police often could not maintain order without calling out the militia; alcohol was cheap and habitually drunk to excess; and vast numbers of new immigrants and unskilled laborers lived perpetually on the edge of destitution. When the Civil War sharpened political conflicts and war-induced infla-tion made the living conditions of the poor even worse than usual, widespread rioting broke out in the great draft riot of 1863.

When the Civil War began, North and South fielded large armies of patriotic vol-unteers, but as the war continued, both sides turned to conscription. Drafts were ineffec-tive and demoralizing, although they did succeed in their main purpose of encouraging more volunteers. Only about seven percent of those whose names were drawn in draft lotteries actually served. Many simply refused or ran off to another district. And both sides allowed those drafted to hire substitutes to fight in their place or to pay a fee of $300 to avoid serving, arousing cries that the conflict was "a rich man's war, but a poor man's fight." In fact, historians have found that draft districts regularly came up with the money to exempt those who did not wish to serve or hired substitutes by offer-ing bounties for enlistment so that roughly equal proportions of men in all classes served.

Still, the Union conscription law was vastly unpopular. The Democratic Party press made the draft a major issue, fanning opposition particularly among urban Irish Ameri-can populations who largely opposed the war and feared black competition for the unskilled jobs that provided their meager livelihoods. One orator told a mass meeting in New York City that "when the President called upon them to go and carry on a war for the nigger, he would be d—— d if he believed they would go." As soon as actual conscription began taking place in July 1863, rioting broke out in several cities. Most horrific was the one in which Ellen Leonard found herself trapped from July 13 through 16 in New York City.

Ellen Leonard, "Three Days of Terror," *Harper's New Monthly Magazine* 34 (January 1867), pp. 225–33.

It remains, in fact, the worst riot in New York City history. Many of the federal troops usually stationed in the city were in Pennsylvania in pursuit of General Lee's retreating army after the battle of Gettysburg. Over one hundred people died, most of them rioters gunned down when troop reinforcements arrived to retake control of the streets. In addition to random looting and vandalism, the rioters lynched several blacks, burned down the Colored Orphan Asylum, and attacked Republican newspapers, the homes of prominent Republicans and abolitionists, and businesses that employed blacks. Ellen Leonard's article on the riot, published in 1867, offers a rare eyewitness account of an innocent visitor accidentally trapped in these dramatic and dangerous events.

BEFORE YOU READ

1. According to Ellen Leonard's account, what seem to have been the main motivators of the mob?

2. How much danger did the mob pose to the citizens of the city and to visitors like Ellen Leonard?

3. How did women behave during the riot? In what ways did they behave more assertively than demanded by the "separate spheres" ideology of the era?

THREE DAYS OF TERROR

On the tenth of July, 1863, my mother and myself arrived in the city of New York. We had set out on a grand tour of visitation. After vegetating year after year in a New England village, we had sallied forth in genuine country fashion to hunt up our kinsfolk in various parts of the land. We were in no hurry. We had the whole summer before us. . . . We hoped now to spend a few days quietly with my brother J., call on various friends and relatives, visit Central Park and a lion or so, shop a little, and move onward at our leisure.

But man proposes and Fate *disposes*, and nothing in New York turned out as we expected. Instead of visiting our friends and meandering leisurely about the city, we were caught in a mob and penned up in our first stopping-place. . . . The streets were dark, dirty, and crowded with ill-looking people. The whole city was enveloped in fog and gloom. The home regiments had gone to drive the rebels from Pennsylvania, and many hearts were trembling. The household which received us had its full share of anxiety. Its youngest member, a youth of seventeen, had gone with the volunteers, and other friends were in the Army of the Potomac. . . .

I [went] to Broadway. But even there I could see nothing attractive. Every thing looked hot, glaring, and artificial, and every body looked shabby, jaded, and care-worn. An overworked horse dropped dead in the street before me, and I was glad to take refuge for a time in the Astor Library.

Returning thence at mid-day I first saw signs of disturbance. A squad of policemen passed before me into Third Avenue, clerks were looking eagerly from the doors, and men whispering in knots all up and down the street; but I was too much a stranger to be certain that these appearances were unusual, though they annoyed me so much that I crossed at once to Second Avenue, along which I pursued my way peacefully, and once at home thought no more of it. We were indulging ourselves in siestas after our noonday lunch, when a great roaring suddenly burst upon our ears—a howling as of thousands of wild Indians let loose at once; and before we could look out or collect our thoughts at all the cry arose from every quarter, "The mob! the mob!" "The Irish have risen to resist the draft!"

In a second my head was out the window, and I saw it with my own eyes. We were on a cross-street between First and Second avenues. First Avenue was crowded as far as we could see it with thousands of infuriated creatures, yelling, screaming, and swearing in the most frantic manner; while crowds of women, equally ferocious, were leaning from every door and window, swinging aprons and handkerchiefs, and cheering and urging them onward. The rush and roar grew every moment more terrific. Up came fresh hordes faster and more furious; bareheaded men, with red, swollen faces, brandishing sticks and clubs, or carrying heavy poles and beams; and boys, women, and children hurrying on and joining with them in this mad chase up the avenue like a company of raging fiends. In the hurry and tumult it was impossible to distinguish individuals, but all seemed possessed alike with savage hate and fury. The most dreadful rumors flew through the street, and we heard from various sources the events of the morning. The draft had been resisted, buildings burned, twenty policemen killed, and the remainder utterly routed and discomfited; the soldiers were absent, and the mob triumphant and increasing in numbers and violence every moment.

Our neighborhood was in the greatest excitement. The whole population turned out at once, gazing with terror and consternation on the living stream passing before them, surging in countless numbers through the avenue, and hurrying up town to join those already in action. Fresh yells and shouts announced the union of forces, and bursting flames their accelerated strength and fury. The armory on Twenty-second Street was broken open, sacked, and fired, and the smoke and flames rolled up directly behind us. . . .

Bells were tolling in every quarter. The rioters were still howling in Twenty-second Street, and driving the firemen from the burning armory. The building fell and the flames sunk, and then darkness came all at once and shut out every thing. We gathered gloomily around my brother in the back-parlor. An evening paper was procured, but brought no comfort. It only showed more clearly the nature and extent of this fearful outbreak. It only told us that the whole city was as helpless and anxious as ourselves. Many were in far greater danger, for obscurity is sometimes safety; but the black, lowering night, and the disabled condition of our only male protector, oppressed us heavily. Our neighborhood was all alive. Men tramped incessantly through the street, and women chatted and scolded in the windows; children cried and cats squalled; a crazy man in the rear raved fiercely for Jeff Davis and the Southern Confederacy; but over every other sound every few moments the bells rang out the alarm of some new fire. Some were very near; some at a distance. . . .

As the clocks struck twelve a great shout startled me, and a light flamed right up before me. A huge bonfire had been kindled in the middle of the street not far below us. Wild forms were dancing about it, and piling on fresh fuel. Great logs and beams and other combustibles were dragged up and heaped upon it. Sleep, now, was of course impossible. From a seat in an upper window I saw it rise and fall, flame up and fade. . . .

[The next day] there was no milk, no ice to be had, and meat and bread were on the wane; and so I ventured out with my sister H. for supplies. We found our street full of people, excitement, and rumors. Men and boys ran past us with muskets in their hands. We heard that a fight was in progress above Twenty-second Street. The mob had seized a gun-factory and many muskets; but the police had driven them off and taken back part of their plunder. It was cheering to find that the police were still alive. . . . Men talked in low, excited tones, and seemed afraid of each other. The stores were mostly closed and business suspended. With difficulty we procured supplies of provisions and a newspaper; but percussion caps and ammunition were stoutly denied us. No one dared to admit that they kept any such articles lest the rioters should take them away by force. A friendly bookseller at last supplied us. He had been out in disguise, he said, and heard the rioters boasting among themselves. One said he had made a hundred dollars already, and now he had arms and meant to use them. All the shops on the avenue had been threatened. The mob were gathering in great force in our vicinity, and things looked every moment more threatening; so we hurried home as fast as possible, and I took my post again at the window.

New and strange sights met my eyes. Such multitudes of people every where; filling street and sidewalks, crowding all the doors and windows, the balconies and roofs of the houses. Many were merely spectators; some not far distant were *actors*. In the First Avenue the crowd was now very dense and clamorous. The liquor store on the corner was thronged with villainous-looking customers, and the women who had welcomed the mob on their first appearance were again talking loudly as if urging them on to action. "Die *at home!*" was the favorite watch-word which often reached our ears. Every thing indicated that a collision was approaching. We caught, after a time, a glimpse of soldiers, and heard the welcome rattle of musketry, distant at first, then nearer and nearer. The soldiers marched to and through Twenty-second Street and turned down First Avenue. The mob yelled and howled and stood their ground. Women from the roofs threw stones and brickbats upon the soldiers. Then came the volleys; the balls leaped out and the mob gave way at once and fled in every direction. A great crowd rushed through our street, hiding in every nook and corner. We closed doors and blinds, but still peeped out of the windows. The soldiers marched slowly back up the avenue, firing along the way; crossed over into Second Avenue, marched down opposite our street and fired again. Again the mob scattered, and scampered in droves through the street. Yet another volley, and balls came tearing down the centre of our street right before us, dashing along the pavements and carrying off frames from the trees. A boy on the sidewalk opposite was struck; he fell in a pool of blood, and was carried away to die. The streets were now cleared, the crowds had vanished, the soldiers withdrew, and the mob was quelled. For two hours peace and quiet prevailed. . . .

The papers brought no encouragement. Fearful deeds of atrocity were recorded. The mob were increasing in power and audacity, and the city was still

paralyzed and panic-struck. The small military force available could only protect a few important positions, leaving the greater part defenseless. Our inflam-
mable neighborhood was wholly at the mercy of the mob. . . .

Scarcely had my head touched the pillow when a new alarm of fire
sounded. Lights streamed through the door of my room and illumined the
houses opposite. "Another fire in Twenty-second Street!" was the cry. The police station had been set on fire, and volumes of smoke and flame were rising
again very near us. From the rear windows we saw it all with the utmost dis-
tinctness; heard the roaring and crackling, and felt the heat of the flames. Soon
they wrapped the house and caught the adjacent fire-tower, whose bell was
clamoring even now for aid. The mob yelled with delight, and drove off the
eager firemen. The flames soon wreathed the tower and rose in majestic
columns. The whole neighborhood was flooded with light. . . . We heard [the
mob] hurrying on to the gas-works, leaving the waning fires at last to the firemen. We could hear them pounding and shaking the gates, swearing at their inability to force them, and then rushing off again for some easier prey.

The fires were now quite subdued, and we ventured to return to our several
rooms. . . .

Another day had come, Wednesday, July 15th. . . . The city was not all
burned down, we found. The newspapers were still alive, and insisting that
more troops were on hand and the mob checked; but we saw no signs of it. The
morning indeed passed more quietly. The rioters were resting from the labors
of the night; but business was not resumed, and swarms of idle men still hung
about the streets and stores. . . .

As night approached we heard drums beating, and gangs of rioters marched
up their favorite avenue. . . . Then some one shouted, "They are coming!" and
a small band of soldiers appeared marching up our street. The mob seemed to
swell into vast dimensions, and densely filled the whole street before them.
Hundreds hurried out on the house-tops, tore up brickbats, and hurled them
with savage howls at the approaching soldiers. Shots were fired from secret am-
bushes, and soldiers fell before they had fired. Then they charged bravely into
the mob, but their force was wholly inadequate. One small howitzer and a company of extemporized militia could do little against those raging thousands.
A fierce conflict raged before our eyes. With breathless interest we watched
them from door and windows. We feared the soldiers would be swallowed up
and annihilated. Some now appeared in sight with a wounded officer and several wounded men, looking from side to side for shelter. Their eyes met ours
with mute appeal. There was no time to be lost; the mob might any moment be
upon them. There was a moment's consultation, a hasty reference to J., an un-
hesitating response: "Yes, by all means"; we beckoned them in, and in they
came. Doors and windows were at once closed, and the house became a hospital, and seemed filled with armed men. The wounded men were carried into my
brother's room; the Colonel was laid on the bed, and the others propped up
with pillows. There were a few moments of great commotion and confusion.
We flew for fans, ice water, and bandages. Some of the soldiers went out into
the fight again, and some remained with the wounded. A surgeon, who had vol-

unteered as a private under his old commander, dressed the wounds of the sufferers. The Colonel was severely wounded in the thigh by a slug made of a piece of lead pipe, producing a compound fracture. The wounds of two others, though less dangerous, were severe and painful.

Twilight was now upon us, and night rapidly approaching. The soldiers had been forced to retreat, leaving the mob in great force and fury. We heard them shouting and raving on the corner, and knew that we were in great danger. Already they were clamoring for the wounded soldiers who had escaped them. We thought of Colonel O'Brien's fate, and could not suppress the thought that our own house might be made the scene of a like tragedy. Could we defend ourselves if attacked? A hurried consultation was held. We had arms and ammunition, and, including J. and the slightly wounded soldiers, half a dozen men able and willing to use them. But we could not "man our lines." We were open to attack at once from the front and rear, the roof, the front basement, and the balcony above it. We might, indeed, retreat to the upper stories, barricade the stairway, and hold it against all the assailants that could crowd into the hall. But if they chose to fire the house below we could not prevent it, and then there would be no escape either for our wounded or ourselves.

The Colonel promptly decided the question; resistance was hopeless, could only make the case worse, and must not be attempted. Not only so, but all signs of the presence of soldiers must be removed. Arms, military apparel, and bloody clothing were accordingly concealed. The Colonel was conveyed to the cellar and placed on a mattress. The young soldier, next to him most severely wounded, was assisted up to the rear apartment on the upper floor and placed in charge of my mother and myself. The soldiers who had remained were then ordered to make their escape from the house as they best could, and to hasten to head-quarters with an urgent request that a force might be sent to our relief. The surgeon was also requested to go, but would not listen to the suggestion. He had been regimental surgeon for two years under the Colonel, and insisted on remaining by his side, to take care of him, and to share his fate whatever it might be. He took his post, therefore, in the cellar, extemporizing as well as he could some scanty means of concealment for both from the boxes and bins which it contained. The remaining soldier, though severely wounded in the foot, could yet walk with pain and difficulty; and it was decided that, as soon as it should be safe or necessary, he should try the chances of escape through the scuttle and over the roofs of the adjoining buildings.

J., with his bandaged head and disabled arm, was liable to be taken for a wounded soldier, and his wife and her sister, Mrs. P——, insisted that he also should betake himself to the roof. He could render no material assistance if he remained; on the other hand, his presence might precipitate a scene of violence which would not be offered to ladies alone. They did not feel that they were personally in danger—so far there was no report that the lawless violence of the rioters had been directed against women; and if he could get away he might be the means of bringing speedier relief. Very reluctantly he yielded to these considerations, and prepared to accompany the wounded soldier. The mother of the household took refuge in her room on the second-floor. To her daughter-in-law, wife of an absent son, was assigned a post of observation at a front window. The two heroic women, H. and her sister, remained below to confront the mob.

Of all these arrangements, made mostly after we had assumed the charge assigned us, we at the time knew nothing. In utter darkness and desolation we sat above by the bedside of our young soldier, receiving his farewell messages for his mother and friends, and knowing not how soon he might be torn from us. There was no human power to help us in this extremity; we could only trust in Him "who stilleth the madness of the people." The suspense was terrible. In the rear, as we stole an occasional out-look through our closed blinds, we could see men here and there climbing the fences; they might be rioters breaking in, or residents breaking out. All was confusion and uncertainty. We knew not friends from foes.

In front the demonstrations were still more alarming. The rioters had taken possession of the street, stationed a guard on both avenues, and were chasing up and down for the soldiers. Then they were seen searching from house to house. . . . Then came a rush up the steps, and the bell rang violently. Not a sound was heard through the house. Again and yet again the bell rang, more and more furiously. Heart throbbed, nerves quivered, but no one stirred. Then came knocks, blows, kicks, threats, attempts to force the door. Come in they must and would; nothing could stay them.

Having gained for the retreating party all the time she could, Mrs. P—— at length unlocked the door, opened it, passed out, and closing it behind her, stood face to face with the mob, which crowded the steps and swarmed on the sidewalk and the adjacent street. What could she do? She knew that they would come in, that they would search the house, that they would find the men; but she was determined not to give them up without an effort to save them. Possibly, in parleying with them, she might at least calm somewhat the fury of the passion that swayed that howling mob; possibly in that brutal and maddened throng there might be a few with human hearts in their bosoms to which she might find a way, win them to her side, and enlist their aid in saving the lives of the intended victims. That was her only hope.

"What do you want?" she asked, while the air was yet ringing with the cry that came up from the crowd, "The soldiers! the soldiers!" "Bring out the soldiers!" One who stood near and seemed to be a leader replied, "There were two soldiers went into this house, and we must have them. You must give them up."

"There *were* two that came in, but went out again. They are not here now."

She spoke in a low but perfectly clear and steady voice, that compelled attention, and the crowd hushed its ravings to catch her words.

"Let us see; if they are not here we will not harm you; but we must search the house."

"We can not let you in; there are only women here—some that are old and feeble, and the sight of such a crowd will frighten them to death."

"They shall not all come in," was the reply; and after some further parley it was agreed that half a dozen only should enter and make the search. The leader gave his orders, the door was opened, and the men detailed came in; but before it could be closed the mob surged up, pressed in, and filled the hall. Many of them were armed with the stolen carbines.

"Light the gas!" was the cry.

"My sister has gone for a light."

It came, and the parley was renewed. The leader again demanded the soldiers; insisted that they were there, and said it would be better for themselves if they would give them up. She persisted in the statement she had made.

"She is fooling us, and using up the time while they are getting away by the roof!" cried one, and pressing forward with his musket pointed at her, endeavored to pass her. Very deliberately she took hold of the muzzle and turned it aside, saying, "Don't do that. You know I am a woman, and it might frighten me."

The leader returned to the charge. "We know the men are here, and if you give them up to us you shall not be harmed. But if you do not, and we find them, you know what a mob is. I can not control them; your house will be burned over your heads, and I will not guarantee your lives for five minutes."

"You will not do that," was the reply. "We are not the kind of people whose houses you wish to burn. My only son works as you do, and perhaps in the same shop with some of you, for seventy cents a day."

She did not tell them that her amateur apprentice boy had left his place to go to Pennsylvania and fight their friends the rebels. A young man, whom she had noticed as one of the few of decent appearance, stepped to her side and whispered to her, advising her compliance with the demand, assuring her that the men could not be controlled. The tone more than the words indicated to her that she had made one friend; and she found another, in the same way, a moment later.

Meantime the leaders were consulting whether they should go first above or below, and decided on the latter. Stationing one man with a musket at the door, and one at the stairs, they proceeded, pioneered by H., first to the parlors, and then to the basement, thoroughly examining both. Most fortunately the sentinels were the two young men in whom Mrs. P—— felt she had found friends, and she was not slow to improve the opportunity to deepen the impression she had made. But now the crowd outside, thundering at the basement door, burst in the panels, and forcing it open, with terrible oaths and threats rushed in and filled the lower hall. Part joined the searching party, and some hurried up the first-floor. One, crowding past the sentinel, was striding up the stairs. We heard his call to his comrades, "Come on up stairs!" and our hearts sunk within us. But the sentinel's stern command, enforced by his leveled piece, brought him back.

The main party, having ransacked the basement rooms, now turned to the cellar. In a moment a loud shout announced that they had found a victim. The surgeon was dragged up, forced out at the lower door, and delivered over to the crowd outside. A blow from a bludgeon or musket felled him to the earth, inflicting a terrible wound on the head. "Hang him, hang him!" "To the post at the Twenty-second Street corner!" were the cries as they hurried him off. The search within proceeded; a moment more and they had found the Colonel. A new and fiercer shout was sent up. An order from a leader thrilled through the hall, "Come down here some of yees wid yer muskets!"

At the first cry from the cellar Mrs. P—— sprung for the basement, intending to make her way at any hazard. A sentinel stood at the head of the stairway; a stalwart brute, reeking with filth and whisky. He seized her, with both arms about her waist, with a purpose of violence quite too evident. She struggled to free herself without raising an alarm, but in vain; then a sudden and piercing shriek, which rung through the house, made him for an instant relax his hold, and, wrenching herself away, she hurried back and sought the protection of the friendly sentinel.

"He will not let me pass; I must go down."

"You must not," he replied; "it is no place for you." And then he added, looking sternly at her, "You have deceived us. You said there was no one here, and there is."

"I would have done the same thing for you if you had been wounded. Look at me; do you not believe me?"

He did look, full in her eye, for an instant; then said: "Yes, I do believe it. You have done right, and I admire your spirit."

"But I must go down. Go with me."

"No; it is no place for you."

"Then go yourself, and save his life."

And turning over his charge to the sentinel at the door, he did go. Meantime the searching party, having found the Colonel, proceeded to question him. He said he was a citizen, accidentally wounded, and had been obliged to seek refuge there.

"Why did you hide, if you are a citizen?"

Because, he said, he was afraid he should be taken for a soldier. They would not believe, but still he insisted on his statement. Then the muskets were sent for, and four pieces leveled at his head, as he lay prostrate and helpless.

"Fire, then, if you will, on a wounded man and a citizen. I shall die, any how, for my wound is a mortal one. But before you fire I wish you would send for a priest."

"What, are you a Catholic?"

"Yes."

This staggered them; and while they were hesitating the sentinel joined the group, and as soon as he looked on the Colonel exclaimed: "I know that man. I used to go to school with him. He is no soldier."

This turned the scale. The leaders were satisfied, and decided to let him go. But before leaving him they rifled his pockets; and here he narrowly escaped falling into renewed danger. While the parley was in progress his fingers had been busily occupied in quietly and coolly removing from his pocket a quantity of bullets which he had forgotten, and which, if they had been found, would certainly have betrayed him.

Those of the mob who had remained above, disappointed of their prey, with oaths and execrations protested against the action of their leaders, and sent the ruffian at the head of the stairway down to see if it was all right. But the positive statements of the friendly sentinel, which Mrs. P—— had the satisfaction of hearing him rehearse, as the two met in the lower hall, disarmed even his suspicions, and the rest could do no otherwise than acquiesce. So well satisfied, indeed, were the leaders, and, as it is not unreasonable to suppose, so impressed with the resolute bearing of the two ladies, that they volunteered to station a guard before the door to prevent the annoyance of any further search. As they had found the two men who had been reported to them as having entered the house, it did not seem to occur to them that there might be still others concealed; and so they took their departure, leaving the upper stories unvisited.

The surgeon in the mean time had been no less fortunate. In the crowd which hurried him off to death there happened to be one or two returned soldiers who had served in the same regiment with him, and when he came where it was light recognized him. They insisted on saving him, and, raising a party in their favor, finally prevailed, and having rescued him escorted him in safety to his home. . . .

It was now, we thought, past midnight. We had no hope of relief, no thought or expectation but of struggling on alone hour after hour of distress and darkness; but as I was listening in my window to some unusually threatening demonstrations from the mob, I heard the distant clank of a horse's hoof on the pavement. Again and again it sounded, more and more distinctly; and then a measured tread reached my ears, the steady, resolute tramp of a trained and disciplined body. No music was ever half so beautiful! It might, it must be, our soldiers! Off I flew to spread the good news through the household, and back again to the window to hear the tramp nearer and fuller and stronger, and see a long line of muskets gleam out from the darkness, and a stalwart body of men stop at our door. "Halt!" was cried; and I rushed down stairs headlong, unlocked the door without waiting for orders, and with tears of joy and gratitude which every one can imagine and nobody describe, welcomed a band of radiant soldiers and policemen, and in the midst of them all who should appear but my brother, pale and exhausted, who had gotten off the house-top in some mysterious way and brought this gallant company to our rescue! . . .

[They are taken to the Central Police Station.]

All now was life and animation. Well-dressed citizens were hurrying to and fro. Stalwart soldiers lined the street and guarded the steps and entrance, through which we were conducted to an inner apartment, and with much state and ceremony presented to the chieftains of civic power. Three days' experience of anarchy had made us feel the blessedness of lawful restraint, and surely no body of men ever looked so beautiful as these executives of law and government. . . .

38

Healing Wounds

Cornelia Hancock

Of about two million federal troops who served in the Civil War, three hundred-sixty thousand died. Among the more than one million who served in the Confederate military, some two hundred-fifty thousand also perished. Only one in three of these died of battle wounds; the others succumbed to disease or accident. There were also about a half million wounded, many of them severely.

A badly wounded man had only a precarious chance for survival. Little was known about infection, and military surgeons performed operations without sanitary precautions. Soldiers contracted gangrene and other deadly infections. Though anesthetics were known, doctors did not always have them on hand, and major surgery often resulted in shock, followed by death. Long delays occurred when transporting casualties to medical aid stations or hospitals. Soldiers suffered as well from the mosquitos, lice, and biting flies that infested the battlefront and that spread diseases such as malaria and yellow fever. Poor diet also undermined health, although the less well supplied Confederate soldiers suffered from malnourishment to a far greater degree than Union troops.

Cornelia Hancock (1840–1927), from a New Jersey Quaker family, was one of thousands of women who worked to improve health care for the Union Army. In 1863, she volunteered to be a nurse, but Dorothea Dix, then Superintendent of Female Nurses, rejected her application, disapproving of nurses who were attractive or under thirty. Cornelia, twenty-three and pretty, simply traveled to Gettysburg, arriving on the third day of the battle and going right to work helping the wounded. Her account vividly renders the many horrors of Civil War battles. It also illuminates the reactions of friends at home to her decision to strike out on such an unladylike course.

BEFORE YOU READ

1. How does Cornelia Hancock respond to the suffering around her?

2. Why do people at home complain about what Hancock is doing? What is her response to them?

3. How does Hancock respond to escaped slaves? How does her response compare to that of those around her?

Henrietta Stratton Jaquette, ed., *South after Gettysburg: Letters of Cornelia Hancock, 1863–1868* (New York: Crowell, 1956), pp. 6–11, 17–19, 42–45, 58–60, 73–77, 91–94.

HANCOCK'S ACCOUNT OF HER
FIRST DAY AT GETTYSBURG

We arrived in the town of Gettysburg on the evening of July sixth, three days after the last day of battle. We were met by Dr. Horner, at whose house we stayed. Every barn, church, and building of any size in Gettysburg had been converted into a temporary hospital. We went the same evening to one of the churches, where I saw for the first time what war meant. Hundreds of desperately wounded men were stretched out on boards laid across the high-backed pews as closely as they could be packed together. The boards were covered with straw. Thus elevated, these poor sufferers' faces, white and drawn with pain, were almost on a level with my own. I seemed to stand breast-high in a sea of anguish. . . .

Learning that the wounded of the Third Division of the Second Corps, including the 12th Regiment of New Jersey, were in a Field Hospital about five miles outside of Gettysburg, we determined to go there early the next morning, expecting to find some familiar faces among the regiments of my native state. As we drew near our destination we began to realize that war has other horrors than the sufferings of the wounded or the desolation of the bereft. A sickening, overpowering, awful stench announced the presence of the unburied dead, on which the July sun was mercilessly shining, and at every step the air grew heavier and fouler, until it seemed to possess a palpable horrible density that could be seen and felt and cut with a knife. Not the presence of the dead bodies themselves, swollen and disfigured as they were, and lying in heaps on every side, was as awful to the spectator as that deadly, nauseating atmosphere which robbed the battlefield of its glory, the survivors of their victory, and the wounded of what little chance of life was left to them.

As we made our way to a little woods in which we were told was the Field Hospital we were seeking, the first sight that met our eyes was a collection of semi-conscious but still living human forms, all of whom had been shot through the head, and were considered hopeless. They were laid there to die and I hoped that they were indeed too near death to have consciousness. Yet many a groan came from them, and their limbs tossed and twitched. The few surgeons who were left in charge of the battlefield after the Union army had started in pursuit of Lee had begun their paralyzing task by sorting the dead from the dying, and the dying from those whose lives might be saved; hence the groups of prostrate, bleeding men laid together according to their wounds.

There was hardly a tent to be seen. Earth was the only available bed during those first hours after the battle. A long table stood in this woods and around it gathered a number of surgeons and attendants. This was the operating table, and for seven days it literally ran blood. A wagon stood near rapidly filling with amputated legs and arms; when wholly filled, this gruesome spectacle withdrew from sight and returned as soon as possible for another load. So appalling was the number of the wounded as yet unsuccored, so helpless seemed the few who were battling against tremendous odds to save life, and so overwhelming was the demand for any kind of aid that could be given quickly, that one's senses were benumbed by the awful responsibility that fell to the living. . . .

I need not say that every hour brought an improvement in the situation, that trains from the North came pouring into Gettysburg laden with doctors, nurses, hospital supplies, tents, and all kinds of food and utensils: but that *first* day of my arrival, the sixth of July, and the third day after the battle, was a time that taxed the ingenuity and fortitude of the living as sorely as if we had been a party of shipwrecked mariners thrown upon a desert island.

LETTERS

Gettysburg, Pa. July 7th, 1863

My Dear Cousin

I am very tired tonight; have been on the field all day—went to the 3rd Division 2nd Army Corps. I suppose there are about five hundred wounded belonging to it. They have one patch of woods devoted to each army corps for a hospital. I being interested in the 2nd, because Will [her brother] had been in it, got into one of its ambulances, and went out at eight this morning and came back at six this evening. There are no words in the English language to express the sufferings I witnessed today. The men lie on the ground; their clothes have been cut off them to dress their wounds; they are half naked, have nothing but hardtack to eat only as Sanitary Commissions, Christian Associations, and so forth give them. I was the first woman who reached the 2nd Corps after the three days fight at Gettysburg. I was in that Corps all day, not another woman within a half mile. Mrs. Harris was in first division of 2nd Corps. I was introduced to the surgeon of the post, went anywhere through the Corps, and received nothing but the greatest politeness from even the lowest private. . . . To give you some idea of the extent and numbers of the wounds, four surgeons, none of whom were idle fifteen minutes at a time, were busy all day amputating legs and arms. I gave to every man that had a leg or arm off a gill of wine, to every wounded in Third Division, one glass of lemonade, some bread and preserves and tobacco—as much as I am opposed to the latter, for they need it very much, they are so exhausted.

I feel very thankful that this was a successful battle; the spirit of the men is so high that many of the poor fellows said today, "What is an arm or leg to whipping Lee out of Penn." I would get on first rate if they would not ask me to write to their wives; *that* I cannot do without crying, which is not pleasant to either party. I do not mind the sight of blood, have seen limbs taken off and was not sick at all.

It is a very beautiful, rolling country here; under favorable circumstances I should think healthy, but now for five miles around, there is an awful smell of putrefaction. Women are needed here very badly, anyone who is willing to go to field hospitals, but nothing short of an order from Secretary Stanton or General Halleck will let you through the lines. Major General Schenk's order for us was not regarded as anything; if we had not met Miss Dix at Baltimore Depot, we should not have gotten through. It seems a strange taste but I am glad we did. We stay at Doctor Horner's house at night—direct letters care of Dr. Horner, Gettysburg, Pa. If you could mail me a newspaper, it would be a great satisfaction, as we do not get the news here and the soldiers are so anxious to hear; things will be different here in a short time.

Cornelia

3rd Division—2nd Army Corps Hospital
Gettysburg, Pa. July 26th [1863]—Sunday

My Dear Mother

Today is Sunday but there is no semblance of it here. It is now about five o'clock in the morning. Our hospital has been moved and our stores have given out. There is nothing to cook with, hence I have nothing to do, and therefore, have time to write.

. . . I have eight wall tents full of amputated men. The tents of the wounded I look right out on. It is a melancholy sight—but you have no idea how soon one gets used to it. Their screams of agony do not make as much impression on me now as the reading of this letter will on you. The most painful task we have to perform here is entertaining the friends who come from home and see their friends all mangled up. I do hate to see them. Soldiers take everything as it comes, but citizens are not inured. You will think it is a short time for me to get used to things, but it seems to me as if all my past life was a myth, and as if I had been away from home seventeen years.

. . . What I do here one would think would kill at home, but I am well and comfortable. When we get up early in the morning, our clothes are so wet that we could wring them. On they go, and by noon they are dry.

From thy affectionate daughter—
C. Hancock

Jan. 1864

Dear William [Cornelia's brother]

Where are the people who have been professing such strong abolition proclivity for the last thirty years? Certainly not in Washington laboring with these people whom they have been clamoring to have freed. They are freed now or at least many of them, and herded together in filthy huts, half clothed. And what is worse than all guarded over by persons who have not a proper sympathy for them. I have been in the Washington Contraband[1] Hospital for the past two months. It is in close proximity to the Camp of Reception [where the patients first arrived]—and I have had ample opportunity to see these people, the persons in charge of them, and the whole mode of proceeding with them. Their wants are great and appeal in every way for aid from the North.

. . . Smallpox has raged here to a great extent but a separate hospital has been established for that now. The order now is to remove all contrabands south of the Potomac. It may be better there than here, but we remain under the same authority and let me state emphatically that nothing for the permanent advancement of these people can be effected until the whole matter is removed from the military authority and vested in a separate bureau whose sole object is the protection and elevation of these people.

---

1. **contraband:** a black slave who escaped or was brought to the North.

. . . There is much charity being extended to our poor soldiers and I would note that any one should withhold one mite from them, but I maintain that persons living in their comfortable homes in the North should give liberally to those so sadly situated as these forlorn contrabands, as well as to the soldiers. A national Sanitary Commission for the Relief of Colored Persons of this class would save lives and a great deal of suffering. The slaves generally get free when our army advances; they come into our lines several hundred at a time, follow the army for a while, then come into Washington, some probably having walked 50 miles. One woman carried one child in her arms and dragged two by her side. Judge of the condition of that woman when she arrives. Should not some comfortable quarters await her weary body?

> Thy sister,
> Cornelia H.

[In February 1864 Cornelia became a nurse with the Army of the Potomac, then headquartered near Brandy Station, Virginia.]

> 2nd Corps, 3rd Div. Hospital
> Feb. 24th, 1864

My Dear Sister
    . . . I hope the army will stand still forever. . . . If it is not enough to sicken one to hear of the condition in which the officers lead our good men into these small fights. Gen. Warren's orderly is sick in hospital here, he says that he will not go on the field when he is drunk and the day of the last fight he could not get out of his Quarters until 4 o'clock. Gen. Hays meanwhile went splashing around on his own hook. I do not care what anyone says, war is humbug. It is just put out to see how much suffering the privates can bear I guess. . . .

> from thy sister, C. Hancock

> 3 Div. 2nd Corps Hospt.
> Near Brandy St., March 1st [1864]

My Dear Sister
    . . . A colored man is now having both limbs amputated from the effects of small pox. Dr. Dudley says he will try my Abolitionism taking care of him. I think I will stand the test. He is down on the coloreds but always does his duty by his patients and will by him for the reason that he is a patient. He would not suit thee the way he talks, but he is young and may change before he dies.

> from thy sister
> Cornelia Hancock

3rd Div. 2 Corps Hospital
March 25, 1864

My Dear Sister
    . . . On Wednesday we received orders to send all the sick and wounded to Washington, along with the order came a snow storm, along with the snow storm came an orderly countermanding the previous order, along with him came a splendid morning, along with it, came another orderly ordering to move on Thursday; and at 8 o'clock we had them all loaded and on stretchers, and proceeded with the long train from the three hospitals to Brandy station. There the platform was strewed full of helpless men wounded at Morton's Ford. How like Gettys[burg] it seemed to me. I had all our worst cases put in a pile, took a whiskey bottle, and sat down and helped the poor souls to live while they were loaded. Two mortal hours we sat in the sun and heard the locomotive hiss, the cars back and go ahead, then back, etc., etc., etc., just what always happens at depots. One of our nice wounded wanted to give me some greenbacks right in the hubbub. There were two women who stay at the station with hot tea, etc. They supplied all hands and retired. There I sat, I suppose five hundred men staring at me, but Dr. Miller and our own steward and hospital boys were with me and I did not care. By dint of great perseverance a hospital car was provided for the worst cases and I went in and saw them lying comfortably upon the stretchers, saw the cars trudge off with their groaning load, and think I to myself, the idea of making a business of maiming men is not one worthy of a civilized nation. By the time I got home over the corduroy [a bumpy road] had a headache of the first water, went to bed, and there could lay, as my occupation is nearly gone now. . . .

from thy affectionate sister
Cornelia Hancock

3rd Div. 2 Corps Hosp.
March 27, 1864

My Dear Mother
    . . . Our hospital will soon fill up with sick unless they move. Then what will become of us is unknown—Ellen is fretting for fear I shall go on a march. My only answer to all such worriments is you ought to have confidence enough in my judgment to think I will do the best thing. After campaigning successfully for 9 months I ought to have some experience. In regard to Salem people thinking I ought to have a woman to sleep with me, I am much better guarded than the lone widows and maids at Isabell's. Another woman is not needed nor would be allowed here. Mrs. Lee is within sending distance if I was sick, so calm all your fears. I go to sleep just as quick as I touch the bed, am used to being alone, like it, and never feel lonely and would not sleep with Mrs. Lee if I could. I am sorry you have any distress on my account, but I cannot help you any and I assure you it is all unnecessary.

. . . Sarah Sinnickson wrote me a letter expressive of great concern from my "way of living." I wrote her a letter that she will not forget soon. They cannot expect everyone to be satisfied to live in as small a circle as themselves in these days of great events. She expresses it as the great concern of the whole family and her approaching sickness made her bold to express it. . . .

from thy daughter
Cornelia Hancock

[May 1864]

Dear Ellen

. . . I am in Fredericksburg city. I do not know where Doctor is. On going ashore at Belle Plain we were met with hordes of wounded soldiers who had been able to walk from the Wilderness battlefield to this point. They were famished for food and as I opened the remains of my lunch basket the soldiers behaved more like ravenous wolves than human beings, so I felt the very first thing to be done was to prepare food in unlimited quantities, so with my past experience in arranging a fire where there seemed no possibility of one, I soon had a long pole hanging full of kettles of steaming hot coffee, and this, with soft bread, was dispensed all night to the tramping soldiers who were filling the steam boats on their return trip to Washington.

. . . when daylight came Dr. Detmold and Dr. Vanderpool, two eminent surgeons of New York, and I boarded [an ambulance] to go to Fredericksburg, where our hospital is established. On arriving here the scenes beggared all description and these two men, eminent as they are in their profession, were paralyzed by what they saw. Rain had poured in through the bullet-riddled roofs of the churches until our wounded lay in pools of water made bloody by their seriously wounded condition. On these scenes Dr. Detmold and Dr. Vanderpool gazed in horror and seemed not to know where to take hold. My Gettysburg experience enabled me to take hold. The next morning these two surgeons came to me and said: "If we open another church under better conditions than these, will you accompany us?" and I said "Yes." After they got their nerve their splendid executive ability asserted itself and they had the pews knocked to pieces; under the backs and seats put a cleat and made little beds to raise the wounded from the floor. 'Tis true the beds have no springs, but it keeps them from lying in the water. Here day by day things are improving. An amputating table is improvised under a tree in the yard where these two good men work indefatiguably.

[May 1864]

My Dear Mother

. . . I was the first and only Union woman in the city [Fredericksburg]. I believe today there were some of Miss Dix's nurses came thru. I have good quarters. We calculate there are 14,000 wounded in the town; the Secesh [rebel

Southerners] help none, so you may know there is suffering equal to any thing anyone ever saw, almost as bad as Gettysburg, only we have houses and churches for the men. I am well, have worked harder than I ever did in my life. There was no food but hard tack to give the men so I turned in and dressed their wounds. It was all that could be done. I hear from my friends at the front one by one. Almost every one I knew was shot dead except the Doctor. Some of them are taken prisoners, Dr. Aiken for one. Dr. Dudley was safe last night. Lieut. Fogg was shot dead, so was Capt. Madison—this battle is still raging. I am glad I am here but I really thought my heart would break as one after another they told me was dead. If they only accomplish getting to Richmond. If not, it is a dear battle. There is very heavy firing today. I hope Dr. Dudley will get thru safe. He sent a Doctor to see me, told him he knew I would get thru. He is out on the front with his Regt. Oh, how awful, it seems as if the great judgment day was upon us now; the Secesh are still in town but we take possession of all churches and houses we want. I am well. Write to me in care of Dr. Davis, 1st Div. 2nd Corps. hospt., Fred'ksburg, Va. . . .

Thine in haste
Cornelia Hancock

39

A Slaveowner's Journal at the End of the Civil War

Henry William Ravenel

In a letter of August 26, 1865, Henry William Ravenel (1814–1887) summarized the immediate effects of the collapse of the Confederacy as well as anyone ever has:

> *A new era opens before us, but alas! with what great changes. Our country is in ruins, and our people reduced to poverty. . . . We had no money but Confederate and that is now worthless . . . all our securities and investments are bankrupt. . . . There is little money in the country, little cotton and other produce, so there is no business or employment for those who are anxiously seeking to make a living. . . .*

Emancipation had altered social relations; the collapse of the Confederacy and then Reconstruction were transforming Southern politics; the war and emancipation had upset every economic arrangement, making currency worthless, land unsalable, and credit — previously based on chattel mortgages on slave "property" — scarcely to be obtained.

Ravenel belonged to a prominent South Carolina slaveholding family. In addition to managing a plantation, he became an important self-trained naturalist whose studies of American fungi achieved international renown. After the war he supported his family by selling seeds and parts of his collections of fungi to collectors and later worked as a naturalist for the U.S. Department of Agriculture. After his death, Ravenel's botanical collections were sold to the British Museum.

Ravenel began his journal in 1859 and continued it to within weeks of his death in 1887. The journal shows how one thoughtful and well-placed member of the Southern elite struggled to understand the collapse of his familiar world.

BEFORE YOU READ

1. How did Ravenel interpret the causes and outcome of the Civil War?
2. What did he expect to happen to former slaves, and how did he explain their behavior?
3. Are his reactions what you expected of a slaveholder or do they surprise you?

November [1864]

F. 18 The Augusta paper of this morning has startling intelligence from Atlanta. There is no doubt that Sherman has burned Rome, Decatur & Atlanta, & has

Arney Robinson Childs, ed., *The Private Journal of Henry William Ravenel, 1859–1887* (Columbia: University of South Carolina Press, 1947), pp. 202–3, 206–7, 210–21 passim, 228–29, 237, 239–40.

commenced a move with 4 or 5 army corps (40 to 50,000) in the direction of Macon & Augusta. The Northern papers say his intention is to move through to Charleston & Mobile, destroy the rail road & bridges behind him & feed his army from the country. I have been apprehending just such a move since Hood's army was withdrawn. It is a bold stroke, & if successful, would bring untold evils upon us, in the destruction of property & the means of subsistance. . . .

Sunday 20 Beauregard telegraphs the people to be firm & resolute — to obstruct his [Sherman's] passage by cutting the woods in his front & flank — to destroy all provisions which cannot be carried away — to remove all negroes, horses & cattle, & leave a scene of desolation in his front, instead of in his rear as it would be if he passed. . . . Should Sherman succeed in taking Augusta, his march will be onward toward Charleston, & his track will be a scene of desolation. I await the developments of the next few days with anxiety, chiefly on account of my negroes. If I send them away & the farm & house is left without protection, my house will be robbed & despoiled of every thing, whether the enemy passes here or not. I must wait before removing them, until I am very sure the enemy will succeed in his designs upon Augusta — & then perhaps it may be too late.

M. 21 I have had a talk with my negroes on the subject, & explained to them the true state of affairs — that should the enemy pass through this place they must escape & take care of themselves for a while until the danger is passed. I am well satisfied from their assurances, that they are really alarmed at the idea of being seized & taken off by the Yankees, & that they will not desert me.

F. 25 We are now at the gloomiest period of the war which for nearly four years has afflicted our land. I cannot conceal from myself the many discouraging features of our situation & the perilous straits in which we stand.

1st Our Finances are in such a condition that universal discontent & real suffering exists. The currency is so much depreciated, that for the ordinary & necessary articles of subsistance, it requires an outlay beyond the means of most people. This involves privation & suffering. There is a want of confidence in the ability of the Govt. to redeem its credits, founded partly on their great amount & partly on the precarious condition of our affairs. If our cause fails the whole Govt. credits are lost, & doubtless this consideration has its weight among capitalists in producing distrust.

Sunday 8 Samuel Ravenel at home on furlough from Measles was here this morning. He told me that the Post Surgeon had offered Harry & himself & three other boys, exemptions on account of their age & size, & that two had accepted. He & Harry & another had declined. I was gratified to hear that our boys took such high views of their duty. Sam says they have no tents, & have to lie on the bare ground, or with such protection as a few bushes or straw can give. They do picket & *vidette* [watch] duty in sight & hearing of the enemy, see them drill & enjoy the music from their bands every day. . . .

M. 9 Sent off two boxes bacon today to the Depot for Aiken via Charleston. I hope these supplies may not be caught in Charleston or intercepted by the enemy on the way. We are in a quandary what to do. I am buying hogs down here, & at the same time sending supplies hurriedly to Aiken. . . .

January [1865]

Sunday 15 My claim for compensation for slave (Jim) lost in Confed. service, has passed the Legislature & $2000 are allowed. I am to send James Wilson a power of attorney to receive it. They have commenced to fortify Columbia. . . .

M. 23 Our currency still continues to depreciate, as is shown by the increasing prices of all articles. . . .

February [1865]

S. 18 It is reported that Columbia has fallen - - - - No mail from Charleston. We are now closed in & cut off from all news from the outside world. . . . We are now virtually in the enemy's lines. I am in doubt what to do with Harry. He is very weak & just able to walk about. If he remains, he may be captured as prisoner of war—if I undertake to carry him away, I then leave my family never to see them until the war is over. I would not hesitate about leaving my family if they were in a region where they needed no protection & could get subsistance —but the thoughts of deserting them here is very distressing to me.

Sunday 19 Dr. Frank Porcher dined here today. He thinks we should remain where we are. The upper country is in danger of famine, & will soon be without salt, now the coast is given up. . . . Charleston was occupied by the enemy yesterday at 10 A.M.—Columbia has been captured. We hear of a great fire in Charleston yesterday, but no particulars yet. Exciting times!

M. 20 In a few days the last of our army will have crossed the Santee, the bridge burnt behind them—& we then become an evacuated & conquered region. We fall under Yankee rule & the laws & authority of the U. States are established during the continuance of the war. What new relations between us & our negroes will be established we cannot tell but there is no doubt it will be a radical change. I do not apprehend destructive raids, or personal violence to citizens who remain, but we will be compelled to conform to the new conditions under which we are placed, as a conquered people. I suppose all the cotton will be seized & confiscated to the use of the U. S. govt,—& probably a system of culture will be adopted & enforced the profits from which will accrue to them. I think it the duty of all slave owners & planters who remain, to be with their negroes. They have been faithful to the last, & they deserve in turn, confidence from him, protection, attention & care. . . .

T. 21 I think masters who are within these lines of the enemy, should remain on their plantations among their negroes;—the first change of conditions should not be volunteered by us. We have always believed we were right in maintaining the relation of master & slave for the good of the country & also for the benefit of the negro. If we have believed firmly in the Divine sanction which the Bible affords to this relation, we should not be the first to sever it, by abandoning them. They have grown up under us, they look to us for support, for guidance & protection—They have faithfully done their duty during this trying time, when the great temptations were offered to leave us. In the sight of God, we have a sacred duty to stand by them as long as they are faithful to us. We know that if left to themselves, they cannot maintain their happy condition. We must reward their fidelity to us by the same care & consideration we exercised when they were more useful. . . .

T. 28 David returned with a cart from PineVille last night, & said Rene told him the Yankees had been, or were, in PineVille, taking poultry & whatever they wanted. The negroes on many places have refused to go to work. . . . I have spoken to some of them here & intend to give them advice as a friend to continue on the plantation, & work—Of course there must be great care & judgement used in preserving discipline & I have advised with the overseer. I think for their own good & the good of the country, it would be best for the present organization of labor to go on, so that all may get a subsistance, the old & young, the sick & disabled, & the other non producers. . . . The freed & idle negroes who are not kept now under discipline or fear will give us trouble. I feel great anxiety for the future. . . .

March [1865]

Th. 2 Half past two o'clock A.M. Night of horrors! How can I describe the agonizing suspense of the past six hours! Thank God who has protected us all we are still alive & have lost nothing but property.—About half past 8 oclock I was standing in the back piazza, when I heard the discharge of 3 or 4 fire arms. The negroes soon came running up to inform us that the Yankees were in the negro yard. They soon after entered the house, (4 or 5 colored men) armed & demanded to see the owner of the house. I called to Pa & he walked up to the back door where they were. They told him that they had come for provisions, corn, bacon, poultry & whatever they wanted—demanded his horses & wagons, his guns, wine &c. That they had come to tell the negroes they were free & should no longer work for him. They used very threatening language with oaths & curses. They then proceeded to the stable & took my pair & Renes horse—Took the 2 sets harness & put in the horses, into the two wagons & Lequeax buggy. They then emptied the smoke house, store room & meat house, giving to the negroes what they did not want. They then took from the fowl house what poultry they wanted, took the two plantation guns, & used great threats about the wine & brandy. To our great relief they did not enter the house again, & at 1.30 A.M. drove off. They told the negroes if they worked for their master again they would shoot them when they came back. What the future is to be to us God only knows. I feel that my trust is still unshaken in his all protecting Providence. I have all confidance in the fidelity of the negroes & their attachment to us if they are not restrained from showing it. We are all up for the night as the excitement is too great to permit sleep - - - - - 9 A.M. at the usual hour this morning the house negroes came in—They seemed much distressed & said the troops told them last night if they came to the yard or did anything for us, they would shoot them—That a large troop would come today. We told them to go back & not bring trouble upon themselves, until we could see the Commanding officer. The fidelity & attachment of some who have come forward is very gratifying. The girls have been cooking our simple breakfast & we have taken our first meal under the new regime. I long for a visit from some officer in authority, that we may know our future condition & whether the negroes will be allowed to hire themselves to us or not. I know if they are not restrained there are many who would willingly & gladly help us. I had heard often of insurrectionary feelings among the negroes, but I never believed they would be brought to it of their own accord. The experience of this war, & especially of last night all tend to confirm that conviction. Even when compelled by intimidation, & fear of the consequences to their lives, many of them evince real distress, & not one has yet joined in any language or act of defiance. Their fidelity & attachment is amazing with the temptations before them. Those who were engaged in the sacking of the store room & meat house, did so stealthily & I believe not until they were commanded to help themselves.

S. 4   Inauguration of Presdt. Lincoln today for his 2d term of 4 years. Will any thing come out of it in respect to the war? The negroes are completely bewildered at the change of their condition. Many are truly distressed, some of the younger ones delirious with the prospect of good living & nothing to do. Some are willing to remain & work, but object to gang work,—all is in a chaotic state. When they were told that they were free, some said they did not wish to be free, & they were immediately silenced with threats of being shot. I fear this region will be a desolate waste in one year hence, if this state of things continue - - On Thursday night when the army was camped here, their troops were among our negroes, distributing sugar, coffee, meats & bread in profusion—they killed 8 or 10 of the sheep & had them cooked in the negro yard. This was all intended as an earnest of the good things which followed their freedom. . . .

M. 6   The events of the past week have brought up vividly before us the horrors of the French Revolution—& those startling scenes which Dickens describes in his "Tale of two cities." We are in a fearful & trying crisis. If those who had unsettled the present order of things in the name of Humanity, were consistent, they would make some effort to order the freed negroes for their good, & ought to take some steps toward restoring order & recommending & enforcing some plan by which such a large number may escape the horrors of insubordination, violence & ultimately starvation. The negroes are intoxicated with the idea of freedom. Many of them are deluded into the hope that their future is to be provided for by the U S. Govt.—& hence they do not feel the necessity of work. Many are disposed to remain, but perhaps will insist on terms which are incompatable with discipline & good management. It is a fearful crisis.

T. 7   No disposition evinced among the negroes to go to work. There seems to be sullenness which I dislike to see. I think those who are disposed to work or to do for us, are restrained. I hear that many of the negroes are armed with pistols & guns. Some were at Black Oak last night firing off pistols. This is a bad feature in this fearful period.—Oh, Humanity! what crimes are committed in thy name. One week ago we were in the midst of a peaceful, contented & orderly population

—now all is confusion, disorder, discontent, violence, anarchy. If those who up-rooted the old order of things had remained long enough to reconstruct another system in which there should be order restored, it would have been well, but they have destroyed our system & left us in the ruins—"God is our refuge & strength, a very present help in trouble" - - - - The negroes are rambling about the country. This morning 4 mounted on horses & mules rode through the negro yard, stop-ping for a while, & some have passed through in vehicles. It is said they were told to go to St Stephens for horses which the army left behind.

W. 8 We heard guns again last night, but cannot learn from the negroes who fired them. The disordered state of affairs keeps us anxious. . . . On this day a week ago the old system of slave labour was in peaceful operation. The breath of Emancipation has passed over the country, & we are now in that transition state between the new & the old systems—a state of chaos & disorder. Will the negro be materially benefitted by the change? Will the condition of the country in its productive resources, in material prosperity be improved? Will it be a benefit to the landed proprietors? These are questions which will have their solution in the future. They are in the hands of that Providence which over-ruleth all things for good. It was a strong conviction of my best judgement that the old relation of master & slave, had received the divine sanction & was the best condition in which the two races could live together for mutual benefit. There were many de-fects to be corrected & many abuses to be remedied, which I think would have been done if we had gained our independence & were freed from outside pres-sure. Among these defects I will enumerate the want of legislation to make the marriage contract binding—to prevent the separation of families, & to restrain the cupidity of cruel masters. Perhaps it is for neglecting these obligations that God has seen fit to dissolve that relation. I believe the negro must remain in this country & that his condition although a freed-man, must be to labour on the soil. Nothing but necessity will compel him to labour. Now the question is, will that necessity be so strong as to compel him to labour, which will be profitable to the landed proprietors. Will he make as much cotton, sugar, rice & tobacco for the world as he did previously? They will now have a choice *where* to labour. This will ensure good treatment & the best terms. The most humane, the most energetic & the most judicious managers have the best chances in the race for success. I expect to see a revolution in the ownership of landed estates. Those only can succeed who bring the best capacity for the business. Time will show. . . .

Sunday 12 Some of the very peculiar traits of negro character are now ex-hibited. John & Solomon left Morefield on Thursday with the black troops wild with excitement & probably drunk—In all this reign of disorder & anarchy I have not seen or heard of any violence or even of rudeness or incivility from the plan-tation negroes. Docility & submissiveness still prevail. There are two exhibitions of character which have surprised us, & which were never anticipated. 1st. On many places where there was really kind treatment & mutual attachment, the ex-citing events of the last week or two, & the powerful temptations brought to bear upon them, have seemed to snap the ties suddenly. Some have left their comfort-able homes & kind masters & friends, & gone off with the army, thinking to better their conditions. We must be patient & charitable in our opinions — They are ignorant of what they have to encounter, mere children in knowledge & experience, excitable, impulsive & have fallen under the tempting delusions presented to them in such glowing terms — Some who are disposed to take a proper view of their condition, & to return to work, are intimidated & kept back by threats from the more strong & overbearing. They do not clearly comprehend this situation — they have been told they are free, & their idea of freedom is associated with freedom from work & toil. In many places there was bad discipline & little care for the negroes. These are generally the foremost in all the acts of disorder, — & their example & word keep back others. We are astonished at this defection when we do not expect it, but on reflection the causes at work are sufficient to account for it. 2nd. Had we been told four years ago, that our negroes would have withstood the temptation to fidelity which have been constantly before them during the war, we would have doubted the possibility — & had we been told further of the events of the last two weeks, the incitements to acts of violence both by the example & the precepts of the black troops all throughout this region, we would have shuddered for the consequences. Except from the black soldiers, I have not heard of a single act of violence, or even of rude or uncivil language. Their behaviour is perfectly civil so far, & I believe, with a judicous course on the part of the whites, will continue so. This whole revolution from its commencement has developed in its progress, a course of events which no human sagacity on either side, ever foresaw. We are carried along by an inscrutable providence to the consummation of great & radical changes, — we are the actors in a Great Revolution where, not civil institutions only, but social polity, must be reconstructed & re-organized. . . .

May [1865]

May M. 1   Gen Lees surrender took place on the 9th.ult,[1] but it only reached us through our papers & the returning prisoners about a week ago. . . . [This] means the loss of our Independence for which we have been struggling for four years with immense loss of life & property. But the fate of nations is controlled & over-ruled by a wise Providence, which sees the end from the beginning, & orders all things in the highest wisdom. Whatever therefore may be the will of God regarding our destiny, I accept His decision as final & as eminently good. I have honestly believed we were right in our revolution, & would receive the divine sanction — if I have erred, I pray God to forgive me the error, & I submit with perfect satisfaction to His decree, knowing that He cannot err.

M. 22   We begin now to realize the ruin to property which the war has entailed upon us. All classes & conditions of men will suffer who had property, except the small farmers who owned no negroes. Confederate securities, I consider a total loss. Bank stock, confederation & private bonds, are all more or less dependent for their availability upon Confed securities, & upon the value of negro property; both of which are lost. The Rail road companies are nearly all ruined by the destruction of their roads & the heavy debt they must incur to rebuild. The only money now in possession of our people is coin in small quantities which had

---

1. **ult:** *ultimo*, Latin for "last month"; that is, April 9.

been hoarded through the war, & some bills of the local banks. There will be but little means of increasing this amount for some time to come, as provisions are scarce, & the cotton has been mostly burnt, captured or sold. The financial prospect is a gloomy one, & there will be much distress before our conditions can improve. . . .

M. 29 I went in to Aiken this morning & called at the hotel to inquire if any officer in Aiken was authorized to administer the Oath of Allegiance. They expected in a day or two to have it done here. It is necessary now in order to save property, have personal protection, or exercise the rights of citizenship, or any business calling. Every one who is allowed, is now taking the oath, as the Confederate govt. is annulled, the state govt. destroyed, & the return into the Union absolutely necessary to our condition as an organized community. As Gen. Gillmore's order based upon Chief Justice Chase's opinion announces the freedom of the negroes there is no further room to doubt that it is the settled policy of the country. I have today formally announced to my negroes the fact, & made such arrangements with each as the new relation rendered necessary. Those whose whole time we need, get at present clothes & food, house rent & medical attendance. The others work for themselves giving me a portion of their time on the farm in lieu of house rent. Old Amelia & her two grandchildren, I will spare the mockery of offering freedom to. I must support them as long as I have any thing to give.

T. 30 My negroes all express a desire to remain with me. I am gratified at the proof of their attachment. I believe it to be real & unfeigned. For the present they will remain, but in course of time we must part, as I cannot afford to keep so many, & they cannot afford to hire for what I could give them. As they have always been faithful & attached to us, & have been raised as family servants, & have all of them been in our family for several generations, there is a feeling towards them somewhat like that of a father who is about to send out his children on the world to make their way through life. Those who have brought the present change of relation upon us are ignorant of these ties. They have charged us with cruelty. They call us, man stealers, robbers, tyrants. The indignant denial of these charges & the ill feelings engendered during 30 years of angry controversy, have culminated at length in the four years war which has now ended. It has pleased God that we should fail in our efforts for independance — & with the loss of independance, we return to the Union under the dominion of the abolition sentiment. The experiment is now to be tried. The negro is not only to be emancipated, but is to become a citizen with all the right & priviledges! It produces a financial, political & social revolution at the South, fearful to contemplate in its ultimate effects. Whatever the result may be, let it be known & remembered that neither the negro slave nor his master is responsible. It has been done by those who having political power, are determined to carry into practice the sentimental philanthropy they have so long & angrily advocated. Now that is fixed. I pray God for the great issues at stake, that he may bless the effort & make it successful — make it a blessing & not a curse to the poor negro.

40

The Fall of Richmond
Thomas Morris Chester

One of the earliest modern-war correspondents and the first Northern journalist to enter the Confederate capital of Richmond, Thomas Morris Chester, born in 1834 in Harrisburg, Pennsylvania, led an extraordinary life deeply intertwined with the major events of nineteenth-century African American history. A Negro writer and activist, he caused controversy among his fellow black abolitionists by "abandoning" his country during the difficult years after the passage of the Fugitive Slave Law of 1850, leaving to help build an African American nation in Liberia. He recruited many to the new colony in West Africa, where he edited a newspaper and set up schools. He soon became restless with life in Liberia and moved to England, where he read law and lectured on politics; he also traversed Europe as the chief negotiator between the Liberian president and European leaders, including the tsar of Russia.

In 1863, two years into the Civil War, the United States government finally decided to allow black soldiers into the Union Army. Chester, like many abolitionists, believed that this would be the turning point for the North, and would ultimately end slavery. He founded and captained a company of African American soldiers from Pennsylvania but was soon driven out of the army by racial violence, prejudice, and the prohibition against black officers. Despite the setback, Chester remained committed to the war effort and took a commission the next year as a war correspondent for the Philadelphia Press. *In this capacity he left his most lasting legacy: eight months of vivid and exhaustive accounts of the lives and deeds of black soldiers in the Civil War. Facing the dangers of battle side by side with frontline soldiers, Chester marched into the Confederate capital of Richmond with the Union Army's 36th Regiment of Colored Troops on April 4, 1865.*

After the war, Chester would make several more trips across the Atlantic to England and Liberia before settling in Louisiana, where he built a successful law practice, served as superintendent of schools, and married a woman twenty-one years his junior who later became a locally famous black educator. In 1884, he was named president of the newly formed, black-owned Wilmington, Wrightsville, and Onslow Railroad in North Carolina. Unable to attract enough investors in the post-Reconstruction political climate of retreat and reaction, no track was ever laid and Chester finally withdrew from public life, dividing his time between Harrisburg and New Orleans, where his young wife rose in the black school system.

Thomas Morris Chester, *Thomas Morris Chester, Black Civil War Correspondent: His Dispatches from the Virginia Front*, ed. R. J. M. Blackett (Baton Rouge and London: Louisiana State University Press, 1989), pp. 288–98.

BEFORE YOU READ

1. Why was an African American regiment the first one into Richmond?

2. Does Chester's description strengthen or weaken the argument that it was African American soldiers who made the difference in the Civil War?

3. Do you think Chester gives an impartial account of the fall of Richmond?

HALL OF CONGRESS[1]

Richmond, April 4, 1865

To Major General Godfrey Weitzel was assigned the duty of capturing Richmond. Last evening he had determined upon storming the rebel works in front of Fort Burnham. The proper dispositions were all made, and the knowing ones retired with dim visions of this stronghold of treason floating before them. Nothing occurred in the first part of the evening to awaken suspicion, though for the past few days it has been known to the authorities that the rebels, as I informed you, were evacuating the city. After midnight explosions began to occur so frequently as to confirm the evidence already in possession of the General-in-chief, that the last acts of an out-generalled army were in course of progress. The immense flames curling up throughout the rebel camps indicated that they were destroying all that could not be taken away.

The soldiers along the line gathered upon the breastworks to witness the scene and exchange congratulations. While thus silently gazing upon the columns of fire one of the monster rams was exploded, which made the very earth tremble. If there was any doubt about the evacuation of Richmond that report banished them all. In a very few moments, though still dark, the Army of the James, or rather that part of it under General Weitzel, was put in motion.

It did not require much time to get the men in light-marching order. Every regiment tried to be first. All cheerfully moved off with accelerated speed. The pickets which were on the line during the night were in the advance.

Brevet Brigadier General Draper's brigade of colored troops, Brevet Major General Kautz's division, were the first infantry to enter Richmond. The gallant 36th U.S. Colored Troops, under Lieutenant Colonel B. F. Pratt, has the honor of being the first regiment. Captain Bicnnef's company has the pride of leading the advance.

The column having passed through Fort Burnham, over the rebel works, where they were moving heavy and light pieces of artillery, which the enemy in his haste was obliged to leave behind, moved into the Osborn road, which leads directly into the city.

In passing over the rebel works, we moved very cautiously in single file, for fear of exploding the innumerable torpedoes which were planted in front. So far as I can learn none has been exploded, and no one has been injured by those in-

---

1. Chester wrote his first dispatch from Richmond sitting in the chair of the Speaker of the Confederate House of Representatives.

fernal machines. The soldiers were soon, under engineers, carefully digging them up and making the passage way beyond the fear of casualties.

Along the road which the troops marched, or rather double quicked, batches of negroes were gathered together testifying by unmistakable signs their delight at our coming. Rebel soldiers who had hid themselves when their army moved came out of the bushes, and gave themselves up as disgusted with the service. The haste of the rebels was evident in guns, camp equipage, telegraph wires, and other army property which they did not have time to burn.

When the column was about two miles from Richmond General Weitzel and staff passed by at a rapid speed, and was hailed by loud cheering. He soon reached the city, which was surrendered to him informally at the State House by Mr. Joseph Mayo, the mayor. The General and staff rode up Main street amid the hearty congratulations of a very large crowd of colored persons and poor whites, who were gathered together upon the sidewalks manifesting every demonstration of joy.

There were many persons in the better-class houses who were peeping out the windows, and whose movements indicated that they would need watching in the future. There was no mistaking the curl of their lips and the flash in their eyes. The new military Governor of Richmond will, no doubt, prove equal to such emergencies.

When General Draper's brigade entered the outskirts of the city it was halted, and a brigade of Devin's division, 24th Corps, passed in to constitute the provost guard. A scene was here witnessed which was not only grand, but sublime. Officers rushed into each other's arms, congratulating them upon the peaceful occupation of this citadel. Tears of joy ran down the faces of the more aged. The soldiers cheered lustily, which were mingled with every kind of expression of delight. The citizens stood gaping in wonder at the splendidly-equipped army marching along under the graceful folds of the old flag. Some waved their hats and women their hands in token of gladness. The pious old negroes, male and female, indulged in such expressions: "You've come at last"; "We've been looking for you these many days"; "Jesus has opened the way"; "God bless you"; "I've not seen that old flag for four years"; "It does my eyes good"; "Have you come to stay?"; "Thank God", and similar expressions of exultation. The soldiers, black and white, received these assurances of loyalty as evidences of the latent patriotism of an oppressed people, which a military despotism has not been able to crush.

Riding up to a group of fine looking men, whose appearance indicated that they would hardly have influence enough to keep them out of the army, I inquired how it was they were not taken away with the force of Lee. They replied that they had hid themselves when the rebel army had evacuated the city, and that many more had done likewise, who would soon appear when assured that there was no longer any danger of falling into the power of the traitorous army. . . .

As we entered all the Government buildings were in flames, having been fired by order of the rebel General Ewell. The flames soon communicated themselves to the business part of the city; and continued to rage furiously throughout the day. All efforts to arrest this destructive element seemed for the best part of the day of no avail. The fire department of Richmond rendered every aid, and to them and the co-operate labors of our soldiers belongs the credit of having saved Richmond from the devastating flames. As it is, all that part of the city lying between Ninth and Fourteenth streets, between Main street and the river inclusive, is in ruins. Among the most prominent buildings destroyed are the rebel War Department, Quartermaster General's Department, all the buildings with commissary stores, Shockoe's and Dibbrel's warehouses, well stored with tobacco, *Dispatch* and *Enquirer* newspaper buildings, the court house, (Guy) House, Farmers' Bank, Bank of Virginia, Exchange Bank, Tracers' Bank, American and Columbia hotels, and the Mayo bridge which unites Richmond with Manchester. The buildings of the largest merchants are among those which have been reduced to ashes.

The flames, in spreading, soon communicated to poor and rich houses alike. All classes were soon rushing, into the streets with their goods, to save them. They hardly laid them down before they were picked up by those who openly were plundering everyplace where anything of value was to be obtained. It was retributive justice upon the aiders and abettors of treason to see their property fired by the rebel chiefs and plundered by the people whom they meant to forever enslave. As soon as the torch was applied to the rebel storehouses, the negroes and poor whites began to appropriate all property, without respect to locks or bolts. About the time our advance entered the city the tide of this inadmissible confiscation was at its highest ebb. Men would rush to the principal stores, break open the doors, and carry off the contents by the armful.

The leader of this system of public plundering was a colored man who carried upon his shoulder an iron crow-bar, and as a mark of distinguishment had a red piece of goods around his waist which reached down to his knees. The mob, for it could not with propriety be called anything else, followed him as their leader; moved on when he advanced, rushed into every passage which was made by the leader with his crow-bar. Goods of every description were seized under these circumstances and personally appropriated by the supporters of an equal distribution of property. Cotton goods in abundance, tobacco in untold quantities, shoes, rebel military clothing, and goods and furniture generally were carried away by the people as long as any thing of value was to be obtained. As soon as Gen. Ripley was assigned to provost duty, all plundering immediately ceased, the flames were arrested, and an appearance of recognized authority fully sustained. Order once more reigns in Richmond. The streets were as quiet last night as they possibly could be. An effective patrolling and provost guard keeps everything as quiet as can be expected.

The F. F. V.'s have not ventured out of their houses yet, except in a few cases, to apply for a guard to protect their property. In some cases negroes have been sent to protect the interest of these would-be man sellers. It is pleasant to witness the measured pace of some dark sentinel before the houses of persons who, without doubt, were out-spoken rebels until the Union army entered the city, owing the security which they feel to the vigilance of the negro guard.

When the army occupied the city there were innumerable inquiries for Jeff Davis, but to all of which the answer was made that he went off in great haste night before last, with all the bag and baggage which he could carry. The future capital of the Confederacy will probably be in a wagon for the facilities which it affords to travel. Jeff's mansion, where he lived in state, is now the headquarters of Gen. Weitzel.

Brigadier General Shepley has been appointed Governor of Richmond, and has entered upon the arduous duties of the office. A better selection could not have been made.

It is due to Major Stevens, of the 4th Massachusetts Cavalry, provost marshal, on the staff of Gen. Weitzel, to give him credit for raising the first colors over the State House. He hoisted a couple of guidons, in the absence of a flag, which excited prolonged cheering. Soon after General Shepley's A. D. C.[2] raised the first storm flag over the Capitol. It is the acme standard which General Shepley laid a wager would wave over the St. Charles Hotel in the beginning of the rebellion, and he also laid another that it would be hoisted over Richmond, both of which he has had the satisfaction of winning.

During the early part of the day a number of rebel officers were captured at the Spottswood House, where they were drinking freely. They belonged to the navy, the last of which disappeared in smoke, excepting a few straggling officers and men. These fellows, when arrested, did not wish to walk through the street under a guard, but solicited the favor of being permitted to go to the provost marshal in a carriage. Their impudence was received as it deserved, with suppressed contempt.

On Sunday evening, strange to say, the jails in this place were thrown open, and all runaway negroes, those for sale and those for safe keeping were told to hop out and enjoy their freedom. You may rely upon it that they did not need a second invitation. Many of these persons will have no difficulty in convincing themselves that they were always on the side of the Union and the freedom of the slave. Great events have a wonderful influence upon the minds of guilty, trembling wretches. . . .

HALL OF CONGRESS

Richmond, April 6, 1865

The exultation of the loyal people of this city, who, amid the infamy by which they have been surrounded, and the foul misrepresentations to allure them from their allegiance, have remained true to the old flag, is still being expressed by the most extravagant demonstrations of joy. The Union element in this city consists of negroes and poor whites, including all that have deserted from the army, or have survived the terrible exigencies which brought starvation to so many homes. As to the negroes, one thing is certain, that amid every disaster to our arms, amid the wrongs which they daily suffered for their known love for the Union, and amid the scourging which they received for trying to reach our army and enlist under our flag, they have ever prayed for the right cause, and testified their devo-

---

2. **A. D. C.:** aide-de-camp; a military aide.

tion to it in ten thousand instances, and especially in aiding our escaped prisoners to find our lines when to do so placed their own lives in peril.

The great event after the capture of the city was the arrival of President Lincoln in it. He came up to Rocket's wharf in one of Admiral Porter's vessels of war, and, with a file of sailors for a guard of honor, he walked up to Jeff Davis' house, the headquarters of General Weitzel. As soon as he landed the news sped, as if upon the wings of lightning, that "Old Abe," for it was treason in this city to give him a more respectful address, had come. Some of the negroes, feeling themselves free to act like men, shouted that the President had arrived. This name having always been applied to Jeff, the inhabitants, coupling it with the prevailing rumor that he had been captured, reported that the archtraitor was being brought into the city. As the people pressed near they cried "Hang him!" "Hang him!" "Show him no quarter!" and other similar expressions, which indicated their sentiments as to what should be his fate. But when they learned that it was President Lincoln their joy knew no bounds. By the time he reached General Weitzel's headquarters, thousands of persons had followed him to catch a sight of the Chief Magistrate of the United States. When he ascended the steps he faced the crowd and bowed his thanks for the prolonged exultation which was going up from that great concourse. The people seemed inspired by this acknowledgment, and with renewed vigor shouted louder and louder, until it seemed as if the echoes would reach the abode of those patriot spirits who had died without witnessing the sight.

General Weitzel received the President upon the pavement, and conducted him up the steps. General Shepley, after a good deal of trouble, got the crowd quiet and introduced Admiral Porter, who bowed his acknowledgments for the cheering with which his name was greeted. The President and party entered the mansion, where they remained for half an hour, the crowd still accumulating around it, when a headquarters' carriage was brought in front, drawn by four horses, and Mr. Lincoln, with his youngest son, Admiral Porter, General Kautz, and General Devin entered. The carriage drove through the principal streets, followed by General Weitzel and staff on horseback, and a cavalry guard. There is no describing the scene along the route. The colored population was wild with enthusiasm. Old men thanked God in a very boisterous manner, and old women shouted upon the pavement as high as they had ever done at a religious revival. But when the President passed through the Capitol yard it was filled with people. Washington's monument and the Capitol steps were one mass of humanity to catch a glimpse of him.

It should be recorded that the Malvern, Admiral Porter's flag-ship, upon which the President came; the Bat, Monticello, Frolic, and the Symbol, the torpedo-boat which led the advance and exploded these infernal machines, were the first vessels to arrive in Richmond.

Nothing can exceed the courtesy and politeness which the whites everywhere manifest to the negroes. Not even the familiarity peculiar to Americans is indulged in, calling the blacks by their first or Christian names, but even masters are addressing their slaves as "Mr. Johnson," "Mrs. Brown," and "Miss Smith." A cordial shake of the hand and a gentle inclination of the body, approaching to respectful consideration, are evident in the greetings which now take place between the oppressed and the oppressor.

Masters are looking through the camps of our colored troops to find some of their former slaves to give them a good character. The first night our troops quartered in the city this scene was enacted in Gen. Draper's brigade limits, his being the first organization to enter the city. His troops now hold the inner lines of works. The rapid occupation of the city cut off the retreat of many rebels, who are daily being picked up by the provost guard.

Every one declares that Richmond never before presented such a spectacle of jubilee. It must be confessed that those who participated in this informal reception of the President were mainly negroes. There were many whites in the crowd, but they were lost in the great concourse of American citizens of African descent. Those who lived in the finest houses either stood motionless upon their steps or merely peeped through the window-blinds, with a very few exceptions. The Secesh-inhabitants still have some hope for their tumbling cause.

The scenes at the Capitol during the day are of a very exciting character. The offices of General Shepley, the Military Governor, and Colonel Morning, the Provost Marshal General, are besieged by crowds, mostly poor people, with a small sprinkling of respectability, upon every kind of pretext. They want protection papers, a guard over their property, to assure the authorities of their allegiance, to take the oath, to announce that they are paroled prisoners and never have been exchanged, and don't desire to be, innumerable other circumstances to insure the protection of the military authorities.

The people in Richmond, white and black, had been led to believe that when the Yankee army came its mission was one of plunder. But the orderly manner in which the soldiers have acted has undeceived them. The excitement is great, but nothing could be more orderly and decorous than the united crowds of soldiers and citizens.

The Capitol building all day yesterday from the moment we took possession was surrounded by a crowd of hungry men and women clamoring for something to eat. The earnestness of their entreaties and looks showed that they were in a destitute condition. It was deemed necessary to station a special guard at the bottom of the steps to keep them from filling the building. These suffering people will probably be attended to in a day or so in that bountiful manner which has marked the advance of the Union armies.

I visited yesterday (Tuesday) several of the slave jails, where men, women, and children were confined, or herded, for the examination of purchasers. The jailors were in all cases slaves, and had been left in undisputed possession of the buildings. The owners, as soon as they were aware that we were coming, opened wide the doors and told the confined inmates that they were free. The poor souls could not realize it until they saw the Union army. Even then they thought it must be a pleasant dream, but when they saw Abraham Lincoln they were satisfied that their freedom was perpetual. One enthusiastic old negro woman exclaimed: "I know that I am free, for I have seen Father Abraham and felt him."

When the President returned to the flag-ship of Admiral Porter, in the evening, he was taken from the wharf in a cutter. Just as he pushed off, amid the cheering of the crowd, another good old colored female shouted out, "Don't drown, Massa Abe, for God's sake!"

The fire which was nearly extinguished when I closed my last despatch, is entirely so now. Thousands of persons are gazing hourly with indignation upon the ruins. Gen. Lee ordered the evacuation of the city at an hour known to the remaining leaders of the rebellion, when Gens. Ewell and Breckinridge, and others, absconded, leaving orders with menials, robbers, and plunderers, kept together during the war by the "cohesive power of public plunder," to apply the torch to the different tobacco warehouses, public buildings, arsenals, stores, flour mills, powder magazines, and every important place of deposit. A south wind prevailed, and the flames spread with devastating effect. The offices of the newspapers, whose columns have been charged with the foulest vituperation against our Government, were on fire; two of them have been reduced to ashes, another one injured beyond repair, while the remaining two are not much damaged. Every bank which had emitted the spurious notes of the rebels was consumed to ruins. Churches no longer gave audience to empty prayers, but burst forth in furious flames. Magazines exploded, killing the poor inhabitants. In short, Secession was burnt out, and the city purified as far as fire could accomplish it.

As I informed you in a previous despatch, the Union soldiers united with the citizens to stay the progress of the fire, and at last succeeded, but not until all the business part of the town was destroyed.

About three o'clock on Monday morning the political prisoners who were confirmed in Castle Thunder,[3] and the Union prisoners who were in Libby, were marched out and driven off. Some of our officers escaped and were kindly cared for by the good Union folks of this city. The rebels also gathered together as many colored persons as possible, and were forcing them ahead with drawn sabres, but before they were out of the city Spear's cavalry came down upon them, rescued the negroes, and captured seventeen of the Johnnies, with their horses.

Yesterday afternoon I strolled through Castle Thunder, where so many Union men have suffered every species of meanness and tyranny which the rebels could invent. The only thing that attracted especial attention was the large number of manacles which were for the benefit of the prisoners. This place has been so often described, that it would be unnecessary to weary the reader again. The Castle is empty at present, and is in charge of Capt. Mattison, 81st New York Volunteers, who, by the way, is a very accommodating officer. The Hotel de Libby is now doing a rushing business in the way of accommodating a class of persons who have not heretofore patronized that establishment. It is being rapidly filled with rebel soldiers, detectives, spies, robbers, and every grade of infamy in the calendar of crime. The stars and stripes now wave gracefully over it, and traitors look through the same bars behind which loyal men were so long confined.

Quite a large number of rebels were brought into the city last night. I did not for a certainty learn whether they were captured, or deserted from a bad cause—most probably the latter.

---

3. **Castle Thunder:** a Confederate prison that housed political prisoners—among them, those who had helped blacks escape to Union lines.

41

African Americans during Reconstruction
Felix Haywood et al.

The Thirteenth (1865), Fourteenth (1868), and Fifteenth (1870) Amendments to the U.S. Constitution decreed an equality between the races that did not become a reality in African Americans' daily lives. At first the federal government established the Freedmen's Bureau and supported Reconstruction governments in Southern states, making vigorous efforts to help the freed slaves gain education, legal and medical services, reasonable employment contracts, and a measure of political power. But within about a decade those efforts were abandoned as the Northern public, tired of disorder in the South and wary of government intervention, abandoned freed slaves to their former masters. African Americans were left to respond however they could to the social revolution brought about by emancipation, the war's impoverishment of the South, and the violence of groups like the Ku Klux Klan. Historians have pieced together the story of their actions from a multiplicity of sources. Interviews with former slaves collected in the 1930s, of which you will here read a sample, are one interesting source.

BEFORE YOU READ

1. What, judging from these accounts, were the major problems that former slaves faced after the war?
2. What did these former slaves expect of freedom?
3. What role did the Ku Klux Klan play in former slaves' lives?
4. Why did some freedmen continue to work for their former masters?

FELIX HAYWOOD

San Antonio, Texas. Born in Raleigh, North Carolina. Age at interview: 88.

The end of the war, it come just like that—like you snap your fingers. . . . How did we know it! Hallelujah broke out—

> Abe Lincoln freed the nigger
>   With the gun and the trigger;
> And I ain't going to get whipped any more.
>   I got my ticket,
> Leaving the thicket,
>   And I'm a-heading for the Golden Shore!

"African Americans React to Reconstruction," from B. A. Botkin, ed., *Lay My Burden Down: A Folk History of Slavery* (Chicago: University of Chicago Press, 1945), pp. 65–70, 223–24, 241–42, 246–47.

Soldiers, all of a sudden, was everywhere—coming in bunches, crossing and walking and riding. Everyone was a-singing. We was all walking on golden clouds. Hallelujah!

> Union forever,
>   Hurrah, boys, hurrah!
> Although I may be poor,
>   I'll never be a slave—
> Shouting the battle cry of freedom.

Everybody went wild. We felt like heroes, and nobody had made us that way but ourselves. We was free. Just like that, we was free. It didn't seem to make the whites mad, either. They went right on giving us food just the same. Nobody took our homes away, but right off colored folks started on the move. They seemed to want to get closer to freedom, so they'd know what it was— like it was a place or a city. Me and my father stuck, stuck close as a lean tick to a sick kitten. The Gudlows started us out on a ranch. My father, he'd round up cattle—unbranded cattle—for the whites. They was cattle that they belonged to, all right; they had gone to find water 'long the San Antonio River and the Guadalupe. Then the whites gave me and my father some cattle for our own. My father had his own brand—7 B)—and we had a herd to start out with of seventy.

We knowed freedom was on us, but we didn't know what was to come with it. We thought we was going to get rich like the white folks. We thought we was going to be richer than the white folks, 'cause we was stronger and knowed how to work, and the whites didn't, and they didn't have us to work for them any more. But it didn't turn out that way. We soon found out that freedom could make folks proud, but it didn't make 'em rich.

Did you ever stop to think that thinking don't do any good when you do it too late? Well, that's how it was with us. If every mother's son of a black had thrown 'way his hoe and took up a gun to fight for his own freedom along with the Yankees, the war'd been over before it began. But we didn't do it. We couldn't help stick to our masters. We couldn't no more shoot 'em than we could fly. My father and me used to talk 'bout it. We decided we was too soft and freedom wasn't going to be much to our good even if we had a education.

WARREN McKINNEY

Hazen, Arkansas. Born in South Carolina. Age at interview: 85.

I was born in Edgefield County, South Carolina. I am eighty-five years old. I was born a slave of George Strauter. I remembers hearing them say, "Thank God, I's free as a jay bird." My ma was a slave in the field. I was eleven years old when freedom was declared. When I was little, Mr. Strauter whipped my ma. It hurt me bad as it did her. I hated him. She was crying. I chunked him with rocks. He run after me, but he didn't catch me. There was twenty-five or thirty hands that worked in the field. They raised wheat, corn, oats, barley, and cotton. All the children that couldn't work stayed at one house. Aunt Mat kept the babies and small children that couldn't go to the field. He had a gin and a shop. The shop was at the fork of the roads. When the war come on, my papa went to built forts. He quit Ma and took another woman. When the war close, Ma took her four children, bundled 'em up and went to Augusta. The government give out rations there. My ma washed and ironed. People died in piles. I don't know till yet what was the matter. They said it was the change of living. I seen five or six wooden, painted coffins piled up on wagons pass by our house. Loads passed every day like you see cotton pass here. Some said it was cholera and some took consumption. Lots of the colored people nearly starved. Not much to get to do and not much houseroom. Several families had to live in one house. Lots of the colored folks went up North and froze to death. They couldn't stand the cold. They wrote back about them dying. No, they never sent them back. I heard some sent for money to come back. I heard plenty 'bout the Ku Klux. They scared the folks to death. People left Augusta in droves. About a thousand would all meet and walk going to hunt work and new homes. Some of them died. I had a sister and brother lost that way. I had another sister come to Louisiana that way. She wrote back.

I don't think the colored folks looked for a share of land. They never got nothing 'cause the white folks didn't have nothing but barren hills left. About all the mules was wore out hauling provisions in the army. Some folks say they ought to done more for the colored folks when they left, but they say they was broke. Freeing all the slaves left 'em broke.

That Reconstruction was a mighty hard pull. Me and Ma couldn't live. A man paid our ways to Carlisle, Arkansas, and we come. We started working for Mr. Emenson. He had a big store, teams, and land. We liked it fine, and I been here fifty-six years now. There was so much wild game, living was not so hard. If a fellow could get a little bread and a place to stay, he was all right. After I come to this state, I voted some. I have farmed and worked at odd jobs. I farmed mostly. Ma went back to her old master. He persuaded her to come back home. Me and her went back and run a farm four or five years before she died. Then I come back here.

LEE GUIDON

South Carolina. Born in South Carolina. Age at interview: 89.

Yes, ma'am, I sure was in the Civil War. I plowed all day, and me and my sister helped take care of the baby at night. It would cry, and me bumping it [in a straight chair, rocking]. Time I git it to the bed where its mama was, it wake up and start crying all over again. I be so sleepy. It was a puny sort of baby. Its papa was off at war. His name was Jim Cowan, and his wife Miss Margaret Brown 'fore she married him. Miss Lucy Smith give me and my sister to them. Then she married Mr. Abe Moore. Jim Smith was Miss Lucy's boy. He lay out in the woods all time. He say no need in him gitting shot up and killed. He say let the slaves be free. We lived, seemed like, on 'bout the line of York and Union counties. He lay out in the woods over in York County. Mr. Jim say all the fighting 'bout was jealousy. They caught him several times, but every time he got away from 'em. After they come home Mr. Jim say they never win no war. They stole and starved out the South. . . .

After freedom a heap of people say they was going to name theirselves over. They named theirselves big names, then went roaming round like wild, hunting cities. They changed up so it was hard to tell who or where anybody was. Heap of 'em died, and you didn't know when you hear about it if he was your folks hardly. Some of the names was Abraham, and some called theirselves Lincum. Any big name 'cepting their master's name. It was the fashion. I heard 'em talking 'bout it one evening, and my pa say, "Fine folks raise us and we gonna hold to our own names." That settled it with all of us. . . .

I reckon I do know 'bout the Ku Kluck. I knowed a man named Alfred Owens. He seemed all right, but he was a Republican. He said he was not afraid. He run a tanyard and kept a heap of guns in a big room. They all loaded. He married a Southern woman. Her husband either died or was killed. She had a son living with them. The Ku Kluck was called Upper League. They get this boy to unload all the guns. Then the white men went there. The white man give up and said, "I ain't got no gun to defend myself with. The guns all unloaded, and I ain't got no powder and shot." But the Ku Kluck shot in the houses and shot him up like lacework. He sold fine harness, saddles, bridles — all sorts of leather things. The Ku Kluck sure run them outen their country. They say they not going to have them round, and they sure run them out, back where they came from. . . .

For them what stayed on like they were, Reconstruction times 'bout like times before that 'cepting the Yankee stole out and tore up a scandalous heap. They tell the black folks to do something, and then come white folks you live with and say Ku Kluck whup you. They say leave, and white folks say better not listen to them old yankees. They'll git you too far off to come back, and you freeze. They done give you all the use they got for you. How they do? All sorts of ways. Some stayed at their cabins glad to have one to live in and farmed on. Some running round begging, some hunting work for money, and nobody had no money 'cepting the Yankees, and they had no homes or land and mighty little work for you to do. No work to live on. Some going every day to the city. That winter I heard 'bout them starving and freezing by the wagon loads. I never heard nothing 'bout voting till freedom. I don't think I ever voted till I come to Mississippi. I votes Republican. That's the party of my color, and I stick to them as long as they do right. I don't dabble in white folks' business, and that white folks' voting is their business. If I vote, I go do it and go on home.

I been plowing all my life, and in the hot days I cuts and saws wood. Then when I gets outa cotton-picking, I put each boy on a load of wood and we sell wood. The last years we got $3 a cord. Then we clear land till next spring. I don't find no time to be loafing. I never missed a year farming till I got the Bright's disease [one of several kinds of kidney ailments] and it hurt me to do hard work. Farming is the best life there is when you are able. . . .

When I owned most, I had six head mules and five head horses. I rented 140 acres of land. I bought this house and some other land about. The anthrax killed nearly all my horses and mules. I got one big fine mule yet. Its mate died. I lost my house. My son give me one room, and he paying the debt off now. It's hard for colored folks to keep anything. Somebody gets it from 'em if they don't mind.

The present times is hard. Timber is scarce. Game is about all gone. Prices higher. Old folks cannot work. Times is hard for younger folks too. They go to town too much and go to shows. They going to a tent show now. Circus coming, they say. They spending too much money for foolishness. It's a fast time. Folks too restless. Some of the colored folks work hard as folks ever did. They spends too much. Some folks is lazy. Always been that way.

I signed up to the government, but they ain't give me nothing 'cepting powdered milk and rice what wasn't fit to eat. It cracked up and had black something in it. A lady said she would give me some shirts that was her husband's. I went to get them, but she wasn't home. These heavy shirts give me heat. They won't give me the pension, and I don't know why. It would help me buy my salts and pills and the other medicines like Swamp Root. They won't give it to me.

TOBY JONES

Madisonville, Texas. Born in South Carolina. Age at interview: 87.

I worked for Massa 'bout four years after freedom, 'cause he forced me to, said he couldn't 'ford to let me go. His place was near ruint, the fences burnt, and the house would have been, but it was rock. There was a battle fought near his place, and I taken Missy to a hideout in the mountains to where her father was, 'cause there was bullets flying everywhere. When the war was over, Massa come home and says, "You son of a gun, you's supposed to be free, but you ain't, 'cause I ain't gwine give you freedom." So I goes on working for him till I gits the chance to steal a hoss from him. The woman I wanted to marry, Govie, she 'cides to come to Texas with me. Me and Govie, we rides the hoss 'most a hundred miles, then we turned him a-loose and give him a scare back to his house, and come on foot the rest the way to Texas.

All we had to eat was what we could beg, and sometimes we went three days without a bite to eat. Sometimes we'd pick a few berries. When we got cold we'd crawl in a brushpile and hug up close together to keep warm. Once in a while we'd come to a farmhouse, and the man let us sleep on cottonseed in his barn, but they was far and few between, 'cause they wasn't many houses in the country them days like now.

When we gits to Texas, we gits married, but all they was to our wedding am we just 'grees to live together as man and wife. I settled on some land, and we cut some trees and split them open and stood them on end with the tops together for our house. Then we deadened some trees, and the land was ready to farm. There was some wild cattle and hogs, and that's the way we got our start, caught some of them and tamed them.

I don't know as I 'spected nothing from freedom, but they turned us out like a bunch of stray dogs, no homes, no clothing, no nothing, not 'nough food to last us one meal. After we settles on that place, I never seed man or woman, 'cept Govie, for six years, 'cause it was a long ways to anywhere. All we had to farm with was sharp sticks. We'd stick holes and plant corn, and when it come up we'd punch up the dirt round it. We didn't plant cotton, 'cause we couldn't eat that. I made bows and arrows to kill wild game with, and we never went to a store for nothing. We made our clothes out of animal skins.

WHY ADAM KIRK WAS A DEMOCRAT

House Report No. 262, 43 Cong., 2 Sess., p. 106.
Statement of an Alabama Negro (1874)

A white man raised me. I was raised in the house of old man Billy Kirk. He raised me as a body servant. The class that he belongs to seems nearer to me than the northern white man, and actually, since the war, everything I have got is by their aid and their assistance. They have helped me raise up my family and have stood by me, and whenever I want a doctor, no matter what hour of the day or night, he is called in whether I have got a cent or not. And when I want any assistance I can get it from them. I think they have got better principles and better character than the republicans.

42

White Southerners' Reactions to Reconstruction

Caleb G. Forshey and the Reverend James Sinclair

The Congressional Joint Committee of Fifteen, assembled to examine Southern representation in Congress, was named in December 1865 as part of the Republican Congress's response to President Andrew Johnson's plan of Reconstruction. In 1866, the committee held hearings as part of its effort to draft the Fourteenth Amendment. Despite the president's veto, Congress had already enlarged the scope of the Freedmen's Bureau to care for displaced former slaves and to try by military commission those accused of depriving freedmen of civil rights. Republicans in Congress, in opposition to the Johnson administration, would continue to evolve a Reconstruction policy that attempted to protect the freedmen's rights.

Of the two white Southerners whose interviews with the committee you will read here, Caleb G. Forshey had supported secession while James Sinclair, although a slaveholder, had opposed it. A Scottish-born minister who had only moved to North Carolina in 1857, Sinclair's Unionist sentiments had led to the loss of his church and then to his arrest during the war. In 1865 he served on the Freedmen's Bureau.

BEFORE YOU READ

1. What effect did Caleb Forshey anticipate from military occupation of Southern states?
2. How did he evaluate the effectiveness of the Freedmen's Bureau?
3. What were Forshey's beliefs about African Americans?
4. What were the strengths and weaknesses of the Freedmen's Bureau according to James Sinclair?
5. How does Sinclair's view of Southern opinion differ from Forshey's?

CALEB G. FORSHEY

Washington, D.C., March 28, 1866

Question: Where do you reside?
Answer: I reside in the State of Texas.
Question: How long have you been a resident of Texas?

The Report of the Committees of the House of Representatives Made during the First Session, Thirty-Ninth Congress, 1865–1866, vol. 2 (Washington, D.C.: Government Printing Office, 1866); Forshey: pp. 129–32; Sinclair: pp. 168–71.

Answer: I have resided in Texas and been a citizen of that State for nearly thirteen years.

Question: What opportunities have you had for ascertaining the temper and disposition of the people of Texas towards the government and authority of the United States?

Answer: For ten years I have been superintendent of the Texas Military Institute, as its founder and conductor. I have been in the confederate service in various parts of the confederacy; but chiefly in the trans-Mississippi department, in Louisiana and Texas, as an officer of engineers. I have had occasion to see and know very extensively the condition of affairs in Texas, and also to a considerable extent in Louisiana. I think I am pretty well-informed, as well as anybody, perhaps, of the present state of affairs in Texas.

Question: What are the feelings and views of the people of Texas as to the late rebellion, and the future condition and circumstances of the State, and its relations to the federal government?

Answer: After our army had given up its arms and gone home, the surrender of all matters in controversy was complete, and as nearly universal, perhaps, as anything could be. Assuming the matters in controversy to have been the right to secede, and the right to hold slaves, I think they were given up teetotally, to use a strong Americanism. When you speak of feeling, I should discriminate a little. The feeling was that of any party who had been cast in a suit he had staked all upon. They did not return from feeling, but from a sense of necessity, and from a judgment that it was the only and necessary thing to be done, to give up the contest. But when they gave it up, it was without reservation; with a view to look forward, and not back. That is my impression of the manner in which the thing was done. There was a public expectation that in some very limited time there would be a restoration to former relations. . . . It was the expectation of the people that, as soon as the State was organized as proposed by the President, they would be restored to their former relations, and things would go on as before.

Question: What is your opinion of a military force under the authority of the federal government to preserve order in Texas and to protect those who have been loyal, both white and black, from the aggressions of those who have been in the rebellion?

Answer: My judgment is well founded on that subject: that wherever such military force is and has been, it has excited the very feeling it was intended to prevent; that so far from being necessary it is very pernicious everywhere, and without exception. The local authorities and public sentiment are ample for protection. I think no occasion would occur, unless some individual case that our laws would not reach. We had an opportunity to test this after the surrender and before any authority was there. The military authorities, or the military officers, declared that we were without laws, and it was a long time before the governor appointed arrived there, and then it was sometime before we could effect anything in the way of organization. We were a people without law, order, or anything; and it was a time for violence if it would occur. I think it is a great credit to our civilization that, in that state of affairs, there was nowhere any instance of violence. I am proud of it, for I expected the contrary; I expected that our soldiers on coming home, many of them, would be dissolute, and that many of them would oppress the class of men you speak of; but it did not occur. But afterwards, wherever soldiers have been sent, there have been little troubles, none of them large; but personal collisions between soldiers and citizens.

Question: What is your opinion as to the necessity and advantages of the Freedmen's Bureau, or an agency of that kind, in Texas?

Answer: My opinion is that it is not needed; my opinion is stronger than that—that the effect of it is to irritate, if nothing else. While in New York city recently I had a conversation with some friends from Texas, from five distant points in the State. We met together and compared opinions; and the opinion of each was the same, that the negroes had generally gone to work since January; that except where the Freedmen's Bureau had interfered, or rather encouraged troubles, such as little complaints, especially between negro and negro, the negro's disposition was very good, and they had generally gone to work, a vast majority of them with their former masters. . . . The impression in Texas at present is that the negroes under the influence of the Freedmen's Bureau do worse than without it.

I want to state that I believe all our former owners of negroes are the friends of the negroes; and that the antagonism paraded in the papers of the north does not exist at all. I know the fact is the very converse of that; and good feeling always prevails between the masters and the slaves. But the negroes went off and left them in the lurch; my own family was an instance of it. But they came back after a time, saying they had been free enough and wanted a home.

Question: Do you think those who employ the negroes there are willing to make contracts with them, so that they shall have fair wages for their labor?

Answer: I think so; I think they are paid liberally, more than the white men in this country get; the average compensation to negroes there is greater than the average compensation of free laboring white men in this country. It seems to have regulated itself in a great measure by what each neighborhood was doing; the negroes saying, "I can get thus and so at such a place." Men have hired from eight to fifteen dollars per month during the year, and women at about two dollars less a month; house-servants at a great deal more.

Question: Do the men who employ the negroes claim to exercise the right to enforce their contract by physical force?

Answer: Not at all; that is totally abandoned; not a single instance of it has occurred. I think they still chastise children, though. The negro parents often neglect that, and the children are still switched as we switch our own children. I know it is done in my own house; we have little house-servants that we switch just as I do our own little fellows.

Question: What is your opinion as to the respective advantages to the white and black races, of the present free system of labor and the institution of slavery?

Answer: I think freedom is very unfortunate for the negro; I think it is sad; his present helpless condition touches my heart more than anything else I ever contemplated, and I think that is the common sentiment of our slaveholders. I have seen it on the largest plantations, where the negro men had all left, and where only women and children remained, and the owners had to keep them and feed them. The beginning certainly presents a touching and sad spectacle. The poor negro is dying at a rate fearful to relate.

I have some ethnological theories that may perhaps warp my judgment; but my judgment is that the highest condition the black race has ever reached or can reach, is one where he is provided for by a master race. That is the result of a great deal of scientific investigation and observation of the negro character by me ever since I was a man. The labor question had become a most momentous one, and I was studying it. I undertook to investigate the condition of the negro from statistics under various circumstances, to treat it purely as a matter of statistics from the census tables of this country of ours. I found that the free blacks of the north decreased 8 per cent.; the free blacks of the south increased 7 or 8 per cent., while the slaves by their sides increased 34 per cent. I inferred from the doctrines of political economy that the race is in the best condition when it procreates the fastest; that, other things being equal, slavery is of vast advantage to the negro. I will mention one or two things in connexion with this as explanatory of that result. The negro will not take care of his offspring unless required to do it, as compared with the whites. The little children will die; they do die, and hence the necessity of very rigorous regulations on our plantations which we have adopted in our nursery system.

Another cause is that there is no continence among the negroes. All the continence I have ever seen among the negroes has been enforced upon plantations, where it is generally assumed there is none. For the sake of procreation, if nothing else, we compel men to live with their wives. The discipline of the plantation was more rigorous, perhaps, in regard to men staying with their wives, than in regard to anything else; and I think the procreative results, as shown by the census tables, is due in a great measure to that discipline. . . .

Question: What is the prevailing inclination among the people of Texas in regard to giving the negroes civil or political rights and privileges?

Answer: I think they are all opposed to it. There are some men—I am not among them—who think that the basis of intelligence might be a good basis for the elective franchise. But a much larger class, perhaps nine-tenths of our people, believe that the distinctions between the races should not be broken down by any such community of interests in the management of the affairs of the State. I think there is a very common sentiment that the negro, even with education, has not a mind capable of appreciating the political institutions of the country to such an extent as would make him a good associate for the white man in the administration of the government. I think if the vote was taken on the question of admitting him to the right of suffrage there would be a very small vote in favor of it—scarcely respectable: that is my judgment.

THE REVEREND JAMES SINCLAIR

Washington, D.C., January 29, 1866

Question: What is generally the state of feeling among the white people of North Carolina towards the government of the United States?

Answer: That is a difficult question to answer, but I will answer it as far as my own knowledge goes. In my opinion, there is generally among the white people not much love for the government. Though they are willing, and I believe determined, to acquiesce in what is inevitable, yet so far as love and affection for the government is concerned, I do not believe that they have any of it at all, outside of their personal respect and regard for President Johnson.

Question: How do they feel towards the mass of the northern people — that is, the people of what were known formerly as the free States?

Answer: They feel in this way: that they have been ruined by them. You can imagine the feelings of a person towards one whom he regards as having ruined him. They regard the northern people as having destroyed their property or taken it from them, and brought all the calamities of this war upon them.

Question: How do they feel in regard to what is called the right of secession?

Answer: They think that it was right . . . that there was no wrong in it. They are willing now to accept the decision of the question that has been made by the sword, but they are not by any means converted from their old opinion that they had a right to secede. It is true that there have always been Union men in our State, but not Union men without slavery, except perhaps among Quakers. Slavery was the central idea even of the Unionist. The only difference between them and the others upon that question was, that they desired to have that institution under the aegis of the Constitution, and protected by it. The secessionists wanted to get away from the north altogether. When the secessionists precipitated our State into rebellion, the Unionists and secessionists went together, because the great object with both was the preservation of slavery by the preservation of State sovereignty. There was another class of Unionists who did not care anything at all about slavery, but they were driven by the other whites into the rebellion for the purpose of preserving slavery. The poor whites are to-day very much opposed to conferring upon the negro the right of suffrage; as much so as the other classes of the whites. They believe it is the intention of government to give the negro rights at their expense. They cannot see it in any other light than that as the negro is elevated they must proportionately go down. While they are glad that slavery is done away with, they are bitterly opposed to conferring the right of suffrage on the negro as the most prominent secessionists; but it is for the reason I have stated, that they think rights conferred on the negro must necessarily be taken from them, particularly the ballot, which was the only bulwark guarding their superiority to the negro race.

Question: In your judgment, what proportion of the white people of North Carolina are really, and truly, and cordially attached to the government of the United States?

Answer: Very few, sir; very few. . . .

Question: Is the Freedmen's Bureau acceptable to the great mass of the white people in North Carolina?

Answer: No, sir; I do not think it is; I think the most of the whites wish the bureau to be taken away.

Question: Why do they wish that?

Answer: They think that they can manage the negro for themselves: that they understand him better than northern men do. They say, "Let us understand what you want us to do with [the] negro—what you desire of us; lay down your conditions for our readmission into the Union, and then we will know what we have to do, and if you will do that we will enact laws for the government of these negroes. They have lived among us, and they are all with us, and we can manage them better than you can." They think it is interfering with the rights of the State for a bureau, the agent and representative of the federal government, to overslaugh the State entirely, and interfere with the regulations and administration of justice before their courts.

Question: Is there generally a willingness on the part of the whites to allow the freedmen to enjoy the right of acquiring land and personal property?

Answer: I think they are very willing to let them do that, for this reason; to get rid of some portion of the taxes imposed upon their property by the government. For instance, a white man will agree to sell a negro some of his land on condition of his paying so much a year on it, promising to give him a deed of it when the whole payment is made, taking his note in the mean time. This relieves that much of the land from taxes to be paid by the white man. All I am afraid of is, that the negro is too eager to go into this thing; that he will ruin himself, get himself into debt to the white man, and be forever bound to him for the debt and never get the land. I have often warned them to be careful what they did about these things.

Question: There is no repugnance on the part of the whites to the negro owning land and personal property?

Answer: I think not.

Question: Have they any objection to the legal establishment of the domestic relations among the blacks, such as the relation of husband and wife, of parent and child, and the securing by law to the negro the rights of those relations?

Answer: That is a matter of ridicule with the whites. They do not believe the negroes will ever respect those relations more than the brutes. I suppose I have married more than two hundred couples of negroes since the war, but the whites laugh at the very idea of the thing. Under the old laws a slave could not marry a free woman of color; it was made a penal offence in North Carolina for any one to perform such a marriage. But there was in my own family a slave who desired to marry a free woman of color, and I did what I conceived to be my duty, and married them, and I was presented to the grand jury for doing so, but the prosecuting attorney threw out the case and would not try it. In former times the officiating clergyman marrying slaves, could not use the usual formula: "Whom God has joined together let no man put asunder"; you could not say, "According to the ordinance of God I pronounce you man and wife; you are no longer two but one." It was not legal for you to do so.

Question: What, in general, has been the treatment of the blacks by the whites since the close of hostilities?

Answer: It has not generally been of the kindest character, I must say that; I am compelled to say that.

Question: Are you aware of any instance of personal ill treatment towards the blacks by the whites?

Answer: Yes, sir.

Question: Give some instances that have occurred since the war.

Answer: [Sinclair describes the beating of a young woman across her buttocks in graphic detail.]

Question: What was the provocation, if any?

Answer: Something in regard to some work, which is generally the provocation.

Question: Was there no law in North Carolina at that time to punish such an outrage?

Answer: No, sir; only the regulations of the Freedmen's Bureau; we took cognizance of the case. In old times that was quite allowable; it is what was called "paddling."

Question: Did you deal with the master?

Answer: I immediately sent a letter to him to come to my office, but he did not come, and I have never seen him in regard to the matter since. I had no soldiers to enforce compliance, and I was obliged to let the matter drop.

Question: Have you any reason to suppose that such instances of cruelty are frequent in North Carolina at this time—instances of whipping and striking?

Answer: I think they are; it was only a few days before I left that a woman came there with her head all bandaged up, having been cut and bruised by her employer. They think nothing of striking them.

Question: And the negro has practically no redress?

Answer: Only what he can get from the Freedmen's Bureau.

Question: Can you say anything further in regard to the political condition of North Carolina—the feeling of the people towards the government of the United States?

Answer: I for one would not wish to be left there in the hands of those men; I could not live there just now. But perhaps my case is an isolated one from the position I was compelled to take in that State. I was persecuted, arrested, and they tried to get me into their service; they tried everything to accomplish their purpose, and of course I have rendered myself still more obnoxious by accepting an appointment under the Freedmen's Bureau. As for myself I would not be allowed to remain there. I do not want to be handed over to these people. I know it is utterly impossible for any man who was not true to the Confederate States up to the last moment of the existence of the confederacy, to expect any favor of these people as the State is constituted at present.

Question: Suppose the military pressure of the government of the United States should be withdrawn from North Carolina, would northern men and true Unionists be safe in that State?

Answer: A northern man going there would perhaps present nothing obnoxious to the people of the State. But men who were born there, who have been true to the Union, and who have fought against the rebellion, are worse off than northern men. . . .

Question: In your judgment, what effect has been produced by the liberality of the President in granting pardons and amnesties to rebels in that State—what effect upon the public mind?

Answer: On my oath I am bound to reply exactly as I believe; that is, that if President Johnson is ever a candidate for re-election he will be supported by the southern States, particularly by North Carolina; but that his liberality to them has drawn them one whit closer to the government than before, I do not believe. It has drawn them to President Johnson personally, and to the Democratic party, I suppose.

Civil War and Reconstruction

The Civil War was the first modern war. Guns with rifled barrels could send a bullet accurately for long distances, and cannons loaded with grapeshot could kill and maim many men at a time. Railroads enabled armies to transport troops and supplies over vast distances, greatly increasing the size of battles—and the number of casualties. Not simply fought between professional armies, the war scarred large proportions of the population on both sides.

The popular culture of the era, intensely romantic and heroic, only gradually began to reflect the reality of the war. The soldiers sang of "The Girl I Left behind Me," looked away to "Dixie land," and marched to the "Bonnie Blue Flag." The first visual images depicting the war were largely patriotic: wood engravings and paintings showing—as in Plate 1—soldiers grasping the flag as they fought. Photography, however, as modern as the war itself, eventually undermined this romantic vision of the war. Photographs of the litter of bodies strewn across battlefields and campsites forced the public to see some of the war's terrible realities.

As photographs came to dominate the public's vision of the war, the technical limits of what the camera could depict defined the way people imagined battle. The photographic process then in use was too cumbersome to allow "action" photographs: there are no Civil War photographs of actual battles. Nonetheless, skilled photographers such as Andrew J. Russell and James Gardner followed the Union Army closely, catching the preparations for battle, the sites where battles were fought, and the dreadful aftermaths of these events. The inability of the Confederacy to support a similar photographic industry has had a major impact on the way we visualize the war.

The works of George N. Barnard (Plates 8 through 13) show how photographic artists of the era selected subjects that might portray their own values. Barnard followed General Sherman's army as it fought its way through the South, photographing when the army paused long enough for him to take pictures, sketching when it moved too quickly for his bulky equipment. After the war, Barnard retraced the route of the army photographing "the principal events and most interesting localities" that he had not been able to capture during the actual march. Gathered together in *The Photographic Views of Sherman's Campaign*, a portfolio of views that Barnard published in 1866, these photographs suggest both the power and the limits of the era's photography for evoking a vision of war.

At first, images of the war kept a polite distance from the actual carnage of battle. Plate 1, the only image in this portfolio that is not a photograph, depicts men in battle. What picture of combat does it offer? What would the people who rioted against the draft (Selection 37) have thought of it? How does the mood of Plates 2 and 3 differ from that of Plate 1? Why do you think photographer Andrew J. Russell chose the scenes he did? What does he include, and what does he leave out?

Below: Plate 1. H. B. Hall from a drawing by F. O. C. Darley, "General Lyon's Charge at the Battle of Wilson's Creek," 1862

Above right: Plate 2. Andrew J. Russell, "Battlefield Aftermath at Chancellorsville," May 1863

Below right: Plate 3. Andrew J. Russell, "Battlefield Aftermath at Marey's Heights, Chancellorsville," May 1863

Plate 4. James F. Gibson, "16th N.Y. Infantry Wounded during Battle of Gain's Mill at Savage Station, Va.," June 28, 1862

Plate 4 is the first stereograph published that depicted wounded soldiers. Plates 5, 6, and 7 take us directly into the world of Cornelia Hancock (Selection 38). The images shown are of Fredericksburg, Virginia, in May 1864, when the entire town was converted to a makeshift hospital for those wounded in the battles of the Wilderness and of Spotsylvania Court House. Given the date and place, the woman sitting in the doorway in Plate 7 could indeed have been Cornelia Hancock herself—if she ever found time to sit. How do you think

Plate 5. Brady & Co., "Burying Union Soldiers at Fredericksburg Killed in the Battles of the Wilderness and Spotsylvania Court House," May 12, 1864

those back home reacted to these photographs, all of which circulated widely as cartes-de-visite or stereo views? What do the images suggest about the problems of caring for the wounded during the Civil War? How do they compare to Cornelia Hancock's descriptions of field hospitals?

Above: Plate 6. Brady & Co., "Wounded Indian Soldiers of the Union Army after the Battles of the Wilderness and Spotsylvania Court House," May 12, 1864

Right: Plate 7. James Gardner, "Soldiers from Grant's Army, Wounded at Battles of the Wilderness or Spotsylvania, at Fredericksburg, Va.," May 20, 1864

Plate 8. George N. Barnard, "Destroying the Railroad Just before the 'March to the Sea,'" Atlanta, November 1864

The photographs on this and the next three pages are from a portfolio of images of Sherman's march by George H. Barnard, one of the best field photographers of the Civil War. The captions indicate—insofar as historians have the information—those plates taken at the time of the march and those completed after the war. Plates 8, 9, and 10 indirectly depict a climactic moment of Sherman's expedition: the capture of Atlanta. This Union victory, in which the Confederacy suffered 8,500 casualties and the Union 3,700, assured Abraham Lincoln's reelection in 1864. One casualty came to symbolize that battle, the death of one of Sherman's leading commanders, General James Birdseye McPherson, on July 22, 1864. What mood is Barnard creating in these images? How does this mood compare to the accounts of Sherman's march that you have read? Do you think Northern audiences would have interpreted these images differently from Southern audiences? How would Pauline DeCaradeuc Heyward (Selection 36) react to these images? How would Ellen Leonard (Selection 37) react?

Above: Plate 9. George N. Barnard, "Rebel Works in Front of Atlanta, Ga., No. 3," 1864

Below: Plate 10. George N. Barnard, "Scene of General McPherson's Death," 1864 or 1865

Above left: Plate 11. George N. Barnard, "Destruction of Hood's Ordnance Train," 1864

Left: Plate 12. George N. Barnard, "Ruins in Charleston, S.C.," 1865 or 1866

Above: Plate 13. George N. Barnard, "Ruins of the R.R. Depot in Charleston, S.C.," 1865

Plates 11 through 13 are images of the destruction and aftermath of war. How would you compare them to other images of the destruction of war with which you are familiar, such as Hiroshima and Nagasaki or the Vietnam War? In Plate 11, you can see the demolition of the rail lines that had brought food and supplies to Confederate troops; in Plates 12 and 13, Charleston, South Carolina, is reduced to a pile of rubble. Think again about how Northern and Southern audiences would interpret these images.

[Plate 3] Mount Vernon, Virginia. Library of Congress, Prints & Photographs Division, HABS, VA, 30-, 2-4.

[Plate 4] Monticello, Virginia. Library of Congress, Prints & Photographs Division, LC-USW36-756.

[Plate 5] Touro Synagogue, Rhode Island, exterior. Library of Congress, Prints & Photographs Division, HABS, RI, 3-NEWP, 29-4.

[Plate 6] Touro Synagogue, Rhode Island, interior. Library of Congress, Prints & Photographs Division, HABS, RI, 3-NEWP, 29-10.

[Plate 7] "View of Mulberry, House and Street," by Thomas Coram, oil on paper, Gibbes Museum of Art/Carolina Art Association, 68.18.01.

[Plate 8] Slave cabins dating from the 1800s, Roseberry Plantation, Dinwiddie County, Virginia. Library of Congress, Prints & Photographs Division, HABS, VA, 27-FORD, V, 1-2.

Slavery and Freedom

[Plate 3] Interior View of the Price, Birch & Co. Slave Dealership, Alexandria, Va., 1865. National Archives, Neg. 111-BA-2145.

[Plate 4] Jack (Driver), a Slave in Columbia, S.C., ". . . from the Guinea Coast," 1850. Peabody Museum of Archaeology & Ethnology, Harvard University.

[Plate 5] Delia, a Slave in Columbia, S.C., ". . . Country Born of African Parents," 1850. Peabody Museum of Archaeology & Ethnology, Harvard University.

[Plate 6] Southern Man, His Two Daughters, and Nanny, St. Louis, Mo., 1848. The J. Paul Getty Museum, Los Angeles.

[Plate 7] Robert J. Wilkinson, Successful Businessman, St. Louis, Mo., c. 1860. Missouri Historical Society, St. Louis.

[Plate 8] Portrait of an Unidentified Woman, Hartford, Conn., c. 1850. Collection of the Library of Congress; photograph courtesy of National Portrait Gallery, Smithsonian Institution.

[Plate 13] "Contrabands." Fugitive Slaves Crossing the Rappahannock River during Grant's Second Manassas Campaign, 1864. Library of Congress, #LC-B8171-518.

Civil War and Reconstruction

[Plate 8] Destroying the Railroad Just before the "March to the Sea," Atlanta, November 1864. Special Collections and Archives Division, U.S. Military Academy, West Point.